Shopping Center Management and Leasing

Professional Review
Robert Oliver, CPM®
Robert Cart, CPM®
Mez Birdie, CPM®

Tulie O'Connor
Manager, Education Publishing

Shopping Center Management and Leasing

Richard F. Muhlebach, CPM®
Alan A. Alexander, CPM®

IREM Institute of Real Estate Management

Library of Congress Cataloging-in-Publication Data

Muhlebach, Richard F., 1943–
Shopping center management and leasing / Richard F. Muhlebach, Alan A. Alexander.
p. cm.
Includes bibliographical references and index.
ISBN 1-57203-101-8 (alk. paper)
1. Shopping centers—Management. 2. Shopping centers—Marketing. 3. Commercial leases. I. Alexander, Alan A. II. Title.
HF5430.M84 2004
658.8′7—dc22

2004056861

To my four favorite retail brokers, my daughter Katherine and her husband Bruce Burns in Seattle, and to my son Eric and his wife Amy in San Francisco. To my partner in all our activities for over thirty-five years, my loving wife, Maria.

R.F.M.

To my loving wife Jeanne, who is always there to encourage and support me in my every effort.

A.A.A.

Preface

Shopping Center Management and Leasing has been written to provide the reader with a practical guide for managing all aspects of shopping centers. The information covers shopping centers of all sizes and types—from a neighborhood shopping center with a supermarket and/or drugstore anchor, to the regional mall with up to seven or eight anchors and hundreds of small shops, to the newest of shopping center types: the lifestyle and entertainment centers. The shopping center types are defined in chapter 1; the chapter also provides an overview of the history and evolution of shopping centers. Development of shopping centers is discussed fully in chapter 2; much of the reasoning for why and how a particular shopping center is developed is covered in the chapter.

Of all income-producing properties, shopping centers are generally considered the most complex to manage, operate, market, and lease. In order for a shopping center to be successful, it must have the right location, easy access, high visibility, good management and marketing, and the right anchor(s) and tenant mix for the demographic and psychographic profiles of its trade area. This book details the components a shopping center needs for success.

Location, Access, and Visibility

The best *location* for a particular shopping center depends on the shopping center type. For example, a neighborhood shopping center must have an adequate population of shoppers and a location at the intersection of two well-traveled streets or, at the very least, facing a well-traveled street. Entertainment shopping centers should be located in densely populated areas and should have good access.

Access is critical for all types of shopping centers. Shoppers value convenience, and they will not spend an extra 20 minutes in their cars waiting to get into a shopping center—they will shop somewhere else. Good access includes convenient, defined, left-turn lanes; safe "stacking" lanes, if needed (for deceleration of inbound and acceleration of outbound vehicles); well-timed signals; wide driveways that are well marked; good internal circulation in the parking lot; and well-designed, appropriately angled parking stalls.

If a town had only one shopping center, it could be located almost anywhere and people would find it readily enough because they would have no other convenient choice. However, shopping centers have competition, and that is where visibility becomes essential. *Visibility* is what reminds customers that the shopping center is there, even when they have no immediate need to shop. The shopping center should be easy to see from the street, and how easily it can be accessed should be readily apparent to customers.

Location, access, and visibility are discussed throughout this book because an understanding of these concepts and how they relate to a particular shopping center's development, operations, marketing, and leasing is essential to the shopping center's success.

Management

The tremendous success of shopping centers over the years can be attributed, in part, to their management. The management of a shopping center provides specific direction to all of its parts. It keeps the merchants focused on the trade area so their merchandise and pricing remain a good "fit" with the customer base. It fosters good business practices, encourages advertising, and provides a clean, attractive environment for shoppers. Good management keeps the ownership informed of changes to the trade area, new competition, and adjustments that are needed to the tenant mix. Management also estimates, monitors, and makes the necessary changes to the shopping center's financial projections. Chapter 3, Developing the Shopping Center's Management Plan, and chapter 4, Management Structure, cover all aspects of shopping center management.

Maintenance and Operations

Chapter 5, Maintenance and Operations discusses successful maintenance and operational concerns for the shopping center. Having all lighting, security, cleaning, heating, ventilation, and air-conditioning (HVAC), and any other systems in the best condition possible is critical to the success of any shopping center. Consumers expect a certain level of décor and professional appearance when they shop; they will go elsewhere if amenities such as parking, security, cleanliness, and landscaping are issues.

Administration

Detailed accounting, budgeting, and other administrative records are essential for the successful management of any shopping center. Many records that were formerly kept manually are now stored in computers. User-friendly software packages are available to help the shopping center's administrative staff maintain detailed, accurate records. The shopping center manager is required to provide accurate reports to the shopping center owner—in the style and according to the timeline that the owner prefers. Chapter 6, Administration, presents the administrative details the shopping center manager must oversee to ensure the success of the shopping center.

Tenant Relations

The key elements of successful relations with tenants are detailed in chapter 7, Tenant Relations. Tenants with varying levels of retailing expertise can be found in any type of shopping center. The shopping center manager must evaluate and understand each tenant's needs and expectations even before the lease is signed. Chapter 7 discusses a number of methods of effective communication the shopping center manager can use as well as how and when to best use them in order to maintain long-lasting, positive tenant relations.

Tenant Mix

Tenant mix is much more critical to a shopping center than to an office building or an industrial property because retail tenants require customer traffic to generate the sales that are the measure of their success. To be successful, a shopping center must have complementary store types that maximize its attraction to prospective customers. The right tenant mix for a particular shopping center depends on many factors, among them the type of shopping center, the anchor tenants, the availability of specific tenant types in the area, and economic and other factors related to the leasing terms. The selection of store types is based on the characteristics of the shopping center's trade area. Details of creating and managing a successful tenant mix are found in chapter 8, Creating the Tenant Mix.

Leasing

The primary objective of most nonretail properties is to fill a rent roll as quickly as possible. The type of tenant is often not a major consideration. That is not true for retail properties. The selection of the right tenants and the evaluation of their ability as merchants are paramount to the success of a shopping center. The leasing process does not end when the shopping center is fully leased. Changes to the trade area, new merchants entering the market, and poor-performing retailers provide leasing opportunities even when a shopping center has no vacancies. Chapter 9, Leasing the Shopping Center, covers all aspects of leasing.

Lease Negotiations

The negotiation of leases is one of the most challenging responsibilities the shopping center manager and the leasing agent face. Chapter 10, Negotiating and Documenting the Lease Terms, provides a comprehensive review of all major retail lease components, including monetary and nonmonetary provisions. The shopping center manager and the leasing agent must fully understand how to best negotiate the retail lease provisions because the outcomes of lease negotiations will have a long-term effect on the shopping center, including the tenant mix.

Marketing

Marketing the shopping center and its tenants is increasingly important. The marketing of shopping centers and malls has evolved from weekend promotions in the 1950s and 1960s to developing marketing and merchandising strategies and implementing the tactics to achieve their strategic goals.

Marketing personnel at lifestyle shopping centers, outlet malls, specialty shopping centers, and regional and super regional malls have long understood the value of marketing. They typically budget large amounts to pay for aggressive advertising, marketing, merchandising, and promotional campaigns throughout the year. Smaller shopping centers usually do not have enough tenants for an annual marketing program. The tenants in smaller shopping centers may periodically join together for joint advertising. Chapter 11, Marketing the Shopping Center, discusses the marketing, promoting, and advertising of shopping centers and malls.

Mixed-Use Developments

Retail has become a profitable component of many property types. Airports, train stations, hotels, resorts, and other nonretail environments now include numerous retail options. Chapter 12, The Retail Component in Multi-Use and Mixed-Use Developments, discusses the components of those developments and the significant benefits they offer communities as well as retailers, property owners, and managers.

Appendices

The four appendices cover information relative to specific areas that require more explanation than is practical to cover in the text of the chapters. Those areas cover retail operations, risk management, basic math calculations for retailers and shopping center managers, and a reference section of publications and organizations that will be of interest to the shopping center professional.

This book will serve as a guide to shopping center managers, leasing agents, marketing directors, finance managers, developers, and shopping center owners. *Shopping Center Management and Leasing* is intended to be a deskside reference tool that can be referred to for long-term planning issues with a shopping center as well as the daily management, operations, marketing and leasing issues.

ACKNOWLEDGMENTS

Professionals in every area of the property management industry are willing to share their knowledge and experiences. This enables the property management profession to continue to improve and enhances the professionalism and competency of property managers and other professionals who serve the industry.

Throughout more than 30 years of managing and leasing shopping centers and malls, each of us has benefited from our association with our peers and various professional and trade organizations that serve the industry. Without these associations we would have never have been able to write *Shopping Center Management and Leasing* or our other books.

We would first like to acknowledge our long and valued association with the Institute of Real Estate Management (IREM). The education we received through courses leading to our Certified Property Manager (CPM®) designation, the networking at chapter and national meetings, and the friendships we developed with fellow CPMs enabled our careers to grow and prosper.

We also would like to express our appreciation to the International Council of Shopping Centers (ICSC) for the value we received attending their education programs and conventions. We wish to thank the Urban Land Institute for publishing *Dollars and Cents of Shopping Centers,* the industry standard for benchmarking the performance of retailers along with other invaluable information; a good deal of information from the publication is referenced with permission in this text.

Several shopping center and related industry professionals contributed to the production of this book. First we want to thank a dear friend, Bob

Bearson, who passed away just before this book was published. Bob was a retailer, educator, and retail consultant to small businesses and the shopping center industry. He contributed much of the information on retailing in appendix A of this book. We would also like to acknowledge Jack Smith of American Building Maintenance and Jim Herbert of Herbert Research in Bellevue, Washington for the forms and information they provided.

We also appreciate the advice and expertise of our fellow shopping center managers who served as editorial consultants for the book: Robert Oliver, Robert Cart, and Mez Birdie.

We are grateful for the excellent editing of the first edition of this book by Caroline Scoulas, Senior Editor at IREM and the excellent editing of this edition by Tulie O'Connor, Manager of Education Publishing at IREM.

Richard F. Muhlebach, CPM®
Alan A. Alexander, CPM®

About the Authors

Richard F. Muhlebach CPM®, SCSM, CRE, RPA is Senior Managing Director of Kennedy Wilson Properties Northwest, a subsidiary of Kennedy Wilson International, a public real estate firm located in Beverly Hills, California. He is responsible for the firm's management and brokerage operations in the Northwest and is located in Bellevue, Washington.

Mr. Muhlebach created TRF Management Corporation, a shopping center management and leasing firm in 1980, and served as its president for 19 years until the firm was sold to Kennedy Wilson Properties. Previously, he served as Vice President of Tishman West Management Corporation and The Lusk Company, both developers in California.

Mr. Muhlebach has over 30 years' experience managing and leasing regional malls, large multi-anchored strip shopping centers, waterfront retail properties and mixed-use developments in urban, suburban, and rural areas. He has also managed high-rise office buildings, mid-rise medical buildings, and residential properties.

In addition to serving as an instructor on the National Faculty of the Institute of Real Estate Management (IREM) for more than 25 years, Mr. Muhlebach has also taught for the International Council of Shopping Centers (ICSC) and the Building Owners and Managers Association (BOMA). He teaches commercial property management and leasing at the University of Washington and has lectured in Spain, Poland, Hungary, Singapore, China, Taiwan and Canada.

As author of approximately 100 articles on commercial real estate management and leasing, Mr. Muhlebach has been published in several national real estate journals and magazines, including *Journal of Property Management (JPM), Shopping Center World,* and *Buildings.*

Mr. Muhlebach was the 1998 National President of IREM and served two terms as a trustee of the Washington Center for Real Estate Research. He also served as the president of several real estate organizations, including the Washington State Commercial Association of Realtors, as well as the Seattle or Northwest chapters of IREM, BOMA, and the Real Estate Educators Association.

In addition to holding the Certified Property Manager (CPM©) designation from the Institute of Real Estate Management, Mr. Muhlebach is a Senior Shopping Center Manager (SCSM) given by the International Council of Shopping Centers, a Counselor of Real Estate (CRE) awarded by the Counselors of Real Estate, and a Real Property Administrator (RPA) from the Building Owners and Managers Institute. Mr. Muhlebach is a graduate of San Francisco State University.

Alan A. Alexander, CPM®, SCSM, is President of Alexander Consultants, specializing in management, leasing, and consulting for income-producing properties throughout the Western United States and South America. With over 35 years' experience in the business, Mr. Alexander is the former Senior Vice President of Fox & Carskadon Management Corporation, with responsibility for a portfolio of commercial and residential properties worth more than $300 million dollars in four Western States. As Director of Leasing for Fox & Carskadon Financial, Mr. Alexander was responsible for the leasing of all shopping centers owned by the company throughout the United States, with a total portfolio in excess of $800 million dollars.

Mr. Alexander was a member of the National Faculty of the Institute of Real Estate Management (IREM) as a Senior Instructor for both "Management and Leasing of Shopping Centers and Retail Space" and "Leasing and Management of Office Buildings" from 1982 to 1998. In addition to classes taught in almost every major city in the United States, Mr. Alexander has taught shopping center management courses in Singapore, Canada, Mexico, Malaysia, Taiwan, Hong Kong, the Philippines, Poland, China, Thailand, Holland, Argentina, Turkey, and Jamaica.

Mr. Alexander is a frequent speaker for the International Council of Shopping Center (ICSC) programs including Idea Exchanges, the Annual Convention, Management Institutes, Maintenance Institutes, and the School for Professional Development. He represented ICSC at their first three Asian Shopping Center Schools as an instructor. Mr. Alexander has been a moderator and speaker for over 200 seminars on "Developing and Leasing of Shopping Centers" and "Office Buildings and Apartment Properties" for the Northwest Center for Professional Education.

Mr. Alexander is the past President of the San Francisco Bay Area Chapter of the Institute of Real Estate Management. He was awarded the "Distinguished Service Award" by the International Council of Shopping Centers in 1992 for his contributions to Education and Publications.

In addition to this work, Mr. Muhlebach and Mr. Alexander are co-authors of several books, including: *Business Strategies for Real Estate Management Companies,* published by IREM, *Operating Small Shopping Centers,* published by ICSC, and the two-volume set, *Managing and Leasing Commercial Properties,* originally published by John Wiley & Sons, Inc.

Contents

Shopping Center Management and Leasing

1

Shopping Centers: Evolution and Change

The shopping center industry is constantly evolving; its evolution is evident in the industry's rapid growth. There were 5,000 shopping centers in 1960 and the number more than doubled to 11,000 by 1970. The industry doubled again to 22,000 shopping centers by 1980. Almost 15,000 shopping centers—the most in any decade—were developed during the 1980s, bringing the total to 37,000 shopping centers by 1990. By the twenty-first century, the United States had over 45,000 shopping centers.

Shopping centers, in all their forms, have become an accepted—indeed a desirable—part of the American landscape, and they will continue to grow and prosper. To ensure that growth and prosperity, developers, shopping center managers, marketing directors, and leasing agents must continually seek to understand the needs and desires of shoppers and to make their shopping centers responsive to the demands of a changing consumer marketplace. Shopping is more than purchasing an item—for many people it is an experience.

EVOLUTION OF THE CONCEPT

The concept of the shopping center dates back to the earliest days of trade in the marketplace. In Europe and elsewhere, the center of town was used as a marketplace where one farmer could exchange vegetables for another farmer's grain, and townspeople could barter their "wares" (e.g., pottery) for agricultural products. The center of town was chosen as the marketplace because it was a prominent, visible location and it offered access to most people in the area. The farmers and merchants understood that by gathering together they could offer a variety of goods and services that would attract more shoppers than any of them could attract individually. Permanent shops were established around the town square to take advantage of the traffic and to offer goods and services the farmers did not provide. Eventually, the town square or main street became the central business district of a bustling city. The market area became not only a place to buy and sell goods but also a social occasion and a gathering place for the community.

A similar pattern has developed around malls. When a regional mall is developed, other shopping centers or retail properties are developed in the immediate area. Within a few years of a mall's opening, the area often becomes one of the community's major retailing centers.

The concepts of location, visibility, access, and demographics that the merchants found to be critical to their success thousands of years ago remain the foundation of a successful retail location today. Just as the town center became the social gathering place then, today several types of shopping centers—malls, lifestyle shopping centers, and entertainment shopping centers—have become gathering places for their communities.

The "first place" in a person's life is considered to be the home and family; the "second place" is the workplace or school; the "third place" is where people interact in the community. Shopping centers and malls have become that third place for people because they provide a venue for shopping and dining as well as a center for recreational, educational, and community activities.

HISTORICAL OVERVIEW

The automobile played a major role in the development and expansion of shopping centers in America. The automobile made it possible to live outside the city and still work and socialize in the city. Individuals could travel where they wanted, when they wanted—provided there were roads to their destinations. The migration out of the city and the rise of the suburbs provided a unique opportunity for developers to create a revolutionary retail experience—the shopping center.

The first planned shopping district in the United States was Country Club Plaza, which J. C. Nichols developed in Kansas City, Missouri, in 1922. Nichols foresaw the coming success of the automobile. He located his retail center south of town and designed it to cater to people who arrived by automobile. He included all the elements considered necessary for a successful shopping center today—easy access, visibility, free paved parking, central management, controlled architecture, pleasant landscaping, and a broad tenant mix that was appropriate for the trade area. The Plaza was designed with a Spanish theme reminiscent of a plaza in Seville and included several courtyards and plazas, more than thirty statues, elegant fountains, and tilt-laced murals. The buildings included twelve ornate towers, red tile roofs, and a 130-foot tall reproduction of the Giralda Tower of Seville. The buildings in the 14-block development housed over 150 stores that were oriented toward the street. Parking was available in the center cores of several of the blocks.

The tenant mix of Country Club Plaza has changed over the years. Once anchored by Sears and Woolworth, the Plaza now has high-end fashion stores and upscale restaurants. Country Club Plaza has remained among the most beautiful of shopping centers since its development over 80 years ago. Since the 1990s, developers have replicated the vision of J. C. Nichols by building shopping centers with an urban main street design, a pedestrian-friendly layout, and convenient parking as well as upscale fashion and fine dining restaurant tenants. These shopping centers are called lifestyle shopping centers.

Several factors converged after World War II and set the stage for the rapid growth of the shopping center industry. Government-backed home loan programs—especially FHA (Federal Housing Administration) and VA (Veterans Administration) loans—made home ownership much more attainable. That fostered home building in suburban areas outside large cities. The development of an interstate highway system made getting from one place to another easier, and more important, it made living in the suburbs and working in the city possible. As the population moved to the suburbs, astute merchants soon realized that they could move their businesses to the suburbs as well.

Retailers' Impact on Shopping Centers

Shopping center development is a response to new and expanding retail concepts. Each type of shopping center and mall has gone through several iterations since its initial development. The neighborhood shopping center was originally anchored by a 25,000-square-foot grocery store and a 5,000-square-foot drugstore and had national and local shop tenants. In time, the size of each anchor grew substantially. That created opportunities to develop new shopping centers anchored by larger supermarkets; it also created leasing challenges for older shopping centers when their smaller grocery stores vacated to build larger stores nearby.

The expansion of department stores into the suburbs after World War II provided the anchors for regional malls. The regional mall started as a one-level, open-air, 400,000- to 800,000-square-foot shopping center anchored by one or two department stores. The rapid development of malls would not have occurred without the expansion of department stores. The creation of the large specialty retailers (known in the shopping center industry as *box stores*) in the 1980s, led to the development of power shopping centers. Examples of box stores are Toys R Us, Home Depot, Bed Bath and Beyond, and Costco. Box stores that specialize in a single category of merchandise are known as *category killers* because small retailers cannot compete with their selection or their low prices.

Manufacturers' need to have an outlet for excessive, discontinued, and flawed merchandise provided the tenants for outlet malls. Large, state-of-the-art, multiscreen theaters provided the anchor tenants for entertainment shopping centers. The larger, upscale specialty retailers became the primary draw for lifestyle shopping centers.

Old-line credit retailers, such as Montgomery Ward and Woolworth, and many regional and national specialty chains and discount stores failed and went out of business. At the same time, new retailers, such as Wal-Mart, Home Depot and Costco, as well as new specialty stores, such as Starbucks, Barnes & Noble, The Gap, and Aveda, became leaders in their fields. The continuing evolution in the retail industry, the failure of chain stores, and the emergence of new merchants requires constant monitoring and changes to the tenant mix of all types of shopping centers.

In the late 1990s, with record numbers of people using the Internet, and dot.com ventures starting up in every area of business, many retailers recognized the importance of building an online presence. While traditional retailers initially feared that consumers would cease to shop in person, the dot.com era rapidly collapsed, and few of these start up businesses survived.

The downfall of the dot.com era made clear that consumers still prefer, and perhaps even enjoy, the opportunity to shop in person—especially when shopping for items such as clothing, housewares, and jewelry. They like to be able to feel and touch garments or browse through a store to find a variety of merchandise. Consumers now seem to view shopping online and shopping at a shopping center as complementary experiences that are not mutually exclusive. Chapter 11, Marketing the Shopping Center, discusses more about the retailing experience.

The Evolution of Shopping Centers

The early shopping centers were developed in the 1950s and 1960s. They were grocery anchored neighborhood shopping centers with a shop tenant mix of fashion, gift, specialty food, and restaurants. Those shopping centers grew with the addition of variety stores and junior department stores as anchors.

During each decade from 1970 to the end of the twentieth century, two new types of shopping centers were developed all across the Unites States. In the 1970s, the regional mall and specialty or theme shopping centers were the "new" and popular retail venues. Though the first mall, Northgate Mall, was developed in Seattle in 1950, and the first enclosed, climate-controlled mall, Southdale Center, was built six years later in Edina, a suburb of Minneapolis, malls were not developed in great numbers throughout the United States until the 1970s. Specialty shopping centers were developed as an adaptive use—the conversion of a nonretail building to a retail use—or built from the ground up.

In the 1980s shoppers were looking for value. Developers responded to the needs of the consumer by developing two new shopping center concepts—outlet shopping centers and power shopping centers. Though outlet shopping centers had existed in a few areas on the East Coast for many years, it was not until the 1980s that they were built throughout the United States. The power shopping center was also built in the 1980s as a response to the need for value-oriented shopping. Power shopping centers had several big box stores as anchor tenants and originally excluded shop tenants. Each of the box stores was a powerful customer draw, thus the name power shopping center.

In the 1990s the consumer was looking for a shopping experience that differed from the large malls surrounded by seas of parking lots and the large, impersonal, self-service box stores. Lifestyle shopping centers and entertainment shopping centers provided shopping and recreational activities in two different social environments. With its urban main street designs and parking in front of stores that included fashion and gift merchants, restaurants, and often a theater, the lifestyle shopping center was reminiscent of a small town's downtown during the 1950s. A multi-screen, state-of-the-art theater anchored the entertainment shopping center, which also boasted restaurants, trendy fashion merchants, and quick service and popular restaurants with lounges.

The new retail venues of the 2000s were a return to the beginning of retailing in America. Neighborhoods and downtowns once again became popular places to shop. Also during that period, lifestyle shopping centers continued to evolve into the second and third generations of their development, and power shopping centers evolved into power towns.

Each type of shopping center mentioned above is described more fully later in this chapter.

TYPES OF SHOPPING CENTERS AND OTHER RETAIL OPPORTUNITIES

The shopping center industry experiences more constant change than any other property type. New retail concepts and failing retail chains as well as changing demographics and consumers' needs and wants create opportunities for shopping center and retail property development, renovations, and adaptive uses.

Shopping centers are classified by their size, tenant mix, anchor tenants, and their roles in the community. Ten basic types of shopping centers are recognized: convenience, neighborhood, community, specialty, outlet, power, lifestyle, and entertainment shopping centers and regional and super regional malls.

Over time, variations of these shopping centers have been and will continue to be developed. In most types of shopping centers, the anchor tenant is the main traffic draw. The tenants in the smaller shops may be local, regional, or national retailers. Depending on the type of shopping center, some stores may be leased to service companies or businesses; others may be leased as office space to medical, dental, or legal professionals. Pads or outlots (freestanding buildings) are typically leased to restaurants or banks, although numerous other tenants—drive-up espresso stands, video rental stores, automotive service stations—are appropriate for such spaces.

In addition to shopping centers, other retail properties and retail components are located in multi-use and mixed-use developments. Retail has been added to office buildings, urban high-rise apartments and condominiums, airports, and resorts. Many neighborhoods and downtowns have vibrant retail cores.

The next sections of this chapter present overviews of the ten basic types of shopping centers, downtown and neighborhood retailing, and other retail opportunities.

Convenience (Strip) Shopping Centers

The *convenience shopping center* is the smallest type of shopping center. It is usually comprised of 5,000 to 30,000 square feet of *gross leasable area (GLA)* and is designed as one continuous row of shops—thus the term *strip shopping center*. Though the ideal location is on a corner, a convenience shopping center can be located anywhere along the street. Most of the tenants are service or food operations. If an anchor tenant is present, it is usually a convenience grocery store such as a 7-Eleven or a large video rental store.

Neighborhood Shopping Centers

The typical *neighborhood shopping center* ranges from 30,000 to 150,000 square feet of GLA. It is designed to provide convenience shopping for the day-to-day needs of consumers in the immediate neighborhood. Supermarkets anchor roughly half of these shopping centers, while about a third have a drugstore anchor. The anchors are supported by stores that offer drugs, sundries, restaurants, and personal services. A neighborhood center is usually configured as a straight-line or L-shaped strip with no enclosed walkway or mall area, although a canopy may connect the storefronts.

The significant change in the concept of the neighborhood shopping center is the size of the supermarket. Originally the supermarket was 25,000

to 30,000 square feet, and the drugstore was 5,000 squa
for up to 50,000 square feet of shop tenants.

Supermarket anchors grew during each decade fr
end of the twentieth century; they reached 50,000 squa
the late 1990s. The other primary anchor, the drugstore
25,000 square feet. Thus, beginning in the 1980s, retaile
cupied less space, and the shop space in shopping centers built since the 1990s, was typically less than 25,000 square feet and consisted primarily of service, specialty food stores, and restaurants.

Community Shopping Centers

The *community shopping center* evolved from the neighborhood shopping center. Community shopping centers typically range from 150,000 to 400,000 square feet of GLA. They usually offer a wider range of apparel and other soft goods than neighborhood shopping centers do. Among the more common anchors are supermarkets, super drugstores, and discount department stores. Community shopping center tenants sometimes include off-price retailers that sell such items as apparel, home improvement/furnishings, toys, electronics, or sporting goods. The shopping center is usually configured as a strip, in a straight line, or in an L or a U shape.

Malls

Malls are special types of shopping centers that play important roles in their communities. Like the early market areas, malls have become not only places to buy merchandise but also gathering places for their communities. They provide fashion and mass merchandising, and their marketing provides entertainment and educational activities. (The marketing and promotional activities of malls are discussed in chapter 10, Marketing the Shopping Center.)

A successful mall usually has a few vacancies and new tenants that are in the process of designing or constructing their tenant improvements. Many successful malls turn over 5 percent or more of their tenants each year. Mall operators must keep the common areas fresh and inviting. New or renovated mall amenities, such as benches, restrooms, children's play areas, and landscaping, are continually evaluated, upgraded, and added.

Because of a mall's size and complexity, a mall operator must constantly reevaluate the tenant mix and the physical plant and make the necessary changes to remain competitive. The refurbishment often includes expanding the mall with new anchor tenants, an entertainment element, and new or more shop tenants. Mall renovation is discussed in chapter 2, Development and Rehabilitation of Retail Properties.

As previously mentioned, the first malls were built in the 1950s, but great numbers of malls were not developed throughout the United States until the

s. Since the first malls, many generations of malls have developed. Two those generations—the regional and the super regional mall—are now specifically recognized as separate shopping center types.

Regional Malls. The *regional mall* was a retail phenomenon when it was first developed, and it continued to be the dominant retail venue through the 1980s. The tenant mix for the small shop spaces, which provide general merchandise, is developed around the quality and price points of merchandise sold by the anchor tenants. If the anchor tenants are high-end department stores, the other tenants should offer medium- to high-end merchandise. Fashion, gift, jewelry, and food service retailers occupy most of the shop space. Many generations of malls have their roots in the regional mall concept.

Open-Air, Single-Level Malls. The first generation of the mall was the open-air, single-level regional mall. It typically ranges from 400,000 to 1,000,000 square feet of GLA and is anchored by two or three major retailers—usually specialty or full-line department stores. Other anchors may include junior and discount department stores. This shopping center type provides general merchandise (a large percentage of which is apparel) and services in full depth and variety. Its main attractions are its anchors: traditional, mass merchant, or discount department stores or fashion specialty stores.

Climate-Controlled, Single-Level Enclosed Malls. In the late 1970s, the second generation of the mall was developed as a climate-controlled, single-level enclosed mall. The stores in this type of mall typically have an inward orientation and are connected by a common walkway. Parking surrounds the outside perimeter.

Super Regional Malls. These large malls are considered the third generation of the mall concept. They have become so important that they are now a separate shopping center type, so they are discussed separately below.

Vertical Malls. A fourth version or generation of the mall is the downtown vertical mall. They typically have four to six levels, are anchored by one or two department stores, and have a shop tenant mix similar to a suburban regional mall. Vertical malls are located in the downtowns of major cities. Water Tower Place, the first vertical mall, was developed on Michigan Avenue in Chicago in 1976.

Vertical malls serve several different customer bases—office workers, residents in the city and surrounding areas, and visitors and tourists. They have the challenge of getting the shopper to the upper levels. A strong tenant draw must be placed on the top level. Often a multiscreen theater, a food court, and/or restaurants are located on the top level. Vertical transportation must be convenient and in a prominent location. Glass-enclosed elevators and escalators are often placed in the center of the mall. Ideally, the department store(s) should have an entrance on every level of the mall except the top level.

Super Regional Malls. These malls are similar to regional malls, but because of their larger size, super regional malls have more anchors and a deeper selection of merchandise, and they draw from a larger population base. They encompass more than 1,000,000 square feet of GLA, have more than 100 shop tenants, and are anchored by at least four full-line or specialty department stores. As with regional malls, the typical configuration is as an enclosed mall, frequently with multiple levels.

Recent Mall Trends. Most malls developed in the 1960s, 1970s, and 1980s are still operating today. Many of them have experienced threats to their market positions from other malls and new shopping center concepts. A mall's tenant mix and physical plant must continually be upgraded to maintain its competitive position.

In major metropolitan areas, such as southern California, a regional or super regional mall can be found nearly every 5 to 10 miles along the expressways. There is often little difference among them. They have similar, if not identical, anchor tenants and similar shop tenants. When one of these malls loses its market position because of neglect to its physical plant or tenant mix, shoppers will travel a few miles further to the next mall.

The 1980s proved to be a challenging time for malls when many department store chains filed for chapter 11 bankruptcy. Some, such as Montgomery Ward, went out of business and closed hundreds of stores. Other department store chains emerged from bankruptcy stronger, but closed several stores in the process. Scores of malls lost one or more of their anchor department stores. Malls did not have strong competition from other property types until power shopping centers and outlet shopping centers were developed in the 1980s and lifestyle shopping centers were developed in the 1990s.

In the late 1990s open-air malls were once again developed, as the open-air concept became the choice of retailers and shoppers. Some of those malls were hybrids that combined the features and components of malls, lifestyle shopping centers, and power shopping centers. They combined the traditional anchors of malls (the department store) with the box stores found in power shopping centers and the upscale larger specialty stores that anchor lifestyle shopping centers. These hybrids are often developed with the same main street design found in lifestyle shopping centers. The lifestyle shopping center is frequently attached as a "tail" to an existing enclosed mall. An advantage open-air malls have over enclosed malls is that their common area maintenance costs are usually significantly lower.

Another change in malls in the 1990s and the early 2000s was the inclusion of major discounters as anchor tenants and the addition of an entertainment element. The competition for the consumer's dollar is fierce, and malls that do not maintain or strengthen their market positions will be replaced with another use. Many regional malls lost and could not replace one or more anchor tenants because they were unable to keep pace with the new competition. Those regional malls have either been de-malled to power or lifestyle shopping centers or changed to other uses. Regional and super regional malls that have strengthened their market positions and remain dominant retail venues in their communities are referred to as *fortress malls.*

Specialty Shopping Centers

Specialty shopping centers are also known as *theme* or *festival shopping centers*. They usually range from 50,000 to 300,000 square feet of GLA. They are often created by conversion of an existing building to a new use (adaptive use), although some are new structures. Many perpetuate an architectural theme suggested by the original use of the building or the location. Specialty shopping centers require a location with a high traffic volume. The tourist trade is a major component of their customer base (most do not have traditional anchor tenants as a customer draw).

The main attractions at specialty shopping centers include food services and entertainment establishments as well as smaller shops that are usually one-of-a-kind boutiques, craft specialty stores, and limited national retailers. Faneuil Hall Marketplace in Boston as well as Ghirardelli Square and Pier 39 in San Francisco are classic examples of such specialty centers.

Faneuil Hall Marketplace was originally a row of three industrial and public market buildings near the waterfront. Today it is a specialty shopping center with over 125 specialty food operators, gift, fashion, and accessories merchants as well as restaurants and entertainment.

Ghirardelli Square was originally a multilevel chocolate factory near San Francisco Bay at the end of a cable car line. This specialty shopping center's tenant mix now consists of restaurants, boutique shops, and upscale fashion merchants.

The two-level Pier 39 in San Francisco has a major entertainment element with unique popular attractions that include an aquarium, the home for a fleet of ships that tour the bay, a cyber arcade, and an underwater world in addition to 110 specialty shops.

Specialty shopping centers offer a unique experience with entertainment in addition to specialty and one-of-a-kind shops, typically in a historic building. A successful specialty shopping center is a major attraction in its area.

Outlet Shopping Centers

Developed in the 1980s due to consumer interest in value shopping experiences, *outlet shopping centers* are usually located in rural areas, although they are occasionally found in tourist locations. They typically range from 50,000 to 400,000 square feet. These shopping centers are usually not anchored. A strip configuration is most common, although some are enclosed malls and others are arranged in a "village" cluster.

Outlet shopping centers consist mostly of manufacturers' outlet stores that sell their own brands at a discount. They sell surplus merchandise, which may be seconds, irregulars, or overruns. Some retailers, known as *off-price retailers,* sell first-quality, brand name merchandise at low prices; they make special bulk purchases and pass the savings on to the customer.

Because manufacturers do not want to compete directly with the retailers that distribute their products, these shopping centers are usually located farther from metropolitan trade areas than more traditional regional shopping centers. Frequently, outlet shopping centers serve an "extra-regional" market, with 25 to 50 percent of their sales being to customers who travel more than 50 miles to shop.

At the beginning of the twenty-first century, 260 outlet shopping centers were in existence. Few outlet shopping centers have been developed since the late 1990s, and the growth of the industry is through the expansion of the existing top-tier outlet shopping centers, which are marketed to tourists and locals. Initially they were developed outside major metropolitan areas, but with the growth of those areas and the proliferation of box stores, some outlet shopping centers are now situated among other retail concepts and closer to their customer bases.

Power Shopping Centers

A *power shopping center* is dominated by several large anchors, including discount department stores, home and garden stores, sporting goods stores, warehouse clubs, and other category killers. This type of shopping center typically consists of several freestanding (unconnected) anchors and a few small specialty tenants. They are large strip shopping centers that have between 250,000 and 600,000 square feet of GLA. They have limited landscaping. A disadvantage of power shopping centers is that most of their tenants offer merchandise that shoppers seek out specifically, rather than items purchased on impulse, and therefore the shopping centers themselves have little of the ambiance of a community shopping center or a regional mall where the tenants benefit from each other's presence.

First developed in the mid 1980s, these shopping centers evolved from promotional shopping centers. *Promotional shopping centers* consisted of five to eight stores ranging from 5,000 to 10,000 square feet. The tenants were not typical mall tenants and did not want to pay the higher rents and tenant charges of a regional mall. They grouped together and located near a regional mall to benefit from the traffic the mall generated. The power shopping center thus evolved from the concept of grouping smaller box stores together.

The first power shopping center, 280 Metro, was developed in 1986 in the city of Colma, California, approximately 10 miles south of San Francisco. An expressway separated this power shopping center from a very successful, enclosed regional mall.

The second generation of the power shopping center was first developed in the early 2000s and is referred to as a *power town shopping center.* It is a hybrid between a power shopping center and a lifestyle shopping center. A power town shopping center is anchored by category-dominant box stores. It has more specialty shop tenants than a power shopping center, and it includes an entertainment element that may have theaters, restaurants, and a food court. The design has a main street element and more landscaping and amenities than the original power shopping centers, and it is larger than the original power shopping centers—ranging from 600,000 to 1,000,000 square feet.

Lifestyle Shopping Centers

Developed in the early 1990s, *lifestyle shopping centers* are open-air shopping centers that have a main street design. They range from 150,000 to over 500,000 square feet. They are developed in more affluent areas and have large trade areas. The role of lifestyle shopping centers in the community is similar to that of regional malls. They provide a broad selection of fashion, jewelry, and gifts together with several fine dining restaurants and an entertainment element.

Three generations of lifestyle shopping centers were developed during their first ten years. The tenant mix of the first generation originally consisted of upscale retailers, fine restaurants, and often a theater. The second generation of lifestyle shopping centers included two- to three-level apartments and boutique hotels above the ground floor retail space. The third generation included department stores that had smaller formats than those of their typical mall stores. Lifestyle shopping centers are relatively new in relationship to power and outlet shopping centers and malls, and they continue to evolve.

Entertainment Shopping Centers

Entertainment shopping centers were first developed in the 1980s. The original entertainment shopping centers were anchored by multiscreen state-of-the-art theaters; leisure-oriented tenants (many of which had a theme), such as resort clothing retailers, bookstores, and restaurants; and unique specialty stores. The next generation of entertainment shopping centers added retailers that had an entertainment element as well as establishments that offered games and activities along with food service and trendy and traditional fashion merchants. Multilevel entertainment shopping centers are developed in urban areas, and single-level entertainment shopping centers are built in the suburbs. They often have oversized signage and unique graphics. The entertainment shopping center's role in the community is to provide entertainment, restaurants, and trendy merchandise in a "shoppertainment" urban design environment. In the early 2000s, some entertainment shopping centers began adding specialty department stores such as Nordstrom's to their mix.

A classic example of the evolution of an entertainment shopping center is the Irvine Spectrum Center. Developed in 1995 on 80 acres in southern California, the Irvine Spectrum Center's first phase was a pure entertainment shopping center anchored by a 21-screen, state-of-the-art theater. Additional phases turned the shopping center into a "shoppertainment" by adding trendy fashion, more restaurants, more entertainment, and a specialty department store. The shopping center grew to over 100 stores, restaurants, and a variety of entertainment elements. In addition to one of the largest multiscreen theaters in the world, the entertainment includes a 108-foot Ferris wheel with gondolas, an antique carousel, and live entertainment venues.

Downtown Retailing

Early retailing in the United States started in the downtown areas of cities. Eventually every major city and many of the smaller cities had vibrant retail cores in their downtowns. Retailing brought people from all over the area downtown for shopping, dining, and entertainment. Multilevel department stores were the main attraction, and specialty merchants lined the streets throughout each city's retail core. Downtowns remained the dominant retail venue in America until the development of malls.

When malls were developed in urban neighborhoods and in the suburbs, people found shopping at the malls—especially climate-controlled enclosed malls—more convenient than driving downtown to shop. The downtowns of smaller cities and many of the larger urban cities eventually lost their retail cores. That was the beginning of the deterioration of most downtowns. Many urban downtowns became "eight-hour cities." When the office workers left their buildings to go home to the suburbs, the downtowns became empty canyons of tall buildings with no evening street life.

One of two retail trends during the early 2000s was the revitalization of the retail cores of many cities' downtowns. Many cities that had lost their downtowns worked aggressively to change from eight-hour cities to eighteen-hour cities. To create a successful, vibrant downtown environment that extends beyond the eight-hour workday requires several elements: 1) a large office population; 2) retailing options with shops that are open during and after the dinner hour and on weekends; 3) entertainment venues, such as movie theatres and live performances; 4) residential living options, such as high-rise apartments and condominiums.

Seattle is an example of the positive turnaround of a city that in years past had a strong downtown retail community. Leading up to the mid-1990s, the downtown had lost much of its retail core and after-work nightlife. Nordstrom's played a major role in the turnaround, as it moved from a small store location into a large, vacated department store. That became the flagship store for Nordstrom's, and it was connected to a new vertical mall by a sky bridge.

Neighborhood Retailing

The other emerging trend during the early 2000s was a return to neighborhood retailing. Prior to the development of malls, many neighborhood streets were lined with fashion, gift, and jewelry merchants, five and dime stores, department stores with smaller formats, restaurants, and one or several single-screen theaters. Many urban neighborhoods lost their retail elements for the same reason downtowns lost their retail cores.

By the late 1990s and early 2000s, though, retailers rediscovered that neighborhoods have good demographics and excellent population density. Typically, moderate- to above-average-priced merchants, trendy specialty stores, national retailers, service tenants, specialty food stores, and restaurants began locating in neighborhoods. They learned that the population—often comprised of two-income families with a moderate amount of disposable income and a need for convenience—would support such retailing efforts.

In terms of retailer success, the stores in neighborhood markets can generate the same sales per square foot they generate in malls—or even greater. Because of site constraints, retailers (especially the larger retailers) must modify their standard formats and occasionally operate in a two-level store. Some of the large box stores have created smaller formats for urban and neighborhood locations. Advantages to a street location over a mall include that merchants are able to establish their own hours of operation and triple net charges are considerably less.

Rents in the best neighborhoods in New York, Chicago, San Francisco, and other high-density cities with good demographics and psychographics equal and sometimes far exceed the rents in the best malls in those areas. Neighborhood retailing, as the name implies, serves the neighborhood. However, some neighborhoods develop a reputation for specializing in a particular product, such as trendy fashions, restaurants, and home furnishings, and they can draw people from other neighborhoods.

Other Retail Opportunities

Retail has always been an important component in other property types. Ground-floor retail is a sought-after amenity in urban high-rise office and residential multi-use buildings. If the property is located in a strong retail area, the rents charged for the ground-floor retail space can far exceed the rents for the office space or apartment units.

Retail always existed at airports. Poor food, limited merchandise selection, and high prices were common at all airports in the United States until the early 1990s. A British firm, BAA, revolutionized airport retailing in the United States starting with Pittsburgh International Airport, which was the first airport to lease to national retailers and to offer street pricing. The new retailing at airports provides significantly increased revenue from the expanded retail areas of airports while providing travelers with mall-type merchants and a variety of fast-food service, quick-food service, and fine dining restaurants.

Cities have used retailing and restaurants to develop their waterfronts, such as San Antonio's River Walk and Baltimore's Inner Harbor. Resorts have reevaluated the benefits of retailing and food services to their clientele and their bottom line. They have brought in brand name retailers as well as nationally renowned chefs and signature restaurants. Many resort operators have leased to or entered into a license agreement or joint venture with some of the best restaurant operators in America. Retailers' sales volumes at resorts can far exceed those of mall merchants. To make that happen, the tourists must be familiar with the merchandise or restaurants.

Retailing has always been a critical component for major mixed-use developments. It not only provides an important amenity to office workers, residents, and overnight guests but it also becomes the main attraction for most mixed-use developments. A mixed-use development is often identified in the community and beyond by its successful retail, restaurant, and entertainment elements. Chapter 12, The Retail Component in Multi-Use and Mixed-use Developments, contains more information about those developments.

IMPORTANCE OF SHOPPING CENTERS

As mentioned above, each shopping center serves a major role in its community, but shopping centers primarily provide an optimum retailing environment for the tenants and meet the shopping, dining, and entertainment needs and desires of consumers. Shopping centers continue to be refined and redeveloped, and new concepts will continue to evolve. They are becoming increasingly important due to the services, activities, and entertainment they provide to their communities and the many ways they benefit the communities in which they are located.

Revenue

Many communities encourage the development of shopping centers—especially the large regional and super regional malls and power, outlet and lifestyle shopping centers—because they are major sources of revenue for local and regional governments. The two primary types of revenue they yield are sales tax and property tax. Almost all states and municipalities assess a sales tax, but they may exempt some items, such as food and, possibly, restaurant purchases.

The fiscal impact a shopping center has on a particular community is evidenced by the amount of sales tax it generates. Take the example of a 135,000-square-foot neighborhood shopping center anchored by a 50,000-square-foot supermarket, a 17,000-square-foot super drugstore, and a 35,000-square-foot home accessories center, with the remaining 33,000 square feet divided into several small shops and pad users. Annual sales for the shopping center are $46,250,000 and the supermarket's share of those sales is $25,000,000; the remaining space yields $21,250,000 in sales. The sales tax is 6 percent, and 90 percent of the supermarket sales are exempt from sales tax. The taxable sales for the supermarket would be $2,500,000; the taxable sales for the rest of the shopping center would be $21,250,000. That is a total of $23,750,000 of taxable sales, which would generate $1,425,000 in sales taxes for the community.

A regional or super regional mall generates significantly greater sales and tax revenues than a neighborhood shopping center. Consider the example of a super regional mall that has 1,250,000 square feet of GLA and is anchored by four department stores. If sales are $500 per square foot per year, and none of the sales are exempt from sales tax, the mall would generate annual sales of $625,000,000. Using the same 6 percent tax rate as in the preceding example, this super regional mall would yield $37,500,000 in sales taxes.

According to the International Council of Shopping Centers (ICSC), shopping centers generated more than $53 billion in sales taxes on $1.23 trillion dollars in nationwide retail sales in 2001. That represented well over half of all nonautomotive retail sales across the United States.

Jobs

Jobs are another major benefit shopping centers provide to their communities. A shopping center offers substantial employment opportunities at several levels, and people are attracted to retailing because it is exciting and fun. Businesses in a shopping center offer numerous entry-level positions that are filled by teenagers and other people who are entering the work force for the first time. Most shopping centers employ people both full time and part time. Nationwide, shopping centers directly employ more than 10,700,000 people. In addition, the development of new shopping centers creates thousands of jobs in the construction trades.

CHANGES IN THE SHOPPING CENTER INDUSTRY

The shopping center industry experiences more changes at a faster pace than any other property type. Shopping center professionals must respond to changing consumer wants and needs, a population that continues to diversify, alternative retail venues such as catalog and Internet retailing, the downsizing and upsizing of retailers, the emergence of new retail concepts, and the failure of retailers whose concepts are no longer accepted by the consumer. These are the driving forces that create opportunities to develop new types of shopping centers, to reposition older shopping centers to once again meet the needs of their communities, and to enhance the market position of successful shopping centers while creating challenges for many retailers and retail properties. Changes that constantly occur in the industry present opportunities for shopping center developers, shopping center managers, leasing agents, and marketing professionals. The coming years will see many changes, and they will offer shopping center professionals many challenges—changes and challenges that will also provide opportunities for success.

2

Development and Rehabilitation

The shopping center industry provides a continual stream of new and redevelopment opportunities. Traditional retail development opportunities follow the growth of cities and suburban areas. Shopping centers of different types and sizes are now developed in nearly every community. New and redevelopment opportunities emerge as the demographics and psychographics in a neighborhood change. The corresponding demand encourages the introduction of new properties as well as renovation and remerchandising of older or obsolete retail properties.

Every decade new types of shopping centers are created and developed in response to retail innovations. Each new retail property concept (e.g., power shopping centers, entertainment shopping centers, lifestyle shopping centers) offers development opportunities not previously available as well as opportunities to convert existing retail properties to a new concept. For example, a renaissance occurred starting in the late 1990s with the popularity of neighborhood and downtown retailing. This presented opportunities to redevelop well-located properties to retail use or to upgrade retail uses in existing retail buildings. As community demographics and psychographics evolve, so too will retail development opportunities.

The first part of this chapter explores the analysis and decision-making processes that are common to the development of a new shopping center and the rehabilitation of an existing one. It presents the developer's objectives and the potential rewards that make the investment and effort demanded by either process worthwhile. The beginning of the chapter also introduces each essential position on the development team and outlines the position's primary responsibilities.

The second part of the chapter considers issues specific to the development of a new shopping center. The details of financing—from an analysis of the project to sources of funds—are discussed. Next it explores site selection and acquisition, including option periods and permits. Then it details the planning and design of the new shopping center—from the locations of anchor and shop tenants to parking requirements.

The last part of the chapter presents considerations specific to the rehabilitation of an existing shopping center. It details the rehabilitation income and expense items and construction costs. The chapter ends with a discussion of special considerations the shopping center owner and the shopping center manager must address during the rehabilitation process.

ANALYSIS AND DECISION

Despite the continuous opportunities for development and rehabilitation of income-producing retail real estate, it has always been and will continue to be a speculative business. The developer builds space for lease based on an understanding of the demand for the type of property. A development that is built as budgeted, leased on a timely basis at the rates anticipated, and opened as scheduled is usually enormously successful. If the project's cost is significantly over budget, or if the rental rates or lease-up time do not meet the leasing projections, the development normally experiences financial difficulties. The magnitude of the difficulties varies widely, but if they are severe, and if they are not resolved, the developer may be forced to sell the property or the lender may exercise its right to foreclose on the property. While the risks can be high, developers are willing to take on the risks inherent in building a shopping center because the potential financial rewards can be significant.

Development Objectives

Developers generally build or rehabilitate a retail property for three reasons: 1) to retain ownership and benefit from the ongoing rental income—i.e., for their own account, 2) to offer their expertise as fee developers, or 3) to serve as a merchant builder and develop the property with the intent to immediately sell it. The primary objective of development—whether the developer owns retail property or manages the development process for an owner—is to generate a substantial profit.

Owner Developer. The developer who retains ownership of the property—the *owner developer*—realizes a number of tangible financial rewards as well as a number of intangible and more personal rewards. The developer also faces a number of risks.

Rewards. When a development achieves its goal and is built and leased per the original projections, substantial value is created in the property. The owner developer can harvest that value by selling or refinancing the property.

In addition to the financial considerations, the owner developer receives numerous intangible rewards, such as the pride of ownership and a sense of accomplishment upon completion of the development or rehabilitation of the retail property. Many developers take great pride in the projects they create. They want the shopping center's design and layout to be compatible with the community's objectives, and they want the property to become an asset to the community.

Lenders and prospective anchor tenants evaluate developers based on their prior shopping center projects. When the developer has a successful track record, lenders and prospective anchor tenants are more inclined to become involved with the project.

Risks. The developer of a shopping center risks losing considerable money. The risks may not always be obvious, but they can be substantial. Perhaps the most important to note here are risks that relate directly to the shopping center as a form of investment property.

Functional risk is the possibility that the shopping center's location, design, size, etc., will adversely affect its utility for retail enterprise. *Interest-rate risk* is the potential that changes in value may occur due to variations in interest rates and the availability of financing. *Inflation/deflation risk* is the possibility that the effects of changes in the consumers' purchasing power due to inflation or deflation will negatively impact the value of the shopping center. *Marketability risk* is the potential that the shopping center will be unsuccessful in retaining quality tenants at acceptable rent levels or that anchor tenants and shop tenants may go out of business or elect to close their stores.

Real estate occasionally loses value and, because real property is usually developed (at least in part) with borrowed money, the value does not have to drop to zero for the owner to lose his or her entire equity in the investment. Risk accompanies most investments, and shopping center developers and their financial advisors are expected to make intelligent estimates of the risks inherent in such projects.

Fee Developer. A *fee developer* builds a retail property or shopping center for another party for a fee. For instance, a retailer may hire a developer to build a freestanding store and an adjacent shop space, or a family may hire a developer to build a shopping center on a site that has been in the family for years. In such cases, profits for the shopping center developer derive from several sources.

Income from Development Activities. A developer will look to make profits from the shopping center in a number of ways. Through the various services they can provide, the developers can achieve profits through the development fee, leasing commissions, management fees, asset management fees, sales commissions and operating income.

Development Fee. The *development fee* typically ranges from 3 to 7 percent of the actual construction costs, which are also known as the *hard costs*. They are the costs to complete the site work as well as to construct the building and any improvements. *Soft costs* include fees to consultants, taxes, insurance, etc., and the cost of financing. The development fee is an important source of income for a development company because it covers the company's overhead. If several shopping centers are developed concurrently, development fees can easily exceed the developer's annual overhead.

Leasing Commissions. Another potential source of income for a developer is *leasing commissions*. A developer can take many approaches to leasing a shopping center, and the approach used determines the commission income earned.

First, the developer may hire a retail broker to lease the shopping center. The broker has the exclusive authorization to lease space in the shopping center, and cooperation with other brokers is limited. Brokers represent many national and some local retailers, and they co-broker a lease with the property's exclusive leasing agent.

In another approach, the developer negotiates the leases with the anchor tenants and hires a leasing company to market and lease the smaller shop spaces. Developers use this approach when they have a rapport with anchor retail tenants and are in a better position than anyone else to negotiate those specific leases. The anchor tenant's lease is often negotiated and executed before construction starts. In this situation, the developer earns only the commissions for the anchor leases. If the developer elects to hire a leasing firm to negotiate the remaining shop and pad leases, the developer does not earn any commission income from those tenants.

Management Fees. Another source of income is *management fees*. If the developer's business includes a shopping center management department or management company, managing the shopping center for the development company can generate a fee.

Asset Management Fees. Some developers charge the partnership that owns the shopping center an *asset management fee*. The developer, who is usually the general partner of the partnership, provides a service similar to that provided by asset management firms. This includes conducting partnership meetings, providing ownership level reports, making ownership management decisions, such as when to refinance or sell the property, accepting or rejecting lease proposals, providing redevelopment analysis and recommendations, etc.

Sales Commissions. If the shopping center is a joint venture with another company or with other individuals, the developer may act as the broker when the shopping center is sold and earn a commission on the sale—in addition to an ownership share of the proceeds.

Operating Income. When the developer retains ownership of the shopping center, there is the opportunity to obtain cash flow from the income of the property.

Development Team

The development and rehabilitation of shopping centers are complex processes that require the knowledge and experience of many individuals, each with a separate expertise. Each member of the development team comes to the project with one objective in mind—to develop a successful shopping center or retail development.

The central or focal point of the development team is the developer who typically assigns a *project manager* to orchestrate the team's efforts and take the project from concept through lease-up to opening. The project manager selects the other members of the team, which include an architect, a general contractor, a leasing agent, and a property manager.

If the development project is the renovation of a large shopping center, the shopping center's marketing director will be a member of the development team. In some projects, the lender is also a team member.

Hiring additional experts as consultants to the development team is often necessary. An appraiser may conduct a market study to verify for the lender and to confirm for the developer that a demand exists for the retail space and that the projected rental rates are achievable. The expertise of civil, structural, and mechanical engineers as well as landscape architects and environmental and wetlands consultants may be needed.

A small development firm or an individual developing a shopping center may hire a consultant or an architect to supervise the development process. In the early stages, differences of opinion should be encouraged in order to obtain a complete analysis of all sides of each issue and aspect of the development process.

Almost every shopping center development has surprises, delays, and financial challenges. Good chemistry among all the team players—especially among the developer, the architect, and the general contractor—is critical to the development process.

Architect. The architect creates a layout and design for the proposed shopping center based on the vision of the developer. Drawing upon such information as the proposed anchor tenants, a suggested number of pads or outlots, and a range of sizes for the other shop spaces, the architect proposes an arrangement of store spaces. The well-developed creative skills of a knowledgeable, experienced shopping center architect augment the developer's vision. The architect should also be able to provide a rough estimate of the costs of constructing the proposed shopping center as designed.

Selection Process. Selection of the right architect is critical. The architect should not only specialize in shopping centers but should also have a subspecialty in the type of shopping center that will be developed. The architect needs to know the anchor and shop tenants' requirements, which include store size, width, and depth as well as preferred location. The architect's design team needs to know how customer amenities differ for a grocery anchored strip shopping center, an urban multilevel enclosed mall, and a lifestyle shopping center with residential units above ground-floor retail. This is especially important when a strip shopping center developer is venturing for the first time into developing another type of shopping center, such as an outlet shopping center or a lifestyle shopping center.

Special Considerations. Careful consideration must be given to selecting an architect. Together with the project manager, the developer should interview two or three. The interview should be conducted in the architect's office so the developer can tour the office and meet the design team that would be assigned to the project. Similar shopping centers the firm has designed should be reviewed. The developer may request that the proposed design team include members who were on the design team of similar projects. The interview should include a discussion of the team's experiences designing the proposed type of shopping center and a visit to similar shopping centers the firm has designed.

The developer should ask the architect several questions to determine how the design team would handle the project. What is the workload of the members of the design team? Will they have sufficient time to complete the design and construction drawings on schedule? What are the firm's technical capabilities? Which consultants (e.g., soils engineer, landscape architect) does the firm recommend? With which general contractors, landscape architects, and subcontractors have they worked and with which have they had the best experience?

The firm should be familiar with the cost to build the project. The developer should inquire about the cost of similar shopping centers the architect recently designed. Often these costs are expressed as a dollar-per-square-foot figure. The developer should request references and follow up on them.

The architect should be told the budget for the project before the final selection of the architect is made. The design team's and the general contractor's awareness of the developer's budget are critical to the success of the project. One of the biggest challenges in developing a project is keeping within the development budget.

The discussion with potential architects should include in-depth details of the requirements of the different categories of tenants found in such shopping centers and the latest trends in this type of shopping center. The developer's team should tour the site for the proposed development with the design team. Before an architectural firm is selected, the firm's services and fees must be discussed. The American Institute of Architects (AIA) has agreements for architectural services that are widely accepted in the industry.

General Contractor. Together with the project manager or the construction manager, the developer interviews and selects a *general contractor* who will construct the project according to the architect's plans and specifications.

Selection Process. Several contractors should be interviewed. The interview process should include a review of similar projects the firm has built, the cost of those projects, and a detailed discussion of the contractor's estimated cost for the proposed project. The contractor's on-site team, which includes the proposed superintendent and any assistants, should attend and participate in the interview.

The development team should request that the contractor's team give them a tour of similar shopping centers they have built. If the project is a renovation or redevelopment of an existing property while the tenants remain open, the contractor's methods of minimizing any interference with the tenants' businesses during construction must be thoroughly discussed. The firm's past performance is important when evaluating a general contractor—especially for rehab projects with tenants in place.

Special Contract Considerations. The developer should check the general contractor's financial strength and references. General contractors use several methods to charge for their services.

Fixed-Price Contract. The contractor may provide a lump-sum or *fixed-price contract* in which the contractor provides a price based on detailed plans and retains any savings. Additional fees are charged for change orders.

Cost-Plus-Percentage Contract. Another method is the *cost-plus-percentage contract.* The developer pays the cost to build the project, and the contractor's fee is based on a percentage of the costs. This method may be appropriate during the early stages of a rehab when a reasonably accurate projection of the construction costs is impossible until more is known about the condition of the building. Then the fees for the balance of the contract can be based on one of the other methods.

Cost Plus a Fixed Fee. A third method is the *cost plus a fixed fee*. In this method, the developer pays the actual cost to build the project plus a negotiated fixed fee to the general contractor.

Guaranteed-Maximum-Price Contract. The last method is the *guaranteed-maximum-price contract*. The general contractor guarantees the construction costs and shares in any savings.

Primary Role/Responsibility. Traditionally, the general contractor's main function is to construct the project according to the plans and specifications previously prepared by the architect and approved by the developer. While that remains the principal role of the contractor, many developers make greater use of the contractor's construction expertise.

During the design stage, developers often ask the general contractor for opinions about other aspects of the property's construction. In an economy in which rising construction costs are the norm, the general contractor's expertise in keeping costs down without sacrificing quality can benefit the developer. To guarantee that the project is economically feasible, the developer should arrange a series of meetings between the architect and the general contractor during the initial design and drafting stages.

Leasing Agent or Team. Land, construction, and financing costs can be estimated with a reasonable degree of accuracy for a new development. The one outcome of the development process that cannot be predetermined, unless a project is fully pre-leased, is the leasing. This makes the leasing agent or in-house leasing team a critical part of the development team. Projected lease-up time and rental rates are estimated based on the best information available to the developer. If space in the shopping center is leased at rental rates significantly lower than those projected, or if the lease-up period extends far beyond the time projected, the development is a candidate for failure—regardless of whether the other projections are on target.

Selection process. The project manager must select the leasing agent who is most qualified to market and lease the shopping center. The person (or persons) selected may be an in-house leasing agent, an agent or agents from a brokerage firm, or the shopping center manager. The leasing agent selected must have extensive experience leasing the proposed type of shopping center. A person who has several years' experience leasing grocery anchored shopping centers is probably not the right person to lease a lifestyle shopping center, an outlet shopping center, or a regional mall. Each type of shopping center has different anchor tenants, a different tenant mix, and a different placement of tenants. Leasing agents have relationships with different retailers, depending on the types of shopping centers they lease.

A large shopping center needs a leasing team in which each team member specializes in one or more categories of merchants. Most regional malls have in-house leasing teams. The developer usually has multiple malls and has developed relationships with most of the national retailers. The leasing team has completed several leases with most of the targeted retailers.

Since each state has relatively few outlet shopping centers, leasing agents who work for brokerage firms seldom if ever get the opportunity to lease an outlet shopping center, develop outlet tenant contacts, or develop an expertise in leasing that type of retail shopping center. The same applies to lifestyle shopping centers. The retail brokerage firm often leases anchored and unanchored strip shopping centers and provides tenant representation services for many national and regional retailers.

The initial lease-up of a shopping center is critical to the success of the development, and the developer must choose the leasing person or team that is the most qualified and can devote sufficient time to leasing the shopping center. Seldom does the shopping center manager have the time to lease a new shopping center, unless it is a small strip shopping center. If a brokerage firm will be given the leasing assignment, at lease two firms should be interviewed, and each firms' leasing agents and their managers should be interviewed.

Special Considerations. Critical issues that should be included in the interview include the following:

- Has the leasing agent leased similar retail properties or shopping centers?
- What have been the terms of recent leases the leasing agent negotiated?
- What types of tenants would lease space in the proposed shopping center?
- What is the leasing agent's opinion of the design of the project and the location and size of each space?
- What are the current market conditions and rental rates?
- How much time does the leasing agent estimate will be needed to reach *occupancy breakeven* and a fully leased project?
- What marketing materials will be developed and who will pay for them?

- How much time does each member of the leasing team have to devote to this development?
- Which, if any, other shopping centers or retail properties is each leasing agent currently leasing?
- How much more time will be needed to lease up those properties?
- Will the leasing agent have other leasing assignments concurrent to leasing the proposed shopping center?
- How often should leasing meetings take place?
- What types of leasing reports will be provided and how often?
- What is the proposed leasing fee and is an incentive fee proposed?

Shopping Center Manager. A shopping center manager can provide valuable insight into the layout of the shop space and assist in the selection of materials to use that will lower the maintenance costs of the shopping center. Chapter 4, Management Structure, details the duties of the shopping center manager.

Selection Process. In the case of a new development, the developer may have in-house property management services. If that is not the case, several property management firms should be interviewed, and the most qualified one should be selected. When a shopping center is being rehabilitated, the shopping center manager may already be in place. In fact, the shopping center manager might initially have suggested the renovation to the developer.

The interview process should include each member of the potential shopping center manager's management team—the shopping center manager, the supervisor of accounting, the property accountant, and the administrative assistant—along with the executive manager or company owner. Issues to discuss include the following:

- The individual's or the firm's experiences managing similar retail properties
- The number of new retail properties the firm and/or the shopping center manager have opened
- The number of retail properties the shopping center manager manages
- The number of retail properties for which the property accountant provides accounting services
- The accounting software and other computer programs the firm operates
- The accounting procedures to process payables and collect and deposit rent

- The types of annual management plans and budgets along with the monthly management and financial reports
- The firm's insurance coverage, including errors and omission insurance

Special considerations. The shopping center manager should be included during the design stage to contribute a management perspective on the development process. The layout of the shopping center should be reviewed to detect any spaces that may be difficult to lease. The shopping center manager should examine the layout of the shopping center and evaluate the proposed building materials from maintenance and operations perspectives (e.g., care, repair, safety, security). Also at this stage, the shopping center manager should review the projected rental rates and lease-up schedule and either verify them or offer another perspective on the market.

Lender. The lender is likely to become a member of the development team. One of the results of the savings and loan crisis of the late 1980s and early 1990s was a tightening of lending practices. Some lenders now require that the developer obtain their approval for over-budget and non-budgeted items. They often retain the right to approve each proposed lease that is below the projected rental rates and/or that requires additional concessions. In essence, these controls include the lender as a member of the development team.

Marketing Director. This person is an important member of the development team for a large property that is being rehabbed. Malls as well as specialty, lifestyle, outlet, and entertainment shopping centers have on-site marketing directors who develop and implement the marketing, advertising, and promotions programs. The marketing director works closely with the tenants to market the property and usually has the best relationship with them.

The marketing director understands the shopping center's customer base, has identified the merchandise mix weaknesses, and knows the strengths and weaknesses of the competition. This person can provide valuable insights and recommendations to upgrade and improve the property's tenant mix. In addition, the marketing director knows how the shopper perceives the property and can make recommendations to the architect regarding the amenities of the property that shoppers enjoy or that need to be added. The responsibilities of the marketing director are detailed in chapter 4, Management Structure and chapter 11, Marketing the Shopping Center.

NEW SHOPPING CENTER DEVELOPMENT

Once the developer has assembled the development team for a new shopping center—and frequently even while the team is being assembled—

many other important tasks must be accomplished. If the developer does not have sufficient funds to undertake the project alone (and few do), financing must be found. The developer may have a potential site in mind, but now the site (and perhaps others) must be evaluated and acquired. Then the shopping center itself must be planned and designed.

Financing

Based on the preliminary site plan, the developer can prepare a *pro forma,* a financial analysis for the proposed development that lists the costs of developing the site and the income, expenses, and cash flow projections. The developer negotiates a loan to finance the project based on the cost to develop the shopping center, the amount of equity the lender will require, and the property's net operating income (NOI). This section details the development pro forma and sources of financing.

Preparation of the Development Pro Forma. A developer prepares and revises the pro forma for a proposed shopping center several times. The pro forma is the financial analysis of the proposed development. It includes land, construction, financing, marketing, and leasing costs. It also includes the projected income and expenses of the property during its initial lease-up and once it is a stabilized, operating property.

The entire development team contributes to the evolving pro forma. The developer contacts major retailers and begins to negotiate the terms of their leases. The leasing agent provides income projections for rents for the shop spaces, pads, and outlots. The project manager obtains firm bids from several general contractors. While the construction costs are being acquired, the developer negotiates with a lender for a loan commitment. The property manager verifies the income projections and prepares estimates of grand opening event costs and operating expenses. If the rough numbers indicate that the proposed shopping center is economically viable, the developer will pursue the project.

The example pro forma in exhibit 2.1 permits analysis of the cost to develop the shopping center, projections of income and the landlord's non-reimbursable operating expenses, and calculation of the NOI and the return on investment (ROI).

Cost Analysis. The costs of developing the shopping center include land acquisition, design and consultation fees, construction costs, and the cost of financing those activities. Also to be considered are off-site infrastructure costs, impact fees, construction and operating permits, etc., all of which can add substantially to development costs.

Income Projection. Projected rental income from the property is based on the gross leasable area (GLA) of anchor tenant spaces, small shop spaces,

Exhibit 2.1

Draft Pro Forma

Date: __________ Project: __________

[*Company Name*]

Areas

Total Site __________ Sq Ft (__________ Acres)
Less Nonusable __________ Sq Ft
Net Site __________ Sq Ft
Building Area __________ Sq Ft
Common Area __________ Sq Ft

Costs

A. Land __________ Sq Ft @ $__________ /Sq Ft $__________

B. On Site __________ Sq Ft @ $__________ /Sq Ft $__________
Off Site __________ Sq Ft @ $__________ /Sq Ft $__________
Total for Site Work (B) $__________

C. Buildings
1. __________ __________ Sq Ft @ $__________ /Sq Ft = $__________
2. __________ __________ Sq Ft @ $__________ /Sq Ft = $__________
3. __________ __________ Sq Ft @ $__________ /Sq Ft = $__________
4. __________ __________ Sq Ft @ $__________ /Sq Ft = $__________
5. __________ __________ Sq Ft @ $__________ /Sq Ft = $__________
6. __________ __________ Sq Ft @ $__________ /Sq Ft = $__________
7. __________ __________ Sq Ft @ $__________ /Sq Ft = $__________
8. __________ __________ Sq Ft @ $__________ /Sq Ft = $__________
9. Tenant Allowances __________ $__________

Total Buildings (C) $__________
Total Buildings *plus* Site Work (B + C) $__________

D. Architecture and Engineering __________ % of (B + C) $__________
E. Annexation and City Liaison $__________
F. Sales Tax __________ % of (B + C) $__________

G. Lease Commissions
1. Anchor __________ Sq Ft @ $__________ /Sq Ft
2. Shops __________ Sq Ft @ $__________ /Sq Ft
3. Pads __________ Sq Ft @ $__________ /Sq Ft
4. __________ Sq Ft @ $__________ /Sq Ft
5. __________ Sq Ft @ $__________ /Sq Ft

Total Lease Commissions (G) $__________

H. Fees and Permits $__________
I. Survey, Soils, Texts, and Inspections $__________
J. Legal, Environmental, Appraisal, and Market Study $__________
K. Real Estate Taxes $__________
L. Assessments $__________
M. Bond/Insurance __________ % of (B + C) $__________
N. Escrow $__________
O. Clean-Up—Punch List $__________
P. Grand Opening and Promotion $__________

Exhibit 2.1 ***(continued)***

Q. Miscellaneous Costs $________
R. Development Fee ________% of (B + C) $________
S. Contingency $________
T. Financing $________
________ Points $________
Interim ________% ________ Months ________% $________
Total Financing (T) $________
U. Land Carry $________

Income Statement

A. Rental Income
1. Anchor ________ Sq Ft @ $________/Sq Ft $________
2. ________ Sq Ft @ $________/Sq Ft $________
3. ________ Sq Ft @ $________/Sq Ft $________
4. Shops ________ Sq Ft @ $________/Sq Ft $________
5. ________ Sq Ft @ $________/Sq Ft $________
6. ________ Sq Ft @ $________/Sq Ft $________
7. Pads ________ Sq Ft @ $________/Sq Ft $________
8. ________ Sq Ft @ $________/Sq Ft $________
9. ________ Sq Ft @ $________/Sq Ft $________
Total Rental Income (A) $________

B. Expenses
1. ________% Vacancy $________
2. Management Fee ________% $________
3. Nonreimbursable Maintenance $________
4. Vacancy CAM/Tax/Insurance @ $________/Sq Ft $________
5. Merchants' Assn/Market'g Fund @ $________/Sq Ft $________
6. Other Expenses $________
Total Expenses (B) $________

C. Net Operating Income (NOI) [A–B] $________

Cash—Loan—Equity Analysis

Economic Value—Cap Rate ________% of NOI $________
Loan ________% of Value—Coverage ________ $________
Debt Service ________%—________ Year = $________K $________
Cash Flow $________

Total Cost $________
= Loan Amount $________
Equity Requirement $________

$________ (Cash Flow) ÷ $________ (Equity Required) = ________% (Rate of Return on Investment)

Common area usually includes space allotted for parking. *Off-site costs* may include infrastructure items. *Equity requirement* would include any down payment (amounts paid upfront by the developer and/or ownership partners) and may reflect the developer's investment of time and expertise (part or all of the "development fee") and prior investment in the land.

Pro forma compilation and calculations are intended to project a reasonably accurate estimate of construction costs and operating income and expenses. Other items may be incorporated as appropriate.

pads or outlot tenants, and possibly temporary tenants. However, developers and lenders are primarily interested in the revenue the shopping center is likely to produce on an annual basis over time, rather than what it could produce if it were always 100 percent occupied and all rents were paid in full.

Anticipating some loss of income due to vacancies is prudent. Lost income from vacancies has usually been projected as 5 percent of the small shop space, with no vacancy factor applied to anchor spaces (anchor leases have long terms, and the tenants are usually creditworthy). However, this varies in practice. *Vacancy loss* may be estimated based on a time period, say three months, at the market rate prevailing at the time of lease expiration. *Collection loss* may be calculated as a percentage of the gross receipts (e.g., 2 percent of the anticipated gross rental income from all tenants except the anchors). Subtraction of vacancy and collection losses from gross rental income yields a projection of *effective gross income* or the actual receipts likely to be collected for the shopping center.

Non-reimbursable Operating Expense Projection. Next, the *non-reimbursable operating expenses* are estimated. These include the pass-through charges—e.g., common area maintenance (CAM), taxes, and insurance—that are attributable to the vacant spaces and that the landlord therefore pays. It also includes other non-reimbursable expenses that cannot be collected from or passed through to tenants, such as merchants' association or marketing fund dues, utility costs for vacant spaces, legal fees, and possibly the management fee.

If anchor tenants' leases exclude them from paying some CAM expenses and the other tenants' leases prorate CAM expenses in relation to the entire GLA of the shopping center (including the GLA of the anchor spaces), the portion of the anchors' shares of the CAM expenses that is not covered becomes the landlord's non-reimbursable operating expenses. That expense should be included in the development pro forma estimates to ensure their accuracy. The lender may require line items for reserves for future major maintenance and replacements, sometimes referred to as a *sinking fund,* and for tenant improvements and commissions.

NOI and ROI Calculations. Subtracting the operating expenses from the effective gross income yields the property's net operating income (NOI). Finally, the annual debt service on the loan (payments of principal and interest) is subtracted from the NOI to determine the *cash flow.* This cash flow figure is used to project the developer's return on investment as part of the development pro forma.

Lender Considerations. Lenders and developers prefer a high percentage of the shop tenants to be *credit tenants.* This is possible in most anchored shopping centers regardless of the shopping center type, but it is not likely in unanchored shopping centers. Lenders for medium and large shopping centers recognize the importance of the anchor tenant to the success of the shopping center. Developers usually cannot obtain a loan commitment until one or more anchor tenants acceptable to the lender have committed to the project. Lenders carefully evaluate the financial status of the anchor tenant because some anchor tenants had financial problems due to leveraged buyouts in the middle and late 1980s.

Lenders may require a certain percentage of the shopping center's income to be from creditworthy tenants. No industry-wide ratio has been established for the percentage of the shopping center's income, the number of tenants, or the amount of GLA to be attributable to creditworthy tenants.

However, shopping center investors prefer that anchor tenants *not* occupy too large a percentage of the shopping center's GLA. For instance, an investment group may set a criterion that not more than 65 percent of the GLA is to be occupied by anchor tenants. Anchor tenants negotiate lease terms favorable to themselves that include long-term leases and limited and small rent increases, typically every five years. For this reason, many investors believe that a shopping center with an extraordinarily high percentage of GLA occupied by anchor tenants will have limited upside income potential. A good balance between anchor tenants and shop tenants is a key factor in a shopping center's success.

Acquiring the Equity. A major source of equity in the 1980s (prior to the tax law changes of 1986) was from private and public syndications that fueled the growth of the real estate industry in general—and of shopping centers in particular. The equity requirements to develop a property are usually 20 to 25 percent of the cost of the development, including the cost of the land. A grocery anchored shopping center can cost between $10 and $20 million. The equity needed for such shopping centers can range from $2 million to $2.5 million for the $10-million-dollar shopping center and $4 to $5 million for the $20-million-dollar shopping center.

Most developers do not have sufficient cash reserves to meet the equity requirements. They need an *equity partner* who will provide a significant portion or all of the equity. Equity partners can be found as individual partners, group partners, or syndicated partners, such as private, public, tax-oriented, or income-oriented organizations.

The equity partner receives an ownership interest in the development, based on the amount of equity provided—which can range from 50 to 75 percent of the development. The equity partner may also receive a *preferred return*. For instance, the equity partner may have a 7 percent preferred return and may be paid this return on its investment before the developer receives any cash distribution. After the equity partner is paid the preferred return, two approaches are followed. In the first, the developer receives the same percentage return on its equity, then all additional distributions are shared equally. In the second system, after the equity partner receives the initial 7 percent return, all additional distributions are shared, based on the percentage of ownership in the shopping center. Countless methods are used to distribute the cash flow and later the sale proceeds of the shopping center.

Importance of Financing. As is clear from the above discussions, financing is a critical element in the shopping center development process. Without an outside source of funds—either a lender or a joint-venture partner—a shopping center will not be developed. A project is usually developed with two loans.

Construction Loan. The first is a *construction loan*—a short-term loan that covers the cost to develop the project and is usually funded by one or more commercial banks. The primary lender negotiates with and provides the loan to the developer. The primary lender often shares the risk of making the loan by having other lenders participate in it. Such participating lenders then provide the funds for a portion of the construction loan. A construction loan is usually a *recourse loan,* meaning the borrower is required to guarantee the repayment of the loan (the lender can claim other assets of the borrower in addition to the property if the loan is defaulted).

Permanent Loan. Subsequently, a *permanent loan* is taken out to replace and pay off the construction loan. In the past, a permanent loan was typically a long-term loan for a period of 30 years. Now, permanent loans may also have a term of 10 to 20 years with an *amortization* (installment payments) comparable to those for a 30-year loan and a final balloon payment to pay off the outstanding principal. Long-term loans typically are *nonrecourse loans* (the borrower, upon default, has no personal liability for the loan beyond the property pledged as collateral).

As mentioned earlier, lenders may require a percentage of a shopping center project to be pre-leased either before construction or before the permanent loan commitment, which includes a lease commitment from one or more anchor tenants.

Sources of Financing. Generally, a developer's goal is to obtain the maximum financing for the development of the shopping center. Prior to the early 1980s, a developer could obtain 100-percent financing. In such a situation, the developer would have no cash invested in the project; he or she would receive a substantial development fee and still own the project. If a developer could demonstrate that the value of a shopping center was 133 percent of the cost to develop it, and the lender was willing to provide a loan at 75 percent of the value, the loan would be for 100 percent of the development cost (133 percent × 75 percent = 100 percent). Once the shopping center was operational and leased-up at or near pro forma rates, its NOI was usually sufficient to service the debt on the loan because interest rates were traditionally below 10 percent.

In the early 1980s, however, interest rates reached the highest levels in the history of the United States; they soared into the double digits and exceeded 20 percent for a period of time. Understandably, few proposed developments would generate sufficient NOI to service a loan at such a high interest rate. Consequently, developers sought alternatives to traditional financing. Two sources of such funding that were common during those high-interest-rate years included equity sharing by institutions and lender participation loans, both of which reduced the developer's *equity* (outright ownership) in the project.

Equity Sharing. Many institutions, especially insurance companies, stepped in to provide the funds to develop commercial projects. For providing all of the development funds, the institution would receive a 50-percent or greater share of the equity—no loan or loan payment as such would be made. Often the institution would receive either a guaranteed or a preferential return on the investment.

A *guaranteed return* provided the institution with an agreed rate of return on the funds it contributed. The guarantee was for a limited period (e.g., two or five years) or the entire term of the joint ownership of the property. If the cash flow from the property were not sufficient to provide the guaranteed return, the developer would have to make up the difference from company or personal funds.

A *preferential return* provided the institution with the first distribution from the cash flow of the property until it received a prescribed percentage return on the amount contributed (e.g., 12 percent). The developer then received the next distribution from the cash flow, which equaled the amount paid to the institution. Any additional cash flow was distributed between the institution and the developer based on their shares of the shopping center. A distinct advantage to this arrangement was that when all the funds necessary to develop the project were contributed, there was no debt service—in essence, the NOI of the property was its cash flow.

Lender Participation Loans. The second source was *lender-participation loans*. The lender provided a loan at an interest rate below the market rate and received either (1) an equity position in the property or (2) a percentage of the cash flow from the property or from its appreciation upon sale.

Equity Partners. During the early 1990s, developers were confronted with another type of financing crisis. The savings and loan industry tightened its lending practices, and lenders required developers to put cash into their projects. The typical loan was for 70 to 80 percent of the project cost, and developers were required to make up the difference between the project cost and the loan amount, either from their own funds or those of an equity partner who would receive a substantial percentage of ownership in the project.

Commercial Mortgage Backed Securities. In the 1990s a new form of financing was created. *Commercial mortgage backed securities (CMBSs)* are securities backed by the cash flow of the property. During the early 2000s interest rates reached an all-time low, and developers were typically able to finance 75 to 80 percent of their developments at very favorable interest rates. The developer often had an equity partner to provide some or all of the funding in addition to the loan needed to develop the project.

Site Selection and Acquisition

Selection and acquisition of the site depend on careful analysis. Several basic criteria are required to determine the best retail site. As mentioned in chapter 1, Shopping Centers: Evolution and Change, the trade area must have the right demographics and psychographics to support the proposed development. The site must also be easily accessible and have good visibility. Finally, the site must have sufficient buildable area to accommodate the proposed development.

In the development process, the developer evaluates the demographic and psychographic information to determine whether the site is viable for a shopping center. (Chapter 9, Leasing the Shopping Center, discusses creating a demographic profile.) If development is feasible from the market standpoint, the developer will take an option on the site or enter into a sales contract contingent on certain requirements being met.

Option Period. Most developers will not acquire the title to a property until they have a commitment from one or more anchor tenants. Developers require that the property have or the seller obtain the proper zoning before purchasing the site. The developer must often take an option on the property to have sufficient time to negotiate a lease with the anchor tenants and possibly to obtain the proper zoning. The option is usually for six months, and it may need to be extended. Developers prefer to have a free "look see," meaning no option fee, but if the option is extended, there often is a fee, which may include paying the taxes and insurance on the land during the option period. Option fees are often applied to the sale price of the land.

Permits. The development process continues during the option period as the developer's architect draws a preliminary site plan of the shopping center that shows the locations of anchor tenants, shops, and pads or outlots.

The site and building plans must be submitted to the municipal building department for approval and permits.

Zoning. The first approval is for zoning. *Zoning ordinances* are the means by which a municipality exercises control over land use. If the site is not zoned for shopping center use, the developer may apply for a variance, and the option to purchase the site will be contingent on appropriate rezoning.

Environmental Audits. Environmental issues are also considered in the analysis of the site. An *environmental audit* is conducted to determine if any hazardous substances are present. Development of wetlands requires a specific permit. Environmental laws issued by state and local governing bodies in addition to the federal regulations enforced by the U.S. Environmental Protection Agency (EPA) can affect a shopping center's development. Requirements for testing, monitoring, and approvals as well as construction and operating permits add to the development costs. The outcomes of some environmental analyses may preclude development of a selected site.

Planning and Design

While financing plans and site selection are underway, the developer and the development team are also working on finding and obtaining commitments from anchor tenants, determining which shop tenants complement the anchor tenants, and analyzing the needs of the shopping center's potential customer base. Once the many pieces begin to come together, they can plan how all the pieces will fit into the architect's design of the new shopping center.

Anchor Tenants. Anchor tenants are crucial to shopping center development. The size and positioning of anchor space affects the design and placement of all the other tenant spaces in the shopping center. The type and price points of the anchor tenants' merchandise affect both the mix of tenants and their placement in the center. The financial arrangements with anchor tenants will affect development costs, and they may affect the leases for the other tenants and the financial arrangements with them. For these reasons, the negotiation of anchor leases takes place very early in the development process.

Anchor tenanted shopping centers cannot be built, nor can construction begin, until some or all of the anchor tenants' leases are negotiated and executed. The developer must be assured of the anchor tenants' commitment to the project well in advance, both to attract other tenants to the shopping center and to secure construction and permanent financing. Lenders often require lease commitments as a condition for shopping center development loans. (Negotiation of anchor leases is discussed in chapter 10, Negotiating and Documenting the Lease.)

Anchor Store Location. Retailers use several criteria when evaluating and selecting a site for a store. The old saying that the three most important things in real estate are "location, location, and location" definitely applies to shopping centers. Major retailers that occupy anchor spaces and many national and regional retailers that lease shop spaces thoroughly analyze a site using criteria they have developed to measure their stores' projected success. Location means more than just the actual site. When retailers or shopping center developers say "location," they also mean the demographic and psychographic profiles of the area and competition in relation to the site as well as site accessibility and any impediments to development.

Demographics and Psychographics. A retailer normally evaluates an area to determine its sales potential. An analysis of demographic and psychographic data for the area allows the retailer to determine if its typical customer is well represented in the proposed shopping center's trade area. The information also allows the retailer to project sales volume figures.

A major retailer's selection of the site is one validation that a shopping center could succeed there. The developer must be cautious, however. The fact that a major retailer has selected a site is no guarantee that other retailers will be successful at that location. An anchor tenant draws customers from a larger trade area than the tenants in the smaller shops can—largely due to its extensive array of merchandise and its ability to promote itself more widely.

Competition. Retailers are also concerned with location in relation to competition and the number of competitors in the area. Another consideration is the location of a site in relationship to the retailer's other stores. All of these factors will affect tenants' sales volumes. The final consideration is the impact future developments in the area could have on a retailer's success at this site. New competition moving into the general area has the potential to reduce an established retailer's market share.

Customer Draw. An anchor tenant usually occupies a large proportion of the available GLA and draws the majority of the customers to the shopping center. The type of retailer that serves as the anchor tenant varies with the type of shopping center.

Department stores such as Nordstrom or Macy's traditionally are the anchor tenants for regional and super regional malls. Since the early 2000s, alternative anchors have become acceptable in many regional and super regional malls. Alternative anchors often provide services, entertainment, specialty products, or price points not found or offered by the traditional department stores. Large discounters, such as Target, major furniture stores, such as Ikea, warehouse stores, such as Costco, and large bookstore chains, such as Borders or Barnes & Noble, are being designed into new malls or shopping centers and are replacing anchors that have closed in existing malls. Department stores are still the dominant anchor tenant, but these alternative anchors are complementing them.

Other retailers that can positively influence customer draw include discount stores (e.g., Target, or Wal-Mart), which more frequently anchor community shopping centers but may also be found in regional malls and other shopping centers. Supermarkets, super drugstores, and home improvement centers serve as anchor tenants for neighborhood and community shopping centers. Multiscreen theaters and entertainment venues most often anchor entertainment shopping centers. Any of these anchors may now be found in some regional and super regional malls and in lifestyle and entertainment shopping centers because fewer and fewer traditional tenants are available.

Specialty or theme shopping centers are an exception to the rule that most shopping centers need traditional anchor tenants. Many such shopping centers are the result of the adaptive use of landmark structures. Along with their specialty and unique merchants, entertainment venues, and restaurants, the location and unique design of the building or its historical nature are traffic draws. For instance, Ghirardelli Square in San Francisco transformed an old chocolate factory at the end of a cable car line near the waterfront into a specialty shopping center. Trolley Square in Salt Lake City combined the uniqueness of an old trolley barn with entertainment facilities and boutiques, and Fanueil Hall Marketplace capitalized on the history, architecture, and traditions of Boston.

Structuring the Anchor Tenant Deal. The negotiation of the anchor tenant deal in a new shopping center development has some unique points. As is most often the case, the anchor tenant is in the strongest position when negotiating with a developer. Because few anchors are interested in any one site and most retail developments prefer to have multiple anchors, seldom do anchor tenants compete for the same location.

The anchor tenant is aware that without an anchor tenant the retail project cannot be developed. The anchor usually negotiates a deal below the developer's cost, at par, which is a break-even deal, or one in which the developer earns a small profit.

The developer is willing to accept such a deal because without the anchor tenant, the project will not be built. In doing so, the developer trusts that the rents from the other tenants will more than make up for what some would call a "give away" deal for the anchor tenant. If the deal is a lease, rather than a store to be owned by the anchor tenant, the developer often has the potential to collect percentage rent in addition to the minimum rent sometime in the future through sales increases. (Chapter 10, Negotiating and Documenting the Lease Terms fully discusses lease negotiations.)

When at least one anchor tenant is definitely committed, all governmental requirements for approval have been met, and financing has been obtained, the developer can exercise the option to purchase the property and proceed with the development.

Shop Tenants and Shoppers. When planning and designing a shopping center, in addition to the anchor tenants, the development team must satisfy two customer bases. The first customer base is the tenant; the second is the consumer—the shopper.

In the early years of shopping center development, tenants represented almost exclusively retail or service uses. More recently, though, the shop tenants have expanded to include offices, medical professionals, and government agencies.

The consumer base has also changed. For example, people who shop at convenience shopping centers are looking for a quick trip. They know what they want to buy, and they want to be in and out of the shopping center and the store or stores as quickly as possible. When the same people shop at an enclosed mall, they have different expectations—usually they want to comparison shop in a more leisurely atmosphere. No matter how beautifully designed, how well-built, or how well-maintained it is, a shopping center will not succeed unless the tenant mix is appropriate, and the community accepts and supports it by shopping there.

Changing Tenant Requirements. The requirements of shopping center tenants vary with the type of center. For instance, most tenants in a strip shopping center are concerned with their visibility from the parking lot or the street. They also want customers to be able to walk directly from their cars into the stores. The design of each type of shopping center must be planned to meet the needs of each type of tenant that will locate there.

The needs of retailers have changed rapidly in recent years. The most obvious change is the increasing size of the supermarket—the primary anchor tenant for neighborhood and community shopping centers.

The larger supermarkets have also changed the tenant mix of the shopping centers they anchor. For example, a 50,000-square-foot supermarket carries a much wider array of merchandise than a 35,000-square-foot grocery store and often includes a fresh fish market, a deli, prepared food for carryouts, a cafeteria, and an extensive selection of wines and liquors. Some even include camera departments and sell film and film processing. All of these departments used to be potential uses for the small shop spaces. When the anchor tenant expands its line of merchandise, it often precludes some other tenants from leasing smaller spaces in the shopping center. An independent fish market or deli may not want to compete—indeed, may not be able to compete—with a supermarket that has greater buying power and an extensive advertising program.

The increasing size of certain retailers, such as supermarkets, combined with the possible downsizing of many of the tenants for shop spaces, has changed the design of the shopping center over the years. Shop size requirements change often, in response to many factors in the retail market. Monitoring the trends in retailing enables a developer to plan and design a shopping center that will meet the space needs of its tenants and have a high probability of success.

Changing Shopper Needs. Just as the requirements of shopping center tenants have changed over the years, so the needs of shoppers have changed, and the shopping center must meet those needs, too. Shoppers' needs also vary with the type of shopping center. For example, a shopper expects a neighborhood or community (strip) shopping center or power shopping center to have easy ingress and egress for cars, convenient parking, a well-lighted parking lot, and stores that are visible and accessible from the parking lot. Alternatively, when shoppers are looking for convenience, they seek out a shopping center that has the right mix of stores; one that is easy and convenient to reach, well maintained, and well-lighted; and one where they feel secure.

Owners of existing shopping centers and developers of new ones must monitor the changing needs of both retailers and shoppers. When the needs of either of these shopping center customers change, the shopping center must be adjusted to remain competitive and avoid losing customers to another shopping center. Adjustments can be made through renovation or a change to a different retail use. Developers must be aware of the changing needs of their prospective customer bases, and the design of a new or renovated shopping center must incorporate adaptations to those changes. Changes can be incorporated most cost effectively during the planning and design stages of a proposed shopping center. When the developer or property owner ignores or is unaware of the changing needs of the retailer or the consumer, the shopping center will have a built-in leasing problem that may or may not be curable.

Site Planning. When the developer and the development team have decided on the anchor tenants and have studied the needs of the other potential tenants and the consumers, they can turn their attention to the arrangement of the tenants in the new shopping center. In this phase, they must determine the optimum gross leasable area, consider specific design challenges, and avoid certain shop design problems.

GLA Issues. One of the developer's early concerns is how the maximum gross leasable area can be designed into the shopping center. That can lead to a critical design error. When the primary design criterion is to maximize the GLA, the result is often a shopping center with built-in leasing problems. Space is designed that is difficult to lease. Shop spaces may be too deep or oddly shaped. They may have little frontage and wide rear areas, or they may have poor visibility to shoppers. They may be isolated from the primary traffic flow of the shopping center or tucked away in a corner.

The developer often attempts to maximize the amount of GLA on the site in the belief that the larger the GLA is, the higher the income projection will be. However, that is a fallacy—the amount of GLA should be based on the demand for space. If the demand for space is less than the total amount of GLA that the site can accommodate, it is usually prudent to develop the shopping center in two or more phases. The cost to carry the undeveloped portion of the shopping center is considerably less than the cost to carry vacant space.

Design Challenges. Though the site plan is the creation of the developer's architect, the anchor tenants will have considerable input into the final layout of a shopping center. An anchor tenant will want to be certain that its store is positioned to meet its needs and the needs of its customers. Among the specific concerns of all shopping center tenants are the visibility of their stores, the accessibility of the shopping center, parking, customer amenities, and service and maintenance facilities.

Visibility. Visibility is critical for most tenants in a strip shopping center. Tenants in small shopping centers (5,000 to 30,000 square feet of GLA) must be visible from the street. Because these shopping centers have no strong anchor tenants, their tenants' success is partially dependent on people seeing them repeatedly as they drive by and eventually becoming regular customers. Store spaces in larger strips—neighborhood and community shopping centers—should have good visibility from the street and the parking lot.

Signage is an important component of the concept of visibility. The shopping center sign criteria should allow each tenant to have a sign that is sufficiently large and properly placed so that it can be seen easily. However, all signs must conform to a coordinated signage program. Enclosed mall tenants have no visibility from the street; they are concerned with visibility to the mall traffic.

Accessibility. In evaluating whether to locate in a particular shopping center, a major concern of all prospective tenants is accessibility. For example, strip shopping centers must be located on streets that have substantial traffic volume, and convenience shopping centers must be convenient for the shopper. Most shopping centers are located on a corner so they are accessible from two streets.

Shopping centers should be accessible to traffic flowing in both directions. If no left turn lanes lead into a shopping center, many shoppers will drive by it en route to the next one. The entrances to and exits from the shopping center should provide a clear view. Landscaping or a large identification sign for the shopping center should not block a driver's view when cars enter or exit.

Parking Lot Layout. After accessibility, the next concern is parking lot layout and traffic flow. The parking lot or parking garage should provide pedestrian walkways. Lighting is a critical element in a shopper's decision to visit a shopping center at night, and all areas of the shopping center, including the parking areas must have adequate lighting. Because of their importance, parking lot requirements are discussed in detail in the next section.

Customer Amenities. Proper customer amenities affect the traffic draw to a shopping center. Adequate seating areas, dining options, bike racks, and restrooms are essential for malls, lifestyle, outlet, and entertainment shopping centers. Most enclosed malls also have information booths.

Service Facilities. Tenants' operations require service facilities. The placement and accessibility of loading areas are important to store efficiency. Loading areas for strip shopping centers are located behind the stores; they must be accessible to large trucks. All of the stores in an enclosed mall may have direct access to the parking lot for loading, but that is not always possible. Usually only some of the stores, primarily the anchors, have such direct access, and the loading areas for the remainder are behind the stores in corridors that lead to a service exit to the parking lot.

Management and Maintenance Requirements. Storage rooms, access to the roof, locations of utility meters, shutoff valves, and hose bibs must be included in the site plan and design for all retail properties. A management office must be designed into the plans for a mall, lifestyle, entertainment, or outlet shopping center.

Shop Design Problems. The design of each space determines its marketability. The anchor tenant provides the design and layout for its premises, and its architect works with the shopping center architect to coordinate the placement of the anchor tenant's premises in the shopping center. The remaining store and shop spaces must have good visibility, and they must be placed where they can benefit from the traffic generated by the anchor tenant or tenants. The following can become individual shop space and leasing problems:

- *Spaces too deep.* Because most retailers have downsized, they seek shallower spaces. Strip shopping centers that have store depths greater than 75 feet find fewer and fewer potential tenants.
- *Spaces too large.* In neighborhood shopping centers, spaces that are larger than 2,500 square feet have fewer potential uses, and spaces larger than 3,000 square feet have limited uses.
- *Spaces too narrow.* Tenants want as much frontage and as little depth as possible. Spaces with more than 1,000 square feet of GLA and widths less than 15 feet are difficult to lease.
- *L- and T-shaped spaces.* Spaces that are L- or T-shaped, with the wider portion in the rear, have limited appeal.
- *Pie-shaped spaces.* Spaces in the middle of an L-shaped strip of shops are sometimes triangular or pie shaped. These large spaces have little frontage and a wide rear area, which is not a desirable configuration.
- *Spaces with poor visibility.* Most small shop tenants need good visibility. Too many buildings on pads or outlots in front of a neighborhood shopping center can block the visibility of small, in-line shops. A shopping center may front on a major street and have shops on the side of the shopping center that face a poorly traveled street.
- *Malls too wide.* The mall area between stores should range from 30 to 40 feet wide. When the width exceeds 40 feet, the customer does not see the stores on both sides of the mall as easily.
- *Side hallways in a mall.* Many malls have secondary exits to the parking lot, usually from hallways that are tenanted by small shops. Because these areas receive little traffic, many retailers find them undesirable.
- *Unanchored malls.* Small shops in an enclosed mall that has no anchor tenant have neither a major draw nor visibility. The small shops collectively are not strong enough to draw shoppers into the mall. Enclosure of the mall eliminates storefront visibility from the street.
- *Unanchored wings of a mall.* Expanding a mall by developing a wing of small shops without an anchor tenant can be deadly. Without a major draw, this area of the mall will have little traffic, poor sales, high tenant turnover, and large numbers of vacancies.
- *Malls with no anchor on second level or higher levels.* Multilevel malls that have an anchor tenant, such as a major department store or a major discounter, on one level, but no anchor tenant on the other levels, will have a great disparity in traffic between the levels. The levels without anchor tenant exposure will be slow to lease and will have high tenant turnover.

- *U-shaped centers.* In U-shaped neighborhood and community shopping centers where the anchor tenants are on the ends of the U, little traffic may be drawn to the small shops in the area of the U between the anchors unless another anchor tenant is in that area.
- *Anchor tenants grouped together.* A shopping center design that groups the anchor tenants together instead of locating them at opposite ends of the shopping center clusters the smaller shops away from the anchors in areas where they receive little traffic.
- *Minimalls.* The division of large vacant spaces, such as former anchor tenant spaces, into multiple small shops to create an enclosed minimall is rarely successful in the long term. However, some malls have replaced a vacant anchor with a food court, which typically has sufficient drawing power to be successful.
- *Second-level office space.* Shopping centers with second-level office space often have incompatible uses. The office space usually becomes less-desirable, Class B space. The office employees who park all day may occupy valuable customer parking. Quite often the office space suffers from a high turnover of tenants and a high vacancy rate. Though second-level office space often is not successful, the second generation of lifestyle shopping centers is successful with two to four levels of residential above-ground-floor retail.

Poor planning and design are either impossible or costly to correct, and they lower the income and the value of the shopping center. In evaluating such errors, it is important to distinguish between *economic obsolescence,* which results from changes in the marketplace or the impact of government regulations, and *functional obsolescence,* which is due to the design or components being out-of-date. The loss of value due to functional obsolescence may be curable, but the desirability of a cure depends on the cost of the replacement being equal to or less than the expected increase in value. If a retail property must be designed with some spaces that do not meet the needs of most retailers, the income in the pro forma must reflect the lower rent and the longer lease-up time that will be required for those spaces.

Parking Requirements. Americans depend heavily on their cars for transportation, and parking can become a critical determining factor in their choice to shop at a particular shopping center. Planning to meet parking lot requirements is an essential component in the design of a new shopping center. This section begins with a list of criteria for the evaluation of parking convenience. It then presents several considerations for determining the appropriate parking allocation for the shopping center.

Evaluating Parking Convenience. The following criteria are used to evaluate the convenience of a shopping center's parking:

- Convenience of access to and exit from the parking area
- Adequacy of the number of parking stalls
- Ease of parking
- Level and quality of maintenance of the parking area
- Level and quality of lighting of the parking area
- Customers' actual and perceived level of safety
- Ease of access to the shopping area from vehicles

A shopper will be discouraged from patronizing a shopping center if any one of these criteria is not satisfactorily met. If several of the criteria are not met, the shopper will patronize the shopping center only out of necessity.

Determining Parking Lot Allocation. One of the objectives in developing a shopping center is to maximize the amount of GLA at the proposed site. The main design criterion that will affect the GLA a site can accommodate is how much of the site is dedicated to parking. The shopping center architect usually designs a shopping center to have the maximum GLA and the minimum parking allowed. To determine the allocation for parking, the parking requirements of anchor tenants as well as municipal parking requirements must be reviewed.

Parking Ratio. The size of a parking area is determined by complying with (1) the number of parking stalls the municipality requires, (2) the number of parking stalls the anchor tenants demand, and (3) the amount of space the municipality requires for landscaping. The specific requirements are expressed as a *parking ratio,* which expresses the number of parking stalls provided for every 1,000 square feet of GLA. A ratio of 5 to 1 means five parking stalls are available for every 1,000 square feet of GLA. The 5 represents the number of parking stalls and the 1 represents 1,000 square feet of GLA. The parking ratio is most frequently used to express the parking needs or requirements of a shopping center—or a particular tenant.

An anchor tenant may negotiate parking requirements to be stated in the lease. For example, the lease for a supermarket may include a provision in which the landlord is required to maintain parking ratios of no less than 4.5 to 1. Alternatively, the anchor tenant's parking requirements may be expressed as the number of stalls in the entire shopping center or within a defined portion of the shopping center. The supermarket lease in the previous example might state a requirement for a minimum of 450 parking stalls in the shopping center and a minimum of 250 parking stalls in a specific area in front of its premises. A site plan highlighting areas of parking requirements is often attached as an exhibit to an anchor tenant lease.

A major consideration in calculating the number of stalls that can be designed in an area is whether stalls for a particular size car are included in the parking layout. Consumers' preferences for vehicle sizes have changed over the years. Minivans were popular in the 1980s and 1990s, and SUVs were popular in the 1990s and into the early 2000s.

Parking Standards. In 1999, the Urban Land Institute published the second edition of their *Parking Requirements for Shopping Centers.* The findings in the second edition are similar to those in a study over 20 years before that found that shopping centers are getting bigger. Additional uses are being included in retail properties. The study included more data for regional and super regional malls than for any other retail property type.

The study found that parking requirements are not dependent on the size of cities, whether they are in urban or suburban areas, nor in which area of the country the shopping center is located. The factors that impact parking requirements are (1) the percentage of the shopping center that is occupied by restaurants, theaters, and entertainment uses; (2) the amount of nonautomobile traffic; (3) the size of the shopping center; and (4) whether employees park on-site or off-site during peak selling periods.

According to the Urban Land Institute study, the recommended parking ratio for shopping centers that have less than 400,000 square feet is 4 parking stalls per 1,000 square feet of GLA. The ratio increases for shopping centers that have between 400,000 and 600,000 square feet to between 4 and 4.5 parking stalls per 1,000 square feet of GLA. The parking ratio increases slightly for centers that have over 600,000 square feet to 4.5 parking stalls per 1,000 square feet of GLA. The recommended parking ratios in the 1999 study are the same as in the 1982 study for shopping centers under 400,000 square feet, but the recommended parking ratios for the larger shopping centers actually decreased from the 1982 study. Restaurants and entertainment uses increase the ratio from a small fraction of one space to a quarter of a space, depending on the amount of GLA of those uses and the size of the shopping center.

The Urban Land Institutes Parking study established the standards for parking requirements in shopping centers. It should be part of every shopping center developer's and shopping center manager's reference library.

Municipal Requirements. Municipalities impose any number of requirements in regard to the appearance of the parking area, the use, and the amount of GLA in relation to the shopping center. The municipality often requires a specific amount of landscaped area to beautify or soften a parking area. It may require that a minimum percentage of the area be landscaped and even specify the types and sizes of plants that must be included in the landscaped areas.

Municipalities may allow for *dual use,* which is the sharing of the same or a portion of the same parking area by different property uses. Dual use can sometimes maximize the use of the parking area. An example is parking shared between an office building and a shopping center in a multi-use development.. Office buildings typically need parking Monday through Friday from 8:00 a.m. to 5:00 p.m. The parking lot for an office building is almost totally empty during peak shopping times—evening hours Monday through Friday as well as late mornings, afternoons, and evenings the entire weekend.

Municipal regulations may allow for an office building and a shopping center to plan for 85 percent dual use of parking, in which each property may share 85 percent of its required parking stalls with the other property. However, caution must be exercised when considering the ratio of dual use parking. If the parking requirements of one property should increase, the amount of parking available for the other property will be reduced.

The final parking area design must take into consideration all of the preceding concerns. It must also be sure to provide parking for employees and all types of shoppers.

SHOPPING CENTER REHABILITATION

As conditions favorable to new developments declined in the 1990s, developers and property owners explored opportunities to rehabilitate existing shopping centers. Good retail sites available for development have become scarce in many areas. Many urban areas and even some suburban areas do not have parcels of land that are large enough and have good enough visibility and accessibility to develop large shopping centers and retail properties. Developers and retailers are exploring development opportunities in urban in-fill locations. Many of these in-fill sites are being developed as multi-use projects that have retail on the ground floor and two to five levels of apartments above the retail. Currently, shopping centers are either rehabilitated to enhance the value of the property, to maintain its existing value, or to halt its decline.

Reasons to Rehabilitate a Shopping Center

Some shopping centers need a major redesign, while others need to be demolished so new shopping centers can be built on the land. Many shopping centers are excellent candidates for rehabilitation for several reasons:

- An existing shopping center has an established trade area. Over time the density of the area may have increased, adding shoppers. New shopping centers are often developed on the fringe of growth, and several years may pass before the trade area is developed.
- An existing shopping center has at least a group of tenants who are successful and whose businesses are well established.

- The shopping center's physical plant is intact; it needs only minor modification.
- The demographics and psychographics of the area have changed, and the current merchandise and tenant mix of the shopping center are no longer targeted to the property's customer base. New merchants have entered the market and are excellent candidates along with existing merchants in the market to remerchandise the shopping center by changing the shopping center's tenant mix.
- Most important, the shopping center that is a candidate for rehabilitation has an existing income stream.

Preparation of the Rehabilitation Pro Forma

The first step in determining whether to rehabilitate a shopping center is to develop a pro forma for the prospective shopping center. A rehabilitation pro forma differs from a development pro forma because the shopping center already exists, has tenants, and has a cash flow. Early in the decision-making process, the developer and the development team should review the leases and the shopping center operating agreement to determine whether any restrictions in them limit rehabilitation or expansion of the shopping center. An important component of the pro forma is a projection of net operating income (NOI) that takes into account the changes that will result from the rehabilitation.

Income Sources/Operating Income. The first component of the net operating income (NOI) formula is income, and evaluation of the rehabilitation of a shopping center starts with an existing income stream. The income from the existing GLA is generally projected based on three factors: (1) rental and other income from existing tenants through the remainder of their lease terms; (2) anticipated rental increases when existing leases expire and the tenants' leases are renewed or they are replaced; and (3) projected income from existing vacancies. Two other factors can sometimes become income sources: One is income from additional GLA if the shopping center is expanded; the other is the potential for reimbursement of operating expenses that are currently not being reimbursed by the existing tenants.

Existing Tenants. The income from existing tenants must be evaluated. Their rents are usually low compared to the rental rates that will be expected from the tenants after the rehabilitation is completed. Some may not be able to generate the sales necessary to support a substantial rent increase. They may only be marginally successful paying low rent and may not have the merchandising ability to produce significantly higher sales, regardless of any changes to the shopping center. The developer can usually easily identify these tenants by evaluating their sales as a percentage of current and projected occupancy costs for the past few years, by visiting their stores, and by evaluating their merchandise and inventory levels. The developer must anticipate that these marginal tenants will not renew their leases. However, if their leases have several years remaining, they will continue to pay the lower rent until they renew or are replaced when their leases expire.

Rent Increases. Some tenants will welcome improvements to the shopping center and will be able to afford the rent increases because their sales will probably increase due to the rehabilitation. Marginal existing tenants may have to be replaced with tenants that can successfully operate in the shopping center while paying market rents. To be prepared to replace those tenants, the developer must be familiar with potential new anchor and shop tenants that are interested in locating or expanding their presence in the trade area of the retail property that is being considered for rehabilitation.

Vacancies. Another step in the income projection is to estimate how long existing vacancies—and the vacancies created when existing tenants do not renew—will endure. The development team should conduct a market survey to accurately project the property's rental rates after the rehabilitation. If new tenants lease and occupy space prior to the rehabilitation, they may have a two-tiered rental rate. Their leases will show an initial rental rate that reflects the value of space in the shopping center prior to the rehabilitation, and the leases will include automatic rental increases to the new market rate for the shopping center that commences on the date the rehabilitation is completed.

Additional GLA. In some instances, income is projected for additional GLA. This could be rent and other income from new pad or outlot space or from space in new buildings.

The GLA of the site might lend itself to expansion without adding land or a parking garage. If the shopping center originally had a parking ratio of 5.5 or 6.0 parking stalls per 1,000 square feet of GLA, additional GLA may be added to the site if the parking ratio can be lowered to 5.0 to 1 or to 4.5 to 1. The developer should check with the municipality to see if the required parking ratios have changed since the shopping center was developed. If the parking ratios have not changed, the developer may petition for a variance or suggest to the city's building department that it consider changing the municipal parking ratios. The developer might provide information from the Urban Land Institute report, *Parking Requirements for Shopping Centers,* 2nd edition, (mentioned earlier) to the building department or city council as supporting documentation.

Before planning to change the parking ratios, the development team should check existing anchor and shop tenants' leases for provisions that restrict the number of parking stalls. The leases and the shopping center operating agreement must be reviewed to determine the existence and extent of any restrictions that limit changes to the parking area or rehabilitation or expansion of the shopping center.

Reimbursed Operating Expenses. Another potential source of income that should be evaluated is the reimbursement of operating expenses that are passed through to tenants, such as common area maintenance, taxes, and insurance. If the shopping center will have a higher occupancy after rehabilitation, additional income from pass-through charges can be projected, but this income will probably only offset any increases in operating the renovated shopping center. If a shopping center is de-malled, CAM charges and operating expenses will typically be reduced because fewer maintenance, heating, ventilation, and air-conditioning (HVAC), and other expenses are involved in operating an open mall.

After projecting the income from all sources, the developer should project a realistic vacancy factor and adjust the projected income accordingly. A vacancy factor is seldom applied to the anchor spaces because of the length of their lease terms and their creditworthiness. For the small shop space, however, the industry uses a rule-of-thumb vacancy rate of 5 percent.

Operating Expenses. Operating expenses are the second component of NOI. The operating expenses for a shopping center are budgeted in two or three separate groupings: (1) the landlord's non-reimbursable expenses, 2) maintenance of the parking lot and exterior common areas, and (3) maintenance of the common areas in an enclosed mall. Each of these groups of expenses will undoubtedly increase after the rehabilitation.

Landlord's Non-reimbursable Expenses. These expenses include the landlord's contribution to the marketing fund dues or the merchants' association (older shopping centers may still have merchants' associations), the cost to maintain the vacant spaces, partnership audits, legal expenses, utilities in vacant spaces, and the management fee if it is not included in the CAM expenses.

Parking Lot and Exterior Expenses. One outcome of the rehabilitation of a shopping center is an upgrade in the appearance of the common areas and the buildings. The exterior improvements that will be most noticeable are those referred to as "curb appeal," such as the landscaping and parking lot, the exterior of the building, and any added or upgraded lighting. The parking lot is usually in poor condition when rehabilitation of the shopping center is needed. Once the parking lot is resurfaced, the layout of the parking stalls should be evaluated. A more efficient way may be found to lay out the parking stalls. That may create additional parking stalls that can support additional buildings. All of these improvements involve additional operating expenses that should be included in the rehabilitation pro forma.

Common Area Maintenance Expenses. Interior improvements in an enclosed mall include new and upgraded lighting, the addition of skylights, new flooring, remodeled restrooms, and renovated entrances. Outdated planter boxes, landscaping, benches, and directories are usually replaced. In addition to an increase in expenses for these items, the overall maintenance cost will increase. The additional value created in the shopping center will also result in increased taxes and insurance costs. Most of these expenses are passed through to the tenants, and that will increase their occupancy costs. If the retail property has many vacancies, the owner will be responsible for the cost attributed to the vacancies until they are leased and occupied.

Components that are not visible but usually need to be replaced or repaired are the roof and the HVAC units. The owner may need to install and/or upgrade life safety systems. These additions and replacements will impact the shopping center's operating expenses.

The tenants in a shopping center that is renovated will have several different lease forms, depending on when they entered into their leases. The developer will use a state-of-the-art lease form with the new and renewing tenants that will be a *triple net lease* (one that passes through prorated shares of all operating expenses to the tenants) or one quite similar. The tenants whose leases do not renew for some time may be on a much older lease form that excludes some of the CAM reimbursable expenses. As a result, it is likely that some tenants will not reimburse the typical CAM expenses for some time.

Construction Costs. Another component in the pro forma for rehabilitating a shopping center is an estimate of the construction costs. Structural and mechanical surveys should be done to determine the integrity of the physical plant. The extent of repairs needed and the costs to make them should be estimated.

Upgrades. Areas that should be considered for upgrading include directories, new or redesigned entrances, removal of large planter boxes, and adjustments to any seating areas. Kiosks and carts are often added to a mall to generate additional income and create a festive atmosphere with small boutique retailers. *Wall shops,* shallow depth stores, can be added to blank walls. A department store in an older mall often has a long stretch of blank walls. A row of stores that are six to ten feet deep may be built in front of a blank wall to provide visual excitement to an area that previously experienced little traffic.

Building Codes. A review of the local building code should reveal any specific upgrades that are necessary to meet code requirements. For example, installation of sprinklers and fire walls as well as compliance with the Americans with Disabilities Act (ADA) requirements (added ramps, special doors, etc.) may be required if they were not part of the original construction. The local municipality may require an environmental impact report (EIR). Certainly if the shopping center is being purchased for redevelopment, an environmental audit will be needed. Potential hazards in a shopping center include wastes classified as toxic substances (e.g., spent dry cleaning fluid), PCBs from transformer leakage, and asbestos used as a construction material. The costs of the surveys and of any changes necessitated for full compliance should be included in the construction cost estimate.

Leasing Costs. Another item in the pro forma is the cost to market and lease the new space and to re-lease existing space when tenants vacate. The amount of this expense can be projected accurately; however, the timing of the payment of commissions can only be estimated because it is based on when space is leased.

Marketing Costs. The next expense to evaluate is marketing and advertising. The landlord, through the marketing fund, will provide additional funds to promote and advertise the shopping center during the period of construction and for a grand reopening. The extra advertising and promotion are necessary to let the community know that the shopping center is open during construction and to promote its new image.

Funding. The cost of the rehabilitation may be funded from the property's cash flow, an equity infusion, financing, or any combination of these sources. Potential sources for financing are discussed in the section on new shopping center development earlier in this chapter. The rehabilitation pro forma, the projected NOI when the property is stabilized, and the stabilized cash flow are used to determine whether to proceed with the rehabilitation.

Proceeding with the Rehabilitation

Once the decision is made to go ahead with rehabilitation of a shopping center, the developer must determine the extent of the work to be done in accordance with the pro forma developed. The developer and the development team must conduct a thorough review of existing leases, develop a realistic leasing plan, and perform a careful tenant mix analysis. Maintaining excellent communication with the shopping center tenants and ensuring the safety of tenants and shoppers are of primary importance during the rehabilitation.

Lease Review. The development team must review all the leases, especially the anchor tenants' leases and the Common Area Agreements or Reciprocal Easement Agreements to determine if any of those documents provides approval rights to a tenant or group of tenants in case the shopping center is renovated. The team must determine if any tenant has the right of expansion, relocation, or cancellation or if any tenant has an exclusive that has been overlooked.

Leasing Plan. A successful marketing and leasing plan will validate the decision to rehabilitate the shopping center. This program starts with the rental or market survey. Once the market rental rates are established for the shopping center, each existing space and all new spaces must be priced based on their value to a retailer or service tenant. Chapter 9, Leasing the Shopping Center, details the leasing plan, the market survey, and the establishment of rental rates.

Tenant Mix Analysis. Next, a survey is conducted to determine which tenant uses are over- and under-represented in the shopping center's trade area. The existing tenant mix is analyzed to determine the shopping center's strengths and weaknesses. The introduction of new anchor tenants may call for a different tenant mix. (See chapter 8, Creating the Tenant Mix.) The marketing and leasing program should be targeted to specific tenant uses. Prior to or during the construction phase is an excellent time to extend some tenants' leases. All tenants that remain should be encouraged to remodel their stores to present a fresh, new image when the shopping center has its grand reopening.

Tenant Communications. The shopping center manager must communicate with the tenants before and during the rehabilitation. A general meeting of all the merchants should be called to announce the rehabilitation. This meeting should include a presentation by the architect. The architect or general contractor should explain the construction sequencing and how each tenant will be affected during the construction phase. The shopping center manager or the marketing director should present the marketing, advertising, and promotional plans for the construction period and beyond.

Following the general meeting, the shopping center manager should meet regularly with each merchant to explain how the rehabilitation is progressing, what will happen next, and what effect this will have on the tenant. Memos or e-mails on advertising and promotions, new tenant leases, and construction progress should be sent out regularly to all tenants.

Tenants will naturally be concerned that the construction phase will have a negative impact on their sales. Surprisingly, many tenants' sales increase during the construction period. The additional advertising and promotion, new tenants moving in, and shoppers' curiosity often result in increased traffic at the shopping center and, thus, in higher sales.

If a tenant's loss of sales is expected to be severe, conversion of the tenant's lease to require payment of percentage rent only for the duration of the construction phase may be appropriate. That is, the retailer would pay a percentage of its sales in lieu of the minimum or base rent required under the lease. For tenants located in an area that will be demolished, the development team may explore buyouts of the leases or temporary (or permanent) relocation within the shopping center.

Operating Issues. The developer must address several operating issues prior to and during the construction phase. Seldom are shopping centers totally vacant during the construction. A plan must be developed to keep the tenants open for business during construction. The plan should incorporate a concern for the safety of shoppers and employees. Safety issues may be addressed by barricading construction staging areas, building protective walkways, and fencing off construction activities. Keeping the parking lot and sidewalk clear of all construction debris is mandatory. The assignment of security personnel may be necessary to keep people out of construction areas and provide a liaison with the construction workers.

The shopping center manager should meet with the property's insurance agent to review the current insurance coverage and increase the coverage due to the renovation. The "new" shopping center will have a higher replacement value and that must be reflected in the property's fire and extended policy. The rental income will increase so the insurance for loss of rental income must be increased.

Rehabilitating a shopping center presents opportunities to enhance the value of the property. For every opportunity to succeed, however, there is a corresponding opportunity to fail. A thorough analysis of the proposed rehabilitation is necessary to ensure that it will be a success.

3

Management Plan and Operations Manual

The *management plan* is an organized collection of information about the shopping center that guides decisions about day-to-day operations and prepares the shopping center manager to meet the challenges of a changing business environment (e.g., market conditions, legal guidelines, infrastructure changes, gentrification, functional obsolescence, financing alternatives, new competition, and interest rates). Flexibility is imperative because the property and the environment in which it exists are changing constantly. Shopping center managers often learn better ways to maintain the property or become aware of specific trends in the area (e.g., more families with small children moving in, increasing commercialization, or changing consumers' buying power because the area is going through a transition), and they must be able to take advantage of their new knowledge.

The *operations manual* contains information about the shopping center for situations that demand quick decisions. It is separate from the management plan, but because it serves many of the same purposes as some parts of the plan, concurrent development is appropriate.

To prepare the shopping center manager to do what is most important—that is, operate a shopping center in a changing economic climate—this chapter focuses on the management plan and the operations manual as meaningful decision-making tools for the individual or entity that owns the shopping center and for the shopping center manager who runs it. To manage effectively, the shopping center manager must know the owner's objectives and have a management plan and an operations manual.

THE OWNER'S GOALS AND OBJECTIVES

As the shopping center manager considers alternatives for operating a shopping center or repositioning it to make the most of changes, analysis of each possibility must include consideration of the owner's goals and objectives. Investors own income-producing properties for many reasons, and their ownership objectives have a major bearing on which alternative they choose for a specific property.

Suppose the property owner is a single, elderly woman who expects the investment's cash flow to provide her with income during her retirement years. This owner will probably reject a plan to use the entire cash flow to modernize the shopping center because doing so would eliminate her income. Because her need for income is immediate, she may have little interest in any long-range plan to improve the shopping center's profitability, especially if achieving that objective would impact her cash flow.

Consider, however, the owner who is an institutional investor, someone seeking long-range capital appreciation. For this type of owner, cash flow is generally secondary, and the appearance of the property and long-term appreciation are primary concerns. The shopping center manager in this scenario should investigate alternatives whose long-term possibilities will maximize the property's value.

Though individual investors may own shopping centers, sole proprietors are more likely to be outright owners of smaller, less-complex properties (e.g., a two- or three-story building that contains one or more street-level store spaces below apartments or offices, or a strip center developed on the corner of a city block).

Large-scale developments such as regional and super regional shopping malls that require the investment of tens of millions of dollars are more often owned by development companies, investment partnerships, Real Estate Investment Trusts (REITs), or other institutions that have access to large amounts of capital. In the United States, institutional ownership of shopping centers—by insurance companies, pension funds, and REITs—has grown tremendously since the early 1990s and is now a major form of ownership.

Equipped with a thorough understanding of the owner's investment needs, the shopping center manager can develop the management plan and the operations manual that flows from it.

THE MANANGEMENT PLAN

Management plans are not only for large shopping centers. To succeed in ever-changing commercial environments, all sizes and types of shopping centers benefit from management plans. Though a strip shopping center or a neighborhood shopping center may not need as complex a management plan as a super regional mall, each needs to have a plan that lays out how to handle issues such as leasing renewals, maintenance, capital improvements, etc. The success of a shopping center depends on a thorough management plan that states the objectives and financial projections of the investment and provides short- and long-range recommendations for achieving them.

An effective management plan is the result of gathering all the pertinent information, analyzing it, presenting the results of the analysis in a usable format, evaluating various alternatives, and making specific recommendations that will guide the operation of the shopping center. In some cases, the shopping center manager will have alternatives to present that must be fully analyzed and compared.

The management plan must be as accurate and specific as possible if it is to provide effective guidelines. Otherwise, decisions based on the plan are likely to have unanticipated outcomes (e.g., reduced income, adverse effects on the tenant mix, and an inability to realize the shopping center's full value). The recommendations contained in the management plan address such considerations as rental rates, lease terms, at-risk tenants, maintenance schedules, tenant sales performance, staffing requirements, long-term capital considerations, alternative programs for improvements, and financing to achieve specific goals.

The shopping center manager must prepare the management plan with a completely unbiased point of view and no preconceived notions. As information is gathered and analyzed, the most probable course of action will emerge, and quite often it will be counter to the initial thoughts and approaches.

To ensure its flexibility as a decision-making tool, the management plan should be updated at least annually and as necessary to reflect changes in the local market (trade area) and in the local (community) and national economies.

A management plan should have the following components:

- Market survey
- Property analysis
- Rental rate analysis
- Budget planning
- Operations
- Analysis of alternatives
- Challenges, opportunities, and recommendations

This section discusses each component of the management plan.

Market Survey

A unique aspect of an investment in a shopping center is how the changes in the trade area impact both the owner and the tenants. In this type of real estate investment, more than any other, the owner's income is directly related to the tenants' economic success. Additionally, the consuming public, which comprises the trade area, determines whether the tenants will be successful. Successful tenants will ultimately lead to a successful shopping center. Therefore a thorough analysis of the market is essential to the management plan.

The *market survey* or *market analysis* notes all of the factors that affect the shopping center. It includes studies of the region (e.g., the Sacramento metropolitan area), the community (the town or neighborhood where the shopping center is located), and the trade area. A major component of these analyses is a *demographic profile* of the population that includes trends and changes in its size and characteristics. A *psychographic profile* of local lifestyles is also helpful.

Analysis of the market is critical to the decision to build a new shopping center. For an existing shopping center, the market analysis defines current conditions. The market may have changed substantially since the center opened, especially if it is more than 10 years old. Changes in the market may suggest or necessitate changes in the tenant mix, operations, or both to make the shopping center profitable now.

Regional and Community Analyses. The shopping center manager is interested in learning the vital statistics of the region, and this usually begins with an analysis of the population—the number of people and their distribution by age and income as well as any past and projected trends (the demographic profile) and the shopping habits of the population (the psychographic profile). Other considerations include family and household composition, income level, and buying habits. Ethnic composition may also be important.

These data can be obtained from census reports, although the shopping center manager should be aware that demographic data can change quickly. Information from the decennial census is updated annually, and more current figures may be found in the *Statistical Abstract of the United States*. The Census of Retail Trade and the American Housing Survey are conducted on five-year and three-year cycles, respectively. The use of information available through the Internet has facilitated comparative analysis of demographic data, and numerous commercial sources are also available (see appendix D, References and Resources).

Many other aspects of the region can affect planning for a shopping center. Climate, available natural resources, tourist impact, local industries, government facilities (such as military bases), recreational facilities, schools, and competing businesses in the area will all affect the investment, and the shopping center manager should analyze each of these factors on an ongoing basis. Information on types and levels of employment is also particularly useful. Evaluation of the dominant industry should provide an indication of the region's stability.

A geographic obstruction, such as a major lake, a river, or a mountain range, will probably affect the region and the shopping center. Any such natural barrier should be mentioned in the management plan along with an expert's opinion of what it means to the area and the shopping center.

Man-made conditions must be analyzed as well. If the shopping center is located in a major tourist area or if office buildings dominate the location, that should be noted in the management plan along with the likely impact on the investment project. Local municipal ordinances, constraints, and regulations (e.g., zoning, signage, and parking changes) should also be evaluated and noted in the management plan because they can affect current and future operations as well as any alterations to the property.

Because the future of the property as an investment is the ultimate concern, the shopping center manager must understand the current economic picture to be able to project the economic prospects for the region. Various federal agencies can provide data on economic trends in a region. The municipal or county government and their planning departments, redevelopment agencies, trade associations, real estate brokers, appraisers, local chambers of commerce, utility companies, financial institutions, and the local library are all possible sources of economic information on the regional and local scenes.

Trade Area Analysis. The management plan for a shopping center should contain an analysis of the *trade area*—the area from which customers come to a shopping center. This represents the shopping center's drawing power. The trade area can be divided into primary, secondary, and tertiary trade areas, often also called "zones" to distinguish the parts from the whole.

The *primary zone* is the area from which most of the shopping center's customers come (70–75 percent of sales). Its size varies from center to center and depends on such things as shopping center size, anchor stores, dominance in the marketplace, and the extent and effectiveness of the competition.

The *secondary zone* is the source of customers who will come to the shopping center less frequently (some 20–25 percent of sales). It extends some distance from the shopping center and is shaped by many of the same center-specific factors mentioned above.

The *tertiary zone* is the source of occasional or one-time customers (perhaps 5 percent of sales) and may extend many miles beyond the shopping center. This small percentage of sales also represents people who may travel a considerable distance to take advantage of a special sale or visitors to the area who may shop on their way to or from somewhere else.

In analyzing the trade area, the shopping center manager should focus on the primary zone. However, the demands of and limitations on shoppers from the other two zones should also be taken into account.

Although identification and analysis of all the trade area zones are important for every type of shopping center, careful evaluation of the primary zone is critical to the success of neighborhood shopping centers because they attract repeat customers from an extremely small geographic area. For any type of shopping center, the population of the primary zone must be sufficient in numbers and buying power. Attracting enough customers from the secondary and tertiary zones to support a shopping center of any size is usually impossible. The exception is the specialty center developed intentionally as a focus for tourists—Faneuil Hall Marketplace in Boston is an example.

The descriptions of the various types of shopping centers presented elsewhere in this book indicate the consumer population they require for survival. Except for those living in isolated rural areas, most people will usually travel only a short distance (1½ miles) to purchase groceries and convenience items, while they will travel much farther (8–10 miles) to comparison shop for a major appliance. These travel distances are another consideration in determining the boundaries of the trade area zones for each type of shopping center.

The market analysis should also include the results of a physical inspection of the area. Valuable insights may be gained from observing the general appearance of homes and noting the average prices at which they are selling, the numbers of factories, businesses, and schools in the area, and the overall condition of highways and expressways. Attitudes at the local government level should also be investigated. A "no-growth" sentiment may be evident from zoning ordinances restricting commercial development; zoning codes can impose strict limitations on changes to an existing shopping center or prohibit development of a new one. (Market analysis is also important to leasing; see chapter 9, Leasing the Shopping Center.)

Property Analysis

The *property analysis* for a shopping center management plan includes physical and fiscal considerations. It should begin with a thorough physical inspection of the shopping center (type of construction, age, general condition of the physical plant) that includes an evaluation of the common areas (including entrances and exits). The property analysis should contain a review of the rental rates as well as a review of the tenant mix that includes an assessment of current vacancies. Finally, the property analysis should include an assessment of the financial status of the shopping center.

The property analysis is the basis for comparing the strengths and weaknesses of the shopping center with its competition. It also provides a basis for the development of the operations manual that will facilitate the day-to-day and long-term management of the property.

After all the property analysis information is compiled, the shopping center manager should compile similar information for all shopping centers in the trade area that compete with or have an effect on the subject property. The objective is to determine how the subject shopping center compares to its competition. Shopping centers that are located just outside the subject's trade area may well have an impact on it. They should be reviewed and their likely impact should be stated.

Inspection. The key to the analysis of the shopping center is a thorough physical inspection and an evaluation of what is observed. Ideally the inspection will be conducted before the survey of the competition because it will give the shopping center manager an idea of minimum standards for the comparison. However, these standards are not essential to the property analysis, and the shopping center manager may want to set specific goals for the property.

A record of the inspection is usually compiled on a specific form. The level of detail may vary, but the objective is to establish the current condition and note any specific repairs that must be made to restore the physical plant to optimal operating condition. Obvious deferred maintenance should be recorded in this initial inspection as well as any other information that can be used to plan and schedule routine maintenance and repairs.

The shopping center manager should conduct the physical inspection in a manner that will maximize familiarity with the property. Carrying a digital camera and taking pictures will provide a record not only of conditions but also of the location and orientation of various elements of the property. Digital pictures can easily be sent by e-mail to supervisors and/or clients and incorporated into the final report.

Of particular concern are those aspects and features of the property that may be important considerations for insurance coverages. Items to be located and photographed should include shopping center signage and directories, lamp hoods, bicycle racks, benches and other seating areas, trash receptacles (baskets or containers, bins or dumpsters), roof access ladders and roof equipment, fire safety equipment (extinguishers, sprinkler heads, controls), timers and switches, sump pumps, ejector pumps and grease traps, directional arrows in parking areas, and locations of utility meters. Additionally, the two largest components of any shopping center—the roof and parking lot—will need to be photographed. Because pictures also serve as reminders, the shopping center manager should photograph items in need of repair. The shopping center manager should also inspect for pests such as termites and ensure that the building is code compliant and meets the Americans with Disabilities Act (ADA) regulations.

The inspection will provide the shopping center manager with a broad view of the property and help familiarize him or her with the location of specific items. Ultimately, the information gathered during this initial inspection will be used to prepare budgets, predict future capital expenditures, allocate funds for maintenance and personnel, determine the need for maintenance and other service contracts, respond to tenants' complaints, and react promptly to emergencies.

Rental Rates. Because the primary source of income for the property is rents, the property analysis comparison data should also include rental rates. This information will be used in the third component of the management plan—a rent analysis. To set optimal rents, the shopping center manager must know what rents other shopping centers charge and how rates at the subject shopping center compare to those of its competitors.

Knowing the terms of those leases is important as well. Are they net leases? Do they have percentage rent provisions? How long are the typical leases? What are the additional costs in terms of common area costs, real estate taxes, insurance and marketing contributions?

Comparison with rental rates at competing properties will indicate the shopping center's position in the marketplace as well as establish a basis for setting new rates at the property. Rental rate analysis is discussed later in this chapter and in chapter 9, Leasing the Shopping Center.

Tenant Mix. The property analysis for the management plan should contain an analysis of each tenant. Because sales volume is often the true measure of retailing success, a review of past sales records is a good starting point for evaluating individual tenants. Each tenant's performance should then be compared to the performance of similar merchants in the trade area.

Sales are the most effective measure of how well the tenants are doing. We can compare each tenant's sales with those provided by the *Dollars and Cents of Shopping Centers,* published by the Urban Land Institute, and determine if each is the best for the shopping center and if not, what might be a better alternative. Sales provide a good look at the general trend of a given merchant, and we can use sales to evaluate categories of merchandise and/or wings of a mall.

Within a particular shopping center, tenants may be evaluated by comparing their total sales as a percentage of total occupancy cost. This offers the landlord a quick test as to the financial viability of the tenant to meet rent and other financial commitments. Generally, 12 to 14 percent or higher would be of concern, and the lower the percentage, the better. The evaluation of the tenant mix should also include and assessment of current vacancies.

Financial Status. A final, critical component of the analysis of the property is an evaluation of its financial status. A straightforward calculation of cash flow will indicate whether the shopping center is being operated profitably at its current level and serve as a benchmark for comparing income and expense projections for other sections of the management plan, especially in the analysis of alternatives. Cash flow is calculated as follows:

	Gross Possible Rental Income
minus	Vacancy and Collection Loss
plus	Miscellaneous Income
equals	Effective Gross Income
minus	Operating Expenses
equals	Net Operating Income (NOI)
minus	Debt Service (Principal and Interest)
equals	Cash Flow

When percentage rent is to be included in the calculation, it should be a separate line item added to the income. Though percentage rents are welcomed by landlords, the ultimate value of percentage rents is lower than base rentals because the sales on which percentage rent is calculated can be reduced by new competition, poor tenant management practices, and changes in customer preferences.

At this point, all the analyses of the market and the property should come together. The market analysis should indicate what types of tenants are most likely to succeed at the shopping center, given the economic conditions and demands in the trade area. The property analysis should indicate whether the property can or does satisfy the needs of the current tenants and whether the tenants are, in fact, suitable for the shopping center. The tenant mix analysis should reveal any disparities between probability and actuality of success, and these should be evaluated further.

A specific tenant may no longer be suitable for the mix of the shopping center based on the current demographic and psychographic profiles for the trade area and the existing competition. In particular, fads in merchandise are usually short-lived. The shopping center may need one or more new tenants to create a new image or to more effectively compete with other shopping centers in the market. The shopping center manager may find that the shopping center is actually outperforming the competition.

Whatever the situation, without this thorough analysis, the shopping center manager and the owner may not know which tenants are best for the trade area and the shopping center, and they could enter into leases that are actually harmful to the future of the property.

Rental Rate Analysis

Establishing rental rates that are fair for all parties is critical for assuring the profitability of the shopping center as an investment. A lower-than-market rent may attract tenants to the shopping center, but it will eventually have a negative impact on the property's value.

For example, if an owner decides to lease a 1,000-square-foot store for $1.20 per foot per year less than the market would actually allow, the rent loss will amount to $100 per month or $1,200 per year. At a conservative capitalization rate of 10 percent, the value of the shopping center will have been reduced by $12,000. Though $1.20 per square foot per year may seem insignificant, it obviously is not especially when all the spaces are being rented below market rate. Any amount of reduced rent is likely to cut deeply into the investor's profits.

If rents are too high, leasing space in the shopping center may be extremely difficult. Spaces that are vacant for long periods—or even multiple short-term vacancies—can give the shopping center a troubled look and compound other problems on the property. Vacancies have a negative impact on the existing tenants, tenant prospects, and the customers of the shopping center. Vacancies also reduce income that can never be recaptured.

Fair Market Rents. Setting rents at the proper level can be challenging, but shopping center managers can take a systematic approach to setting optimal rental rates. First, they should check rental rates at competing shopping centers by requesting information about rental rates when "For Lease" signs are seen in retail spaces, reading classified ads in newspapers, contacting local appraisers, talking to other shopping center managers and leasing agents, and directly approaching retailers in the trade area. Information from these sources should provide an idea of the "going rate" in the trade area.

After these figures have been obtained, more objective comparisons must be made. The shopping center manager should evaluate the competing shopping centers, scrutinizing their geographic locations and the populations they serve as well as the availability of public transportation. Vacancy rates at competing shopping centers—the ratio of vacant space to total leasable areas—should also be determined. All of these factors relate to rental rates.

The shopping center manager should then analyze specific aspects of the subject shopping center. Prospective tenants will want to know particulars about the retailing mix (types of tenants and merchandise) and the anchor tenants, the aesthetics of the interior of the shopping center and maintenance of the property as a whole, and the convenience of the location. All of these factors affect their willingness to lease space at a specific rental rate.

After all this information has been compiled, the shopping center manager should prepare a grid that lists positive and negative aspects of the subject and the competing properties. Many decisions about rental rates will depend on this final comparison. Typically, new shopping centers can command a higher rental rate than older shopping centers. If small-sized shop spaces rent for $20 per square foot at competing sites and the subject shopping center is new, the new space probably can command $21 or $22 per square foot, assuming all other factors, such as location (quality of anchor tenants) and visibility, are equal.

Still other factors must be considered, however. Space built out for a tenant, rather than leased as a shell, may command a higher rent. The type of lease is also especially important. A *triple-net lease* may yield a lower base rent than a *gross lease* because it requires the tenant to pay both rent and a proportionate share of some or all of the costs of operating the shopping center, usually including common area maintenance, repairs, insurance, and taxes. Under a gross lease, the landlord pays the operating expenses, and the tenant pays only the base rent.

Ultimately, the rental rate is a subjective decision, but it should be based on objective market conditions. The shopping center will suffer if rents are too high or too low. The shopping center manager must understand how optimal rents will increase the income and therefore the value of the property.

Actual Rents. Once a fair market rent has been set, the base rate will actually apply only to some of the spaces in the shopping center. Different types of retail businesses will command different rental rates based primarily on their size or use.

For example, most supermarkets operate on a high volume of sales with a low markup. They occupy large store spaces and pay low base rates and low percentage rates (often only 1 percent). Jewelry stores, on the other hand, operate on a high volume of sales per square foot and a high markup; they occupy small store spaces and pay substantial base and percentage rental rates (the usual range is 6–8 percent for jewelers and 5–8 percent for service tenants). A supermarket that occupies more than 35,000 square feet of gross leasable area (GLA) may have sales approaching $550 per square foot and pay total rent amounting to only 1 percent of gross sales, including percentage or overage rent. A jewelry store may occupy only 1,500 square feet of GLA and have sales of $800 per square foot but pay a total rent approaching 10 to 15 percent of gross sales when percentage or overage rent is included.

Generally, smaller spaces rent for higher rates per square foot than do larger spaces. Although fewer potential tenants are available for very large spaces, the laws of supply and demand are only a partial explanation for the rate variations. Smaller spaces actually cost more per square foot to build than do larger spaces—restrooms and doorways, for example, cost the same, regardless of the size of the store. The rent a particular tenant pays depends on several factors.

- *Size and location* of the leased space in the shopping center. Small spaces with good visibility in areas of heavy pedestrian traffic (e.g., kiosks in the main corridors, corner locations, and spaces close to anchors) command higher rental rates than odd-shaped spaces and those on side corridors away from the anchors. Usually the more frontage a small space has, the higher the rent.
- *Type of business* determines the potential for percentage rent. As mentioned above, supermarkets have large volume sales at a low markup and usually pay a low base rent and a low-rate percentage rent (this can be very profitable for the shopping center owner because a 1-percent rate will yield $1,000 of percentage rent for each $100,000 of sales over the amount of the base rent); a jeweler or furrier usually pays a high base rent and a substantial percentage rate because these types of businesses have comparatively fewer sales at high unit prices and a substantial markup.
- *Desirability* of a particular tenancy. If having a store of the premier local chain of stores in the area will add to the shopping center's attraction, image, sales, or all three, negotiation of a lease may require a compromise or concession that provides for a reduction in the rent (although a reduction in base rent may be compensated by percentage rent).

If all spaces were leased at the same rental rate, prospective tenants would seek out only the best locations, and the owner would be left with vacancies in the less-desirable spaces. Only when one or two less-desirable spaces remain to be leased are rent reductions as such usually discussed.

Budget Planning

Providing a plan for how the operating and capital budgets will be handled is a critical component of the management plan. The *operating budget* for a shopping center is an estimate of how much income the property can be expected to generate on a regular schedule. It also provides a projection of what the operation and maintenance of the center during that period will cost. The *capital budget* for a shopping center shows the amount to be set aside each month to build a capital reserve for major work that is anticipated at a future date (e.g., roof replacement).

Operations

The management plan must have a section that describes the general parameters for how the shopping center will be managed, operated, and maintained. The shopping center manager will recommend to the owner any on-site staffing for larger shopping centers and which services—such as cleaning the common area, landscaping, security, etc.—will be maintained in-house or contracted, and how marketing and leasing activities will be managed. Those topics are covered thoroughly in chapter 4, Management Structure.

That the shopping center is clean and functioning smoothly will remain ongoing concerns of the shopping center manager (see chapter 5, Operations and Maintenance). A well-maintained property will help foster good management-tenant relations, and it serves as one of the best promotions for attracting a continual flow of shoppers.

Analysis of Alternatives

An *analysis of alternatives* is a study of the property to determine its highest and best use. Few properties would not benefit from having a lot of money spent on them, but the objective of the shopping center manager's analysis is to determine the optimum investment by comparing expected benefits to likely costs. Such an analysis should include the economic feasibility of leaving the property as is and compare that with the benefits of investing in modernization, rehabilitation, expansion, or a change of use. If the management plan recommends changes to the shopping center, the analysis of alternatives should also include a recommendation for financing the changes. Finally, the analysis of alternatives should include an analysis of the value of the shopping center before and after the change that the shopping center manager can use to make the case for the selected alternative.

Highest and Best Use. In analyzing the alternatives for an established shopping center, the shopping center manager searches for the *highest and best use* of the property. At first, this is a subjective determination, but it is validated through the analysis in the management plan. *Highest use* refers to financial returns, which suggests that the success of an investment depends purely on economic factors. However, each developer's expectation of the return on an investment will be different. *Best use* refers to that which makes one use more appropriate than another—that is, whether a shopping center or apartments would be more beneficial for the site. If the shopping center is also likely to prosper, the developer has chosen the highest *and* the best use. If an existing property is doing well financially, and it fits into the growth patterns of the area, then it is probably at its highest and best use—in which case, the appropriate "alternative" would be to maintain the status quo.

Assume, however, that the shopping center is operating at less than its highest and best use. The owner in this situation faces a major decision about the shopping center—whether to continue trying to optimize profits in the context of its limitations or to change it. Basically, five options can be considered: (1) do nothing, (2) modernize, (3) rehabilitate, (4) de-mall/enclose, or (5) convert to another use. Each alternative will have a different cost, so investors analyze them all very carefully.

The evaluation of alternatives should include a *cost-benefit analysis* that projects the impact of the particular change on the net operating income (NOI) and cash flow and compares that impact to the cost of making the change. The costs to be considered should include any financing and the time required for the change to pay for itself. If a change is to be economically feasible, the projected increase in income (and related increase in property value) must clearly outweigh the costs involved.

Doing Nothing. Note that though the choice to do nothing has no up-front costs, financial projections for long-term operations without change should be made as a basis for comparison. This may, indeed, be the preferred option. The other four alternatives require investment up front.

Modernization. With the exception of doing nothing, this is generally the least costly option. *Modernization* refers to the removal or upgrading of original or existing features primarily to reflect technological improvements (e.g., installation of energy-saving light fixtures in the parking lot). The purpose of a modernization program is to replace outdated equipment that is adding significantly to the cost of operating the property. Modernization should reduce financial losses due to changing modes of operation, a process referred to as *functional obsolescence.*

Sometimes modernization is more important for a shopping center's image. Many shopping centers built during the 1950s and 1960s were well planned and are still architecturally sound. They are in good locations, but their exteriors date them. A modernization program can benefit these shopping centers greatly. Many older shopping centers are recognizable from the steel columns along their walkways and the corrugated metal overhead. Though functional, these elements are not aesthetically pleasing and appear dated compared to more recently designed shopping centers. For a reasonable cost and with minimal disruption of operations, the property owner often can remove and replace such elements that age a shopping center.

Signage, in particular, quickly becomes dated. In the past, shopping center owners generally imposed few limitations on signage. Each tenant tried to surpass the others' signs in size, brightness, or attractiveness. That has changed, however, and most shopping centers now have sign criteria that all tenants must follow. The idea that the shopping center is a unit (and that tenants must plan all their marketing and promotional efforts in relation to the whole) is the basic purpose for such coordination.

The same philosophy holds true for all design elements at the shopping center, from paint colors to sidewalks and lighting. The design must be coordinated or the shopping center will look chaotic. In shopping centers where the anchors own their own sites and build their own buildings, the design elements are still coordinated between the anchors and the rest of the other tenants' spaces to maintain one architectural theme.

A modernization program related to signage can be inexpensive. New signs can be leased with little capital outlay, and that will improve the appearance of the center. A request that merchants remove paper advertising signs from their windows costs nothing, and yet this simple act may greatly improve appearances.

Other cosmetic changes that can be made at a relatively small cost are installing new benches and trash receptacles, sealing and striping the parking lot, upgrading landscaping, and replacing the lens covers on canopy lights. Items that are no longer useful can be removed. Unsightly or incorrect signs, old flag poles, broken roof drains, and abandoned pipes fall into this category.

Many early shopping centers had little landscaping, but those built more recently have extensive landscaping. New shopping centers frequently have 15–20 percent of the site landscaped to comply with local governmental requirements. Although existing landscaping may be updated, extensive changes may exceed the objectives of a modernization program.

Modernization alone can accomplish much for little cost, but it will correct only minor, mostly cosmetic, problems. It cannot change a poor layout of buildings, nor will it solve such problems as poor access or poor visibility. The management plan, if properly prepared, will distinguish between those problems that can be corrected by simple modernization and those that require major renovations.

Rehabilitation. The next option relates to major structural changes on the property. Rehabilitation may involve complete removal of a building or addition of a new one. It can entail complete relandscaping or total remodeling of tenant spaces. Sometimes the creation of additional leasable space by altering (reducing) the common area or adding a parking structure to accommodate additional buildings is possible or desirable. Whatever the changes, rehabilitation is intended to restore a property to its original condition without changing its basic use.

Rehabilitation is generally done in an operating shopping center, which creates the added concern that the construction may disturb customers and tenants. How much rehabilitation is necessary will be determined largely from evaluation of the competition in the area. Remodeling programs frequently look good on paper at first but do not make sense when fully analyzed. Because a compromise on the improvements could eventually preclude the best merchants from leasing space at the shopping center (or mean that rents will be below the market rate) the analysis of alternatives should indicate the proper level of improvements to the shopping center to make it competitive once more.

Generally, rehabilitation becomes necessary either because of neglect of the property or because of major changes in the trade area. If the underlying problem is a complex socioeconomic condition within the trade area population, no single project—no matter how extensive—is likely to change that situation. However, changes in the shopping center and retailing industries are more likely to make a particular center obsolete. The shopping center's trade area might also improve over the year with higher density that will help support the changes desired.

Economics are always a consideration. Nearly all investors work with limited funds, and the shopping center manager must recognize what the demands of the property will mean in financial terms. The solution to the problem may be clear, but the owner may not have the resources to see it through. The shopping center manager must determine what the actual problems are and, using the resources available, work toward the best solution within the limitations that exist. Without sufficient capital, however, even a well-prepared shopping center manager will face great obstacles in trying to turn a decaying property into a prosperous one.

In planning a rehabilitation program, the shopping center manager should consider every aspect of the shopping center and ensure that each part of the program conforms to the owner's objectives. The basic layout of the property may be a detriment, or improvements may reduce insurance costs. Each retail space should be evaluated for deficiencies as well. When these spaces are re-leased, they should be able to command higher rents.

If the improvements appear to be economically sound and the necessary financing has been secured, if practical, the owner would be well advised to proceed with the rehabilitation program as soon as possible, despite any limitations related to leases. In an inflationary economy, the cost of construction will only escalate. Though *phased construction*—completing small, discrete projects and rehabilitating the property gradually over a longer period—is an alternative, it can affect the earning power of the investment and reduce the impact of having an "all new" shopping center to promote to the public. The cost-benefit analysis of making improvements over an extended period must also examine the attendant disruption of tenants' business and loss of rents, and all of these considerations must be weighed against the specific costs and benefits of completing the work quickly and efficiently.

De-malling and Enclosure. Converting enclosed minimalls to strip shopping centers, or *de-malling,* is a growing trend, even in areas with severe weather conditions. De-malling generally has to do with the size of the shopping center, the nature of the market, and the merchants that are likely to be attracted to the site. A regional mall may no longer be able to attract the shoppers necessary to support an enclosed mall, but the conversion to an open lifestyle shopping center or a power shopping center may well be supported in the area.

Two shopping centers in the Southwest have been de-malled. Both properties were small regional shopping centers and both are more than 40 years old. Neither property has the available space to turn it into a full-scale regional mall in today's environment, but the locations are good. The owners in both cases have decided to completely change the shopping centers from small, enclosed malls to open town shopping centers. In each case the shopping center will retain some of the tenant mix, but tenants more attuned to the town shopping center, or lifestyle shopping center, will replace much of it.

Enclosure is the conversion of part of the common area of an open shopping center to a "mall" that is fully enclosed by a roof and walls. This can be the erection of a simple canopy or a complex, million-dollar project (most enclosures are also heated and air conditioned). In the 1970s and 1980s, most open-air malls were converted to enclosed malls.

Many factors must be considered in the decision to enclose a shopping center. Though economic issues are paramount, they are not the only considerations. The owner will want to know if enclosure will yield additional income and whether that will justify the cost. Enclosure can be a rationale for raising rents, but other considerations will also be important to the decision. If the competition is enclosed and the subject shopping center is not, the open shopping center may lose customer support and tenants may be more likely to move out when their leases expire, especially if the fact that it is not enclosed is a deciding factor. In such circumstances, enclosure is preferable even if it offers no immediate economic benefits. The intent would be to preserve the asset rather than to achieve immediate financial gain.

Change of Use. As trade areas change and the shopping center industry evolves, many opportunities for shopping center development exist that did not exist when some of the first shopping centers were built as early as the 1930s. Change of use is becoming more common as a development alternative. Examples include the specialty shopping centers developed in strong markets through adaptive use of old nonretail buildings, many of which were once landmarks (e.g., train stations, post offices, warehouses). Even the conversion of existing shopping centers provides developers with many possibilities. To a large extent, the market survey will determine how the property should be altered.

For example, if the owner is considering changing a convenience shopping center into a discount shopping center, the demographic and psychographic profiles of the trade area will indicate whether the latter would be more profitable. The location and success of other discount operations in the area—the competition—should also be evaluated because the market may already be saturated. Several examples of obsolete shopping centers being converted to other uses exist throughout the United States. One regional mall was converted into a public school. Others have been converted into general office buildings. For some older shopping centers, the physical and functional obsolescence was such that the best alternative was to tear them down and start over with a new building and a different use. Chapter 12, The Retail Component in Multi-Use and Mixed-Use Developments discusses change of use properties in detail.

For any contemplated change of use, the data for the area must indicate a real need for the proposed shopping center. Otherwise, the project will be a mistake. The demographic and psychographic profiles must be appropriate for the types of stores that will be at the center, and tenants must be found whose merchandise fits the proposed product array. In some parts of the United States, anchor tenants for new sites are plentiful but tenants for small shop spaces are not. In other areas, the reverse is true. A market (tenants) must be present for all the space that will be created, and tenant mix must be given special consideration.

A modernization program that permits more efficient operation of the shopping center may effectively lower operating expenses (e.g., heating, air conditioning, and lighting). A rehabilitation program for individual store spaces may increase efficiency, lower operating expenses, and generate additional income by commanding higher rents. Enclosing an open mall will increase operating costs, especially if a new common area is created. However, enclosure should also make increases in rental rates possible. Another consideration is that common area maintenance expenses are among those most commonly passed through to tenants. (Whether and how much expense can be passed through will depend on the language of existing leases, which the property management firm's accounting staff should review. When existing leases expire and are renewed, there may be a need to renegotiate the pass-through provision.)

Before proceeding with plans for an alternative, the shopping center manager and the owner must review the profitability of the property in its present state and anticipate the effects of each proposed change. Income and expenses must be scrutinized. A comparison of current income and expenses to projected income and expenses will indicate how the net operating income and, ultimately, the cash flow of the shopping center will be affected by the change.

Many of the improvements that we have discussed to this point are considered *capital improvements*—items that add to the asset base of the shopping center and are expected to last for several years. These capital improvements must be evaluated based on return on investment as well as what they contribute to the overall success of the shopping center. Capital expenditures are not direct tax write-offs. They require a large initial capital outlay, but the tax advantages are spread over the life of the asset as determined by tax codes. Additionally, even if the capital expenditure shows a reasonable return on investment, it must also be evaluated in terms of the financing available.

Financing. Financing is an important consideration in the analysis of alternatives. Many excellent real estate projects have not been developed because the would-be investor could not obtain proper financing. That can be a statement about the project or about the marketplace. In some instances, the high cost of funds may render a project unfeasible. Interest rates can change dramatically—for the benefit or detriment of a specific shopping center. In the early 1980s, interest rates were in the midteens, and 20 years later, they were at all-time lows.

The shopping center manager should approach several lenders with a brief explanation of the project and a description of its current financing to find out if they are active in the market. This type of loan shopping should yield an acceptable form of financing that is suited to the project. However, financing is a specialized subject, especially in relation to a shopping center, and a professional mortgage banker or a loan broker who is familiar with the various lenders and the types of projects they prefer to finance may obtain more suitable financing. Assuming more than one choice is available, the shopping center manager should select the financing package that best meets the owner's goals for the investment.

The terms of any loan should be considered carefully, including the fees that must be paid. *Points* paid for loans are up-front fees intended to increase the yield to the lender—one point equals 1 percent of the face value of the loan. Points play a big part in the financing of shopping centers. Because such loans are often for millions of dollars, points will be measured in tens of thousands of dollars. On a long-term loan, the points will not have much impact, but on a short-term loan (3–5 years), the points can make a substantial difference in the yield to the lender. On a construction loan with a term of 24 months, the points are a critical consideration. Investors frequently pay additional points up front in exchange for a lower interest rate (and, as a consequence, lower debt service payments), thereby making the loan possible.

If the analysis of alternatives includes refinancing, the shopping center manager should be able to provide valid reasons for selecting one form of financing over another, taking into account the financial structure of the shopping center and the likely alternatives. To be able to make such recommendations, the shopping center manager must understand available financing and be able to choose which type best suits the investment. However, because financing is such a complex and important matter, the shopping center manager and the investor would be wise to obtain the advice of a mortgage banker. Common types of financing include refinancing, wraparound financing, recasting an existing loan, and commercial mortgage-backed securities (CMBSs).

Refinancing. Evaluation of the financial condition of a shopping center often provides specific insights. It may be appropriate to refinance the investment as a means to lower periodic debt service payments or to make more money available for improvements. The decision to refinance an existing shopping center should not be taken lightly. The shopping center manager must determine how the owner's short- and long-term goals for the property will be affected by refinancing before a decision is made.

Because points have to be paid on a new loan, refinancing may not be worthwhile if the property will be sold in the short term. However, refinancing an assumable loan may make the property more attractive and therefore easier to sell. The terms of the existing debt should be considered. If the owner has a first loan with a low interest rate, seeking secondary financing for the short term and retaining the original loan for the long term may be more advantageous.

Wraparound Financing. Wraparound (or wrap) loans have a specific application and are generally used when current interest rates are significantly higher than the rate on the existing first mortgage. With a wraparound loan, the first loan remains in place and the amount of the first loan is combined with (wrapped around) the terms and amount of the additional funding needed. The combined debt is the basis for a new loan at an interest rate somewhere between that on the existing loan and the current market rate. The borrower receives the difference between the face amount of the wrap loan and the amount of the existing debt, and the wrap lender assumes responsibility for payment of the debt service on the prior loan. The borrower then makes payments only to the wrap lender.

For example, assume that a property owner has a current loan balance of $4 million and needs $2 million to make improvements to the property. Instead of creating a second mortgage, the wrap lender writes a loan for $6 million with a single periodic payment due from the borrower, and the wrap lender assumes responsibility for the $4 million loan.

Recasting an Existing Loan. For many shopping center investments, a logical means of obtaining additional funds is to recast an existing loan. The original lender puts up the additional funds and renegotiates the interest rate. Because the lender is already familiar with the property, its owner, and the existing financial arrangements, the recast loan closes faster. Not only is this an efficient way for the owner to obtain the needed funds but it also generally reduces the loan fees and penalties.

Commercial Mortgage-Backed Securities. Since the 1990s, commercial mortgage-backed securities (CMBSs) have been a popular form of financing. They are single property loans for which many investors make up the required loan funds. They generally apply to larger, class "A" properties, but they have been used for many new shopping centers with good success. Their lending requirements are generally more stringent than those of the mortgage companies, but CMBSs are also deemed to be more flexible in the overall terms.

Once the owner and the shopping center manager have considered the alternatives for financing the shopping center, they must remember that the financing plan they discuss with a lender today may not be available for long if interest rates fluctuate. Though a lender may agree to commit to a project, the borrower must realize that market conditions will dictate the final terms of a specific loan. Additionally, a sizeable commitment fee may be required and be at risk if for some reason the owner does not close on the loan. All of these considerations must be part of the management plan because they are central to the success of the shopping center investment. Not all shopping center managers are involved in the financing of the shopping centers they manage, however. The amount of responsibility granted to the shopping center manager will vary depending on the owner.

Valuation. Value is a driving force in the decision-making process and therefore in the creation of the management plan. The shopping center manager must evaluate alternatives in terms of what they cost and what value they add. Some decisions are made based on fending off competition and may not make current economic sense, but most of the decisions will require a realistic return on investment. The management plan is the vehicle to make the case for the selected alternative.

The principal goal of most investors who buy shopping centers is cash flow and long-term appreciation of the property's value, but it is not always that simple. The shopping center manager must understand the two types of value that apply to investment real estate: market value and investment value.

Market value is the price at which an "arm's-length" seller would willingly sell the property and an "arm's-length" buyer would willingly buy it if neither were acting under unusual pressure. Market value is based on the implication that both buyer and seller are acting as "typical" participants in the transaction.

Investment value is the price that an investor bound by special circumstances and restraints will agree to pay. Investment value relates to equity ownership and may be more useful in decisions regarding refinancing or sale of a property already owned. The return on the investment, income taxes, and alternative investment opportunities also affect investment value. Investment value and market value will be equal only when the investor's requirements are typical of willing buyers and sellers in the prevailing market situation.

There are three approaches to determining property value: (1) replacement cost, (2) comparable sales in the market, and (3) income the property generates. Each approach has some inherent problems. Ideally, the shopping center manager will use all three methods, and each method will serve as a cross-check on the others. Ultimately, however, only a willing buyer and a willing seller will decide the real (market) value of a property. (A professional appraiser should be consulted to obtain an accurate estimate of property value.)

Cost Approach. This method determines the value of a property based on the cost to replace the improvements on it. That cost will depend on whether the intent is to reproduce the improvements using the same materials or to replace them using modern materials and techniques. Though the cost approach may be used as a cross-check on the other approaches, in reality, replacement cost has little bearing on the value of an income property—a single-use concrete building may cost a lot to replace but have little actual value in the marketplace. Used along with the other approaches to valuation, however, and assuming that the property itself is useful, the cost approach may reinforce a decision about the property.

Underlying the theory of replacement is the *theory of substitution*. The theory implies that a buyer will not knowingly pay more for an existing property than building a new, identical property would cost. If this were true, however, why would developers ever build shopping centers in the first place? They simply would not. An older shopping center in a prime location should be able to achieve higher rental rates than a newer shopping center in a secondary location, all other factors (e.g., tenant mix, anchor tenants) being equal. As tenants prosper in the shopping center, asking rental rates are likely to increase and tenants are likely to pay increased percentage rent.

In computing value based on replacement cost, the shopping center manager takes into account each element in the building and prices each component part in the current market. The shopping center manager may also confer with architects, engineers, cost estimators, and developers to determine how much replacement of the improvements on the property would cost at current prices. The calculation must include the value of the land (estimated as vacant), development costs (including the developer's overhead and profit), and an allowance for depreciation (loss of value). When all of these factors are taken into account, the value determined for the property using the cost approach should be close to the values obtained using the other approaches.

Market Approach. This method determines the value of a property by comparing it to similar properties that have recently been sold. The main advantage of this approach is that it directly reflects the market. However, no two properties—in particular, no two shopping centers—are exactly alike, and this is the basic problem with comparable sales analysis as a basis for value. If the shopping center manager does use this approach, special care must be taken in selecting "comparable" properties. Factors such as age, location, condition, layout, tenant mix, financing, surrounding area, and possibly even a personal problem of the seller may all affect the final sale price in a transaction. In some cases, the seller may offer favorable financing terms in exchange for a higher price, or a higher interest rate may be paid for financing in exchange for a lower selling price. Therefore the shopping center manager must learn as much as possible about each sale before accepting it as a basis for comparison.

Income Approach. In this method, value is determined based on the property's ability to generate income. Although the method is not perfect, it is considered the most accurate way to determine the market value of income-producing property. Most investors use the income approach to value.

Because the ability to generate income is dependent on the property remaining in good condition, all long-term improvements (e.g., roof replacement) must be taken into account, even if the property has only recently been built. Shopping center managers often prepare an income statement without accounting for vacancies or possible emergency maintenance. The developer or former owner may agree to manage the property for an extremely low fee, which will lower expenses for the new owner, but only for a short time. An appraiser will adjust for such variations to develop a "stabilized" net operating income (NOI)—for use in estimating value. Regardless of the specifics, the more accurate the estimation of stabilized NOI, the more accurate the estimation of value. Value is estimated by dividing NOI by a capitalization rate—the formula follows:

$$V = \frac{I}{R}.$$

The *cap rate* is a rate of return used to estimate value based on the net operating income. *Capitalization* is therefore the process of translating a property's estimated income stream into an estimate of value. The cap rate is the percentage rate of return (yield) on the investment (purchase price) that the investor expects to obtain from the property. Ultimately, the market cap rate reflects the "typical" buyer's evaluation of risk. The higher the cap rate, the greater the risk—assuming that the real estate market sets prices efficiently—but the higher the return from the investment. Because the cap rate is divided into NOI to estimate market value, a high cap rate yields a lower value for the property and a low cap rate yields a higher value for the property using the same NOI.

In the real estate market, the cap rate for a particular property can change for many reasons. The condition of the property, the safety of the investment and, above all, market conditions—the rental levels of the property compared to others in the market and competing non-real estate investment opportunities—may change for the better or the worse, and these factors are all reflected in the cap rate. Too many investors chasing too few available properties can have the effect of driving down cap rates, whereas too much property for sale in a poor market will have the effect of driving up cap rates. Ultimately, the market determines the prevailing cap rate. If many investors in the area are willing to buy property at a 7 percent cap rate, the investor who is only willing to buy at a 9 percent cap rate is unlikely to find many properties of similar perceived risk available for purchase. The rate difference does not make either investor right or wrong. In this case, the other market participants have bid the cap rate—that is, the rate of return—to a level lower than the investor is willing to accept.

Income Capitalization. As noted, the income approach is the most accurate of the three methods of determining property value, yet it, too, has inherent problems. The main problem is finding an accurate cap rate. Through the years, practitioners have used many different methods to obtain cap rates. Some of the more common methods are described in the following paragraphs.

In the early years of real estate investment, shopping center managers often calculated a cap rate using *comparable sales* in the market—the net income of the property at the time of the sale divided by the purchase price produces a percentage (yield) rate for each transaction. Unfortunately, many problems are inherent in this method, including the difficulty in finding comparable properties. Also, the buyer's net income figure may be higher than the seller's, or vice versa, and the method ignores the cost of improvements. Furthermore, financing arrangements (terms), which do affect the value of the investment, will change from one transaction to the next. Rarely are two real estate transactions alike in all respects.

Another method divides the sales prices of comparable properties by their effective gross incomes to arrive at a *gross rent multiplier* (GRM) for the specific investments. Multiplying the income of a property by a GRM gives an estimated sale price or market value. Expressed as a percentage, the GRM is similar to a cap rate. Although this method is straightforward, it implies that expenses will be the same among properties in the sample, and that is seldom true. In actuality, a GRM is rarely used for commercial properties. Too few comparable shopping centers are available to permit the development of a statistically accurate model. However, the method does reflect the market, and from that standpoint it can be a useful check on other methods.

The *band-of-investment method* paved a new road for investment real estate. It was the first method to use elements of first and second loans and equity in establishing the cap rate. However, this method relies completely on the current availability and terms of financing and does not take into account individual buyers' behavior. A refinement of the band-of-investment considered more accurate by practitioners today is the *debt equity band-of-investment method*. This combines two critical elements of investment real estate, namely, debt constant and equity dividend. The method recognizes the principles that the market depends on financing and that interest rates often change over time and from one property to the next. It also recognizes that investors want to measure their equity cash flow. The debt equity band-of-investment method takes into account both debt and equity components and assumes that the investment can and will be financed or refinanced at conventional rates with conventional terms.

Many factors in the present U.S. economic picture frustrate attempts to arrive at an acceptable market cap rate. The cap rate reflects the relative risk of an investment. Under normal economic conditions, a new property with no deferred maintenance would be expected to have a lower cap rate and, therefore, a higher price than an older, neglected property, and the buyer of the new property could expect a higher rate of return.

The cap rate can change dramatically if the investor obtains a large loan on attractive terms. The better the financing package, the more affordable the investment. For instance, the seller may be willing to offer a 7 percent loan for a specific period in exchange for a higher selling price. All else being equal, the price paid may, indeed, be higher.

Early in the 1990s when the Resolution Trust Company was active in selling off failed savings and loan properties, they often held firm on the purchase price but gave attractive, below-market loans as an inducement for the buyers. The approach was quite successful.

Value Enhancement. The shopping center manager's role is to meet the owner's goals and objectives, and most often one of the owner's goals is value enhancement. There are many ways to enhance the value of a shopping center. In good markets the shopping center manager should look for opportunities to buy out weak tenants and replace them with better tenants, at better rental rates. The addition of kiosks and wall shops can add tremendous income, but the shopping center manager has to be careful not to harm existing uses. In some shopping centers the parking can be restriped to gain sufficient parking to add outlot or pad tenants. The addition of ATMs (automatic teller machines) to the common areas can provide an excellent boost in income. Splitting larger stores into two or more smaller shops can often create more income as the small shops generally lease for higher rates than the larger spaces. Sponsorships—where a company such as Boeing or Coca-Cola have the naming rights to the center court area of a shopping center—are becoming an important source of income, especially for larger shopping centers with high traffic counts. The effective shopping center manager will always be looking for additional sources of income without jeopardizing the other merchants or the image of the shopping center.

Although the management plan is an analysis of the shopping center, its recommendations must also reflect consideration of the financial capability of the owners, their reasons for owning the property, and their short-term and long-term objectives for it. Equipped with the management plan and a thorough understanding of the owner's investment needs, the shopping center manager is in a position to recommend the best course of action, including advantages, disadvantages, risks, and costs for the shopping center. The property owner should receive a complete copy of the management plan, including a list of the steps the shopping center manager and the management team must take to achieve the owner's stated goals for the shopping center.

Challenges, Opportunities, and Recommendations

The management plan culminates in specific short- and long-range recommendations that will guide the operation of the shopping center. These may include changing the tenant mix, adding a new anchor tenant, eliminating curable obsolescence, adding a pad tenant or anything else that would increase the value of the property.

THE OPERATIONS MANUAL

The *operations manual* is a separate document, but it serves many of the same purposes as some parts of the management plan. The shopping center manager is well advised to develop the two documents concurrently.

The operations manual should be a ready reference to answer most of the operating and management questions that arise on a daily basis and to provide information in situations that demand quick decisions. Use of a loose-leaf binder will facilitate organization of the contents and addition of new information. When the shopping center manager is out of the office or away from the shopping center, the operations manual serves to guide the other staff members in maintaining the status quo.

Operations Manual Components

The operations manual should include the following items:

- A site plan showing the locations and names of all tenants
- Plot plans that indicate the locations of essential features, fixtures, and controls
- A list of key personnel to contact for each tenant (store owner, store manager) with store phone numbers plus their home addresses and emergency phone numbers
- A lease summary sheet for each tenant

- Lists of exclusives granted by the landlord (owner) and restrictions that are imposed on the tenants—either by other tenants (usually the anchors) or to comply with legal requirements (e.g., zoning)
- A list of property files and their contents
- A list of employees who comprise the management staff, including their positions and their home addresses and phone numbers
- A list of maintenance and service contractors, including company and individual names, addresses, and business and emergency phone numbers
- Emergency procedures for disasters such as fire, flood, or earthquake

Plot plans are scale drawings of the site that indicate locations of such key elements as parking lot light controls; roof access points and ladders; incoming water lines and distribution piping as well as effluent piping and storm and sanitary sewer lines; fire sprinkler valves, extinguishers, and alarms; electrical wiring patterns and master controls; and various utility meters, including a complete list of what they serve at the shopping center. Plot plans make it easy to pinpoint problems and facilitate access to control systems to shut off utilities during repairs.

A *lease summary sheet* is a computer-generated record of the tenancy and the leased space that includes such information as the store area, rental rates (base rate, rent escalations, percentage rate), pro rata bases for pass-through charges, utilities, marketing fund contributions, insurance requirements, and specific lease terms (including options, if any, and lease restrictions). The information on this form provides ready answers to questions about specific tenants and specific leases. (An example form is included in chapter 6, Administration, and its use is discussed in detail.)

An *exclusive use provision* reserves to the tenant the exclusive right to conduct a certain business in the shopping center during the term of the lease. A list of these special provisions prevents violating rights granted to other tenants when new leases are negotiated. A complete list of restrictions that apply to the shopping center should also be included. These may include local zoning ordinances, planned unit development (PUD) guidelines, reciprocal easement agreements (REA), common area agreements, and separate agreements negotiated with anchor tenants, such as easements granted or parking rights or limitations. (Restrictions are addressed in more detail in chapter 10, Negotiating and Documenting the Lease Terms.)

Property Files and Record

The shopping center manager is responsible for maintaining the property files and records even though they belong to the property owner. Preparation of a list for the operations manual is one way to ascertain the completeness of the property files. The shopping center manager may need to have some or all of the following in their files:

- Deeds of trust and mortgage papers for the property
- Agreements that apply to the shopping center (e.g., easements, etc., negotiated with anchor tenants)
- Current zoning laws that apply to the property
- Records of property taxes
- Insurance policies and premiums
- Tenants' leases and records
- Covenants, conditions, and restrictions in the leases
- Rent increases
- Sales records (bases for percentage rents)
- Common area maintenance expenses and prorations
- Property tax allocations to tenants
- Tenant correspondence and payment records
- Correspondence from public officials
- Contracts
- Employee and payroll records

Like the management plan, the operations manual must periodically be updated. Whenever the management plan changes, the shopping center manager must ensure that the operations manual reflects the changes.

THE SHOPPING CENTER MANAGER'S ROLE

Regardless of the owner's specific objectives, the shopping center manager should always prepare a thorough management plan and operations manual. Their development is an integral part of the shopping center manager's job regardless of whether the information is used. The shopping center manager must present a comprehensive plan for the property, complete with a program for its current operation and recommendations for its future. The property manager is a professional—an expert who should understand all aspects of the property—and a well-prepared management plan and operations manual are evidence of the shopping center manager's professional expertise.

The shopping center manager's responsibilities for the management, maintenance, and remodeling of a shopping center remain constant, regardless of the owner's objectives. If appropriate action is not taken to maintain or improve the present position of a shopping center in the marketplace, it is likely to decline economically as an investment.

Ultimately, if the present owner is unwilling to invest the necessary money, the shopping center manager may want to recommend selling the shopping center to someone who is willing to invest in the necessary improvements. Once a shopping center has reached the latter stages of deterioration, to turn it back into a positive investment is difficult and expensive. Not every investor is prepared to undertake major remodeling of a poorly producing property. Many investors are adept at keeping a good property going; however, few are adept at making the changes and taking the risks necessary to turn a poorly performing property into a top-producing investment.

Once the owner has approved the management plan, the progress is tracked with monthly management reports (e.g., income and expense analyses, capital improvements, leasing progress, sales analysis, delinquency reports, budget comparisons, cash flow forecasts, and construction progress reports). By analyzing the position of the center on a monthly basis, the shopping center manager is in a good position to detect potential problems as well as opportunities early on and make the necessary adjustments to resolve the problem or take advantage of the opportunity.

4

Management Structure

The management of shopping centers has become much more sophisticated for many reasons, including an increasingly competitive retail environment and new ownership entities. Many new types of shopping centers have been created since the early 1980s—power shopping centers, outlet shopping centers, entertainment shopping centers, lifestyle shopping centers—and now urban retailing is experiencing a renaissance. Each new type of shopping center requires new leasing and management skills; each has a different tenant mix and must be marketed and promoted to a different market or shopper base.

The type of ownership and the investment goals the owners have for a particular property determine how the shopping center will be operated day to day and over the long term. Real Estate Investment Trusts (REITS) and institutions, as owners, have brought a higher level of analysis and evaluation to shopping centers. Recent economic difficulties demand that shopping center managers find ways to optimize their resources and improve net operating income. All property owners expect to profit from their investments, and the best way to accomplish that is to hire professional management.

As mentioned in chapter 3, Management Plan and Operations Manual, though individual investors may own shopping centers, sole proprietors are more likely to be outright owners of smaller, less-complex properties.

Large-scale developments such as regional and super regional shopping malls that require the investment of tens of millions of dollars are more often owned by development companies, investment partnerships, REITs, or other institutions that have access to large amounts of capital. In the United States, institutional ownership of shopping centers—by insurance companies, pension funds, and REITs—has grown tremendously since the early 1990s and is now a major form of ownership.

KEY MANAGEMENT PERSONNEL

The success of any shopping center depends on two critical factors: (1) the relationship between the landlord and the tenants and (2) the acceptance of the shopping center by the community. To achieve good results in both areas requires effective management of the shopping center by certain key personnel—the asset manager, the shopping center manager, and the marketing director.

Professionals within the real estate industry sometimes use the terms "asset management" and "property management" interchangeably. The differences between the terms can be drawn more clearly by describing them within a hierarchy of management. The Real Estate Research Corporation, a national real estate advisory and appraisal firm, distinguishes among three different levels of involvement. *Portfolio management* is the allocation of investor equity among various types of assets (e.g., stocks, bonds, venture capital, and cash), including real estate. *Asset management* focuses on one type of asset (e.g., real estate) and the addition of value to it. *Property management* is involved with the day-to-day management, operations, and leasing of specific buildings or land.

In the context of shopping center management, the asset manager assumes the role of the landlord and authorizes the expenditure of funds. The shopping center manager implements the plans of the asset manager/landlord and works directly with the tenants to create the property income. The marketing director promotes the shopping center to consumers and prospective tenants.

Asset Manager

When institutions own shopping centers, the management of the investment is usually complex. Prior to institutional ownership, individuals who oversaw all facets of the operation owned many shopping centers. As institutions take over, operations become departmentalized, and better and more sophisticated reporting becomes critical. Additionally, the coordination between departments in the institutions takes time and tends to delay and complicate the decision-making process. Institutional owners commonly appoint an *asset manager* to oversee the financial management and operation of the shopping center. The asset manager acts as the representative for the institutional owner and may be responsible for several shopping center holdings.

Asset management has eight key functions; each represents a way in which the value of a property is increased during the period of ownership:

1. *Acquisition* includes the review of candidate properties (particularly their operating expenses and revenue potential) and performance projections as well as the assessment of future opportunities for re-tenanting and rehabilitation.
2. *Property management* includes the supervision of property management companies, authorization of operating expenditures, review and approval of leases, and monitoring of conditions in the local market.
3. *Performance monitoring and control* involves generation of management information at regular intervals (monthly, quarterly, annually), periodic visits to the site, strategic review of the property's potential, preparation of long-term capital budgets, and analysis (and sometimes appeal) of property tax assessments.
4. *Re-tenanting and rehabilitation* involves design and execution of planned programs.
5. *Peripheral development* includes the review of assets for existing expansion opportunities, preparation of development plans, and implementation of necessary additional construction, or selling or leasing part of a property to generate cash.
6. *Refinancing* involves monitoring the national financial market and current techniques for restructuring debt, renewing mortgages at more attractive terms, and securing new financing as a means to reduce equity or to fund improvements.
7. *Restructuring of ownership* considers transfer of partial ownership via sale or lease of a portion of a property or evaluates buyout options in a joint venture.
8. *Disposition* involves the monitoring of the life-cycle position of a property to identify an optimum time for sale, consideration of a sale if the local market position is threatened, and evaluation of all unsolicited offers to buy.

The asset manager selects and hires the property management firm and works directly with the shopping center manager. Because asset managers' schedules usually do not allow them to visit an individual property frequently, day-to-day management, operations, and leasing responsibilities are assigned to the shopping center manager. However, some of the duties and responsibilities of the asset manager and the shopping center manager overlap as they work together to enhance the value of the property.

Shopping Center Manager

The shopping center manager has six areas of responsibility: administrative, fiscal, operations, tenant relations, leasing, and marketing and promotions. Many of the specific duties of management are delegated to administrative or operations personnel.

Administrative

- Collect rent
- Obtain and review tenants' sales reports
- Administer risk management (e.g., insurance policies and certificates)
- Hire, train, supervise, and terminate management staff
- Evaluate tax assessments
- Assist with litigation
- Administer leases
- Handle estoppel certificates for sale and financing
- Coordinate tenants' move-ins
- Risk management

Fiscal

- Develop net operating income (NOI) projections as well as operating and capital budgets (annually)
- Prepare operating statements (monthly)
- Authorize expenditures within approval limits
- Monitor financial activities (budget versus actual)

Operations

- Develop the management plan (annually)
- Prepare management reports (monthly)
- Develop and implement emergency procedures
- Develop and implement programs for maintenance management
- Evaluate and, if necessary, establish a program for the property's security and loss prevention
- Coordinate or supervise tenant improvements
- Coordinate remodeling and rehabilitation

Tenant Relations

- Develop a program to retain tenants
- Establish lines of communication with tenants
- Be responsive to tenants' needs

Leasing

- Keep the lease current with state-of-the-art provisions in conjunction with the owner's legal representative
- Determine market rental rates and concessions
- Develop and implement a program to identify, contact, and follow up with prospective tenants
- Conduct market surveys
- Negotiate leases and renewals
- Coordinate leasing activities

Marketing and Promotions

- Supervise the marketing director
- Develop the community relations program
- Represent the property owner in the marketing fund

The shopping center manager works closely with the marketing director to develop and administer specific programs directed to the community at large (discussed later in this chapter). Subsequent chapters of this book address the shopping center manager's role in shopping center operations, fiscal responsibilities and reporting requirements, tenant relations, and leasing activities. They also discuss the contents of the lease document. The roles of the shopping center manager and the marketing director in marketing the shopping center to consumers are the subject of chapter 11, Marketing the Shopping Center.

Marketing Director

One of the key members on the management staff of a large shopping center is the *marketing director*. This individual must have the creative skills to develop and implement programs to effectively promote the shopping center to consumers. In addition, he or she must have strong observational and analytical skills because the marketing director will be called on to help evaluate the competition and promote the shopping center to prospective tenants. This person works closely with the shopping center manager and with the tenants in the operation of the marketing fund. The responsibilities of the marketing and promotions director include:

- Communicating with merchants via a newsletter that is mailed, e-mailed, or delivered by the security guards
- Conducting periodic market research
- Preparing annual advertising and marketing calendars
- Developing a public relations program
- Implementing advertising, marketing, and public relations programs
- Maintaining rapport with the media
- Developing an annual marketing budget
- Reviewing and approving invoices for marketing expenses and funds management
- Developing and operating the accounting system for the marketing program
- Visiting periodically with merchants
- Maintaining a close working relationship with the managers of major stores
- Directing the merchants' association or managing the marketing fund meetings
- Adhering to the bylaws or rules and regulations of the merchants' association
- Hiring, training, and supervising marketing staff

MANAGEMENT STAFFING

The proper level of management staffing is critical to the success of any shopping center. If it has too much staff, the shopping center is overloaded with the cost of excess personnel; if it has too little, essential issues may be overlooked. Regional and super regional malls have large, experienced staffs. Generally, a regional mall has a general manager, an assistant manager, one or two administrative assistants, a marketing director, a chief of security, and a director of operations. Additionally, if accounting is handled on-site, the shopping center has an accounting supervisor, and if there is a food court, it has a food court supervisor. A regional mall also has security guards, janitorial personnel, landscaping crew, and food court service staff. Other on-site personnel may include a leasing agent and a specialty leasing or temporary tenant leasing person.

Specialty shopping centers tend to have on-site shopping center managers because they have a tremendous number of smaller merchants and extensive marketing programs. Lifestyle and outlet shopping centers operate with a shopping center manager as well as administrative and marketing staff on-site. Community shopping centers tend to be operated by off-site staff, as do most neighborhood and strip shopping centers. Depending on the shopping center type, size, and number of tenants, an experienced shopping center manager can handle 6 to 10 neighborhood shopping centers from off-site. Having strong staff backup is essential to effective management. The shopping center manager should consider the distance between the shopping centers, as timely travel between them to handle any problems that arise could be difficult.

MANAGEMENT AGREEMENT

If a management firm is employed to manage the shopping center, the *management agreement* will detail the shopping center manager's responsibilities between the management firm and the shopping center owner. It is a legal contract between ownership and management that establishes the shopping center manager's duties, authority, and compensation and states the owner's obligations to insure the shopping center, provide sufficient funds for its operation, and ensure its compliance with building and construction codes and environmental regulations.

The typical management agreement is for one year, with a 30- or 60-day cancellation right for each party. The term for a regional or super regional mall is generally longer. The issues that involve the most negotiation include accounting and financial reporting, management fees, and the indemnification and hold-harmless provisions. Institutional owners typically require that their management agreements be used. Most other owners use the property management firm's agreement.

For the management services provided, the shopping center manager is compensated with a *management fee* that is usually defined in the agreement as a percentage of the gross rental income of the property. A minimum monthly amount may also be stated to ensure compensation for management regardless of the level of rental income. Calculation of this fee should take into account the full range of duties and activities to be undertaken by the shopping center manager or the management firm and, if not otherwise specifically provided, the wages and benefits paid to employees who work as on-site management staff. Provisions may be appropriate for additional specific fees to compensate the shopping center manager for services such as supervising renovations, tenant improvements, and major maintenance repairs.

The shopping center manager usually receives additional compensation for leasing and lease renewals because the leases for shopping center store space are usually for three years or longer and negotiation of the specifics related to them—rents, renewals, prorated operating expenses, and tenant improvements—is complex. A specific commission schedule and the leasing parameters acceptable to ownership may be appended to the management agreement and incorporated into it by reference.

The management agreement should state the types and frequencies of reports to the ownership and the timing and issuance of the budget for the following year. It should designate responsibility for compliance with employment laws and for the filing of reports on employment taxes withheld from wages. The shopping center manager may seek indemnification from certain liabilities, as may the ownership, and the indemnifications they agree to should be stated. Because federal, state, and local laws determine liability under and compliance with environmental and other specific regulations, legal advice should be sought regarding what regulations may apply in a particular situation.

The management agreement may cover other particulars related to the legal arrangements for the management of a shopping center. The specific property to be managed and the names of the parties to the agreement (ownership and management) should be stated, along with the authority of the parties to enter into the arrangement. These agreements usually cover a specified period and are subject to renewal by mutual agreement. The beginning and ending dates of the term and conditions of renewal should be specified. Provisions for termination of the agreement other than at the expiration of the term and for compensation to the parties if such termination occurs may also be included.

Provision for notification of the parties and a statement of the relationship between ownership and management are other important inclusions. The shopping center manager is authorized to act as the owner's agent and, as such, is not an employee of the owner. Also to be included are statements regarding the ownership of records related to the management of the property and provisions for the transfer of records from ownership to the shopping center manager at takeover of the property and their return to ownership at termination.

The specific provisions of a particular management agreement should reflect the responsibilities the shopping center manager assumes to achieve the owner's objectives for the investment in the property. The complexity of the document varies with the size and complexity of the property and the shopping center manager's duties. Both parties to the agreement should consult their respective legal advisors to ensure that the provisions of the management agreement properly represent and protect their interests.

MANAGEMENT DUTIES AND RESPONSIBILITIES

Included among the shopping center manager's specific duties is the responsibility for administering the property's *risk management program*. This includes maintaining records of insurance coverage and ensuring on-time payment of the premiums. The shopping center manager also administers the details of individual leases. In working directly with individual tenants to ensure compliance with lease requirements, the shopping center manager has frequent opportunities to observe the tenants' business operations and identify potential problems. Sometimes the shopping center manager can help solve those problems.

Risk Management and Insurance

The shopping center manager administers the insurance program for the shopping center. However, shopping center managers usually do not determine the types and amounts of insurance coverages because few have specific expertise in insurance and, in case of a loss, they could be held liable for inadequate coverage. The owner should determine the insurance requirements in consultation with a qualified insurance agent. A shopping center should be insured against losses resulting from physical damage to the structure (due to fire, natural disasters, and so on) and against liability for injury to persons or damage to others' personal property. The types of risks involved and the range of coverages that can apply to shopping centers are described in more detail in appendix B, Insurance and Risk Management.

A property management firm employs individuals who perform a variety of specific functions, ranging from administrative activities performed in an office (accounting and record keeping) to maintenance of property and equipment at a managed site. Most often, the firm's personnel handle clients' funds (e.g., rent collections and bank deposits). Insurance for a management firm includes fidelity and other surety bonds, coverage for damage to or loss of office equipment and personal property, automobile liability for company cars, and workers' compensation. The firm may also offer insurance as an employee benefit—most commonly including life, health (hospitalization, major medical, dental), and disability coverage. The property management company is subject to liability as the owner's agent, so the firm should carry *errors and omissions insurance* (professional liability coverage).

In terms of managing a shopping center, the shopping center manager is responsible for the following:

- Conducting periodic risk management inspections and implementing incident reporting procedures
- Developing an emergency procedures manual
- Communicating with the local police and fire departments
- Ensuring that contractors have specific insurance with the owner named as an additional insured, along with the management company
- Ensuring that the shopping center complies with all government regulations

Lease Administration

The relationship between the shopping center manager and the tenant begins with a review of the shopping center's operations. The shopping center manager is responsible for ensuring that the tenants abide by the rules that regulate store hours (opening and closing times), employee parking, trash removal, deliveries, and use of the common areas. Because each of those issues affects the tenant mix and the shopping center's image in the community, the leases the tenants sign should specifically address those issues. (Lease provisions are discussed in chapter 10, Negotiating and Documenting the Lease Terms.)

A tenant who moves into a shopping center is prepared to operate a business, but the tenant may be unaware of how to do that within the shopping center environment. The shopping center manager should meet with the tenant just before or after the lease is executed and begin work to form a positive relationship. They should discuss the tenant's operation and the shopping center's rules and regulations, including the tenant manual, rent payment compliance, shopping center and store hours, employee parking, and merchandising beyond the lease line.

Tenant Manual and Letter of Welcome. The shopping center manager should provide the merchant newcomer with a manual that contains pertinent information regarding shopping center operations that apply to all tenants and aid in maintaining the shopping center as a special place to shop. A personal welcome letter from the shopping center manager should accompany the manual.

Tenant Manual. The manual should include information on utility providers (telephone, electricity, heating oil), garbage pickup, the shopping center's marketing fund, employee parking, the operation of the heating and air-conditioning equipment, and mailbox keys or combinations. A statement of house rules (proper use of plumbing, disposal of hazardous substances, fees for late payment of rents, etc.) may also be appropriate.

The tenant manual should include suggestions for handling emergencies (fires, accidents, bomb threats, arson, terrorist incidents, and power outages) and good housekeeping practices to prevent fires and accidents. Depending on the geographic location of the shopping center, specific natural disasters (earthquakes, floods, tornados) should also be mentioned. The manual should have sufficient extra capacity to keep correspondence from the shopping center manager and the marketing director at the back.

Letter of Welcome. A personal letter from the shopping center manager should accompany the tenant manual. The letter should welcome the tenant as a new member of the shopping center, and it should include an offer to be of help if needed. The welcome letter should request the following items from the tenant:

- Certificate of insurance
- Certificate of occupancy
- Construction drawings
- Signage drawings
- Estoppel certificate
- Tenant emergency information (home phone numbers of the store manager and the assistant manager) and the home office (headquarters) phone number. (This should be updated at least annually or whenever there is a change of store management or other key personnel.)

Rent Payment Compliance. The shopping center manager monitors compliance with the financial requirements of the lease. On-time receipt of rents, operating expenses, common area charges, and other payments from the tenants is imperative because those funds are critical to the shopping center's net operating income and cash flow. (Collections and other economic factors of lease administration are discussed in chapter 6, Administration.)

Shopping Center and Store Hours. A critical component of a successful retailing community is uniform store hours. The consumer wants to know that most (if not all) of the stores will be open during specific periods each day. Most consumers have limited times during the day when they can shop, and they prefer to shop at those shopping centers where they can accomplish as much of their shopping as possible at one time. Shopping center managers should ensure that tenants adhere to the hours stated in their leases.

Uniform Store Hours. In addition to being important to the customers, uniform store hours are important to the tenants. The primary benefit for a tenant to locate in a shopping center is the synergy created by the variety of retailers and service tenants. Each tenant plays an important role in creating that synergy because each merchant's customer traffic benefits the other merchants. In the same manner, every vacant space and every merchant that is closed while the other stores are open may weaken the synergy and lessen the traffic draw.

Uniform store hours are extremely important to the shopping center's tenant mix and its leasing program. When retailers are open longer hours, they often have higher levels of sales. Extended hours and the increased sales that result enable a tenant to be more successful and increase the likelihood that the tenant will pay percentage rent.

A shopping center lease usually requires tenants to maintain specific store hours. In an enclosed mall, tenants that do not have a customer entrance from the parking lot generally are not allowed to remain open when the mall is closed with the exception of movie theatres. Anchor tenants, as well as some restaurants in malls, have both mall and parking lot entrances. Tenants that have such outside entrances may open earlier and close later than the mall. When the mall includes a movie theater, the entrances near the theater are kept open 30 to 60 minutes after the last movie is over.

Neighborhood and strip shopping centers often establish minimum core opening hours but allow merchants to open earlier and stay open later—even 24 hours a day. By establishing core hours, the shopping center is able to publicize those hours to the public with the expectation that all stores will be open during those times.

Monitoring Tenant Compliance. All tenants must maintain the hours specified in their leases. When tenants do not maintain their required store hours, the tenant mix, the shopping center's reputation, tenant morale, and the potential for percentage rent are all affected. Some leases provide for a penalty if the tenant opens late or closes early. The penalty for repeated violations can range from a monetary fine to lease termination. Closing for an entire day may be a violation of the continuous operation provision, and some shopping center leases give the landlord the right to cancel the tenant's lease if a store is closed for a day or longer.

The shopping center manager should develop a program to monitor tenant compliance with shopping center hours. If management, maintenance, or security personnel are on-site, one person can be assigned to walk past all the stores each morning and evening and provide a report to the proper management authority.

In the absence of on-site personnel, store hours will probably not be monitored on a daily basis. In that case, the shopping center manager should periodically visit the shopping center at the times when the stores should open or close and note their posted (and actual) opening and closing times. Frequent visits and discussions with the merchants may disclose violations of the store hours provision.

Employee Parking. The occupancy of a prime parking stall can change 8 to 10 times a day at a regional mall, and even more frequently at a convenience shopping center. This turnover refers to the numbers of shoppers who park in the stall each day. One of the criteria for a successful shopping center is convenience. When tenants' employees take prime parking stalls, the shopping center becomes less convenient for shoppers. To avoid this problem, employee parking rules and regulations should be established and enforced.

Parking Program. An important early step in an effective program for the enforcement of employee parking is to explain to the store operators (owners, managers) the importance of providing convenient parking for shoppers.

Another key step is to designate a specific area for employee parking. This may be an area in the parking lot that is some distance from the shop buildings or behind them. A map of the parking lot with the employee parking area highlighted should be provided to each tenant. (For security, the parking lot itself should not be marked.)

Office tenants in a shopping center may cause parking problems because they are likely to have more employees than a retailer leasing the same amount of space. For example, a real estate office may have more than 20 salespeople attending weekly meetings. The office manager of the real estate firm must tell these employees where they are required to park.

Some regional malls rent nearby parking areas or garages during the busy holidays and require employees to park in those areas during peak traffic periods—evenings and weekends. Free shuttle service between the off-site parking areas and the regional mall may be provided. Off-site parking possibilities include the parking lots of adjacent office buildings and schools, both of which are usually empty in the evenings and on weekends. In locations where safety is questionable, use of security guards in off-site parking areas may be necessary or appropriate. A buddy system, in which employees walk together to their vehicles, should also be encouraged.

Monitoring Parking. Regular monitoring is necessary to ensure that tenants' employees are parking in the designated area. The level of occupancy of the assigned area will indicate the level of compliance. For a regional mall or a larger shopping center, a more effective method is for the management to require the tenants to supply the license number for each employee's vehicle or to issue a numbered sticker and require that each employee place it in the vehicle window.

Tenants' leases should include a provision that allows the landlord to fine the tenant for its employees' violations of the parking rules. If a tenant has the potential to become a major violator of this lease provision, the monetary penalty should escalate with each violation. The fine should be assessed against the tenant because the landlord's relationship is with the tenant and not with the employee.

Merchandising Beyond the Lease Line. The *lease line* is the divider between the tenant's premises and the common area. Except for center-wide sidewalk sales and similar promotional events, shopping center reciprocal easement agreements (REAs) and common area agreements usually prohibit tenants from using the common area for selling. Nevertheless, tenants frequently place merchandise in front of their premises. Mall tenants frequently position "Sale" signs in holders two or three feet into the mall corridor. Some place tables of sale merchandise outside their lease lines. In a strip shopping center, tenants may stack merchandise in front of their stores.

The shopping center manager is responsible for enforcing the reciprocal easement or common area agreement and the lease. Before discussing possible lease-line violations with a tenant, the shopping center manager should review the documents. If any of them prohibits lease-line violations, the shopping center manager should visit the store owner or the store manager and explain the rule and its purpose. Because many store managers never see the lease itself, they may be unaware that they are violating a lease provision, or they may be unaware of the limitations established through an REA or a common area agreement.

If lease-line violations are permitted, the shopping center may develop an unsightly appearance. Eventually more tenants may move merchandise beyond their lease lines, and the shopping center may soon take on an unkempt appearance.

Avoiding Tenant Problems

Shopping centers have the potential to have many tenant problems. Apart from business failures, a particular tenant's use may create a problem. Use and disposal of hazardous substances, offensive odors, unruly clientele, and long-term parking (usually by tenants' employees) are a few of the problems associated with specific uses. The best way to handle tenant problems is to anticipate their potential, address them in the lease, and establish a positive relationship with the merchant.

Tenants, leasing agents, and shopping center managers may all bemoan the length of a shopping center lease, but this complex document has evolved out of necessity. Almost every provision in a lease addresses a problem experienced by a landlord at one time or another. While the lease is intended primarily to protect the landlord's investment, the value of the lease frequently is not appreciated or fully understood until the shopping center manager has to resolve a tenant problem.

Most retail tenants do not intentionally cause problems. However, some categories of businesses have greater potential to create disturbances and problems than others, and the shopping center manager must be aware of these types of tenants and address the potential problems they can cause both in the lease document and in the shopping center's operational procedures. Common potential problems are hazardous waste, offensive odors, disruptive behavior by some customers, and business failures.

Hazardous Waste. The unlawful use, storage, and disposal of hazardous substances are major concerns of landlords and property owners. The cost to remove hazardous waste and clean up a site usually starts in the tens of thousands of dollars and can easily exceed $100,000. For example, when a landscaped area behind a shop building at a shopping center (managed by one of the authors) was contaminated with cleaning fluid, the cost to clean the site was more than $75,000. (In that case, one of the tenants was thought to have disposed of the material—without the shopping center manager's knowledge.)

Businesses that handle or use hazardous materials in their operations include service stations, automotive service centers, dry cleaners, and photo-processing plants. Doctors and dentists generate uniquely hazardous wastes because medical wastes can create problems related to the public health. Tenants' leases should prohibit illegal use and disposal of hazardous materials and require appropriate safeguards when such materials are used legally. Hazardous wastes also require special labeling and transport for disposal. The landlord or the landlord's representative (i.e., the shopping center manager) must be allowed to inspect the premises periodically, and the tenant should be required to pay all fines and cleanup costs associated with the use or disposal of hazardous substances (both legal and illegal). The shopping center manager should inspect the premises personally and, if a problem is suspected, seek out services for inspection with a consultant. If the tenant violates the hazardous waste provision of the lease, the landlord should have the right to terminate the tenant's lease, to charge the tenant for the cleanup, or both.

Offensive Odors. Adjacent tenants and their businesses can be adversely affected by unpleasant odors that penetrate their premises from businesses such as hair salons, nail sculpture studios, or pet stores. A possible solution is to build the demising walls of such tenants' spaces all the way to the roof. Such operations may require additional ventilation as well. Their leases should state that the cost to eliminate the transfer of odors to adjacent stores is a tenant expense.

Disruptive Behavior. When a tenant's clientele become disruptive or vandalize the shopping center, not only the landlord but also the other tenants and their customers are affected. Taverns and sports bars are among such businesses where poor behavior among the clientele can prove problematic.

Some landlords will not lease to businesses that may foster poor behavior because they do not fit the tenant mix or because their potential problems outweigh the potential benefits of their presence. If the clientele of a particular business may cause problems, that business should not be considered a prospective tenant. When a lease is offered to such a business, it should include provisions to minimize or eliminate potential problems. One solution is for the lease to require the tenant to have a uniformed security guard on the premises. The landlord should have the right to charge

Exhibit 4.1

Example Lease Provision—Entire Agreement

This lease contains the entire agreement of the parties hereto and any and all oral and written agreements, understandings, representations, warranties, promises and statements of the parties hereto and their respective officers, directors, partners, agents and brokers with respect to the subject matter of this lease, and any matter covered or mentioned in this lease shall be merged in this lease and no such prior oral or written agreement, understanding, representation, warranty, promise or statement shall be effective or binding for any reason or purpose unless specifically set forth in this lease. No provision of the lease may be amended or added to except by an agreement in writing signed by the parties hereto or their respective successors in interest. This lease shall not be effective or binding on any party until fully executed by both parties hereto.

the tenant for security personnel in the parking lot or other common areas if problems arise there.

Business Failures. Occasionally when a local business in a shopping center fails, the operator may blame the landlord. The tenant may try to get the landlord to cancel the lease with no penalty or threaten to sue the landlord for an alleged breach of promise. The promise may have been an inferred "guarantee" from the landlord or the leasing agent that a particular retailer would lease space in the shopping center or that a certain percentage of the shopping center's spaces would be occupied by a particular date.

This is a difficult situation to avoid. However, as with other types of problems, a well-crafted lease provision that specifically addresses this issue may avert it. (An example of an "entire agreement" clause is shown in exhibit 4.1) As additional protection against an alleged breach of a promise to lease only to retailers, the leasing brochure should state "retail, service, and office space for lease," rather than "retail space for lease."

Helping Tenants Succeed

Shopping center managers generally have more interaction with their tenants than do managers of office buildings or industrial properties. This occurs because the tenant's business is affected by the operation of the shopping center, and the success of the shopping center is determined by how well the tenant conducts its business. Sometimes when a tenant has difficulties, the shopping center manager may be able to help turn the situation around. To do this effectively, however, the shopping center manager must understand how retailers operate their businesses (see appendix A, Retailing Basics).

Seminars for Merchants. The rent a retailer can afford to pay is often directly related to its sales volume. Parent corporations of national shop tenants and franchisees commonly provide them with ongoing education and training. However, local merchants have limited opportunities and little time to pursue education. Consequently, they generally do not have the expertise and sophistication of the national retailers. Local merchants also represent the majority of so-called problem tenancies—rent collection difficulties and reluctance to advertise and participate in promotions—and have the highest percentage of business failures. The shopping center manager can help these merchants succeed by providing sources education and training they need.

One approach is to develop a series of seminars for presentation once a month at night or in the morning. Retailing consultants can be brought in to discuss markdown timing, window displays, merchandise presentation, in-store promotions, and other merchandising issues. If the merchants' selling skills need polishing, motivational sales training can be included. A banker can discuss financing to purchase inventory and the availability of and requirements for loans from the SBA (U.S. Small Business Administration). A police representative can discuss shoplifting, nonsufficient funds (NSF) checks, and credit card fraud.

Another approach is to have retail consultants present a series of three or four miniseminars during the course of a week, followed up with one-on-one meetings with the merchants to discuss their store operations. Such seminars can be invaluable to the local merchants, but they may have to be encouraged to attend. The tenants should be involved in the selection of topics and speakers from the beginning. After the program is developed, the shopping center manager should meet with each of the merchants and personally encourage them to attend and bring along as many of their staff as possible. To further promote the program, the shopping center manager should send a bulletin to the merchants a month before the start of the program, followed by a reminder notice a week before the program and a telephone call the day before.

Landlord sponsorship of these seminars is appropriate because investment in the tenants' merchandising abilities is an investment in the shopping center. Regardless of whether seminars are feasible, the landlord may want to consider purchasing copies of *The Retail Challenge* (the International Council of Shopping Center's newsletter for retailers) for distribution to the merchants.

Working with Financially Troubled Tenants. Throughout the life of a shopping center, some merchants will experience financial problems. These problems may be the result of an economic downturn, a consequence of the shopping center losing its competitive edge, or an instance of a merchant not being adept at retailing; alternatively, the problems may be related to a merchant's personal situation, such as a divorce, death of a spouse or partner, or other problem.

In some situations, the landlord and the shopping center manager may decide to work with the tenant to try to resolve the problem. Careful evaluation of the situation beforehand and continuous monitoring throughout the period of recovery are essential. In choosing to work with the merchant, the landlord may offer monetary or nonmonetary assistance.

Evaluation. One of the first signs that a merchant is having financial problems is slow rent payment. This problem must be addressed immediately. Other indications of a tenant wrestling with financial difficulties are a shortening of store hours (closing earlier), a reduction in inventory, a lessening of advertising, and layoffs of personnel. The shopping center manager must decide whether to evict the delinquent tenant or to work with him or her to turn the situation around. To make this decision, the shopping center manager must consider several factors.

First and foremost are the owner's objectives and the impact on the shopping center of the tenant's failure and another vacancy. If the shopping center already has several vacancies, one more will weaken the tenant mix further, lower the morale of the other tenants, and add to the difficulty of leasing space in the shopping center.

The condition of the leasing market (how soon the space can be released, what the size and location of the space are, and how much replacing the tenant will cost) is another important factor to consider. The turnover cost will include loss of income in the forms of rent and tenant charges for an unknown period; added to this are payment of a leasing commission and, possibly, the cost of new tenant improvements. However, if the shopping center has a high occupancy, or the leasing market is strong, or both, the best course may be to replace the tenant.

The value the tenant has contributed to the shopping center should also be considered. If the tenant has been successful for many years but is now experiencing personal problems or is being affected by a downturn in the economy, working with the tenant to overcome this short-term problem may be desirable. The prospect of a successful turnaround—and its costs—must be weighed against the likelihood of the tenant becoming so far behind in rent payments that recovery is impossible. If the decision is made to work with the tenant, the shopping center manager and owner must determine the type of assistance to offer.

Monetary Assistance. This type of assistance is usually some form of rent relief, either a deferral or a waiver of rents for a specific period. When rent is *deferred,* payment of present and future rent is delayed until a future time. For example, a tenant's monthly rent of $2,000 may temporarily be lowered to $1,000 (e.g., for the next 12 months), and the tenant may be required to pay back the deferred amount during another specific period (perhaps the last 12 months of the lease).

When rent is *waived,* part or all of past and/or future rent is forgiven. A requirement to *pay percentage rent only* is a waiver of the minimum rent for a specific period, during which the tenant has to pay only a percentage of its sales. Waiver of a portion of the future rent may require the tenant to spend part of the waived amount on additional advertising. Alternatively, the tenant's security deposit may be applied to past due or future rent. The program for a particular tenant should be tailored to that tenant's needs, and ways to address the problem over the longer term should be explored.

Rent relief should be considered carefully before it is granted to a merchant. Most shopping center managers are aware of tenant problems even before the tenant brings the situation to their attention. The shopping center manager should always be assessing rental payments, store hours, merchandise levels, help levels, store cleanliness, and the store owners' and managers' involvement. A tenant "watch list" to track tenants who may be in financial trouble can be useful. When rent relief becomes an issue, the tenant must be willing to provide up-to-date financial information on the business as well as on a personal basis, and management must carefully evaluate that information.

If rent relief appears to be the only viable option, the shopping center manager should consider the following: (1) review the landlord's right to terminate the lease; (2) create an addendum to the lease that specifically addresses the conditions (e.g., time frame as well as details on whether the tenant pays common area and triple net charges during the rent relief period); and (3) obtain a release from the tenant for any claims. Ultimately, depending on the cause of the current problem, the relief may not be needed, the relief may only have to be temporary, or the best solution may be to suggest closing the store.

Nonmonetary Assistance. This type of assistance may also take different forms (e.g., reduction of the size of a tenant's premises or relocation to a space where the rent is lower). However, a tenant's particular problems may require a different approach altogether, in which case, the landlord may choose to hire a retailing consultant to evaluate the tenant's operations and recommend ways to improve them.

When monetary or nonmonetary assistance is offered, the tenant's lease must be amended appropriately. The lease should be reviewed, and onerous provisions (from the landlord's perspective) should be renegotiated. While elimination of an exclusive option or an option previously granted to the tenant may be most desirable, other provisions should be scrutinized as well—specifically, the provisions on use, assignment, merchants' association or marketing fund, signage, store hours, and advertising.

Although monetary or nonmonetary assistance is not advocated (or appropriate) for every merchant that has financial problems, it can offer a temporary solution to a shopping center's immediate problem—in some shopping centers, it may be the only solution. Partial rent and a merchant in operation may be better than no rent and another vacancy.

Other Tenant Programs

In large shopping centers and malls in particular, supplementary programs that benefit both the tenants and the shopping center can often be developed. Examples of effective programs are employee discounts, display cases, and merchandising vacant space.

Employee Discounts. Many shopping centers develop an employee discount program to encourage shopping throughout the center, create loyalty to the shopping center, and provide a benefit for working at one of the stores. To make such a program work, a special identification card and a list of the stores that offer the discount should be issued to tenants' employees. Each merchant should be encouraged to participate; however, some may not. While for some businesses nonparticipation may be related to a corporate policy, others may not participate because their merchandise and pricing policies preclude such discounting.

When an employee discount program exists, the shopping center management and operations staff may be included as participants in an employee discount program, unless objectivity or conflict issues are present. However, if no such program exists, the shopping center manager should never ask for a discount or seek any special favor from a tenant. Such requests only lead to problems. If a shopping center manager accepts a special favor or a discount not offered to all employees of the shopping center, he or she may be indebted to the merchant and may develop a reputation for being "on the take" or using the management position to take advantage of tenants. In addition, such indebtedness may render the shopping center manager unable to deal objectively with the tenant on other issues (e.g., lease violations).

Display Cases. Though department stores and other major retailers usually have ample space in which to promote their merchandise, smaller merchants—especially those whose stores are in less-frequented areas of a shopping center—may welcome additional, low-cost display opportunities. Strategically placed display cases are one such opportunity. Similar use of vacant storefronts is a productive alternative to boarding them up.

Display cases are four-sided, freestanding rectangular units, four or five feet high. Their top halves are glass enclosed and include shelves for displaying merchandise. Display cases are used to generate additional income, focus attention on a particular area of the shopping center, and allow merchants the opportunity to promote their stores in other areas of the center. When display cases are planned, they should be designed to match the architecture of the shopping center, and they should be constructed from quality materials.

Merchants may be allowed to use the display cases on a rotating basis, and a fee may be charged for their use. If the display cases are intended to attract attention to an area of the shopping center that has poor traffic or where tenants have poor sales, the fee may be waived. Regardless of how or why they are used, overuse of display cases reduces their impact and may give the shopping center a cluttered appearance and detract from nearby merchants' stores.

Merchandising Vacant Space. Whether true or not, vacancies send two messages: (1) that some businesses at the shopping center have failed and (2) that the shopping center is having leasing problems. To overcome these negative impressions, vacant spaces can be merchandised, albeit on a temporary basis. This can benefit the community as well as the shopping center's merchants and eliminate the unsightly appearance of an obvious vacancy.

The shopping center manager can offer retailers in the shopping center free use of the display windows or areas in vacant spaces and allow them to decorate the spaces with merchandise and signs indicating their store locations. The vacant spaces can also be leased in whole or in part on a temporary basis. Possible users include card shops; bookstores; hobby and craft stores; clothing, accessories, and music stores; and service tenants.

Another idea is to allow community groups to place displays in the windows of vacant stores. The YMCA, Scout troops, Little League, school classes, and senior citizens' groups are just a few organizations that may welcome such an opportunity. Vacant space may be donated to charitable organizations for short-term use for fundraising and other activities they sponsor (e.g., collecting toys for needy children during the December holidays, a haunted house at Halloween). Use of vacant space as a community room is discussed later in this chapter.

CUSTOMER SERVICES AND COMMUNITY RELATIONS

In the 1980s, malls became the meeting places and shopping areas of the nearby communities, and shopping centers and malls continue to serve communities that way today. When a shopping center gains prominence, it has an opportunity to provide valuable services to the community, especially in suburban areas. Various services and activities sponsored by or offered at the shopping center can be valuable to the community. The size of the shopping center or mall will often determine the extent of the specific programs.

Customer Services

Shopping center services and programs that benefit individuals generate additional traffic and create goodwill in the community at large. Senior citizens and teenagers frequently patronize malls, and those groups deserve special attention.

Information Booth. Most large shopping centers and malls have an information booth. During the hours the shopping center is open, staff in these booths are available to handle such things as addressing shoppers' questions, providing assistance to find lost children, and helping people with car problems. The information booth may also be the answering service for the shopping center. Services commonly offered at such booths include rentals of strollers and wheelchairs, sales of bus passes or lottery tickets, sales of shopping bags (imprinted with the shopping center's logo) and gift certificates that can be used at any store in the shopping center.

Senior Citizen Programs. The number of senior citizens in the United States is increasing steadily, and shopping center managers can encourage senior citizens to patronize a shopping center by providing services directed toward them. Some shopping centers offer discount programs; others sponsor a free or reduced-fare shuttle or bus service between local senior housing facilities or recreation centers and the shopping center.

The "Mall Walkers" is a popular program which may be coordinated with a local hospital or a community agency. Usually established in enclosed malls, the doors are opened early in the morning for senior citizens and other members of the community to exercise. Registered participants receive special walkers' pins; their distances are recorded; and they receive a certificate when they reach specific milestones.

Teens at the Shopping Center. Malls and shopping centers are often favorite places for teenagers to socialize. Regardless of the weather or the time of year, there is always something to do there. Fashion fads, restaurants, music stores, video games, theaters, and promotions all attract teens. They can meet their friends and be seen. Parents often encourage teens to spend time at the shopping center or mall because they are among the safest places in the community.

The wise shopping center manager will welcome teens for several reasons. They have much more disposable income than their parents did when they were teenagers, and in a few years they will represent a major segment of the mall's customer base. However, the teen years are a period of growth and high energy levels, and sometimes teenagers become unruly. Such behavior can be frightening to others in the shopping center, especially elderly shoppers. Teens monopolize some shopping centers during certain times of the day or night.

The shopping center manager may want to welcome teens, but maintaining an orderly and safe shopping environment for all customers is important. Any program developed to encourage all the consumers in the community—including teenagers—to shop at the shopping center must include means of preventing groups of teens from creating problems for other shoppers. The Mall of America has implemented a program called "Mighty Moms" in which local mothers help with the teen problems in the shopping center.

Gangs, Graffiti, and Other Problems. Graffiti may be the first indicator of potential gang problems. Gangs mark their turf with messages and symbols, and the police can often identify which gang is active in the area by the types of graffiti. (Graffiti removal is discussed in chapter 5, Maintenance and Operations.) If teen behavior or gang activity becomes a problem, the police should be asked to participate in the development and implementation of a solution. Teens are more likely to congregate in or near a food court, a center court, video game rooms, music shops, and areas near theaters. Security staff should be alert, and teens who become unruly should be informed that they are welcome only as long as they do not disturb others. Preventing large crowds from gathering in one place and discouraging teens from loitering in one area can help prevent problems.

Some malls have adopted a "get tough" policy. They ban teens on Friday and Saturday evenings if they are not accompanied by an adult and bar unruly teens from returning to the shopping center for a time. Teens are given pocket-sized cards listing the rules and regulations, and parents are called when a teenager's behavior is unacceptable. Shopping center managers have differing opinions as to whether such a policy is effective or only serves to aggravate the situation.

Shopping center security staff must be trained to deal with teenagers. A bully approach may not work and may aggravate a sensitive situation. Some shopping centers have a customer representative whose responsibility includes working with teens and handling teen problems. Good lighting in the parking lot and other areas of the shopping center is a particular deterrent to disorderly behavior. Music affects behavior, and many restaurants have changed the music they play specifically to discourage unruly clientele.

A Positive Approach. The shopping center manager can take a number of approaches to dealing with teenagers, including having the police act as advisors to the shopping center management.

One effective approach is to develop and implement a specific program to cultivate a relationship with the youth of the community. This can be accomplished by creating an advisory board at each high school in the mall's primary trade area and a teen board at the mall. A representative from each school's advisory board is appointed to the teen board. The advisory board may be invited to suggest promotions, assist in presenting fashion shows, and coordinate school-related activities at the mall.

In conjunction with the merchants through the marketing fund, development of a work-study program with the local high schools may be possible. The school's advisory board would then serve as the job-placement liaison with the shopping center management and the stores.

Specific promotional events can be developed in honor of the schools and the students. If the area has only one or two high schools, the shopping center may become a sponsor or supporter of an athletic team or another student activity or organization.

Holiday Community Programs. Holidays bring out people's charitable instincts, and community programs can be initiated that will benefit those in need, generate goodwill in the community, and promote the shopping center.

One popular program for the December holidays is an angel tree—a tree decorated with paper angels, each bearing the name and age of a needy child. Shoppers can select an angel, purchase a gift, attach the angel to the gift, and place it under the tree. The program is coordinated with a local social service agency (e.g., the Salvation Army) that provides the names and ages of the children, and the gifts are distributed just before the holidays. It may be appropriate to stipulate that gifts should not be wrapped. Otherwise, wrapped gifts may have to be unwrapped (to ensure that the gift is safe and appropriate) and rewrapped. An angel tree program may also include the names of needy adults.

Another popular offering is a gift-wrapping service provided by a community group. Space in the shopping center may be donated to a local charitable organization to set up a gift-wrapping booth. No rent or fee is charged for the space, and the organization is expected to provide the gift-wrapping materials. The fees received fund the organization's other activities. In addition to providing a source of funds for a worthy cause, the gift-wrapping booth provides an added service for shoppers.

Charitable groups may also sell other holiday-related items, such as handmade seasonal decorations. However, specific offerings must be scrutinized beforehand. Items sold to benefit charities should not compete directly with the tenants' merchandise. Remember that holiday sales represent a major portion of most retailers' annual sales, and a successful holiday season is the measure of their business year.

Valet Parking. During the holiday season, some malls and large shopping centers provide valet parking as a convenience to shoppers loaded with purchases who have a long walk to their cars. Valet parking also relieves the concerns some shoppers may have about safety late in the evening. If shoppers feel more comfortable and secure, they are more likely to patronize the mall or shopping center. Valet parking may be provided at no charge or for a standardized fee. While valet parking may well have started as a holiday offering, some malls, lifestyle shopping centers, and entertainment shopping centers have instituted valet parking on a year-round basis, and it is very well received.

Community Services

Programs geared toward the larger community strengthen the shopping center's position in the community by providing valuable services to those who live and work nearby.

Community Room. A community room in a large shopping center or mall provides a place for organizations to meet. Many developers design a permanent community room for a shopping center, usually in an area that would be difficult to lease to retailers. However, provision of a community room may have to be on a temporary basis. If a strip shopping center or an enclosed mall has several vacancies, one of those spaces may be converted to a community room. If the demand for the community room is great and other vacancies are expected to continue for a while, additional community rooms may be created. Because some community rooms may be easily reconverted to leased space, reservations for their use should not be accepted more than two months in advance to facilitate future leasing.

To allow as many groups as possible to use the community room, and to minimize problems that can arise from such use, policies and guidelines should be developed. Such policies may establish conditions for use, set priorities for accepting reservations, and prohibit specific activities. The following are examples of issues the policies should address:

- Reservations should be made no less than two weeks and no more than two months before the intended use.
- No group should be permitted to use the room more than twice a month.
- Use of the room may be limited to nonprofit organizations only, or nonprofit groups may be given priority.
- A fee may be charged for use of the room (nonprofit groups may be allowed to use the room at no charge).
- A security deposit may be required.
- Certain activities may be prohibited—sales of services or merchandise, preparation of food, distribution of handbills outside the room, loudspeakers, and loud music.

- The user should be required to clean the room and return the tables and chairs to their original positions.
- Hours for the use of the room should be established.
- Organizations should be required to sign a hold-harmless agreement that indemnifies the shopping center and its management against liability arising out of the organization's activities on the property and includes rules and regulations for the use of the community room.

Other conditions or limitations may be required for a community room in a specific shopping center. The program and policies governing its use should be thought through carefully before the first use of the community room, and the landlord's (owner's) potential for liability should be investigated. Insurance coverages may preclude some kinds of activities, and state and local laws may proscribe others. The shopping center manager should seek the advice of legal council before proceeding.

The establishment of a community room offers a unique opportunity to market the shopping center to a captive audience. The walls can display a list of the merchants and restaurants, a calendar of upcoming promotional events, and posters promoting past events and photos of them.

The community room itself should be promoted. It offers an opportunity for publicity and community goodwill. A description of the community room and an invitation to use it can be sent to local nonprofit organizations, and announcements (press releases) can be sent to all the media. Basic equipment for a community room consists of folding tables (at least two, usually eight feet long), a number of folding or stacking chairs (usually at least 20 to 30), and possibly audiovisual equipment, a projection screen, flip charts, and a coffee pot if a kitchen is available.

Community Booth. Though to permit individuals or groups to promote their activities at a community booth in the shopping center may be desirable, such permission may also require provision of time and space for promotion of controversial issues and organizations. The U.S. and state Supreme Courts have issued varying and conflicting rulings regarding the right to use the shopping center as a public forum. State and federal laws and court cases as well as local ordinances may have to be researched to understand the situation fully.

Allowing use of the common areas for dissemination of information may be required under the law. Because this can be a sensitive issue, legal advice should be sought regarding public rights and the owner's (landlord's) obligations to allow individuals or groups to disseminate information at the shopping center. Development of a specific policy regarding use of the shopping center as a public forum may be appropriate.

If the shopping center owner chooses or is required to permit such a use of the common areas, reasonable and nondiscriminatory rules regarding such use must be established. Specific rules may (1) require an application and advance reservations and payment of a reasonable and refundable deposit; (2) set limitations on the duration of use, location, and signage; (3) prohibit use of a public address system and interference with the tenants; and (4) require a security deposit and insurance.

To accommodate such public use, a booth may be set up in a mall in an area that is visible to and accessible by shoppers. In a strip shopping center, a discrete area may be designated in lieu of a booth. Participating individuals should be required to remain in the booth or designated area, and they should be prohibited from distributing handbills outside of their area.

Other Use of the Shopping Center. Many shopping centers donate space or charge a nominal rent for city and county agencies to use space. Space leased to the U.S. Postal Service for a post office, a postal substation, or an express mail drop box provides a customer convenience and is therefore a useful amenity. Many shopping centers now include a branch of the city hall, which makes contact with city officials and payment of municipal fees more convenient.

Space that is difficult to lease or less desirable from a retailing standpoint may be donated for local use as a branch public library, a police substation, a youth community room, or an art museum. Police and fire departments and area hospitals may be provided space to conduct training sessions (e.g., cardiopulmonary resuscitation classes). Space may be set aside in the parking lot for recycling bins. The shopping center manager should explore and understand the legal responsibilities and liabilities before making any specific arrangements.

Customer Surveys

Keeping up with population changes, evolving tastes, and new competition requires frequent monitoring of consumers' needs and preferences. Formal research of such factors should be conducted approximately every three years. The shopping center is designed, leased, marketed, promoted, and managed to meet the needs of the community. An effective means to discover what area residents want is to ask them. Surveys may be conducted prior to the development of a new shopping center or when a property owner is planning to rehabilitate an established one. Surveys are designed to find out which categories of tenants and which specific merchants should be in the shopping center—that is, what the shoppers want.

Regular customer surveys provide valuable information for evaluating and assisting the leasing, marketing, and operations of a shopping center. A customer survey can be conducted to determine the demographic profile of a trade area or to characterize a shopping center's regular shoppers and

Exhibit 4.2

Example Customer Survey Questionnaire

Advertising and Promotions

1. To help us in the proper placement of our advertising, please indicate which newspaper(s) you regularly read.

   ______ Seattle Times
   ______ Seattle Post Intelligencer
   ______ Eastside Journal American
   ______ Redmond News
   ______ Kirkland Tribune
   ______ Highlander
   ______ Other ______________________
   ______ None. Do not regularly read a newspaper

2. Which radio station(s) do you listen to regularly?

   ______ KING-AM
   ______ KOMO-AM
   ______ KIXI-AM
   ______ KPIX-AM
   ______ KROO-AM
   ______ KIRO-AM
   ______ Other AM ________
   ______ KTIP-FM
   ______ KUOW-FM
   ______ KROX-FM
   ______ KOLD-FM
   ______ KREX-FM
   ______ KING-FM
   ______ Other FM ________

3. What do you think is the best medium for advertising Northway Mall?

   ______ Newspaper ads
   ______ TV
   ______ Radio
   ______ Mailers
   ______ Ads in weekly shopping news
   ______ None of the above
   ______ Other ______________________

4. Which newspaper is delivered to your home?

   ______________________________ ______ None

5. Do you subscribe to cable TV? ______ Yes ______ No

6. Did you or anyone in your household attend the following events at Northway Mall?

   ______ January sidewalk sale
   ______ February Valentine's promotion
   ______ Easter show
   ______ Boat show
   ______ Bridal show
   ______ Summer fashion show

Leasing and Tenant Mix

1. At which store(s) did you shop during the past week?
   ____
2. Which store(s) did you visit today?
   ____
3. In which store(s) did you make a purchase?
   ____
4. Are there any additional stores you would like to see at Northway Mall?
   ____
5. Which stores do you shop that are not located at Northway Mall?
   ____

Exhibit 4.2 *(continued)*

Management and Operations

1. Please rate all of the following aspects of Northway Mall.

	Excellent	Good	Fair	Poor	No Opinion
Selection of stores	____	____	____	____	____
Selection of merchandise	____	____	____	____	____
Quality of service	____	____	____	____	____
Parking facilities	____	____	____	____	____
Access to the center	____	____	____	____	____
Mall cleanliness	____	____	____	____	____
Decor/attractiveness	____	____	____	____	____
Mall amenities/facilities	____	____	____	____	____
Eating facilities	____	____	____	____	____

2. If you are dissatisfied in any way with Northway Mall, please tell us about it. (Please be as specific as possible.) ____________________

Frequency of Shopping and the Competition

1. How often do you shop at Northway Mall?

   ____ Twice a week or more　　____ Once a month
   ____ Once a week　　____ Less than once a month
   ____ Twice a month　　____ This is my first visit

2. Which of the following describes the length of your typical shopping visit?

   ____ Less than one hour　　____ Two to three hours
   ____ One to two hours　　____ Three hours or more

3. How did you arrive at the shopping center?

   ____ Car　　____ Walk
   ____ Bus　　____ Bicycle
   ____ Other ____________

4. Please tell us which shopping center you shop regularly.

   ____ Southcenter　　____ Bellevue Square
   ____ Northgate Mall　　____ Alderwood Mall

5. At which shopping center do you shop most frequently?
   ____

6. What do you like best about that shopping center?
   ____

7. Why don't you visit Northway Mall more often?
   ____

determine their preferences. Surveys are used to determine the most effective media for advertising, and shoppers' preferences for radio and television stations and newspapers are commonly sought. Shoppers may be asked which promotions they attended and what other types of promotions they would like presented as well as their opinions of the security, maintenance, and convenience (or inconvenience) of the shopping center.

A customer survey may include questions regarding advertising and promotions, leasing and tenant mix, management and operations, frequency of shopping, and the competition as well as specific demographic information. (A sample questionnaire is shown in exhibit 4.2.) The customer survey is intended to evaluate many aspects of the shopping center and to compare it to its competition. Once a survey is completed, the results are tabulated, evaluated, and shared with the tenants, if appropriate. Customer surveys can be invaluable for maintaining the shopping center's competitiveness.

Several methods are used for conducting customer surveys. Different methods obtain different types of information, and the cost of each varies. Five methods are described below.

Intercept. This type of survey is conducted at the shopping center. The shopper is intercepted and asked questions regarding the leasing, marketing, and operations of the shopping center. Interviews take between 7 and 12 minutes, and 300 to 500 interviews are required for the results to be valid. An intercept surveys only consumers who shop at the shopping center; it does not obtain the opinions of consumers who do not shop there.

Bag Stuffer Questionnaires. A simple questionnaire may be placed in the bag along with the purchased item. A center-wide survey might ask questions about where the purchase was made (store name), what was purchased and the price paid, when the purchase was made (time of day, day of the week), whether it was an intentional (destination) or unintentional (impulse) purchase, how often the shopper visits the shopping center, and some basic demographic data (e.g., the shopper's age and the distance traveled).

The shopper who returns the questionnaire may be given a token gift, or the survey may be included in a drawing for a larger item, in which case a name and address are required. Zip codes or city information taken from the drawing entries can provide some useful information. The response rate for this type of survey is low, and the validity of the results is questionable. However, it is an inexpensive method of collecting data and may produce good public relations. Some surveys include prepaid postage for mailing the questionnaire back to the shopping center management.

License Plate Survey. Copying license plate numbers and asking the state department of motor vehicles to identify the town and street address where the owner of the vehicle lives was popular for many years. Today, however, many states will not give out this information. So, a license plate survey can only be useful in determining the percentage of shoppers from another state. Shopping centers located in states that border on Canada may use this method to determine the number of Canadian shoppers. A more effective methodology is to track vehicle stickers. Most municipalities tax vehicle owners, and the windshield stickers (decals) they issue prominently feature the town's name.

Focus Groups. *Focus groups* consist of six to eight randomly selected individuals who are recruited by telephone to meet in the office of the research company or in a community room at the shopping center. Usually they are compensated for their time with cash or merchandise. The results are subjective rather than objective and are not statistically significant, but the forum-like environment fosters conversation and can provide interesting information and opinions.

Direct Observation. This has become a popular survey technique. It primarily involves counting exercises, from which patterns of shopper behavior in a particular shopping center can be determined. Specific observations include people leaving the shopping center with bags, traffic counts, and the times of day people shop at the mall.

Direct observation yields some interesting specifics and answers the questions who, when, and how many. Estimated percentages of shoppers leaving with bags indicate customers (buyers) as compared to shoppers (lookers). Traffic counts taken in different areas of the shopping center, at different times of the day (especially evenings), and on different days of the week (especially Sundays) indicate peak shopping times and areas. Observation of specific groups at specific times pinpoints customer habits. This information can be used to help plan specific events. *People counters*—sophisticated cameras and computers—can provide an accurate way to actually count the people who come into the shopping center

Prospective tenants may conduct their own observation surveys to determine which areas of the shopping center have the highest traffic or where particular groups of shoppers spend more time. Observation techniques are inexpensive compared to other types of surveys.

5

Maintenance and Operations

The day a shopping center is complete, its physical plant begins to depreciate. Shopping centers are often high traffic properties run with sophisticated plants, especially as they approach square footages above 500,000 square feet, are enclosed, or have escalators, elevators, alarm systems, etc.

It is incumbent upon the shopping center manager to delay the deterioration of the shopping center with a good maintenance management program. The shopping center manager may choose to develop an in-house maintenance program or contract for these services. The daily appearance of a shopping center must be consistent to foster a positive perception in the minds of customers. Every customer gains a feeling about the shopping center on each visit; should it appear unkempt or neglected, the customer may never come back. Keeping the shopping center in first-class condition at all times should be a primary goal of every effective shopping center manager.

The operation of a shopping center goes beyond the maintenance of specific areas and equipment. The shopping center manager's operational responsibilities include the provision of security to protect the property and the people on it (tenants and shoppers), development of procedures for rapid (and appropriate) responses to emergency situations, disposal of trash and waste materials generated on the property, and conservation of energy.

MAINTENANCE

An effective maintenance program is important for several reasons. The economic life of a building is a consequence of its physical condition. Value diminishes when a property is neglected and maintenance is deferred. Good maintenance extends a building's physical life. Most maintenance problems get worse if they are not addressed immediately. For example, cracks in a parking lot are easy to repair early on, but if they are not repaired when they first occur, a larger problem will ensue, eventually requiring removal and replacement of the asphalt. The landlord has a responsibility to the tenants and the community to provide a well-maintained facility. Pride of ownership is another reason to have a maintenance management program, but the most important reason is to assure the safety of shoppers and tenants.

Maintenance Management

An effective *maintenance management program* assures a high-quality shopping environment while preserving and upgrading the condition of the shopping center and enhancing its value. The program includes custodial, corrective, and preventive maintenance. *Custodial maintenance* is the ongoing cleaning and upkeep of a property that includes janitorial activities as well as daily activities such as mowing the lawn, sweeping the parking lot, handling snow removal, etc. *Corrective maintenance* refers to the ordinary repairs that must be made to a building and its equipment on an ongoing basis. *Preventive maintenance* refers to a program of regular inspection and care that prevents or identifies potential problems early and facilitates the proper maintenance activities before major repairs become necessary. It includes routine servicing of major equipment—e.g., the heating, ventilation, and air conditioning (HVAC) system—to assure its smooth, continued operation and helps control the cost and frequency of repairs.

Excellent software programs are available to assist the shopping center manager in the administration of a maintenance management program. Many of the programs can track major functions and details of a maintenance program. They can even remind the proper personnel of inspection dates, keep track of maintenance requests, and alert the user when a work order is not closed out. The programs can assist the shopping center manager in keeping track of stock on hand and maintaining a list of approved contractors. The system can produce printouts to track past calls, which can help the shopping center manager identify trouble areas that may require special attention.

Inspections. The first step in implementing a maintenance management program is an inspection of the shopping center. This initial inspection is necessary to determine what types of maintenance tasks have to be performed on the property, how frequently each task should be performed, and whether the work should be done by the shopping center's maintenance personnel or outside contractors. The common areas, including the roof, landscaping, and parking lot as well as vacant spaces, should be inspected thoroughly, not only to assess the need for specific maintenance but also to identify requirements for capital improvements. Inspection is vital to estimating future maintenance costs for consideration in the development of operating and capital budgets.

The shopping center manager is responsible for conducting all inspections. Periodic inspections reveal the general physical state of the shopping center. Most shopping center managers inspect portions of the center on an informal basis every time they are there, but more formal inspections are necessary as well. Management and maintenance personnel other than the shopping center manager should inspect the property periodically as each person will observe the property differently. The maintenance schedule may require the shopping center manager to conduct every other inspection and to assign the in-between inspections to various maintenance, management, and administrative personnel.

How often a shopping center is inspected depends on its age and condition. An older property or one that is in disrepair will normally need more frequent inspections than a newer shopping center or one in good condition. The volume of customer traffic is another consideration. Heavier traffic usually necessitates more frequent inspections. Other variables include the relative locations of the property to the shopping center manager's office and the time the manager has available to conduct such inspections.

As a rule, a shopping center—including the parking lot—should be thoroughly inspected on a formal basis at least once a month. High-traffic areas and areas where trash receptacles are located should be inspected more frequently. Daily or even hourly inspections of restrooms, center court amenities, and food courts may be necessary, especially during busy periods (e.g., the holidays or the grand opening of a shopping center), and janitorial employees may conduct these inspections.

Inspection of an occupied space is the responsibility of the tenant. The exception is the property's insurance inspection, which includes the interiors of the tenant spaces. This generally is done either yearly or every other year. The shopping center manager can take that opportunity to accompany the insurance inspector and watch for any situations within the tenant spaces that may be violations of codes or violations of the lease provisions. The rest of the year, the shopping center manager can use visits to the store to meet with the tenant as opportunities to observe any code violations (such as material stacked too close to fire sprinkler heads).

Unoccupied store spaces should be inspected each time a property inspection is conducted. Roofs should be inspected no less than twice a year. (Roof and parking lot maintenance are discussed later in this chapter.)

To ensure a thorough inspection, an appropriate form should be used. Separate inspection forms are used for the exterior common areas and the interior common areas for an open or enclosed mall. Use of the same form each time a property is inspected provides a historical record of maintenance and repairs. That record can become important documentation if someone is injured on the property (i.e., in a slip-and-fall suit), and inspection forms may provide the evidence that the shopping center is well maintained.

Extra effort should be made to locate and inspect hidden equipment such as sump pumps, sewer ejection pumps, and grease traps. The person who conducts the inspection should be required to note the status of each item listed on the form. This will ensure that every item is properly inspected. Administrative and maintenance personnel should give inspection forms they complete to the shopping center manager who should review them, take necessary and appropriate actions, and file them as a record. Copies may be provided to the property owner in the monthly management report. Any digital photos the inspector took can serve as a visual record of a problem and can easily be sent to clients and/or supervisors. These inspections should be conducted with the aim of identifying all physical problems in the shopping center.

Maintenance Personnel. In developing a maintenance management program, one of the shopping center manager's earliest decisions is whether to contract for maintenance services or establish an in-house maintenance staff. Each approach has its advantages and disadvantages, so each should be weighed to determine the most efficient and cost-effective approach for a particular shopping center.

Two variables that affect the decision to contract or have an in-house maintenance program are the size of the shopping center and its location. A strip shopping center with less than 300,000 square feet of gross leasable area (GLA) usually cannot support a full-time maintenance person. Because the tenants are responsible for maintaining their premises, the maintenance person would only be responsible for the common areas—in this case, primarily the parking area—and the roofs. Unless the shopping center has unusual maintenance or security requirements, there would not be enough work to occupy someone on the site full-time. Policing the grounds, minor repairs, and landscape maintenance for neighborhood, community, and strip shopping centers often can be done by one person working part-time. A small, enclosed mall may need one or more people working full-time to maintain the mall and the parking lot. As an alternative, a management firm responsible for numerous properties may employ one maintenance person or a maintenance crew to travel between and maintain several shopping centers.

Contract Labor. The advantages of contract maintenance are many. First, the price is known and agreed upon before the work commences; the fee for a particular job is the same, regardless of how long it takes. Often a contractor's technical knowledge exceeds that of any in-house person. Contractors can usually meet short-term needs for specialized labor. The contractor provides supervision of the maintenance staff, and the shopping center manager communicates primarily with that supervisor. The shopping center manager is relieved of the responsibility for interviewing, hiring, training, and—when necessary—terminating maintenance personnel as well as employee administration and replacement of workers when they are ill or on vacation. The shopping center may not have the expense of purchasing, storing, and maintaining equipment, and the contractor's insurance covers damage caused by its personnel.

While most regional and super regional malls have their own staff to perform most of the maintenance and repairs, some services are best provided by outside contractors. The HVAC service is usually performed by outside contractors. A few of the largest shopping centers in the United States may have the capacity to have their own staff for this function, but that is rare. Virtually all shopping centers contract escalator and elevator service because of the regulations, potential liability issues, and complexity of the equipment. Landscaping and sweeping are generally contracted by all but the largest shopping centers and malls.

Larger shopping centers and malls may have their own security officers so they can train them and have better control. In the 1990s, many mall owners shifted from in-house security to contract services. Smaller shopping centers contract for security services because of the difficulty of hiring, training, and retaining a small staff of security personnel. A cost-benefit study of the various personnel requirements will assist the shopping center manager in deciding whether to contract for services or maintain them in-house.

In-House Staff. Having an in-house maintenance staff has certain advantages, including direct control over scheduling and the quality of work. The cost to perform a particular task may be less because the contractor's profit is saved, but the time required to perform the job may be a concern. Employees are often more loyal to their direct employer—in this case, the shopping center. Having additional personnel available to handle emergencies is also an advantage; their schedules can often be adjusted to respond more quickly to maintenance problems.

Using Both Contract and In-House Personnel. The shopping center manager's analysis of the shopping center's maintenance needs and the owner's objectives largely determine whether in-house staff or contract maintenance is the most effective way to maintain a particular shopping center. For large shopping centers, a hybrid approach is frequently taken, with contractors handling technical maintenance and security and in-house personnel handling minor repairs and maintenance tasks that require general labor. Smaller shopping centers typically contract all maintenance or contract the technical maintenance and hire a part-time employee to police the grounds. Enclosed malls generally have the most complex systems and equipment. For these properties, maintenance and repairs that require specific expertise are contracted (e.g., HVAC, elevators, escalators), while tasks that can be performed by less-skilled labor are assigned to in-house staff.

Janitorial Specifications. No other commercial income property type has as much daily traffic as a shopping center. Shopping centers are open to the public between 70 and 75 hours a week; during the December holiday season, they may be open 80 or more hours a week. They must be kept clean, regardless of the amount of traffic or the weather. In addition to cleanup, rain poses a hazard because it makes the floors slippery. In winter, long periods of accumulated snowfall mean that melted snow, sand, and salt will be tracked in and deposited on the flooring. Ongoing cleanup is necessary, not only for its own sake but also to minimize the potential hazard of a slippery floor surface and to prevent possible damage to the flooring material.

All types of shopping centers and malls are unique in that they are cleaned while they are in use. The number of janitorial or housekeeping personnel needed for a particular shopping center varies with the selling season, the size of the shopping center and the volume of promotional activity. To facilitate housekeeping, the design of large shopping centers and malls should include janitorial closets and storage areas located strategically throughout the complex. Hot and cold running water and drains are required for scrubbing machines, so storage areas should include appropriate plumbing.

Janitorial work is scheduled in two phases: (1) general cleaning and policing the grounds while the shopping center is open and (2) heavy cleaning and floor care when the mall closed. There are three approaches to handling janitorial tasks:

1. Contract all such work.
2. Establish an in-house program.
3. Contract the after-hours heavy cleaning only and have an in-house crew that has direct control over the cleaning while the mall is open.

The combination approach precludes the purchase of heavy equipment and supervision of late-night work crews. Daytime janitors at a mall or lifestyle shopping center are assigned duties that include dusting prominent surfaces, polishing the floor, cleaning the restrooms, keeping the glass in directories and doors clean, and policing the shopping center and the parking lot—including the landscaped areas.

The key components of an effective program are (1) supervision and (2) comprehensive janitorial specifications. The shopping center manager or the maintenance supervisor must communicate regularly with and supervise the janitorial foreman, who must then closely supervise the janitorial staff—each of whom must have a job description listing all of his or her duties.

The janitorial specifications are provided to the supervisor of the in-house janitorial staff or attached to the janitorial contract as an addendum. These specifications differ with the type of shopping center. For example, strip shopping centers do not have the amenities, restrooms, and common areas found in enclosed and open malls, and their requirements for janitorial work per se may be limited to such activities as policing the parking lot, emptying waste containers and washing the outsides of windows. Almost all services in the strip shopping center are contracted, as there just is not enough activity to warrant in-house employees. Most shopping center managers try to combine services with one or a few contractors in strip shopping centers to save money and gain efficiency.

Food Court Operations. Food courts are popular components of many malls; they often become major gathering places. The typical food court has 9 to 12 small food vendors and common seating of approximately 35 to 40 seats per vendor. (Food courts and their tenants are discussed in chapter 9, Leasing the Shopping Center.) Ideally, restrooms and a janitorial closet with hot and cold running water and floor drains should be adjacent to the food court. A sufficient number of trash receptacles is essential. Natural lighting, interior landscaping, a music system, colorful décor, and attractive signage create a special ambience.

The combination of food service with high traffic requires special attention from the shopping center manager. Some food courts have a food court manager who is responsible for the overall operation of the food court, but that does not lessen the shopping center manager's responsibility to ensure that the food court is operated in a first-class manner.

No other area of a mall has such fluctuations in traffic volume during the day. The food court generally has a primary traffic peak at noon and a second peak period for the evening meal. The number of janitorial staff working in the food court changes throughout the day; some individuals are reassigned to other areas during slow traffic periods. Although the concept of a food court is one of self-service, and customers are expected to dispose of their food and paper waste in the receptacles provided, substantial policing of the area is still required.

The main janitorial responsibilities are wiping tables and chairs, cleaning (possibly mopping) the floor, emptying trash receptacles, and keeping the adjacent restrooms clean. If the food court area is not cleaned properly, grease deposits will accumulate on the surfaces. This, together with a dirty floor, can make the eating area uninviting. Care should be exercised in selecting the cleaning agents, as they must be authorized for use in areas where food is prepared and served. Cleaning is especially important because food wastes are breeding grounds for insects and bacteria.

Waste disposal is another potential problem. Receptacles for wet trash (including food waste) should be stored in close proximity to the food court.

If the trays used in the food court have to be cleaned for reuse, facilities and equipment to wash the trays must also be nearby. The alternative is vendor-provided, disposable trays, which are expensive and add to the volume of waste.

A separate budget should be established for maintenance of the food court, and food court common area maintenance (CAM) costs are passed through to the vendors. Some malls also have a separate marketing fund to promote the food court and its tenants. Because a food court is an amenity and a traffic draw and has the potential to generate high revenue, it should be managed with great attention and care.

Graffiti. A common problem that demands immediate attention is the presence of graffiti. Although graffiti may be the result of enthusiasm for a local event (a winning team, a graduating class), they are usually intentional acts of vandalism and may signal the presence of gang activity. Buildings covered with graffiti messages are not inviting. Shopping centers, with their numerous daily visitors and long, massive walls, are prime targets for graffiti artists.

Photographs of any such markings should be sent to the local police so they can try to identify the people responsible; then the graffiti must be removed as soon after their discovery as possible. If not removed, the markings may inspire additional graffiti. Also, when graffiti are not removed, the public may rightly assume that the property owner does not care about the exterior of the building and that the interior is equally uninviting.

Shopping center personnel should be on the lookout for graffiti every time they inspect the property. Even if graffiti are not present, development of an action plan to combat this potential problem is a good idea.

The first phase in effectively dealing with graffiti is preventive action, which may include applying an anti-graffiti coating to surfaces that are easy targets. Be aware, however, that the coating material can penetrate the surface of the wall and may darken it, an effect that may be aesthetically undesirable. Other preventive approaches to combat graffiti may be more desirable. They include providing good lighting and adjusting the schedules of maintenance and security personnel to place them in specific areas at particular times of the day or evening.

The second phase of dealing with graffiti involves denying the artist a showcase by removing or painting over graffiti as soon as possible. Graffiti artists use a wide array of media that include spray paint, felt tip markers, lipstick, nail polish, and shoe polish, none of which is water soluble. The appropriateness of a particular removal procedure is dependent on the finished surface of the building—i.e., whether it is porous or nonporous, rough or smooth, layered or nonlayered. The type of surface will also determine the materials that can be used to remove the graffiti. The safest, gentlest process that will yield the best results is the best choice.

There are two basic approaches—the use of chemicals such as acids and alkalis (both water-based) or solvents (oil-based, organic) and mechanical treatments such as water blasting, sandblasting, and steam. Because each of these methods can damage a building, an experienced chemical or equipment contractor or supplier should be consulted before any attempt is made to remove graffiti.

Tenants' and Landlord's Responsibilities. The maintenance responsibilities of the landlord and the tenant are spelled out in the lease. Typically, the tenant is responsible for maintaining the area inside the demised premises, the storefront (including the windows), bathrooms, and the entrance and rear doors. The landlord is usually responsible for maintenance of the common areas, the roof, and the HVAC unit. Roof maintenance is typically a common area maintenance (CAM) charge, and the contractor bills maintenance of the HVAC unit for the particular tenant space directly to that tenant.

Some managers and assistant managers of retail stores may not have seen the leases for their stores and therefore do not know all of the tenants' responsibilities. On-site maintenance personnel for the shopping center should be instructed *not* to perform maintenance in the tenants' premises except in an emergency or a special situation. Because store personnel may not know whom to call for specific maintenance work, the shopping center manager should provide each merchant with a list of acceptable maintenance contractors and vendors. Usually this is included in the tenant manual (see chapter 4, Management Structure).

Access to Occupied Spaces. Once a store space is occupied, responsibility for everything inside the store is usually transferred to the tenant. Unlike the arrangements in office buildings, *the shopping center manager should not keep keys to occupied store spaces.* When a space is leased, all the keys should be turned over to the tenant; the lock should be taken off the master key; and the tenant should be encouraged to re-key the doors. When the shopping center management retains keys, it has greater liability. If a tenant's store is broken into and merchandise is stolen, the shopping center manager and shopping center staff could become suspects.

If an after-hours emergency requires entering a tenant's locked space, the tenant can be called out to the store, the door can be forced open, or if necessary, the glass in the door can be broken to provide immediate access. This particular situation may only occur once or twice in a shopping center manager's career—or not at all.

Some argue that keys should be retained in case of fire or police emergency, but that can be resolved by installing a "knox box" in the shopping center that houses keys to the stores and can only be opened by the police or fire department. That way, the shopping center manager never touches the tenant keys and does not have access to them.

Maintenance of Vacant Spaces. Vacant spaces must be ready to show to prospective tenants at all times. This means provision of electrical power (for lighting) and water for the restroom(s) must be continued at the landlord's expense, and the spaces must periodically be inspected and cleaned.

Vacancies should be inspected no less often than once a month, and maintenance personnel should be reminded about the need to have vacancies ready to show at all times. When a store is vacated, the prior tenant's signs and fixtures should be removed, and the space should be returned to broom-clean condition. The windows should be washed on the inside at least once every six months and on the outside every two to three months. Two areas in vacancies are frequently overlooked—restrooms must be cleaned, and water-stained or missing ceiling tiles must be replaced. Anything stored in a vacant space should be stacked neatly in the rear. Windows should not be covered with paper unless something inside the premises should not be in public view. If the vacancy does not have a storefront, a plywood wall can be built to keep people out and eliminate the unsightly appearance. The plywood can be painted or covered with wallpaper-like material showing graphic designs or the name of the shopping center.

Specific Maintenance Requirements

A shopping center is a large, complex property, and several major areas require regular, detailed inspections and ongoing preventive maintenance—the heating, ventilating, and air-conditioning (HVAC) system, the roof of the building, the elevators and escalators, and the parking lot.

The HVAC System. Customers will spend little time shopping in a store or an enclosed mall that is too hot or too cold. The HVAC system should provide a comfortable, safe environment in which to shop. The adequacy of heat and air conditioning depends on the type and size of the HVAC system. In particular, the HVAC units should be appropriate to the climate of the region, the tenant's specific use (e.g., bookstore versus hair salon), and the size of the enclosed mall. Correct equipment, a good preventive maintenance program, and proper use of the system components and controls will ensure year-round comfort for all.

HVAC Maintenance. Responsibility for the maintenance of the HVAC system varies according to the type of shopping center. For example, the landlord is responsible for maintenance of the heating and air-conditioning units in an enclosed mall. The cost is prorated and billed to the tenants as a CAM expense.

In the past, strip shopping center landlords required tenants to maintain their own HVAC units. That resulted in different levels of maintenance. The units broke down more frequently and were more costly to repair because of the lack of proper maintenance. Since the early 1980s, some landlords have modified the lease provision covering the HVAC maintenance so the tenant remains responsible for the cost to service and repair the HVAC unit, but the landlord assumes responsibility for having the work done. This allows the landlord complete control over the standard of preventive maintenance for shop tenants' HVAC equipment and helps minimize the number of contractors walking and working on the roof. Regardless of the arrangements for the shop tenants, major shopping center tenants are typically responsible for the maintenance of the HVAC equipment for their stores.

HVAC Maintenance Contracts. The volume of service required at one site should enable the shopping center manager to negotiate a very competitive service contract. When only one service contractor is used, traffic on the roof is reduced and so is the potential for damage. More important, when a tenant vacates, the landlord knows that the HVAC unit has been properly maintained and is in good working condition.

When the shopping center manager seeks bids on HVAC service and repairs, each contractor should be required to bid on the same specifications. The type and number of filter changes and the number of times the units are serviced should be standardized. The specifications should be developed from the manufacturers' recommendations for the specific equipment. (If copies of service manuals are not in the property files, the shopping center manager should obtain them.) The type and frequency of service will vary with the type of equipment and the geographic area. If each contractor provides a bid based on its own specifications, the maintenance tasks to be performed under the service contracts will not be comparable.

When bidding HVAC service contracts, the following points should also be considered:

- The contractor's experience with the type of equipment
- The contractor's ongoing training of service personnel
- The contractor's availability and charges for after-hours service
- Any limitations on the amount of time to be spent servicing each unit
- Parts routinely carried in service trucks
- Extra charges for filters
- The types of insurance coverage the contractor carries

A good preventive maintenance program will extend the life of the HVAC equipment, reduce the frequency and cost of repairs, and provide a comfortable, climate-controlled environment for shoppers and tenants.

The Roof. The roof of a neighborhood shopping center may cover a total area of 2 to 4 acres; that on a super regional enclosed mall may extend over 15 to 25 acres of both tenant space and common areas. A roof that is not well maintained will eventually deteriorate and damage the building, resulting in extensive, costly repairs and premature failure of the roofing system.

The Roofing System. The basic components of a roofing system are a roof deck, a vapor-retarding barrier, insulation, and a surface membrane. The majority of commercial (low-slope) roof systems have *built-up roofing (BUR) membranes*—two or more alternate plies of saturated or coated felts or similar materials layered in place and cemented together with asphalt or pitch to make the system waterproof. A typical BUR membrane has between three and five felt plies, with three plies generally considered the minimum for a BUR membrane (finished thickness less than one-half inch). The felts reinforce the roofing system, protect the bitumen from water degradation, and add fire-retardant properties to the membrane.

Single-ply roofing (SPR) systems that consist of only one layer of a watertight, weatherable membrane are also used. However, this type of roofing is more vulnerable to piercing than are BUR membrane systems.

Roof Maintenance Program. A roof is a major investment for a property owner. The most important reason for regular roof maintenance is to protect that investment. A good maintenance program will not only add years to the life of the roof but it will also help shopping center managers detect minor problems before damage is widespread. To facilitate development and execution of a roof maintenance program, the shopping center manager should have as-built drawings of the roof deck, flashings, and roof system, plus a roof plan showing construction details (all vents and rooftop installations), updated to show additions. A history of the roof should be kept on file, including its age, the dates and descriptions of any resurfacing, and copies of inspection reports.

An effective roof maintenance program consists of inspections and corrective action (removal of debris, cleaning of drains, minor repairs, consultation with a roofing contractor as appropriate). Inspections should be conducted no less than twice a year—preferably in the late spring or early autumn—and after any severe weather (e.g., torrential rains, high winds) or other natural occurrences (e.g., earth tremors). The inspection and maintenance schedule for the roof should incorporate other related elements as well. Skylights require frequent inspection and maintenance, and drains and gutters require regular cleaning.

Items to inspect include the parapet walls, counter flashing, metal work, coping, roof penetrations, equipment supports, curbs, condensate lines, drains, gutters, and downspouts. During the inspection, the roof material should be observed for the following conditions: water ponding, bubbles and blisters, splits, dry felts, wrinkles, exposed laps and fish mouths, oxidation, and alligatoring. Each of these defects requires immediate action. Four courses of action are possible when a roof requires repairs:

1. *Patching* with material that is compatible with the existing roof materials
2. *Recoating* of the roof surface when the felts are in good condition

3. *Recovering* by applying another roof system over the existing one
4. *Replacement* of the old roof system with a completely new one

Roof Access. In general, traffic on the roof should be kept to a minimum, and a professional roofing contractor should be consulted about major problems. The lease should require tenants to receive advance written approval by the shopping center manager for access to the roof. Because every penetration threatens the integrity of the roof membrane, installation of a special walkway may be desirable or necessary. This is particularly true for SPR membrane roofs. If a tenant wants to install equipment on the roof, permission to do so should require the work to be performed to strict specifications, and the shopping center manager or assigned maintenance personnel should be present during the installation. The installation should be inspected as soon after completion as possible.

Elevators and Escalators. In enclosed malls and shopping centers that are designed with more than one level, elevators and escalators require special considerations. Though service for each is contracted, the shopping center manager can monitor many details on a regular basis to ensure that the elevators and escalators are operating properly.

The location, efficiency, safety, and appearance of each will affect shoppers' perceptions of the shopping center. For example, elevators are expected to have good speed, adequate lighting, good ventilation, and easily understood controls. If escalators are frequently out of service, shoppers may develop the impression that the shopping center is not well managed; service issues should be addressed immediately. Regular maintenance should alleviate the problems that can arise if the elevators or escalators are not well maintained.

The Parking Lot. At a small strip shopping center, the parking area may be only a quarter of an acre, but the parking lot at a super regional mall can cover more than 50 acres. Regardless of the size of the shopping center, the parking lot typically covers the largest area of the property. When a shopping center first opens, the parking lot is attractive and safe, but its condition deteriorates over time as it is damaged by weather and use. An appropriate maintenance program will extend the useful life of the parking lot and minimize repairs and liability issues.

General Maintenance. At the very least, a parking lot should be swept regularly, especially when landscaping debris (fallen leaves, seed pods, etc.) makes it look unkempt. Because it is the shopper's first impression of the shopping center, the maintenance schedule should include daily policing and removal of wastepaper and other litter.

The parking lot should be inspected regularly by walking the area from side to side and from one end to the other. Large parking lots can be divided into sections and each section can be inspected on a different day. A well-maintained parking lot improves the aesthetics and safety of the shopping center and reduces maintenance and repair expenses.

Snow Removal. The best retail selling period during the year is the December holiday season. Most retailers generate 15 to 35 percent of their annual sales between Thanksgiving and Christmas. In many areas of the United States, this holiday period is also the snow season. In the North, snow may fall as early as October, and periodic snowfalls continue through April.

The shopping center manager must develop and implement a cost-effective snow-removal program that allows for safe, convenient access to the shopping center. If snow removal is ineffective, the parking lot will be unsafe; traffic to the shopping center will be reduced; and sales will be lost. After the first substantial snowfall, the tenants will know just how effective the snow removal plan is.

The first step in developing a snow removal plan is deciding who will remove the snow. On-site personnel are usually responsible for keeping the sidewalks and shopping center entrances clear of snow and ice. To do this effectively, they need the proper equipment—snow shovels, a snowblower, and possibly salt or other chemicals. If on-site staff have access to a pickup truck with a blade, they may be able to move light snow out of prime parking areas.

The shopping center manager may hire a contractor to augment the work of the on-site staff or to handle all the snow removal. Parking lot sweeping companies often provide snow removal service, and some highway and road construction contractors use their equipment for winter snow removal. Before a contract for snow removal is signed, the contractor's references should be checked. The contractor should be asked to provide a list of equipment the company has available and to indicate whether it is owned, leased, or rented on an as-needed basis. (Rented equipment may not be available to the contractor during heavy snowfalls.)

Once a contract is signed, the shopping center manager should walk the parking lot with the contractor and the drivers of the equipment to point out features such as curbs, signs, and speed bumps that may later be hidden by snow. During this inspection, the current condition of the parking lot should be noted so that when the snow season ends, the contractor will not be held responsible (or billed) for preexisting damage.

Completely removing snow from the parking lot is not always necessary. During months when sales are slow (e.g., January and February), snow may simply be moved to areas of the parking lot that are not being used. When snow removal is necessary, however, arrangements may sometimes be made with the owner of a nearby vacant lot to pile snow there. The entire parking lot must usually be kept clear during December.

Each time snow removal is required, the contractor must be told which areas are to be cleared of snow and where the snow is to be taken. Snow moved to the perimeter of the parking lot must not be piled too high because it can reduce the shopping center's visibility from the street. Also, a large accumulation may not melt for months, and eventually it will become an unsightly mass of dirty snow and debris.

Throughout the snow season, sand and hot gravel may be laid down in the parking lot to improve vehicle traction and reduce slickness from ice buildup. Salt or other chemicals may be used on sidewalks to eliminate ice and minimize slippery areas. Care should be taken in using any of these methods, however. Chemicals may be tracked into the mall area or the stores, and the residue can damage the flooring or floor coverings. The residues are also harmful to grass and landscaping. When the snow season is over, the parking lot should be thoroughly cleaned. Several sweepings are often necessary to remove all the sand and debris.

In the northern states, snow removal is usually budgeted as a separate line item, and the expense is based on slightly more than a year's average snowfall. Weather information published in local newspapers and historical data available from the U.S. Weather Bureau can help increase the accuracy of the budget projections. In a year of heavy snowfall, the annual snow removal budget may be exceeded in one or two months; despite the additional cost, efficient show removal is necessary to provide for shoppers' convenience and safety and to maintain strong tenant sales.

Pavement Repairs. The majority of parking lots are constructed of asphalt pavement. The parking lot may become a victim of spending cutbacks because it is installed during the final phase of shopping center construction. As the final phase approaches, the developer may determine that construction costs are over budget and attempt to make up for it by laying down too thin a pavement or by skimping on the preparation of the underlayment. The result is an inadequate parking lot.

Improper thickness of the asphalt pavement is one of the major causes of parking lot failures, but the primary cause of asphalt failure is water underneath it. Proper drainage is essential to a well-maintained asphalt parking lot. Excessive moisture underneath the pavement weakens the foundation layers and reduces the ability of the soil to absorb traffic-induced stress. Water enters through cracks and other breaks in the pavement. When the water freezes, it expands, eventually cracking the asphalt and breaking it apart. Once this occurs, the deterioration will continue until the area is properly repaired—or the pavement is replaced.

Asphalt pavement in need of repair or maintenance usually exhibits one or more of the following characteristics:

- *Raveling* is the undoing of the texture of the pavement due to a progressive separation of aggregate particles. The most common cause is lack of proper compaction during construction, but disintegrating aggregate or poor mix design can also cause raveling.

- *Shrinkage cracks* are interconnected breaks in the pavement that form a series of large blocks, usually with sharp angles. They are caused by volume changes in the base or subgrade of the pavement, and they can sometimes be repaired by simply filling the cracks. If the problem is severe, the pavement must be replaced.
- *Alligator cracks* are also interconnected, but they form a series of small blocks that resemble alligator skin or chicken wire. The remedy is similar to that for shrinkage cracks.
- *Potholes* (or chuck holes) are common and easy to recognize. They are often the result of the neglect of other types of pavement distress. The remedy is usually replacement of an area that extends beyond the borders of the hole.
- *Upheaval* is the upward displacement of a pavement area due to the swelling of either the subgrade or some portion of the pavement structure. In colder climates, upheaval is commonly caused by the expansion of ice in the lower courses of the pavement or the subgrade, and replacement of the area may be the best and only remedy.
- *Grade depressions,* also known as birdbaths, are localized sunken areas of limited size that may or may not be accompanied by cracking. They are usually caused by the settling of the lower pavement layers, poor construction methods, or heavier traffic than that for which the pavement was designed. The remedy is either to build up the asphalt paving to support the load levels or to replace it.
- *Seal coating* is an important, cost-effective treatment in the preventive maintenance of asphalt parking lots. A seal coat is a thin layer of asphalt or coal tar sealant applied to the surface to waterproof it, stop oxidation and pavement deterioration, and improve the texture of the asphalt surface. Seal coating protects the pavement from the effects of water, traffic, fuel spills, chemicals, and weather. There are two types of sealers—emulsified asphalt (derived from crude oil) and coal tar—and one application usually lasts three to five years.

OPERATIONS

The shopping center manager fulfills the landlord's lease obligations and responds to community needs and government mandates. The operational responsibilities of the shopping center manager have evolved to include the establishment and implementation of programs that will enhance the value of the shopping center. Waste management, recycling, energy conservation, and water conservation are not only sound economic measures but they are also socially responsible actions. From establishing security and emergency procedures to providing adequate parking, the shopping center manager's role in the operations of the shopping center has an important impact on the tenant, the community, and the value of the shopping center.

Security

Customers need to feel safe while they are shopping and when they are walking to and from their vehicles. The security needs of a particular shopping center depend on its size, type, and location. Small strip shopping centers seldom if ever have security personnel, while regional malls and entertainment shopping centers typically have full-time security forces.

Determining Security Needs. When reviewing the security needs of a shopping center, the shopping center manager may need to meet with the police to collect data on criminal incidents in the area and maintain a log of security-related incidents at the shopping center. The log will indicate if any area of the shopping center is particularly vulnerable and whether a pattern of crime is developing.

Neighborhood, community, and strip shopping centers usually do not need on-site security officers. Any incidents are most likely to occur between midafternoon (after school lets out) and late evening, and any necessary security can be provided by a patrol that periodically drives through the shopping center during that time. If on-site security is needed, an officer can be present from midafternoon until the shopping center closes. Sometimes the officer may be needed for only a month or two to address a temporary situation. If security concerns warrant the presence of a full-time security officer, a round-the-clock security program should be implemented.

Small enclosed malls usually do not need security 24 hours a day, but part-time security may be warranted. The schedule might provide for an on-site officer Monday through Friday from 3:00 p.m. until one-half hour after the shopping center closes and during all the hours it is open on Saturdays and Sundays. The workdays of maintenance, janitorial, and security personnel may be scheduled so that at least one person is on-site at any given hour of the day or night.

Regional and super regional malls typically have security personnel on-site for all the hours the mall is open or 24 hours a day. Several security officers are usually on duty during the hours the mall is open; one or two officers are generally assigned to the parking areas while others are inside the mall. Additional security personnel are needed during special promotions, during the holiday season, and on Halloween and New Year's Eve.

Depending on the size of a lifestyle shopping center, the security force may range from one as large as that of a regional mall to one as small as

Exhibit 5.1

Advantages and Disadvantages of Contracted Security Services

Advantages of Contract Security Services

1. **Selectivity**—Employer retains only those persons personally approved.
2. **Flexibility**—More or fewer personnel, as required.
3. **Absenteeism**—Replacement of absentees on short notice.
4. **Supervision**—Supplied at no additional cost to the client.
5. **Training**—Supplied at no additional cost to client; may be superior to in-house training program.
6. **Objectivity**—Judgment not clouded by personalities.
7. **Cost**—Generally 20 percent less than in-house, not counting administrative savings (e.g., insurance, retirement pension, social security, medical care).
8. **Quality**—May be of higher caliber than an in-house officer.
9. **Administration and Budgeting**—Brunt borne by security company.
10. **Variety of Services and Equipment**—Security company may be specialists in various criminal justice skills or provide expensive equipment unavailable to home security.
11. **Hiring and Screening Costs**—Borne by security company.
12. **Better Local Law Enforcement Contacts**—May know more law enforcement personnel.
13. **Sharing Expertise and Knowledge**—May have developed security skills, as a result of many jobs, that can be shared with a client.

Disadvantages of Contract Security Services

1. **Turnover**—Extremely high industry-wide.
2. **Divided Loyalties**—Serving-two-masters quandary.
3. **Moonlighting**—Low salary for officers may force them into secondary jobs, resulting in tired and unalert personnel.
4. **Reassignment**—Some agencies send in the best men at inception of contract and then replace with others as new contracts open.
5. **Screening Standards**—May be inadequate.
6. **Insurance**—Determine liability and ensure individual officers are bonded and insured.

The preceding are conclusions drawn following a nationwide survey by a task force funded by the federal government.

Reproduced with permission from *Management Insights*. Copyright by American Building Maintenance Industries.

that of a small enclosed mall. Entertainment shopping centers, on the other hand, often have theaters, interactive video centers and fast food operations that attract great numbers of teenagers, so they usually have a strong security contingent.

Establishing a Security Program. A proprietary (on-site) force or a contracted service can provide security. Each has advantages and disadvantages that are spelled out in exhibits 5.1 and 5.2. As with any contracted service, the shopping center manager must know the types and extent of insurance

Exhibit 5.2

Advantages and Disadvantages of Proprietary Security Forces

Advantages of Proprietary Security Forces

1. **Loyalty**—A positive quality.
2. **Incentive**—Promotion possibilities within the entire company structure.
3. **Knowledge**—Of operation, products, personnel of the company because of permanent employment.
4. **Tenure**—Less turnover than contract officers.
5. **Control**—Stays inside company structure.
6. **Supervision**—Stays inside company structure.
7. **Training**—Can be specifically geared to the job performed.
8. **Company Image**—May become a status symbol.
9. **Morale**—A hoped-for state maintained by security manager.
10. **Courtesy**—Can render courtesies to VIPs because of familiarity with company personnel.
11. **Better Law Enforcement Liaison**—Security manager can informally develop law enforcement liaison with less conflict.
12. **Selection**—Company selection procedures apply.
13. **Better Communication**— More direct.

Disadvantages of Proprietary Security Forces

1. **Familiarity**—May become too familiar with personnel to be effective on job.
2. **Cost**—Expensive (salary, benefits, workmen's compensation, social security, liability insurance, work space, equipment, training).
3. **Flexibility**—Hard to replace absent personnel.
4. **Administrative Burdens**—Must develop an upper-level staff to handle these personnel.

The preceding are conclusions drawn following a nationwide survey by a task force funded by the federal government.

Reproduced with permission from *Management Insights*. Copyright by American Building Maintenance Industries.

coverages the contractor carries. Ideally, the contractor's insurance will act as a liability buffer for the owner of the property where security services are provided.

A proprietary security program should include specific training of security personnel and development and distribution of a security handbook that outlines their duties. Periodic refresher sessions should be held to review procedures, discuss recent incidents and problems, and obtain feedback and suggestions.

Security officers may or may not wear uniforms when on duty at a shopping center. If officers are to maintain a low profile and serve in a public relations role, wearing a blazer and contrasting slacks is better. If high visibility is necessary, they may wear a police-type uniform. "Uniform" expenses (cleaning, repairs, replacement) may be a consideration in the employment or contract discussions.

Shopping center security personnel rarely need to be armed. An unarmed guard can usually handle most situations. When a gun is necessary, the police should be brought in to handle the incident. Catching criminals is not the primary responsibility of the security force at a shopping center. A guard carrying a gun sends a message to the public that the shopping center may be an unsafe place to shop.

Representatives of the police department may be invited to speak at security training sessions. Such interaction develops rapport with the police department and facilitates good communication and respect between the guards at the shopping center and the police. Some shopping centers offer the police department free space that they can use as a substation where officers patrolling the area can make telephone calls, write reports, and take coffee or meal breaks. Off-duty police officers can be prime candidates to serve on the shopping center's security force. Police departments in some cities have programs under which a shopping center manager can contract with the city government or the police union for the services of uniformed police officers.

If security is needed at a shopping center, it must be implemented regardless of whether it was budgeted. A shopping center cannot afford to have inadequate security. A well-planned security program is comprehensive and anticipates possible problems. As part of the security program, every guard should be required to fill out a daily or shift report. (A seemingly unimportant incident may be the lead to solving a crime.) An important component is a review and upgrade, if necessary, of parking lot lighting. A well-lighted parking lot is a deterrent to criminal activity. As an added precautionary measure, especially when employee parking is in a remote section of the lot or off-site, a guard may be assigned to walk employees to their vehicles after the shopping center is closed. When guards are not available, employees should be encouraged to implement a buddy system and never to go to their vehicles alone.

Emergency Procedures

Appropriate security and an emergency procedures plan address shoppers'—and tenants'—concerns about safety. Development and implementation of emergency procedures is a major responsibility of the shopping center manager. Natural disasters, terrorist acts, and manmade emergencies can occur at any time. Shopping centers, especially enclosed malls, present unique challenges in this regard. Unlike office buildings or industrial properties where the same groups of people are present every day, most of the people in a shopping center at any one time are shoppers, and they cannot be trained to respond to an emergency. In addition, many of the shoppers are young children and elderly adults, which makes evacuation or even simple crowd control more challenging. The shopping center manager should develop an emergency procedures plan that is tailored to the shopping center.

Emergency Situations. The first steps are to determine the likelihood of particular natural disasters, terrorist acts, or manmade emergencies occurring at the shopping center and to learn the most appropriate responses to them.

The U.S. Weather Bureau can provide information on weather-related natural disasters (tornados, floods); the U.S. Geological Survey can indicate the possibility of earthquakes. If an area is susceptible to these types of phenomena, the plan should include specific responses to them. A good basic plan can easily be adapted for a particular emergency that was not anticipated.

Manmade situations—medical emergencies, arson (fires), theft, assaults, bomb threats, vandalism, hostage situations, random shootings, terrorist acts—are not limited by geography. The sociopolitical climate of an area may make it a more likely target for bomb threats and acts of violence. Local police and fire departments can provide assistance in developing responses to these situations. Professional organizations that focus on educating the public about fire safety, hazardous spills, first aid responses, etc., are other possible resources. Consultation with insurance professionals can provide valuable insights and minimize liability and problems with insurance claims.

Emergency Teams. To ensure the most appropriate response to a particular emergency, the shopping center manager should designate two emergency teams—a primary team whose members are assigned specific responsibilities based on the type of emergency and a support team to provide assistance in specific situations.

If the shopping center has an on-site staff, all management, administrative, marketing, maintenance, and security personnel should be members of the primary response team. In a strip shopping center that has no on-site personnel, staff from the property management company should be expected to provide the primary response to emergencies, and they should be trained to handle a variety of emergencies. Members of the support team include the local police and fire departments, service contractors, and utility company representatives, in addition to the insurance agent and the attorney for the property. In some situations, tenants may also function as part of the support team.

The plan should be designed so the teams are prepared to handle every likely emergency. Each member of the primary team should have a specific task to perform for any particular situation. For instance, if a shopping center received a bomb threat, the receptionist would call the police; the janitor would check the restrooms; maintenance personnel would inspect the corridors for foreign objects, etc. (Some of the most recent thinking on the subject of searching for a bomb indicates that the inexperienced shopping center staff should not look for the bomb. That should be left up to the local police and fire department personnel.)

As another example, if a tenant received the threat, he or she should first call the police, then notify the shopping center manager, who would implement the bomb-threat plan. The shopping center manager would have to decide whether to evacuate the mall—in which case, an announcement could be made over the public address system if one exists. (To avoid possible panic, the stated reason for evacuation should be something other than a bomb threat—e.g., the mall is losing electrical power.) The security guard would then direct shoppers into the parking lot, and the marketing director would respond to any media inquiries about the evacuation.

Once emergency procedures are established, practice sessions should be held at off hours for the primary team. Local police and fire departments may be invited to assist in the training.

Tenant Procedures. The shopping center manager should meet with the store managers to review the emergency procedures section of the tenant manual and encourage them to go over that information with their employees. If asked to do so by the store manager, the shopping center manager should arrange a time to meet with the tenant's employees. In multilevel malls where response to emergencies is more difficult, providing employee training sessions for all tenants and their staffs may be necessary.

The emergency procedures for tenants to follow will be less extensive than those for the primary and support teams; however they should suggest ways for the tenants themselves to respond to such emergencies as fires, bomb threats, assaults, and natural disasters (e.g., earthquakes). Training seminars for tenants and their employees would also be less comprehensive. (Adequately training tenants' work forces is difficult because of the large numbers of seasonal and part-time workers—and the high rate of turnover among retail workers in general.)

Emergency Public Relations. The media usually report disasters and emergencies, so an emergency public relations program should also be developed. Its objective is to provide accurate and timely information to the press, the tenants, and the community. Only one person should be authorized to talk to the media. This may be the marketing director rather than the shopping center manager or, if a public relations firm is employed, the assigned spokesperson. Everyone else should refer media inquiries to the spokesperson. Hiding information from the media will raise concerns and can lead to an unnecessary (and sometimes potentially harmful) investigation. The sooner the media receive precise information, the more likely they will be to report the incident accurately and promptly, and the sooner the incident will be over. Care should be taken, however, that information given to the media will not impede a fire or police department investigation. Appendix D provides a number of resources to consult when dealing with emergency situations at the mall or shopping center.

Emergency Procedures Manual. The responses to particular types of incidents should be written down and collected into an emergency procedures manual. The manual may not address every possible emergency, but it should address the ones most likely to occur. Periodic evaluation of established procedures, in particular their applicability to specific incidents that have occurred, will indicate the strengths and weaknesses of the program and provide an opportunity to update the manual.

The manual should include a list of emergency contacts with the names and telephone numbers of all the members of the primary and support teams plus the same information for the tenants. The latter may need to include both home and business numbers for store owners. A plot plan showing the locations of fire extinguishers and fire hydrants as well as fire department call boxes will expedite the response to a fire.

The manual should also include a plan for restoration of the property after a disaster. Equipment needed to respond to an emergency should be located on-site or be readily available from a local rental company. A list of specialized equipment and services, and sources for them, should be a part of the manual as well.

After an emergency, the shopping center manager (and any other staff members involved) should evaluate the response to the incident and write a report. Copies of the report should be sent to the owner and retained in the property files. (Insurance claims for property damage or loss may require additional information.)

Waste Management

Waste management is often overlooked in managing a shopping center, yet it is an important part of operations. Modern waste management includes waste collection and recycling.

Waste Collection. An effective waste collection system should be properly designed into the shopping center because the location and design of trash disposal areas will affect the aesthetics of the property. Dumpsters are unsightly and, if set in the parking lot, will create additional litter. Dumpsters or compactors should be conveniently located, easily accessed by the tenants, and shielded from public view. In small shopping centers, dumpsters are often located behind the shops, and each tenant is required to contract separately for waste disposal. Alternatively, the landlord may contract for trash removal for the entire site and include the cost in the common area charges the tenants pay or bill the tenants individually based on the size of their dumpsters.

Larger shopping centers often purchase or lease trash compactors, which offer many advantages over dumpsters, the most important being a reduction in the volume of waste. (Lower volume means fewer pickups and lower transportation and disposal costs.) Compactors are totally enclosed and lockable, and their use reduces or eliminates such negative conditions as offensive odors and vermin. In fact, they may contain odor- and insect-control chemicals or devices. Because they are enclosed, unauthorized disposal at the site is precluded. Access can be controlled by a special key or card that activates compaction. A card-activated system may also record each tenant's usage, thus permitting more equitable tenant billings. Otherwise, tenants may be billed for waste disposal on a pro rata basis (i.e., based on their square footage). The compactor can be programmed to automatically alert the contractor when full. This eliminates regularly scheduled pickups of less-than-full containers and reduces the cost to the tenants.

Many restaurants have special bins for discarding cooking grease and oils. These are generally placed near the dumpsters. They must be monitored to ensure that the exterior of the container is kept clean, the lids are kept closed, and grease is not spilled onto the asphalt surface, as it will damage the surface.

Recycling. Disposal of solid waste has become a priority issue as landfill sites throughout the United States reach capacity and limitations are imposed on the volume and composition of wastes disposed in them. To reduce the impact of these volumes of waste on landfill sites, municipalities across the country are requiring residents and businesses to separate their wastes for recycling. Paper, glass, aluminum cans, and various types of plastic containers are among the most common items that can be reprocessed into usable products.

A shopping center should have a recycling program for several reasons:

1. Businesses are major generators of waste materials, and as such, they have a responsibility to control the wastes they generate and minimize their impact on landfills.
2. The cost of disposing of solid wastes keeps rising as the numbers and capacities of landfill sites dwindle.
3. Recycling conserves natural resources and energy and lowers the cost of waste removal and disposal.
4. Recycling creates goodwill in the community and boosts employee morale.

Developing a Recycling Program. The first step in developing a recycling program for a shopping center is to determine which specific wastes are recyclable and in what volumes and how rapidly they are generated.

For example, corrugated cardboard from shipping cartons accumulates very quickly in large volumes at shopping centers. If food vendors sell beverages in aluminum cans or glass bottles, these items are candidates for recycling. Other recyclable materials include batteries, metallic items (e.g., steel and tin cans), cooking grease, paper, motor oil, and paper and polystyrene packing materials. Many federal, state, and county agencies as well as nonprofit organizations can be called on for assistance in developing a recycling program.

Granted that recycling is desirable and that sufficiently large volumes of specific recyclable materials warrant their separation, the planning process must address storage space and the costs and logistics of a recycling program. A place must be selected to store the recyclable materials, and separate containers must be provided for glass, metals, paper, etc. A contractor is then selected to remove the recyclable wastes. The volumes of specific materials and their value for recycling determine the cost of the program. The recycler may pay the shopping center for some waste materials and charged it to have others hauled away. The recycler may provide a dumpster or other container, or the shopping center manager may have to arrange for a container. The specific contractual arrangements will depend on the types of waste materials, their volumes and quality, and the facilities available locally for their recycling.

In some communities, for example, recycling firms will provide a large container for the accumulation and storage of cardboard. At the shopping center, the tenants themselves or someone on the maintenance staff may place the cardboard in the container. The accumulated cardboard may be hauled away on a regular schedule, or the hauler may be called to remove the container when it is full. To prevent unauthorized dumping of trash in the container, it should be locked when not in use. Some major tenants have participated in cardboard recycling programs for many years, and they often have their own balers to compact and tie the cardboard. The volume of cardboard generated by all the tenants at a shopping center determines whether a baler or compactor for cardboard only is warranted and, if so, whether such equipment should be purchased or leased.

Once a recycling program is planned, the tenants must participate in the program for it to be successful. Containers for the collection of recyclable materials must be conveniently located and easily accessed by the tenants. If the containers are too far away from the tenants' premises, they may balk at participating. Tenants will better appreciate their role and responsibility in the program once they are educated to the benefits of recycling.

A well-planned program should reduce the volume of waste for disposal and thus lower the amount tenants pay toward this expense item. Some recyclables may generate income for the shopping center, and those funds should be used for the common good of the tenants. Conversely, if there is a charge for the removal of a recyclable material, appropriate proration of that expense may mean that only the generators of a waste pay for its removal (i.e., food vendors who sell beverages in bottles may have to bear the expense of glass recycling). Because volume and quality affect the costs of recycling, costs may also affect individual tenant participation. Once a program is established, however, participation can be mandated when the lease is renewed by adding a provision covering waste disposal or adding a separate provision to cover recycling.

Executing the Recycling Program. To effectively execute the recycling program for a shopping center, a member of the management staff may be assigned the role of recycling coordinator. This person may be responsible for launching the program, educating the tenants and their employees, and encouraging active participation by everyone at the center. The tenant education program may include a recycling kick-off event, a one-on-one discussion with the manager of each store, a regular newsletter for tenants, and publicity for those stores that participate fully.

The community at large may also be invited to participate. If that is the case, the recycling program should be publicized in the community. Large metal containers for the collection of paper, glass, and aluminum can be placed in a side or back area of the parking lot.

Some counties have a mobile unit for pickup of household hazardous waste. It travels to different areas of the county and stays for three to five days at a time to collect household paints, motor oil, and hobby chemicals. Such a mobile unit may be permitted to set up in a remote area of a shopping center parking lot. As a safeguard against liability, however, posting a special security guard may be necessary or appropriate during the hours the unit is closed to ensure that residents do not drop off or spill hazardous wastes at the site. Residents who bring wastes during those off hours must be encouraged to return when the unit is open.

To complete the cycle, so to speak, the program should encourage tenants and others to purchase and use recycled materials. Bags and printed items that utilize recycled paper and boxes made from recycled cardboard are the most obvious examples. There are greater opportunities to develop and implement a recycling program for a mall than any other shopping center type.

Energy Conservation

Even though shopping centers are not major energy users, energy conservation should be one of the design considerations in the development of a new shopping center. (Energy efficiency is often considered equitable with cost-effectiveness.) During development is the ideal time to plan for and install energy-efficient lighting and mechanical systems and to meter each tenant separately for electricity, gas, and water. Tenants have an additional incentive to conserve energy when they are aware of their own usage and pay for it directly.

For an established center, an evaluation of energy use should be part of the management takeover, and the astute shopping center manager will develop, implement, and monitor an appropriate energy conservation program as part of the shopping center's operations. The goals of such a program should include substantial permanent reduction in energy usage.

The first step is to involve representatives of the utility companies in the conduct of an energy audit and development of a chart of energy consumption that covers a period of years. (Some information should be readily available to the shopping center manager because utility bills state amounts of electricity and gas used.) The charting process will reveal trends that the utility representative can compare to the energy consumption of similar shopping centers. The utility representatives should walk through the shopping center with the shopping center manager to identify specific causes of energy wastage. The shopping center manager should periodically conduct a similar energy audit, perhaps as part of the periodic inspection of the property as a whole.

At a shopping center, the two areas with the greatest potential for energy savings are the HVAC system and the lighting. A service contractor can determine whether the HVAC system is operating at maximum efficiency. As an item of preventive maintenance, frequent filter changes are necessary for HVAC units to operate efficiently. However, the most obvious consumption of energy is for lighting. Lighting in the parking lot and the common areas of the mall is one of the most costly energy uses in a shopping center. However, specific conservation of energy used for lighting must be weighed against the need to maintain adequate lighting for security purposes. Security certainly takes precedence over a reduction of lighting levels in the parking lot. The possibility of replacing existing lamps with more efficient lighting sources should be investigated. Lighting that is strictly decorative may be a candidate for replacement or removal.

Some specific energy-conserving procedures for a shopping center are listed below:

- Whenever possible, use fluorescent rather than incandescent lighting.
- Use light-colored paint on shopping center walls to increase reflected light.
- When practical, schedule cleaning and maintenance work during the hours the shopping center is open.
- Use time clocks or delay switches to phase on the HVAC or lights.
- Avoid changing thermostat settings. (Frequent changes increase heating costs in winter and cooling costs in summer.)
- Use economizers on the HVAC when the weather permits.

- Keep fans and coils clean and in good condition, and change filters often.
- If possible, turn off the HVAC in storage rooms and unoccupied spaces, or reduce it substantially.

The shopping center manager has responsibilities to the property owner (to maximize the property's net operating income), to the tenants (to operate the common areas as cost-effectively as possible), and to the community (to minimize energy usage on the property). An effective energy conservation program should be publicized to the community and the tenants. The tenants, in particular, should be informed of the progress the shopping center is making in conserving energy. In fact, the tenants should be actively involved in the energy conservation program. The shopping center manager can arrange meetings between the tenants and representatives of the utility companies and give the tenants a list of things they can do to conserve energy in their stores. The cost savings that result from everyone's efforts should lower the prorated CAM charges.

Tenant Improvements

In shopping centers, unlike in office buildings, tenants are usually allowed to construct their own improvements to their store spaces, such as finishing the interiors and installing display fixtures. The primary reasons are that retail tenants' improvements seldom have a direct impact on the structural components and mechanical systems in the building and most chain stores have their preferred contractors who can build out their stores cost effectively and efficiently. While improvements to their leased spaces are typically the tenants' responsibilities, the landlord must establish the guidelines for such construction to ensure that the integrity of the building is maintained, and the shopping center manager must ensure that the tenants follow the guidelines.

In a new strip shopping center, space is usually leased for the first time as a *shell,* which typically includes a storefront, demising walls, a dropped ceiling, a restroom, and the HVAC. The tenant is responsible for the installation of wall and floor coverings, and a divider wall (partition) may be constructed in the back of the store, along with any necessary decorative platforms and dressing rooms. A build-out of a coin-operated laundry, a hair salon, or a restaurant would also require extensive plumbing and electrical work.

Space in an enclosed mall may be leased in a similar shell state or with only stud demising walls and a dirt floor. The tenant must build out and finish the store proper. Because most mall tenants are sophisticated retailers with the expertise to coordinate extensive tenant improvements, they generally prefer such an unfinished state.

Whether the shopping center tenant has leased a shell or a previously built-out space, the lease will require that the tenant submit a construction or remodeling plan for the landlord's written approval before the improvements can be made. The shopping center manager, the construction manager, or the shopping center architect will review the plan. Particular attention must be paid to such items as changes to the storefront; adequate electrical capacity for the tenant's equipment; grease traps in the drains if the tenant serves food; proposed openings in the roof, bearing, or sheer walls; and changes to the coverage by the fire sprinklers.

The tenant's contractor should be required to have appropriate insurance coverages, and the shopping center owner and management firm should be listed as additional named insured parties for the work to be done. The tenant may also be required to purchase a performance bond to ensure that the contractor will be paid and that the improvements will be completed. The amount of such a performance bond is often one and one-half times the estimated cost of the improvements. Subcontractor lien waivers may be provided to the landlord in addition to or instead of a performance bond.

The shopping center manager should assign specific areas for placement of a construction dumpster (usually behind the leased space) and parking of construction vehicles. To minimize problems and inconvenience to other tenants and shoppers at the shopping center, some specific policies or rules for construction of improvements should be established, such as the following:

- Construction vehicles must park in the assigned area.
- Construction activity that may be disruptive to other tenants and shoppers (e.g., core drilling) must be performed before the shopping center opens—usually not a problem because most shopping centers open between 9:00 a.m. and 10:00 a.m.
- The shopping center manager or an on-site maintenance worker should be present during any penetration of the roof (e.g., by an antenna or other equipment) to ensure that the penetration is properly repaired and sealed.
- The shopping center manager should review the installation of the tenants' improvements and fixtures to ensure that the integrity of the building is not violated.

Assistance for the Marketing Director

Marketing directors often work alone; some have administrative assistants. They rarely have their own staff. However, to assure that marketing and merchandising events run smoothly, and especially to expedite the assembling and dismantling of promotional displays, the marketing director will require assistance in the form of physical labor. Workers can be hired from temporary employment agencies, or maintenance personnel can be assigned to assist the marketing director (provided their work schedules can be adjusted). The second option has the desirable advantage that shopping center staff are familiar with the property. This works best, however, when the workers' duties are well planned.

Event Coordination. The marketing director should give the shopping center manager an advance schedule of the dates of each month's events and the amount of time necessary to set up and take down the equipment and decorations for each promotion. A particular promotion may require building a stage and setting up chairs as well as placement of props and decorations. Once the promotion is over, all of the equipment and decorations must be dismantled immediately. Additional security personnel may be necessary to guard the props, control crowds, or direct traffic. The cost of temporary labor and extra security guards to protect the equipment and decorations should be charged to the marketing fund budget, along with the rental or purchase of equipment or props.

Holiday Decorations. The shopping center's decorations for the December holidays and other holidays may be purchased outright or leased. A particular display may be used for three or four years and then replaced with a new and different one, or decorations may be added each year to continually change the scene. Some shopping centers sell or trade the parts of their holiday displays and decorations that they no longer use.

Installation of an extensive holiday display requires a well-coordinated plan. Traditionally, December holiday decorations were put on display the Friday after Thanksgiving. In recent years, most retailers have started their holiday selling seasons earlier and earlier. Some stores now begin showing Thanksgiving and Christmas decorations in early November or even before Halloween. In any shopping center, the ideal situation would be for all the retailers' own decorations to be on display concurrently with those in the shopping center itself. However, that may not always be possible or practical.

Coordination of the installation of the holiday decorations requires careful planning and extensive labor. The decorations are installed while the shopping center is closed, and large crews must work rapidly to have everything ready at the same time. When a holiday season is over, the decorations must be taken down immediately. Holiday decorations are usually elaborate and expensive, and they must be stored in a dry, safe place when not in use. If storage facilities are not available at the shopping center, rental of a self-storage space may be wise so decorative display elements can be stored intact.

Peak Traffic Parking

Generally, most shopping centers have quite adequate parking for most shopping days; however, peak selling times such as the December holidays, the fall back-to-school weekend, the day after Thanksgiving, Mother's day, and Valentine's day can be especially difficult. A shopping center manager can take some measures to make sure that the customers are properly served during those times.

The most effective tool is the use of traffic officers to help direct traffic and keep it moving smoothly and to help direct customers to open spaces. The officers should be instructed to pay special attention to ensure that handicap spaces are policed and driving and fire lanes are kept clear. Additionally, employees' vehicles can be moved off-site to other parking areas to free up employee spaces for customers. Such areas as nearby churches, office building garages, and sports stadiums are good off-site parking locations.

Any open areas behind the shopping center should be surveyed for possible striping and use by the public. The existing striping should be analyzed to be sure it is optimum for the shopping center and in some cases, compact spaces can be considered for a portion of the lot to increase the number of parking spaces.

6

Administration

The heart of a good management program is a good administrative program. Even the best shopping center manager cannot manage effectively if the records and accounts are not in order. Control of the administrative activities is a key step toward successful shopping center management. An effective administrative system ensures accurate billing, maintains the property's income stream, and helps the shopping center manager fulfill the landlord's obligations under established leases and other agreements. However, while the shopping center manager is responsible for the overall administrative responsibilities for the shopping center, the day-to-day work may be delegated to administrative and accounting personnel hired for that purpose.

ADMINISTRATIVE RECORD KEEPING

Keeping accurate records of collections, payments, and other operational activities at a shopping center is an extremely important part of the administrative function. A good administrative system includes comprehensive policies and specific procedures. An efficient system minimizes the amount of work and the time required to do it, yet provides the information needed for day-to-day operations and for reports to the owner. Shopping center managers increasingly use computers to increase the accuracy and efficiency of their record-keeping systems in every facet of shopping center management. Software programs are available that are designed for shopping centers.

Every administrative system has a number of records that list information on all the tenants in the shopping center. The best way to keep such records is to list every space in the shopping center in the order in which it appears on the site plan or on another schematic layout. (Using such a system, visualization of the individual spaces will be easier because of the natural tendency to associate adjacent spaces and tenants with each other.) Each occupied space should be identified by the tenant's name, and all unoccupied spaces should be identified as vacant, so the shopping center manager can be sure that no tenant or store space is omitted.

In setting up administrative records, using the store name is the best way to identify the tenant; the name of a corporation (or a person) may be difficult to recognize as the tenant in a specific space. However, cross-references are also important. Most software that tracks the administrative and accounting processes for the shopping center provides fields for indicating individual store names as well as the parent company.

Accounting

Accounting for income and expenses is typically done in one of three ways. In *cash-basis accounting,* income is recorded when it is received and expenses are recorded when they are paid. In *accrual-basis accounting,* income and expenses are recorded when they are due—regardless of when they are received or paid. In *modified accrual basis,* most income and expenses are recorded when received, but large items such as insurance premiums and tax bills are handled on an accrual basis. The method used depends on the need for specific types of information. Because most such information will be incorporated into reports to the owners, the owner typically requires a particular method of accounting. Consultation with a professional accountant or accounting firm for assistance may be appropriate before establishing a particular system or specific accounting procedures.

The accumulation of income and expenses throughout the year is usually recorded in a general ledger, and accounting for specific items is facilitated if a chart of accounts (exhibit 6.1) is used. A *chart of accounts* establishes a specific distribution of income sources and recurring expenditures. Most categories of income and expense are subdivided to account for specific expenses and items that are likely to represent substantial dollar amounts by themselves. The assignment of account numbers to major categories and their respective subcategories facilitates tracking of recurring items because it ensures they will be handled the same way. Using these account numbers as codes to identify receipts and expenditures ensures consistency of recording and, in turn, makes development of an accurate budget easier.

Exhibit 6.1
Example Chart of Accounts—Alphabetical List of Expenses

Administrative—70000 series
Accounting fees 77100
Advertising 71100
Airfare 79100
Automobile expense 74100
Bank charges 76105
Entertainment and promotion 71105
Insurance—life 80115
Insurance—medical/dental 80120
Leasing commissions 77120
Legal fees 77110
Management fees 74810
Merchants' assn contributions 71101
Office supplies 76120
Payroll taxes 80105
Permits 78110
Postage 76125
Real estate tax 78120
Telephone expenses 76135

Building Supplies—83000 series
Alarm 83150
Licenses and permits 83100
Security 83250
Trash removal 83500

Repairs and Maintenance—85000 series
Elevator 85600
Flooring 85200
Landscaping 85400
Parking lot 85800
Roof 85500

Utilities—81000 series
Electricity 81100
Gas 81200
Sewer 81500
Water 81400

This abbreviated listing is intended to suggest the range of items that may be accounted separately. Such an alphabetical list is a handy reference for identifying account numbers for particular types of expenses. A comprehensive chart of accounts will usually include numbers for discrete sources of income, specific assets and liabilities, and capital expenditures—as well as the entire spectrum of operating expenses—displayed in numerical order.

Forms and Files

Accounting and record keeping are by nature detail-oriented activities. In shopping center management, these activities require high levels of precision and accuracy that are typically met by using a variety of forms. Chapter 3, Management Plan and Operations Manual, discusses the components of the Operations Manual and lists the property files and the records the manual should include. Many useful forms are presented below; some may be used in the Operations Manual, others may become part of individual tenant files. Shopping center managers are increasingly turning to computerized forms and filing systems, and many of the forms discussed may be stored as electronic documents.

Management Takeover Checklist. The shopping center manager's administrative functions typically begin with the takeover of the management account, and the operating records are often received at the time of the management takeover. The shopping center manager should develop a man-

Exhibit 6.2
Example New Account Check List

Shopping Center ______	Takeover Date ______
Contact ______	Phone Number ______
Company ______	FAX Number ______
Address ______	

Administrative

Contract signed ______	Accounting Notified ______
Obtain Former budgets ______	Obtain Tenant list ______
Notification of Tenants ______	Notification of Suppliers ______
Copies of All Leases ______	Copies of Project files ______
Set of Plans (As Built) ______	Keys for Project ______
Copies of Service Contracts ______	Notify Police/Fire ______
Prepare Emergency Lists ______	Notify City Hall ______
Pending Insurance claims ______	Pending Litigation ______

Accounting

Tenant account files ______	CAM estimates ______
Special Billings ______	Delinquency list ______
Security Deposit Register ______	Deferred Conditions Report ______
Percentage Rent Information ______	Tax Billing Files ______
Bank Accounts ______	Tax ID numbers ______
Mortgage Information ______	Reporting Formats ______

Site Activity

Site Inspection ______	Vacancies Inspected ______
Safety Inspection ______	Meet Contractors ______
Meet Tenants ______	Verify All Meters ______
Inventory Personal Property ______	Verify Employees ______

agement takeover checklist (exhibit 6.2) to help speed the transfer of specific information and records as well as to expedite the development of an appropriate administrative system. (Maintaining contact with the previous shopping center manager is a good idea because that person or company may be helpful in obtaining needed information.) A suitable form ensures that the manager obtains all pertinent records, notifies all appropriate personnel and agencies, and performs all necessary inspections and other tasks related to the takeover of management. Once all the items on the list have been checked, the checklist can be discarded. However, some shopping center managers prefer to note the dates when items were accomplished and retain the forms for future reference.

Lease Summary. In a shopping center, most interactions between the shopping center manager and the tenants stem from particular provisions within the leases. They determine the property's income (base rents, per-

Exhibit 6.3

Example Tenant Lease Summary Form

Shopping Center ______________________ Date ____________
Prepared By ______________________
Tenant Trade Name______________ Corporate Name ____________
Mailing Address ______________________
Home Office Contact ______________ Phone ____________
Store Address ______________ Phone ____________
Store Manager ______________ Phone ____________
District Manager ______________ Phone ____________
Lease Date ________ Commencement ________ Termination ________
Square Footage______________ Security Deposit ____________
Lease Term______________ Options ____________

Monthly Rental Rate

$__________ for the period __________ to__________
$__________ for the period __________ to__________
$__________ for the period __________ to__________
$__________ for the period __________ to__________
Percentage Rate________ Breakpoint ________ Reports Due ________

Reimburse Landlord (dollar amounts)*

Common Area Estimate ________ Tax Extimate ________ Insurance Estimate ________
HVAC Maintenance ________ Utilities ________ Supervision Fee ________
Merchants' Assn ________ Roof Maint ________ Environmental Exp ________

Tenant Responsibility

HVAC Maintenance ________ Utilities ________ Liability ________
Fire & EC ________ Plate Glass ________ Boiler________
Miscellaneous Items ______________________

____

*Estimated from CAM Budget

centage rates), the prorations of operating and common area management (CAM) expenses passed through to the tenants, and the rules and regulations that govern how the merchants are expected to operate their businesses in the shopping center. However, much of the information in the lease itself is not needed for the day-to-day operation of the property. Operations are much easier for the shopping center manager if the data are compiled on a lease summary form. Many types of forms are available for this purpose, but one that is more than three pages long tends to defeat the purpose of summation—even though it is better than handling a 60-page lease each time information is needed. For most managers' purposes, a one- or two-page lease summary form (exhibit 6.3) will suffice.

Even if the former shopping center manager has provided lease summaries, those summaries may have been compiled differently or not kept up-to-date. A new shopping center manager should compile his or her own summaries. The compilation process will help the shopping center manager understand the lease document itself and the variances in its specific terms and conditions. Once new summaries have been compiled, they can be compared to earlier records for accuracy, consistency, and completeness, and any discrepancies can be rechecked against the original leases.

Lease summary data are used to set up records of tenant payments, common area prorations, percentage rent schedules, insurance requirements, and a myriad of other documents that facilitate analysis and comparison of tenant and lease information. Because the lease summary includes terms and conditions of the particular lease, it also serves as a ready reference regarding restrictions, exclusives, options, etc., when current leases come up for renewal and whenever new leases are negotiated with prospective tenants.

Tenant Rent Roll. An important record that is prepared from the lease summaries is a tenant roster. Typically, it lists each tenant's square footage, the rental rate per month and per square foot, the percentage rate, and the amount of any security deposit. The length of the lease term and the lease commencement and termination dates may also be included, but a tenant rent roll usually does not show any specific payments made by the tenant. The example shown in exhibit 6.4 is sufficiently comprehensive for most shopping center managers' needs.

Some shopping center owners may require a more complete roster that shows, for example, estimated common area charges, the date of the next rental increase, the breakpoint, the number of options (to extend the lease), and the terms of the options in addition to the items shown in exhibit 6.4. In fact, each shopping center owner is likely to have a preferred format for a tenant rent roll, and the shopping center manager should try to accommodate those preferences. However, the owner's rent roll may not fulfill the shopping center manager's information needs, which are generally secondary to those of the owner. While the manager may be responsible for only one shopping center, an owner who possesses several properties must have consistent records for all of them.

Expense Prorations. A list of tenants' prorated operating expenses and CAM charges (sometimes called a *billback* analysis as in exhibit 6.5) is also compiled from the lease summaries. Data to be included are tenant name, store size, the natural proration percentage based on the area of the store (square footage), and any variances that may apply to individual tenants. Once the listing is properly prepared, the actual billings are easily computed.

With regard to tenant prorations, tenants often have a negotiated percentage instead of the computed rate. For example, a supermarket may occupy 27 percent of the center's gross leasable area (GLA) but only pay for 25 percent of the operating expenses. Nor is it unusual for a strong retailer

Exhibit 6.4

Heartland Shopping Center—Tenant Rent Roll

Suite	Tenant	Sq.Ft	%	Monthly Rent	Security Deposit	Term	Lease Date	Start	End	Options	Cam Cont
101	Restaurant	4,140	5%	7,377.34	7,000.00	10	3/15/95	7/1/95	6/30/05	2–5 yr	P/R
102	Johnsons	675	6%	1,805.24	1,542.15	5	4/10/00	6/15/00	6/14/05	0	P/R
103	Vacuum Center	2,108	5%	2,630.77	2,400.00	5	5/12/01	7/1/01	6/30/06	1–5 yr	P/R
104	Shoe Store	519	0%	985.66	827.55	3	8/13/02	9/1/02	8/31/05	1–3yr	P/R
105	Restaurant	3,127	6%	5,320.34	0.00	10	2/1/99	2/1/99	1/31/09	1–10 yr	P/R
106	Pet Store	1,210	5%	1,941.22	1,711.87	5	1/16/02	2/01/02	1/31/07	0	P/R
107	Book Store	1,623	5%	2,486.33	2,100.00	5	6/17/01	8/1/01	7/31/06	0	P/R
108	Athletic Shoes	1,320	5%	2,016.34	1,824.34	5	8/23/01	9/1/01	8/30/06	0	P/R
109	Specialty Shoes	1,320	4%	2,240.47	2,002.33	5	10/16/00	11/1/00	10/31/05	0	P/R
110	Dress Store	1,277	5%	1,912.44	1,912.00	3	12/1/02	12/1/02	11/30/05	0	P/R
111	Photo Shop	1,100	5%	2,156.22	2,100.00	5	12/3/00	3/1/00	2/28/05	0	P/R
112	Restaurant	1,060	5%	2,252.17	2,311.46	3	10/1/01	1/15/02	1/30/05	1–3 yr	P/R
113	Jewelery	1,232	5%	1,704.44	1,522.34	3	1/12/03	3/1/03	2/28/06	0	P/R
114	Beauty Salon	1,006	5%	2,024.33	1,826.56	5	3/22/01	4/1/01	3/31/06	0	P/R
115	Cleaners	2,100	5%	3,351.21	2,725.44	10	4/10/94	6/15/94	6/14/04	1–10 yr	P/R
116	Benny's Ice Cream	1,275	5%	3,200.12	3,000.00	10	9/14/95	10/1/95	9/30/05	1–5 yr	P/R
117	Ice Cream	904	0%	1,408.33	1,408.00	5	7/16/01	8/1/01	7/31/06	0	P/R
118	Florist	670	0%	1,084.12	891.55	2	1/18/03	2/1/03	1/31/05	0	P/R
119	Electronic Repair	550	5%	820.34	722.34	3	6/22/03	8/1/03	7/31/06	0	P/R
120	Dresses	1,560	5%	3,120.25	2,134.55	5	11/10/99	12/1/99	11/30/04	1–5 yr	P/R
121	Nail Salon	1,100	0%	2,632.45	1,724.55	5	8/4/01	0101	8/31/06	0	P/R
122	Mexican Fast Food	1,100	5%	2,452.14	0.00	5	8/3/01	9/1/01	8/31/06	0	P/R
123	Medical Office	3,200	0%	5,980.27	3,800.00	10	3/12/94	6/1/94	5/31/04	1–5 yr	P/R
124	Dental Clinic	1,820	0%	4,095.00	5,000.00	10	2/9/96	4/14/96	4/30/06	1–5 yr	P/R
125	Burgers	4,030	5%	12,090.00	0.00	15	6/11/92	8/1/92	7/31/07	1–10yr	P/R
Totals:		40026		77,087.54	50,487.03						

Anchor Tenants Own Their Own Parcels And Maintain Their Own Buildings	
Supermarket	48,600
Drug Store	17,400
Entire Center Footage	106026

Developments Limited

Exhibit 6.5

Heartland Shopping Center—Example-Bill Back Analysis—Buildings & Site

Suite	Tenant	Sq.Ft	Bldg %	Site %	Formula	Super Vision	Notes:
101	Restaurant	4,140	0.1034	0.0390	P/R	15%	Pays Own Water And HVAC Service
102	Johnsons	675	0.0169	0.0064	P/R	10%	
103	Vacuum Center	2,108	0.0527	0.0199	P/R	15%	
104	Shoe Store	519	0.0130	0.0049	P/R	15%	Pays Own Water
105	Restaurant	3,127	0.0781	0.0295	P/R	0%	Handles Own Trash Removal
106	Pet Store	1,210	0.0302	0.0114	P/R	15%	
107	Book Store	1,623	0.0405	0.0153	P/R	15%	
108	Athletic Shoes	1,320	0.0330	0.0124	P/R	15%	
109	Specialty Shoes	1,320	0.0330	0.0124	P/R	15%	
110	Dress Store	1,277	0.0319	0.0120	P/R	15%	
111	Photo Shop	1,100	0.0275	0.0104	P/R	15%	
112	Restaurant	1,060	0.0265	0.0100	P/R	15%	
113	Jewelry	1,232	0.0308	0.0116	P/R	15%	
114	Cleaners	1,006	0.0251	0.0095	P/R	15%	
115	Cleaners	2,100	0.0525	0.0198	P/R	15%	
116	Ice Cream	1,275	0.0319	0.0120	P/R	15%	
117	Florist	904	0.0226	0.0085	P/R	15%	
118	Real Estate	670	0.0167	0.0063	P/R	15%	
119	Electronic Repair	550	0.0137	0.0052	P/R	15%	
120	Dresses	1,560	0.0390	0.0147	P/R	15%	
121	Nail Salon	1,100	0.0275	0.0104	P/R	15%	
122	Mexican Fast Food	1,100	0.0275	0.0104	P/R	15%	
123	Medical Office	3,200	0.0799	0.0302	P/R	15%	
124	Dental Clinic	1,820	0.0455	0.0172	P/R	15%	
125	Burgers	4,030	0.1007	0.0380	P/R	15%	Include Copies Of Invoices
Totals:		40026	1.0000				
Anchor Tenants Own Their Own Parcels And Maintain Their Own BuildingsLs And Maintain Their Own Buildings							
	Supermarket	48,600		0.4584	P/R	10%	
	Drug Store	17,400		0.1641	P/R	10%	
	Total Center:	106,026		1.0000			

Developments Limited

to agree to pay prorated common area costs but negotiate a cap on its share (paying a maximum amount per square foot or a maximum total dollar amount) or an offset against percentage rent (deducting CAM charges and real estate taxes from overage rent due). Many tenants negotiate different administrative or supervision fees, and some may successfully exclude one or more items from the list of operating expenses and CAM charges they pay.

Major repairs, insurance premiums, and taxes are commonly excluded from the calculation of administrative fees; usually the administrative fee applies expressly to CAM and related charges. Many national retailers have specific exclusions in their leases—security, trash removal, some insurance premiums, etc. If a tenant is exempted from paying a particular prorated expense such as security, that tenant will also be exempt from any administrative charges for that expense. (Lease negotiations and administrative fees are detailed in chapter 10, Negotiating and Documenting the Lease Terms.)

The shopping center manager must be aware of any rights or privileges granted to major tenants. In particular, the anchor tenant may have negotiated the right to preapprove large expenditures (e.g., a parking lot pavement repair). All specific rights and exemptions that relate to tenants' payment of operating and CAM expenditures should be noted in the analysis of tenant charges. Failure to make such notes can lead to expensive problems—for example, if the shopping center manager proceeds with a large repaving job without obtaining the required anchor tenant approval, he or she is risking the tenant's refusal to pay its portion of the bill because the shopping center manager did not comply with the lease agreement.

Note that the example in exhibit 6.5 includes taxes and insurance. However, if any tenants' leases require them to pay anything other than their store-size proration of taxes or insurance, those two expenses should be analyzed separately. Particular lease terms of which the shopping center manager should be aware are operating expense exclusions, caps on taxes or insurance premiums, exclusions on insurance premiums (types of coverages), and any specific agreements regarding administrative fees for those items.

Leases in older shopping centers, such as regional malls, differ widely in their calculation of tenant charges because of changes in lease formats that have occurred over the years. As expenses have increased, national tenants have negotiated caps on expenses and have required amortization of capital improvements and limitations on administrative fees. Thus, older shopping centers frequently have numerous methods of calculation. For example, some leases may allow the landlord to prorate the cost of roof repairs to the tenant, and others may not. The same is true of administrative fees, capital improvements, etc.

Security Deposit Register. Being certain that security deposits are actually received is one of a shopping center manager's greatest accounting

Exhibit 6.6

Example Security Deposit Register
Heartland Plaza Shopping Center

Tenant	square footage	deposit	date paid
Fast food	1,250	$3,750	01/10/97
Restaurant	4,215	-0-	N/A
Dress Store	2,400	$4,800	07/15/02
Computers	1,152	$2,780	12/04/01
Video Rental	4,800	$9,600	08/17/99
Photo Shop	900	$2,700	05/22/98
Shoe Repair	440	$2,400	07/23/99
Insurance	880	$1,960	01/22/02
Real Estate Office	1,200	$2,400	07/06/98
Pool Supply	1,200	$3,000	02/14/02
Bicycle Shop	2,230	$4,620	09/23/01
Florist	1,200	$2,700	09/28/02
Travel Agent	1,400	$2,800	07/11/02
Dental Office	1,860	-0-	N/A
Pet Store	3,216	$5,600	10/03/02

NOTE: None of the deposits require interest to be paid and none are required to be kept in a separate trust account. Security deposits on residential properties are handled differently; their requirements are much stricter.

difficulties. When a security deposit is required, most shopping center owners insist that the deposit accompany the signed lease from the tenant. However, that can lead to the assumption that a deposit was received when in fact it was not. The shopping center manager should establish a straightforward policy on security deposits and a precise procedure for their collection. The accountant should maintain a record of all security deposits received (exhibit 6.6) and keep the list current as tenants move in and out. This record is typically included in the report the shopping center manager sends to the owner each month. That report is detailed later in this chapter.

Security deposit funds should be kept separate from operating funds because part or all of those monies will be returned to the tenants when they vacate the leased premises. If the landlord uses the deposit to offset a tenant expense, an accounting receipt should be given to the tenant along with a request for reimbursement. As long as a security deposit is required, the full amount should be in the landlord's hands.

Tenant Ledger. Rent payments are recorded on a tenant ledger that is set up from the lease summaries. In accounting for tenant payments, some shopping center managers enter the rent and pass-through amounts due each month and identify specific payments when the money is received. Others enter only the amounts received. The advantage of prelisting the amount due is that it provides a cross-check for what is paid and when it is received.

Tickler File. One of the most useful administrative systems is a so-called "tickler file" that reminds the shopping center manager and others of what must be done and when. The purpose of the tickler file is to provide a means to prepare for specific changes. Many software programs include tickler files for all types of computers—from desktops to handhelds.

A good way to start a tickler file is to review the lease summaries. From them, such information as rent increases, lease termination dates, and related events can be noted. In a system that covers more than one center, the name of the shopping center should be included as well. Thus, if a tenant's lease calls for an annual Consumer Price Index (CPI) rental increase effective April 1 of each successive year of a five-year lease, that information should be recorded appropriately in the system for each of the four future years.

A one-month lead time may be adequate for many tickler items (e.g., scheduled rent increases, as noted above). However, some require more lead time and may need reminders for subsequent follow-up. For example, lease expiration dates may be recorded in duplicate to provide reminders both six months and 60 days prior to the expiration. The extra time is important because the shopping center manager must evaluate the tenant's performance of the current lease and, assuming a continued relationship is desirable, determine the terms of a renewal lease. The tenant must also be given time to evaluate the new lease and decide whether to sign it. For some tenants, setting up reminders for 90 days and one year prior to expiration may be appropriate. These time frames should be adequate for most small shop leases. However, anchor lease renewal can require many months and even years of negotiations. The same may apply for some national shop tenants.

The tickler file can also be used to track other lease requirements such as option terms and dates, cancellation rights, and submission of insurance certificates as well as recurring activities for the shopping center as a whole—property tax assessments, payment of insurance premiums, etc.

General Files. Files are the repositories of specific information on a shopping center's tenants as well as its operations. Record-keeping systems for most shopping centers now involve computer files as well as traditional paper files.

In addition to tenant files, separate files should be maintained for different types of expenses as well as for specific management activities and reports (e.g., common area maintenance, property taxes, insurance premiums and certificates, correspondence, service contracts, budgets, monthly reports to ownership). Separate files should be created for individual employees and for management personnel employment and payroll records. When a management company is responsible for several shopping centers, each center should have separate files.

Electronic Files. Many existing computer software programs are designed to track all the financial components of shopping center management—from budgets and payroll to customized reports on income and expenses. Other software programs can organize contacts, generate tickler files, and create specialized mailings. Owners of large shopping centers or multiple shopping centers may have computer programmers write proprietary software programs that combine all the necessary information into one system.

A backup system is essential for all information that is kept in electronic files. A *backup* is a copy of information that is made on a separate medium such as a floppy disk, compact disk (CD), or digital video disk (DVD). A backup of all new or changed information should be made at least daily. For large shopping centers, backups may need to be made more frequently. The shopping center manager should ensure that a duplicate backup of critical information is stored in a fireproof vault away from the shopping center.

Paper Files. No matter how much of the shopping center's information is kept in electronic files, traditional paper files are still essential. Leases, insurance policies, correspondence, and even hard copies (paper copies) of computer-generated information, must be filed. A color-coding system or another systematic method of coding can be used to distinguish the files of different shopping centers. If the management records are maintained strictly on-site, color codes can be helpful in the organization of different types of records.

Even more important, the contents of individual file folders should be maintained in chronological order, with the newest material at the front of the folder. Each folder should be labeled to show its contents. In a property management company office, folders should show the shopping center name in addition to the other specific contents. A separate file folder should be prepared for each tenant, and a copy of the lease, any other pertinent documents, and all correspondence with that tenant should be filed there.

Reports to the Owner

A good administrative system starts with an annual management plan or business plan (see chapter 3, Management Plan and Operations Manual), that is followed up with monthly progress reports to determine how the property is performing. A key responsibility of the shopping center manager is to provide the owner with regular reports on the financial status of the property and its management, operations, and leasing activities. The reports may have to be prepared in specific formats, especially if the owner is an institution. A standardized format facilitates comparison of the reports for the property over an extended period. Accuracy of information and on-time submission of reports are critical; delays in reporting or information that is incomplete or incorrect can create problems when data from reports on several properties are merged. Repeated problems with a shopping center manager's reports can result in the loss of the management account.

Shopping center managers usually prepare and submit reports monthly, and the package usually includes several financial analyses. The *operating statement,* which is the main record of money received and paid, is a key document. A monthly bank account reconciliation should be a minimum requirement. When it is included, it assures the owner that the bank balance is generally in agreement with the operating statement (except for items in transit). Most of the other reports are statistical in nature. (The tenant rent roll, security deposit register, and a list of vacancies may not be included with each month's reports unless the tenancy has changed.) Monies not received are noted in a delinquency report, and percentage rent income is supported by a sales analysis. Leasing activity is covered in a separate report. A narrative summary of the operating results and other statistics should always accompany the reports. The reports to the owner are detailed below.

Financial Statement. The *financial statement* shows the current month's income and expenses. It compares actual and budgeted amounts, indicates specific variances, and compares the year-to-date cumulative figures. Typically, this is presented as a cash statement, but institutional clients often prefer accrual or modified accrual statements. Some owners want to see copies of bills sent to tenants and invoices for expenses. However, most prefer that the shopping center manager retain such backup documentation and have it available for inspection.

Delinquency Report. The delinquency report lists each tenant who owes rent or other payments due the landlord and shows how much is owed and how long it has been delinquent. The report should also include a statement of what is being done to expedite collection—agreement on a payment plan, submission to a collection agency or to an attorney, etc. The owner must be advised of delinquencies and how they affect the shopping center and its income stream.

Sales Analysis. An effective report includes a sales analysis for all tenants comparing the current year's sales to the previous year's sales for both the current month and the year to date—in total dollars and sales per square foot. The format for display of information varies from owner to owner. (An example in current use is shown in exhibit 6.7; note that it includes the breakpoint for calculation of percentage rent and an evaluation of the overage, or

Exhibit 6.7

Property: Heartland Plaza Shopping Center
Tenant Sales And Percentage Rent Report

Tenant Information	Sq Ft	Yr	Jan	Feb	March	April	May	June	July
Restaurant	4240								
Sales Y/E 12/31/2003		01	57,355	50,661	56,167	56,643	57,949	59,578	59,31[illegible]
Report Frequency: Monthly		02	60,225	53,493	59,331	64,803	67,736	70,749	70,28[illegible]
Pay Frequency Monthly		03	60,987	57,446	68,641	65,833	66,015	69,609	71,20[illegible]
Jewelry Store	675								
Sales Y/E 12/31/2003		01	1,979	2,071	2,123	2,058	2,214	1,932	2,74[illegible]
Report Frequency: Monthly		02	3,419	2,843	3,042	3,511	3,219	3,149	3,21[illegible]
Pay Frequency Monthly		03	3,995	5,015	5,417	4,932	5,164	5,626	4,86[illegible]
Vacuum Center	2108								
No Percentage Rent Requirement									
Shoe Store	519								
Sales Y/E 12/31/2003		01	4,500	5,055	4,054	4,201	4,974	4,653	4,43[illegible]
Report Frequency: Monthly		02	4,544	3,568	4,071	4,149	3,961	4,200	3,94[illegible]
Pay Frequency: Monthly		03	4,621	4,426	4,997	4,769	4,235	4,183	4,12[illegible]
Restaurant	3127								
Sales Y/E 12/31/2003		01	22,940	23,830	23,135	24,465	25,370	24,240	23,18[illegible]
Report Frequency: Monthly		02	22,715	23,755	21,860	23,855	22,665	22,055	22,78[illegible]
Pay Frequency: Monthly		03	23,127	24,667	22,341	24,688	23,546	22,706	24,66[illegible]
Pet Shop	1158								
Sales Y/E 12/31/2003		01	10,107	11,343	12,142	16,880	23,499	23,148	21,36[illegible]
Report Frequency: Monthly		02	8,353	7,372	10,273	13,127	14,271	18,015	19,01[illegible]
Pay Frequency: Monthly		03	8,101	8,151	8,668	10,175	16,052	18,695	21,02[illegible]
Shoe Store	1320								
No Percentage Rent Requirement									
Book Store	1623								
No Percentage Rent Requirement									
Shoe Store	1320								
No Percentage Rent Requirement									
Dress Store	1277								
No Percentage Rent Requirement									
Photo Shop	1060								
Sales Y/E 12/31/2003		01	95	96	14,550	19,970	17,860	17,020	19,44[illegible]
Report Frequency: Monthly		02	15,013	13,766	9,919	9,789	13,287	15,700	13,10[illegible]
Pay Frequency: Monthly		03	12,230	7,967	10,196	12,238	11,332	14,511	15,37[illegible]
Restaurant	1142								
Sales Y/E 12/31/2003		01	11,925	10,029	11,161	11,615	13,618	10,730	11,88[illegible]
Report Frequency: Monthly		02	12,031	10,574	10,821	10,480	11,163	11,366	10,50[illegible]
Pay Frequency: Monthly		03	11,035	10,133	10,320	11,368	12,103	11,777	10,96[illegible]
Jewelry Store	1232								
No Percentage Rent Requirement									

Aug	Sept	Oct	Nov	Dec	Ytd Total	% Inc/ Dec	Ytd Psf	Annual Breakpoint	% Rent	Actual Amount of % Rent
									5%	
56,752	53,835	59,103	58,830	62,756	688,942		172	1,433,280		0
67,901	64,616	63,305	58,673	67,847	768,960	+11.6%	192	1,433,280		0
70,888					530,625		97	1,433,280		0
									6%	
2,551	2,912	3,111	3,325	4,213	31,231		62	324,515		0
2,951	3,200	3,555	3,745	4,019	35,849	+14.7%	72	331,138		0
3,120					38,135		60	337,896		0
									6%	
4,175	4,073	4,010	4,208	4,037	52,377		106	172,191		0
3,628	3,918	4,108	3,382	3,576	43,473	−17.0%	88	175,706		0
3,921					35,274		55	179,272		0
									6%	
24,727	22,166	22,607	23,143	19,355	279,159		87	1,051,234		0
24,218	22,423	25,057	23,720	25,520	255,105	−8.7%	80	1,072,688		0
					165,741		0	1,094,580		0
									5%	
21,037	12,190	11,064	7,832	6,214	176,819		168	390,755		0
14,208	12,779	10,769	7,601	6,934	135,786	−23.3%	68	398,730		0
16,734					107,598		67	411,062		0
									6%	
19,515	17,256	20,930	21,750	20,576	189,063		195	432,334		0
14,108	12,033	12,571	8,994	15,703	138,280	−38.2%	121	432,334		0
					83,852		80	432,334		0
									6%	
11,262	11,196	10,474	10,768	10,592	135,252		118	461,857		0
10,275	9,931	10,991	10,588	10,881	118,720	−12.3%	104	471,283		0
					77,703		38	480,902		0

(continued)

Exhibit 6.7 *(continued)*

Tenant Information	Sq Ft	Yr	Jan	Feb	March	April	May	June	July
Beauty Salon	1006								
Sales Y/E 12/31/99		97	3,277	3,541	3,597	3,750	4,020	4,821	4,931
Report Frequency: Monthly		98	6,498	8,331	8,819	9,370	6,972	6,055	6,803
Pay Frequency: Monthly		99	7,041	8,442	8,912	9,423	7,004	6,577	7,301
Quick Cleaners	2100								
Sales Y/E 12/31/99		97	16,668	13,697	15,997	16,114	15,479	16,812	17,956
Report Frequency: Monthly		98	16,706	12,171	14,453	15,453	13,080	14,810	16,157
Pay Frequency: Monthly		99	15,157	13,015	13,501	16,800	12,942	12,700	
Benny's Ice Cream	1275								
Sales Y/E 12/31/99		97	9,444	9,916	13,652	14,136	15,129	16,671	17,066
Report Frequency: Monthly		98	10,716	10,068	13,979	14,343	16,545	17,545	17,520
Pay Frequency: Monthly		99	10,574	11,728	13,170	13,327	13,652	15,275	
Array Florist	904								
Sales Y/E 12/31/99		97							
Report Frequency: Monthly		98							
Pay Frequency: Monthly		99							
Lease Commences October 1, 1999									
Real Estate Office	670								
No Percentage Rent Requirement									
Electronic Repair	550								
No Percentage Rent Requirement									
Smoke Enders	1560								
No Percentage Rent Requirement									
Nothing But Nails	1100								
No Percentage Rent Requirement									
Mexican Fast Food	1100								
Sales Y/E 12/31/99		97	3,497	3,474	3,645	3,806	3,879	3,911	3,959
Report Frequency: Monthly		98	3,091	8,000	9,500	12,000	8,200	8,500	9,200
Pay Frequency: Monthly		99	7,650	7,900	13,250	10,500	9,302	9,122	9,323
Medical Office	3200								
No Percentage Rent Requirement									
Dental Clinic	1820								
No Percentage Rent Requirement									
Lofty Burgers	4030								
Sales Y/E 12/31/99		97	67,201	68,307	68,002	71,304	78,445	81,604	83,556
Report Frequency: Monthly		98	79,645	78,665	81,056	84,887	90,334	91,559	102,345
Pay Frequency: Annual		99	128,566	131,689	132,599	135,721	136,721	139,222	141,795

Developments Limited

Exhibit 6.7 *(continued)*

Aug	Sept	Oct	Nov	Dec	Ytd Total	% Inc/ Dec	Ytd Psf	Annual Breakpoint	% Rent	Actual Amount of % Rent
									6%	
5,445	7,792	7,591	8,333	6,873	63,971		66	358,104		0
7,192	7,350	5,877			73,267	+13.6%	75	365,412		0
					54,700		0	365,412		0
									6%	
15,349	14,291	15,424	13,311	14,821	185,919		95	625,638		0
13,903	14,707	15,786	13,279	14,383	160,505	−13.7%	82	638,407		0
					84,115		43	651,436		0
									6%	
15,171	14,118	12,589	10,621	8,548	157,061		113	554,401		0
17,301	14,291	13,857	9,790	8,848	155,955	−1.7%	111	565,716		0
					77,726		55	577,262		0
									5%	
					320,664					
									6%	
3,991	3,527	3,348	3,254	3,302	43,593		42	411,106		0
7,500	7,450	7,500	7,000	7,500	87,941	+100%	84	419,496		0
					67,047		37	428,058		0
									5%	
85,600	88,444	89,201	90,223	91,445	963,332		265	963,332		0
105,541	106,777	114,566	121,378	122,433	1,179,186	+22%	324	1,179,186		0
					946,313		235	946,313		0

percentage rent, income.) For purposes of comparison to prior year figures, the sales analysis should include figures for spaces that are presently vacant but whose previous occupants contributed sales figures in the prior year. For large shopping centers that have multiple tenants, sales are also analyzed by tenant category (e.g., jewelry, women's clothing, restaurants).

Leasing Report. Leasing is a critical component of shopping center operations, and a monthly report on that activity is essential. The report usually covers signed deals versus leasing projections; current deals under negotiation; prospects contacted, including any comments regarding the contact made; and the interest level of the prospects.

Litigation Report. Litigation is an unfortunate part of property ownership and management should track it. Generally, such a report tracks any specific incidents, their current status, any costs incurred to date, and the likely outcome.

Three-Month Forward Cash Comparison. Most owners need to track their cash position and therefore a three-month forward cash forecast is provided. This report compares the budgeted cash flow against the likely cash flow so the owners can make adjustments if necessary.

Narrative Report. This is a summary explanation of each financial report. Each report should cover such considerations as occupancy, move-ins and move-outs, lease expirations and renewals, the condition of the property, capital expenditures in progress, legal issues, marketing activities, and specific issues. Detailed explanations of substantial variances from the budget are usually reported here as well. When prepared properly, the narrative report gives the owner an overview of the month's activities, identifies particular successes, and calls attention to specific problems.

BUDGETING

A budget is necessary to a full understanding of the financial status of a property. A good budget is the result of a good management and/or business plan (see chapter 3, Management Plan and Operations Manual). Property owners and managers regularly rely on budgets.

A budget can be simple or complex; it can be handwritten or computerized. The best budgets project income and expenses on a monthly basis, account for several categories of income, and divide (or subdivide) expense categories as appropriate. The budget will be more accurate if it shows specific income amounts in the months in which they should be received and expenses in the months in which they should be paid. A budget is easier to use if it is prepared in a format that matches the monthly reports, so variances—both favorable and unfavorable—can be identified more precisely when comparing actual versus budgeted figures for the current month and the year to date.

Projecting Income

Preparation of the annual budget begins with a projection of income for the coming year. A shopping center has many sources of income, including base rent, percentage rent, miscellaneous income, and tenant payments of pass-through expenses.

Base Rents. A shopping center's primary income is the base rent paid by each tenant. Once the rental rates are recorded on lease summary forms, the shopping center manager uses those forms as the basis for projecting income. Information for each tenant should be compiled in a budget format that permits itemization for each month as well as the total for the year. If the rent is constant, the same amount is entered for each month. If a CPI increase is scheduled during the year, the percentage increase should be estimated, and the higher rent amount should be recorded for the months in which it will be paid. Scheduled increases should also be recorded in a footnote or be noted in the budget explanation because actual CPI increases will not be known until they go into effect.

Vacancies negatively affect the shopping center's income, so they are a consideration in budgeting. The budget can list a space that is currently vacant in several ways. One approach is to enter the market rent for each month and include a vacancy factor in the budget computations. Another approach is to show no income until occupancy is expected and then enter the expected income for the remaining months. Still other approaches do not account for vacant spaces in the budget and omit a line item for a vacancy factor. However the system accomplishes it, the shopping center budget should show the full potential income stream and an accounting for vacancies. Displaying the cost of vacancy serves as a strong reminder that money is lost each month a store space is empty.

Percentage Rent. After accounting for base rental income (adjusted for vacancies), the shopping center manager next records additional sources of revenue. Percentage rent is difficult to estimate accurately. However, if leases call for payment of percentage rent, the amounts should be estimated for the budget, but they should be based on very conservative calculations. Percentage rent is more likely to be collected in an established shopping center. Shopping centers that are less than three years old generally are not expected to yield percentage rent, although a few tenants (restaurants in particular) may pay overages from the beginning of their leases.

In estimating percentage rents, an incremental increase in annual sales is projected from a review of the tenant's sales history. The potential for percentage rent based on the increased annual sales is then estimated, along with any negotiated offsets of tenant charges, and the amount is entered in the budget. Percentage rent should be indicated in the month or months in which it will be paid. When an anchor tenant reports annually in February, the percentage rent payment is expected in March unless the lease states a different due date. If tenants report and pay each calendar quarter, income is normally received in the month following the quarter (first quarter—January through March—would be paid in April). Monthly reports and payments are also received in the following months (January sales are reported and the percentage rent is paid in February). Percentage rent is always variable; individual tenants may report and pay on very different schedules. While anticipating this income is important in budgeting for a shopping center, the shopping center manager must remember that percentage rent is not an absolutely reliable source of income.

Miscellaneous Income. Income from miscellaneous sources such as bank interest, late fees, and otherwise unscheduled reimbursements from tenants should be considered. Other possible income sources are temporary tenant rents and charges, stroller rental fees, income from vending machines, sponsorship programs, etc. The previous year's actual records (if available) are usually the best source for this information, and forecasts of future income should account for operational changes over the past year. It is better to be conservative in projecting additional funds than to be disappointed because anticipated funds did not materialize.

Pass-Through Expenses. One other major source of income is tenant payments of pass-through expenses. However, this is typically calculated *after* expenses have been budgeted so the figures will be accurate. Each tenant's payments should be estimated separately—whether prorated based on GLA or computed using an agreed formula. This allows the shopping center manager to consider exclusions, caps on CAM payments, differing payment schedules, and other exceptions that affect the amounts paid. Each tenant's expected payments for different items should be computed, and the amounts for each item from all the tenants can be totaled and entered in the months in which they will be received.

One pass-through expense that sometimes poses problems is the CAM administrative supervision fee. That fee is included in the lease to reimburse part of the landlord's expense of administering the maintenance of the common areas, and it is usually stated as a percentage to be added to the CAM proration. Some shopping center owners want this fee shown as part of the budgeted income, but that can distort the figures for some shopping centers—the larger pro rata payments can indicate that the owner is collecting more than 100 percent of the pass-through expenses. However, the

CAM administrative fees can be a significant part of the owner's cash flow, so they are worth including.

Ideally, the proration of pass-through expenses will be distributed over the twelve months of the year so tenants can make equal monthly payments. (Adjustments for the difference between estimated and actual expenses are normally made after the year-end.) However, anchor tenants' leases may call for a different distribution of payments, and those who are permitted to do so may pay for an item when it becomes due (e.g., taxes may be paid twice a year and insurance premiums may be paid annually). Such exceptions should be noted in the budget summary to explain the significant fluctuations in cash flow that will result.

In shopping centers that have marketing funds or merchant's associations, tenants' leases usually require monthly contributions to fund them. The specific amounts and payment schedules are stated in the leases. Most owners prefer to have this income displayed as a separate line item so tracking receipts will be easy. The total collected from the tenants determines the amount to be contributed by the landlord, and these funds are intended to be used exclusively for promotion of the center.

Estimating Expenses

Once income has been projected, the next step is to estimate expenses. This, too, can be approached in different ways. In its most simplified form, the budget shows each type of expense as a line item, and amounts are entered when they are scheduled to be paid (exhibit 6.8). However, shopping centers frequently have three or four separate sub-budgets that distinguish among owner expenses (those that cannot be passed through to the tenants), common area expenses (those commonly prorated to the tenants), marketing and advertising expenses (budgeted separately for a marketing fund), and capital expenses (tenant improvements, leasing commissions, building repairs). Separation of these types of expenses allows them to be analyzed more readily and precludes separate reporting.

Owner's Expenses. This budget item usually consists of business licenses, the landlord's contributions to the marketing fund, legal fees, partnership auditing costs, costs to maintain vacancies (utilities and cleaning the space), and any of the shopping center's business expenses that are not chargeable to the tenants.

Fees for business licenses are usually fairly stable. The previous year's actual fees are a good starting point. The fee paid to the shopping center manager (or property management firm) is typically a contractual item and is easily calculated. However, if the tenants reimburse the fee, it is accounted for under common area costs. The landlord's marketing and advertising contribution is based on lease requirements. It can be calculated from the estimated marketing fund or merchant's association income from the tenants.

Exhibit 6.8

Example—Expenses Budget
Heartland Plaza Shopping Center

Description	Jan	Feb	Mar	Apr	May	June	July	Aug	Sep	Oct	Nov	Dec	Total
Management Fees	3,600	3,600	3,600	3,600	3,600	3,600	3,600	3,600	3,600	3,600	3,600	3,600	43,200
Insurance		8,300						8,300					16,600
Real Estate Taxes				43,500								43,500	87,000
Licenses								265					265
Electricity	9,800	9,600	7,400	6,800	6,800	6,800	6,800	8,100	8,300	9,000	9,400	9,700	98,500
Water/Sewer	300	300	350	350	400	400	400	350	300	300	300	250	4,000
Gas	1,500	1,500	1,200	900	900	800	800	800	900	900	1,000	1,200	12,400
Security	800	800	800	800	800	800	800	800	800	800	800	800	9,600
Signs	100			250			250						600
Supplies	300	300	300	300	300	300	300	300	300	300	300	300	3,600
Trash Removal	2,100	2,100	2,100	2,100	2,100	2,100	2,100	2,100	2,100	2,100	2,100	2,100	25,200
Landscaping	1,300	1,300	1,300	1,300	1,300	1,300	1,300	1,300	1,300	1,300	1,300	1,300	15,600
Building Repair	300	300	300	300	300	300	300	300	300	300	300	300	3,600
Roof Repair			4,500						1,500				6,000
Plumbing	150	150	150	150	150	150	150	150	150	150	150	150	1,800
Parking Lot Repair		2,000								5,000			7,000
Sweeping	1,800	1,800	1,800	1,800	1,800	1,800	1,800	1,800	1,800	1,800	1,800	1,800	21,600
Hvac Service	600			600			600			600			2,400
													0
Total	22,650	32,050	23,800	62,750	18,450	18,350	19,200	28,165	21,350	26,150	21,050	65,000	358,965

NOTE: This example shows only the range of expenses budgeted for the shopping center. The completed budget will include items of income and total expenses. Other information may be included as well (e.g. account numbers for line items, calculation dollars per square foot, etc.) The budget would include the date prepared, who prepared it, and the dates of any revisions.

Legal expenses should be based on anticipated issues, and that can be difficult to determine. Some properties have heavy legal fees year after year and others have none. The shopping center manager's prior experience with legal expenses may be the sole guideline, although previous years' actual expenses should also be reviewed along with any current tenant issues.

Common Area Expenses. The total for common area expenses may be derived from two separate lists of items. Most owners distinguish between site expenses and building expenses because major tenants frequently pay for the former, but not the latter. If they own their buildings or are responsible for maintaining them, anchor tenants are often exempted from some CAM expenses.

Site Expenses. Such items as sweeping, landscaping, pest control, security, site utilities (e.g., parking lot lighting and water for the common areas), and liability insurance premiums are considered site expenses. Last year's budget is a good starting point, especially to identify specific items. The previous year's actual expenses, if significantly different from the budget, should be the basis for estimating amounts. The total amount spent for an expense should be analyzed to determine whether the following year's expense will be higher or lower. Estimates should be distributed across the twelve months as appropriate. In many instances, the amount of an expense will not be the same for each month. For example, landscaping fees vary with the seasons and the climate; fertilization, trimming of excessive growth, removal of dead plants and addition of new ones are all activities that recur—but rarely on a monthly schedule.

If the previous year's budget is not available, the shopping center manager can use other resources. The Institute of Real Estate Management publishes *Income/Expense Analysis: Shopping Centers* each year and the Urban Land Institute publishes *Dollars & Cents of Shopping Centers*. Both are valuable sources for budgeting information. Because *Dollars & Cents of Shopping Centers* is published every two years, the shopping center manager must be careful when extrapolating figures for a budget. However, the publication does provide a good sense of the proportional relationship of specific expenses. Managers of other shopping centers in the area can help pinpoint local costs, and utility companies, local government, suppliers, and contractors can provide useful information on rates, taxes, materials, and labor expenses, respectively.

In evaluating expenses, each line item should be analyzed separately as individual line items can vary dramatically from year to year. This is a reflection of local and national economic conditions as well as climatic and geographic variables. In some areas, utility rates have increased much more rapidly than the general cost of living. On the other hand, contractors' fees have tended to hold steady because of the competition; most would rather not lose an account because of an increase in their charges.

Insurance premiums have varied markedly, and only the owner's insurance agent can provide valid figures for the next year's premium costs. Premiums are typically paid once a year, but large premiums may be paid in installments. Also, different coverages may be paid individually. The budget should show insurance payments in the months they are due.

Specific site expenses often vary with the time of year. Utility rates vary with usage, and parking lot lighting costs less in summer when the days are longer and the lights are on for shorter periods. In areas with heavy snow, there may be a high landscape watering expense in summer and no expense in winter. After each expense has been analyzed, the spread of payments should show amounts in the months they will be paid. If electricity is billed monthly, the amounts should be varied appropriately, remembering that payment follows use.

Building Expenses. A similar approach should be taken in evaluating building expenses. In this case, utilities include gas, which is used primarily for providing heat and hot water. In the northern states, the gas expense is much higher in the winter months and the electricity expense is very high in the summer months because of air conditioning. Maintenance of heating, ventilation, and cooling (HVAC) systems and elevators or escalators is covered by service contracts; last year's expenses and anticipated contractual changes should help the shopping center manager budget accurately for them. Union contracts, changing utility rates, and expenses that do not recur monthly are of particular concern.

Marketing and Advertising Expenses. These are often estimated separately, especially when the shopping center has a marketing fund or merchants' association. Although the income collected from the merchants and the landlord is intended primarily to pay for advertising, decorations, and centerwide promotional events, the funds may also be used to pay part or all of a marketing director's salary and benefits as well as the related administrative costs. When a landlord controls a marketing fund, the income and expenses may be included in the shopping center budget as separate income and expense items. In this instance, the reason for distinguishing them is to ensure that collections cover expenditures.

Capital Expenses. Major roof repairs, parking lot repaving, and similar expenses are difficult to classify. Often they are paid out of funds accumulated in reserve for just such a use. Whether or not a reserve fund is used, these major improvements are recorded in a capital budget, not in the operating budget.

Distinguishing between capital and operating costs can be difficult. Leasing commissions and construction of tenant improvements are examples. If the manager is budgeting for a new shopping center, the expenditures for marketing and initial lease-up are substantial, and leasing commissions and tenant improvements may be included in a separate lease-up budget. However, for an established center, the shopping center manager budgets for rental income beginning when a new tenant takes occupancy of a vacant space, and the lease commission is due on the rent commencement date. Similarly, tenant improvements are usually provided and paid for when the lease commences. In general, inexpensive tenant improvements are considered operating costs and may be included in the operating budget. More extensive tenant improvements might be included in the capital budget. The shopping center manager should consult an accountant when unsure whether an item is an operating or a capital expense.

Debt Service. While not actually an operating expense, debt service is paid out of the income of the property. Most owners do not require the budget to show a breakdown between principal and interest, but they can be separated if desired. Debt service is not considered until all operating expenses have been accounted for; debt service is deducted from the shopping center's net operating income.

Budget Overview

The shopping center budget is generally developed with the intention of estimating potential cash flow—what the owner will collect as profit from the investment. The following flow chart indicates how the budget works.

	Gross possible rental income
minus	vacancies and collection losses (actual or factored)
plus	miscellaneous income
plus	percentage rents
plus	collected pass-through items
equals	effective gross income
minus	owner's expenses
minus	CAM, taxes, and insurance
equals	net operating income (NOI)
minus	debt service (principal and interest) payments
equals	cash flow

All possible sources of income should be identified and the various operating expenses should be deducted from them. Marketing fund contributions may be included as income and promotional costs may be deducted as expenses—as separate line items—if appropriate. Deducting operating expenses from effective gross income yields net operating income (NOI), and it is from NOI that debt service is subtracted to determine the actual cash flow. Capital expenditures are funded out of the cash flow.

Budget Explanation

In discussing both income and expenses, reference was made to a budget explanation, which is a narrative statement that indicates the assumptions made in preparing the budget and anticipates the kinds of variables that may be encountered during the budget year. It helps the owner understand the reasoning behind the budget and reminds the shopping center manager of contingencies when he or she must report actual income and expenses as variances from the budget. For example, if the shopping center manager assumed a 6-percent increase in utilities expense based on then-current information, but utility regulators actually approved a 9-percent increase, the budget explanation would provide the reason for the discrepancy between the budgeted and actual figures.

The shopping center manager should be aware that the budget process between owners and shopping center managers usually involves some discussions. Owners frequently make adjustments to the proposed budget. The shopping center manager should sign, date, and forward the completed budget to the owner for approval. Most shopping center managers work closely with their shopping center owners during the budgeting process. This helps avoid assumptions that the owner cannot or will not accept; major changes in the budget are also less likely to be needed. If changes are made, the new version should be identified as "revised" and should carry a new date. That ensures that everyone recognizes the various generations of the budget. Once the owner approves the budget, it should be marked "approved," and it should show the approval date.

LEASE ADMINISTRATION

The lease grants both landlord and tenant specific rights; it also imposes specific obligations on both parties. One of the shopping center manager's major responsibilities is monitoring tenants' compliance with the specific terms of their leases. The shopping center manager's most important and, perhaps, most difficult task is collection of rents when they are due. In addition to the base rent, tenants often are required to pay a percentage of their sales as rent. They are also required to provide proof that they have adequate and appropriate insurance coverage, and if the landlord asks them to do so, tenants must execute estoppel certificates that affirm the lease terms. (Estoppel certificates are discussed later in this chapter.) The shopping center manager must enforce numerous other lease provisions for the safety and security of tenants and shoppers and for the maintenance and preservation of the shopping center (see also chapter 5, Maintenance and Operations).

Rent Collection

The shopping center manager's job is to collect the rent and maintain the owner's cash flow, which can be difficult when tenants do not pay their rent on time—or at all. The shopping center manager must develop a system for collecting the rent and, when all else fails, for evicting tenants who do not pay their rent.

Collection Procedures. The shopping center manager can collect rent and prorated pass-through expenses from tenants a number of ways. Some choose to send the tenants a statement each month as a systematic approach to rent collection. Other shopping center managers choose not to bill tenants in order to save accounting time and office supplies. Still others may send 12 invoices in December—one for each month of the following year—so the tenant simply needs to submit the payment with the prepared invoice. No matter which method the shopping center manager chooses, the bill-paying habits of each tenant is unlikely to change—those who typically pay on time will continue to do so, and those who usually pay late will continue to pay late.

On-time Payment. Regardless of the system used for rent collection, the shopping center manager should generally stand firm on issues related to rents and on-time payment. Effective collection of rents is critical to the owner, and the shopping center manager is not doing the tenant a favor by allowing delinquencies to occur or by permitting them to continue. The amount of a delinquency can grow very quickly and can become even more difficult to pay. When that happens, the tenant may just give up.

To encourage tenants to pay their rent on time, the lease should state a specific due date (typically the first of the month). It should also state a definite delinquency date and a penalty for late payment. The amount of the penalty is generally dictated by local practices and the attitude of the courts (when such situations have been prosecuted). Common lease requirements include a delinquency date of the fifth of the month and a $50 to $100 penalty or a percentage of past due rent that must be paid after that date.

Collection Techniques. The most effective means of collection is to telephone the responsible party. (Mailed or hand-distributed notices are generally not effective, but some leases require written notice and specify a time for a response.) However, if the shopping center manager anticipates possibly going to court, written evidence of notice and attempts to collect is necessary. The tenant should be reminded that the rent has not been received, and the conversation should not end until an agreement has been reached as to when the rent will be paid. The agreed date should be noted on the delinquency report. If the rent is not received on that date, a follow-up telephone call is warranted. Additionally, the shopping center manager typically issues a notice of default to the tenant after sending the late notice and then follows the lease provisions for working with the tenant to cure the nonpayment.

Handling collections requires diplomacy and tact, and the shopping center manager usually attends to collections personally. Whether the contact is by telephone, personal visit, or written notice, the tenant should be given an opportunity to discuss the reason for the nonpayment. A misunderstanding or extenuating circumstances may need to be addressed.

Actual delinquency may provide the context in which a late charge may be used as leverage. The shopping center manager may express concern about having to add to the tenant's burden, but that should be accompanied by an affirmation that the shopping center manager has no choice but to assess a late charge if the amount due is not received by an agreed date.

Eviction Procedures. The ultimate collection tool, of course, is the threat of default and eviction, but most shopping center managers prefer to avoid that step. Eviction should not be threatened unless the owner and the shopping center manager intend to follow through with it.

Eviction is a legal proceeding, and the local jurisdiction defines the specific procedure to be followed. The shopping center manager should not start an eviction without the express approval of the owner. Advance instructions from the owner may take the form of a specific policy on eviction, i.e., the shopping center manager may proceed with eviction only after certain conditions have been met. However, owners frequently prefer to be consulted on each specific situation. Nonpayment of rent is not the only reason for eviction, and substantial documentation is usually necessary. The services of an attorney are usually required and desired.

Percentage Rents

The shopping center manager should develop a schedule for collecting tenants' sales reports and analyzing them to determine percentage rents due. The system should include a policy and a procedure for determining whether any of the tenants' sales should be audited to ensure accurate reporting and collection of all monies due the shopping center owner.

To develop an analysis of percentage rents, the shopping center manager should compile a list of all tenants that shows their percentage rates, when reports and payments are due, and any qualifying conditions. If a tenant is not required to report sales or pay percentage rent, that fact should be noted. A tenant may have a split percentage or a cap on the amount to be paid. The lease may also provide for exclusions from gross sales for the purpose of calculating percentage rent. (These elements are considered in detail in chapter 10, Negotiating and Documenting the Lease Terms.) The

Exhibit 6.9
Example Tenant's Sales Report Form

Monthly Sales Report

Date ______________________ Reporting Month of: ______________________
Merchant: ____

A. Gross Receipts for month as defined in Lease Agreement			A. $ ________
B. Exclusions: Sales tax	$ ________		
Other exclusions	$ ________		
Exclusions Subtotal			B. $ ________
C. Sales for Rental Calculation		(A–B)	C. $ ________
D. Percentage Rent = C × rate (________%)			D. $ ________
E. Monthly Minimum Rent			E. $ ________
F. AMOUNT DUE		(D–E)	F. $ ________

I hereby certify that the above is true and correct.
By: ______________________________________

Please forward, with any monies due, to:
[Management Company Name]
[Street Address]
[City, State, Zip Code]

The same format is used when sales reports are collected quarterly. Note that this format assumes a natural breakpoint and a single percentage rate applied to all sales.

breakpoint that applies should also be shown. This is usually the *natural breakpoint* (when the base rate divided by the percentage rate equals the natural breakpoint), but negotiated artificial breakpoints will adjust the figure up or down. The breakpoint can also change as rents escalate over the term of the lease. The shopping center manager needs all of this information in order to complete the analysis.

Sales Reports. The lease stipulates when sales reports are due, but it does not tell the tenant how to present the information. Major tenants usually provide sales reports in their own formats (on time and without prompting). However, independent merchants usually need instructions and support to report on time and to present the information accurately and completely. A sample form for tenant use is shown in exhibit 6.9.

A letter reinforcing the importance of sales reports and encouraging on-time submission should be sent to each new tenant when the lease commences. If reports are not received on time, the shopping center manager should call the tenant to request the information and ask that the written report follow immediately. When the reports are received in the management

Exhibit 6.10

Example Sales Volume Report

Percentage ____________ M Q A

Monthly Rent ____________

Square Footage ____________

Base ____________

Tenant Name ____________

Address ____________

____

Notes:

Project ____________

Commencement Date ____________

Lease Term ____________

Month	2003	2004	2005	2006	2007
January					
February					
March					
April					
May					
June					
July					
August					
September					
October					
November					
December					
Total					

office, each tenant's sales are recorded on a cumulative sales volume report (exhibit 6.10) that permits comparison of the tenant's month-to-month sales over a period of five years.

Sales reports are the basis for the payment of percentage rent. The tenant's report should be checked for accuracy and then the percentage rent should be calculated. If the percentage rent is due but not paid, a bill should be prepared and sent to the tenant to ensure that all monies due the landlord are collected in a timely manner. Tenants are typically required to provide a year-end report in addition to the monthly reports. Analysis of this annual report will determine whether the tenant has overpaid or underpaid the percentage rent, and appropriate adjustments can be arranged.

Tenants' individual sales reports are also used for a centerwide sales analysis comparing both total dollars and dollars per square foot. Sales in total dollars and dollars per square foot are compared to the same period in the prior year. These analyses are reported each month to the owner. In large shopping centers, merchants are separated into categories (women's wear, shoes, gifts, etc.), and each tenant's sales are compared to those for the category as well as those for the shopping center. Comparisons can also be based on location in the shopping center to help identify a particular area or group of stores where sales are weak.

Ultimately, analysis of tenants' sales assists the shopping center manager in evaluating each tenant. When a tenant reports low sales, it can be an early warning sign that the tenant is having problems, or it can provide insight regarding a tenant that might benefit from relocation or a change of store size. Such signals can help the shopping center manager fine-tune the mix of tenants and merchandise, and they can provide a partial basis for minimum or base rental rates.

Compilations of centerwide sales figures and comparisons within merchandise categories can also be useful in the leasing process. However, sales figures of individual tenants should not be released to other tenants or to prospects. Tenants consider such information confidential.

Sales Audits. The sales data used for centerwide analyses must be accurate. If it is not, the data could be misleading, and decisions based on them could be questionable or invalid. To help eliminate errors and misrepresentations of results, selected tenants' reports should periodically be audited. The lease typically grants the landlord the right to conduct such audits.

In addition to discovering errors, audits may disclose any dishonesty in the reports. The shopping center manager has a fiduciary responsibility to ensure that all monies due the landlord are collected. However, the shopping center manager need not conduct the audit personally. In fact, having an impartial third party conduct such audits is preferable because of their delicate nature. Many companies provide professional auditing services, and the shopping center manager can hire one that is familiar with retail leases and retailing sales records.

Rarely is every tenant audited every year. The cost of the service prohibits that. (At the time this book was written, the cost of an appropriate audit was likely to exceed $700.) The wisest course of action is to establish a specific program to monitor tenants' sales and audit a percentage of the tenants in a shopping center each year on a rotating schedule. Ideally, every tenant in the shopping center whose sales volume approaches (or should be exceeding) the breakpoint should be audited at least once within a period of three to four years. The shopping center manager should plan to audit all classes of tenants, whether national, regional, or local chains or independents. Underreporting is bound to happen, intentionally or otherwise, so no tenant should be exempt from the process.

Likely candidates for audits are tenants whose reported sales warrant concern—those whose total sales hover just below the breakpoint every year, those who have not shown any increase in sales over a period of two or more years, those who are known to have good traffic but report low sales, and those who have complicated leases with exclusions and other provisions that can lead to erroneous reporting. Other likely candidates include those tenants whose leases require percentage rent only (waivers of base rent), whose reported sales are well below the normal averages (in dollars per square foot), whose sales are running counter to the trend within the shopping center or local area generally, or whose leases will expire within the next six months to one year.

The audit should be conducted in a business-like manner. If the audit discovers a problem, the problem should be discussed with the tenant privately. The shopping center manager's approach should be one of seeking a solution to the problem and not an accusation of any wrongdoing. The shopping center manager's objective is to collect the monies due the landlord *and* to preserve the relationship with the tenant.

Prorated Expenses

Each year after the budget has been approved, the tenants' pro rata shares should be estimated. The ratio of the tenant's GLA to the shopping center's GLA is usually the proration basis, and that percentage may be applied to all operating expenses. For example, a tenant occupying 1,000 square feet of GLA in a 100,000-square-foot shopping center would pay one percent of the shopping center expenses; however, the proration cannot always be so straightforward. The size of the common area to which a particular expense applies often varies because of tenant exclusions and other lease concessions. When that is the case, individual expense items are divided by a specific number of square feet to calculate a cost per square foot (exhibit 6.11), and that cost is multiplied by the individual tenant's square footage to determine the pro rata share.

Exhibit 6.11

Example Statement of Common Area Estimates
Heartland Plaza Shopping Center

Base CAM	**$/Yr**	**Square Footage**	**$/Sq.Ft. Month**
SITE COSTS			
Landscaping	$21,600		
Sweeping	18,700		
Steam Cleaning	14,750		
Parking lot repair	7,600		
CAM electricity	9,800		
Liability Insurance	7,400		
General Repairs	4,600		
Supervision 10%	8,400		
Sub total (site)	$92,850	128,283	.1151
BUILDING COSTS			
Trash removal	$28,800		
Building Insurance	14,200		
Alarm monitor	4,200		
Roof repair	6,700		
Water & sewer	24,000		
Electricity	7,200		
Building repair	6,400		
Taxes	97,800		
Supervision 10%	19,000		
Sub total (building)	208,300	32,640	.5318
Total CAM	301,150		

Merchant ____________________

Footage ____________________ Monthly estimate ____________________

Estimated Assessments. Tenants should be notified of their common area and operating expense assessments in advance so they can pay the correct amounts for the entire year. Most budgets are for a calendar year, so tenants should receive their payment estimates early in December.

Estimates should be presented in considerable detail. Two items should be readily apparent in the statement—what the tenant is paying for and how the tenant's proration was computed. If major or unusual expenses (e.g., roof repairs) are included, an explanation should be provided when the estimates are distributed to the tenants. Budget estimates are usually rounded to the nearest whole dollar to minimize bookkeeping problems and make year-end reconciliation easier. (It is reasonable to round to the nearest five dollars, especially on large dollar items, but whole-dollar rounding is appropriate and recommended.)

Year-End Reconciliations. After the end of the year, the actual common area expenses should be calculated and reconciled with the budgeted amounts. Reconciliations should be timely and accurate, and they should be provided in sufficient detail so the tenant can readily understand the difference between budget and actual—and the reasons for the difference.

Some tenants question the reconciliation as a matter of course. Others may ask to see the invoices on which it is based. Unless their leases prohibit it, tenants may be permitted to inspect invoices in the shopping center manager's office so they can audit their prorated shares. However, unless their leases provide for them to receive copies of invoices—a right usually only granted to major tenants—the invoices need not be provided. It is appropriate to provide a copy of an invoice when that is the only item in question.

A tenant who challenges the accuracy of the year-end billing may be signaling a lack of funds to pay for it. Usually this can be resolved fairly readily by meeting directly with the tenant and working out a payment program. Sometimes year-end adjustments can be substantial, and a tenant may find the difference between budget projections and reality difficult to accept. The manager should monitor expense variances closely and, if warranted, advise the tenants about increases and follow through with them regarding a possible adjustment. Showing a level of understanding for a difficult situation but providing a specific time-payment plan usually ensures receipt of the funds due and preserves the landlord-tenant relationship. Adjusting the payments before the end of the year—with the tenant's agreement—may be even more helpful.

Tenants' concerns over large reconciliation bills are only one reason to strive for accuracy in preparing the budget. Another reason is that a large discrepancy can mean a lack of funds when they are needed. Sometimes the year-end reconciliations do go the other way. A high estimate compared to low actual expenses means the tenant overpaid. When this occurs, the important step is to acknowledge the overpayment. Some owners prefer to pay tenants back directly by check. Others prefer to handle it as an accounting exercise—they issue a credit memo and apply the overpayment against the next monies due. Regardless of how the overpayment is handled, the check or the credit memo should always be accompanied by the reconciliation calculations.

Insurance Certificates

The lease requires the tenant to obtain insurance and to list the landlord and the shopping center management firm as additional named insured parties on the policies. Shopping center tenants should be insured against liability for injuries to persons and damage to others' property. Those who employ others are required by law to carry workers' compensation insurance. Anchor tenants and those who own their buildings are likely to require fire and other casualty coverages. Crime insurance is important for all retail tenants, as is business interruption insurance. Plate-glass insurance may also be appropriate. Specific coverages may vary with the type of business (see appendix B, Insurance and Risk Management). When insurance is purchased, the insurer issues a "certificate of insurance" that shows the types of coverages, the names of all insured parties, and the term of the policy (beginning and expiration dates).

To administer tenants' insurance coverage, the shopping center manager should prepare a schedule that shows the insurance requirements for each tenant. The shopping center manager is responsible for collecting certificates of insurance from all the tenants and for checking them for completeness. Notes should also be made of expiration dates so reminders can be sent to the tenants 30 days before their certificates expire. A certificate should be submitted to the shopping center manager each time the policy is renewed, and tenants must often be reminded to submit the current ones.

Although it is spelled out in the lease, the insurance requirement may be reiterated in the tenant manual, which is distributed at move-in, or in a letter that is sent to each new tenant. Chapter 4, Management Structure, discusses the tenant manual and the letter of welcome to new tenants. A letter is especially helpful in guiding the store owner who has no prior experience in a shopping center and may not fully understand the insurance requirements. (The letter can be provided to the tenant in duplicate with a recommendation to forward one copy to the insurance carrier.)

Tenant Audits of Common Area Expenses

This practice was quite uncommon until the early 1990s; however, tenants now audit the common area billings much more frequently. While tenants have every right to determine if the costs billed are in agreement with the leases, the landlord will want to make sure that the auditor does not go on a hunting expedition beyond the scope of the audit. Here are some suggestions for preparing for a tenant audit if the lease requires it:

1. Provide the auditor with a printout of all reimbursable expenses, the vendor name, description of service, date, and amount of invoice.
2. Place invoice files in a box for the audit rather than allowing the auditor to rummage through all of the file cabinets.
3. Be certain that the auditor has access to only the reimbursable expenses and that they are for the shopping center being audited and no other property.

4. Provide copies of invoices only as specified in the lease.
5. Provide auditors only the time frame for the audit as specified in the lease.
6. Hold the audit at the location where the records are maintained.
7. Allow only one tenant to hold an audit at a time.

Be as professional as possible during the audit process, and be prepared for a time-consuming process; considerable time may be required for preparing for the audit as well as answering the auditor's questions. Chapter 10, Negotiating and Documenting the Lease Terms, discusses items that should be included in leases to make the audit easier and more confidential for both parties.

Estoppel Certificates

An *estoppel certificate* is an affirmation of the lease terms by the tenant. Most leases require the tenant to execute an estoppel certificate if the landlord requests it. An estoppel states the lease commencement and termination dates, the amount of rent and any deposits paid, and that the tenant and landlord are not in default. In the past, this document was a brief paragraph, but this is no longer the case, and tenants may show a reluctance to sign the expanded version of the estoppel certificate.

To ensure uniformity and consistency of presentation, the shopping center manager usually gets the lender's or buyer's form of estoppel certificate and hand delivers it when possible. The shopping center manager may need to explain the document and its purpose to small shop tenants; major tenants usually have their legal departments examine estoppel certificates, and that can take a few days. The shopping center manager is responsible for collecting the signed certificates and may have to follow up on them repeatedly.

Enforcement of Lease Provisions

Various lease provisions require tenants to take, or not to take, a variety of actions. People make lease contracts in the first place, and people ultimately break them. Chapter 4, Management Structure, addresses issues related to store hours, employee parking, and merchandising beyond the lease line. Other specifics are described in detail in chapter 10, Negotiating and Documenting the Lease Terms. The shopping center manager is responsible for ensuring that violations of the lease contract are corrected. However, he or she must obtain the tenant's compliance without damaging (or destroying) the landlord-tenant relationship. The keys to accomplishing this delicate task are diplomacy, tact, and education.

An informed tenant who understands why something is required is more likely to accept the requirement and comply with it. An excellent means of educating tenants is the tenant manual, which is described in chapter 4, Management Structure. It provides an informal reminder of their lease responsibilities. However, neither the manual nor the lease itself is a guarantee of perfect performance of all lease obligations. While the tenant should be given the benefit of the doubt on a first-time offense, the shopping center manager should explain the business reasons for having the clause in the lease. The tenant must understand that any lease default—not just nonpayment of rent—can lead to eviction.

When the shopping center manager becomes aware of a lease infraction, a telephone call or a personal visit is an appropriate way to communicate a straightforward reminder that an activity is not permitted under the lease. The tenant should be given a reasonable time to cure the problem, and when it is cured, the shopping center manager should thank the tenant for cooperating. However, if the cure is not expedited in a reasonable time, the shopping center manager should make a call to remind the tenant of the need for compliance and to establish a firm date for a cure. For a problem that persists, a written "notice of default" may be the first step toward official documentation of actions leading to eviction.

Enforcement of lease provisions is an important responsibility. Although at times ignoring a lease infraction may seem easier for the shopping center manager, the usual result of inaction is further infractions by that tenant and, ultimately, by other tenants who become aware that the lease is not being enforced for the one tenant. In enforcing lease provisions, it is important to agree upon a deadline for curing a problem and then to follow up on that deadline. Notes should be made of the problem, the required cure, and the time allowed for the cure. The documentation of the shopping center manager's actions may become an important issue if a problem persists and eviction becomes necessary.

Problems relating to the lease are not always defaults by the tenant. Sometimes it is not clear who is responsible for a specific maintenance task, and tenants may ignore their responsibilities. When such situations arise, the shopping center manager should investigate the problem and the cure, with the understanding that if an item is the tenant's responsibility, the tenant will have to pay the expense. Often the shopping center manager is in a better position to identify and arrange solutions for maintenance problems than a shop tenant is. A major tenant, on the other hand, is likely to investigate the problem and call the shopping center manager's attention to the question of responsibility.

Whatever the issue, from rent collection to the enforcement of lease provisions, the shopping center manager's role is to sensitively and diplomatically work with all tenants to maintain good tenant relations while accomplishing the owner's goals for managing and leasing the shopping center.

7

Tenant Relations

Establishing positive relationships with the tenants is one of the most important considerations in managing a successful shopping center. Shopping center owners and managers must consider tenant relations from the moment the development of a particular shopping center is considered. Retail tenants and their landlords have some of the closest and most interdependent relationships found in income-producing properties. In no other property type does the success of the tenant reflect on the landlord as much as it does in retail properties. If an office tenant fails, the consequence is essentially a vacancy and the possible loss of rent; the vacancy will not impact the tenant mix of the property. The failure of many retail tenants, however, can have a dramatically negative effect on a shopping center. The loss of an anchor tenant or a major national retailer can ripple through the shopping center, impacting those tenants who depend on that specific retailer for much of their traffic.

The success of a shopping center depends on the success of all its tenants, and it is measurable in sales volumes which impacts base and percentage rents. Every aspect of the shopping center must be planned to maximize sales and to minimize the physical and procedural obstacles to achieving them. A good working relationship between the shopping center manager (landlord) and the tenant is a prerequisite to success. The tenants must understand how the shopping center operates and what its operations mean in terms of their businesses. Maintaining good relationships with the tenants and helping them achieve their goals through positive tenant relations programs are essential steps toward lease renewals and tenant retention.

ESTABLISHING RELATIONSHIPS WITH TENANTS

Tenant relations begin when the shopping center project is conceived. After the selection of the proper site, the development of a carefully designed plan for the center is the first critical step toward successful tenant relations. The leasing representative plays an essential role in finding and attracting suitable tenants and beginning positive relationships with them. After the lease is signed, the shopping center manager takes over the relationship with the tenant and works to maintain positive relations throughout the tenancy.

The Basics of Good Tenant Relations

The operation of the shopping center must be considered in detail during the planning stage in order to avoid problems later. The lease itself, the landlord's workletter, and the construction punch list must receive careful attention.

Potential Problems. Examples of potential problems abound. Imagine the merchant who moves a business into a new shopping center and is paying a share of the common area maintenance (CAM) expenses. That merchant may well become disenchanted with the CAM charges if maintenance people are repeatedly observed hauling out a 300-foot hose to wash down the outside walkways because no water faucets are available next to the walks. The merchant can correctly conclude that the maintenance requirements of the shopping center were not well conceived at the design stage.

To prevent such disenchantment, and the complaints that can result, the shopping center planners should create and follow a checklist of the specific details that must be included in the design. The following list identifies only a few examples of the types of operating details that can lead to problems:

- If a major tenant requests lighting in the parking lot throughout the night, arrangements should be made for separate circuits and, perhaps, separate meters for those lights.
- If a common collection point is to be designated for trash disposal, its location should be convenient to all of the tenants' spaces.
- Receptacles for customers' disposal of trash should be convenient for shoppers but should not block walkways. The size, use, and labeling of the receptacles are other considerations.
- If bicycle racks are provided, they should be accessible to bike riders but should not intrude on automobile or pedestrian rights-of-way.
- Trees and other landscaping elements must not block tenants' or shopping center signage.

- Provision should be made for extra electrical outlets in the common areas for seasonal or holiday decorations.
- Large shopping centers should have well-placed tenant directories.

Careful planning and management review can avoid future problems and allow the tenants to concentrate on their business objective, which is sales.

The Lease. The lease document must be carefully planned, and shopping center operations are an important consideration in its contents. In particular, the allocation of operating expenses and the method of their proration to the tenants must be appropriate and fair. Common area maintenance, utilities, and taxes are among the expenses most commonly passed through to the tenants. If the utilities are master metered, the lease must state the method of allocation to the individual tenants. Taxes may be allocated for the entire center or parcel by parcel. Ownership and values of multiple parcels of land may be the determining factors. A carefully crafted lease takes all of these issues into consideration.

The Workletter. Another important document that applies to all tenants and must therefore be carefully thought out is the landlord's *workletter*—the addendum that lists all the work the owner is to do for the tenant. It becomes a part of the lease, usually as an exhibit. With the inevitable confusion that goes along with moving in, the new tenant who discovers that the promised telephone conduit was not installed will be very unhappy. Most landlords will rectify such a problem eventually, but in the meantime, the tenant's move-in is off schedule and the tenant is aggravated. Because such problems can and do occur, the landlord's workletter must be compared to the construction documents to ensure that the tenant gets everything that is promised.

Punch Lists. Also important in a newly constructed shopping center are tenant *punch list* items (improvements that should be made) and responsive follow-up on them after the tenant moves in. This is a management responsibility because the general contractor is quite often from another city. When the shopping center construction is completed, the contractor and the construction crew often move on to other projects in other cities, leaving the local management to resolve move-in issues.

The Role of the Leasing Agent

Good tenant relations are the responsibility of the shopping center manager and owner. They begin with the tenant's first contact—the leasing representative. The leasing agent must be thoroughly familiar with the lease document and with the method of management of the shopping center, as both will affect the tenant throughout the lease term. Knowing the size of the rental spaces and the rental rate per square foot is not enough. The leasing agent must also know how common-area and other charges will be prorated and passed through. New tenants will want to know where to pay the rent and whom to call if they have a problem. It is critical that the leasing agent fully understand the lease document and the tenant's obligations under the lease.

The leasing agent's job is to prospect for tenants and acquire signed leases. Once a space is leased, the agent should move on to the next prospect. Overseeing tenant improvements or working on management problems may distract the leasing agent from key responsibilities such as filling vacancies and upgrading the shopping center's tenant mix.

For that reason, the shopping center manager must be available to take over the relationship with the tenant once the lease is signed. When a lease is signed, the leasing agent should deliver a copy of the lease to the new tenant along with a *letter of introduction* that identifies the shopping center manager and sets forth the particulars of the turnover of the premises—e.g., the move-in date, the first rent payment date, and the contractors to contact for tenant improvement construction. A copy of the letter should be sent to the shopping center manager.

The ideal next step toward making the transition is for the leasing agent to introduce the tenant to the shopping center manager in person. If that is not possible, the letter accompanying the lease may have to suffice.

The Role of the Shopping Center Manager

Upon receiving the copy of the letter of introduction that the leasing agent sent to the tenant, the shopping center manager should send the tenant a personal letter of welcome along with a tenant manual. The tenant manual includes basic information on the shopping center's operations and a detailed list of resources. Chapter 4, Management Structure, discusses the letter of welcome and the tenant manual in detail. The contents of the tenant manual are important for all tenants. If a store manager represents the tenant, that individual may have little or no knowledge of the details of the lease agreement. In the absence of a copy of the lease, the tenant manual may be the store manager's sole guideline for operating in the shopping center.

A telephone call from the shopping center manager to the new tenant is also an effective way to quickly establish more personal communication. The shopping center manager is often called upon to serve as liaison between contractors and tenants. Moving a business into a shopping center—especially a newly built center—is often a totally new experience for tenants, and they need assistance to get through the process. During construction of the tenant's space, it is helpful if the shopping center manager stops by or calls to see if everything is moving along according to plan. The shopping center manager should keep in mind that the shopping center owner has a vested interest in opening a tenant's store as soon as possible, so working with the tenant benefits both the tenant and the landlord.

A letter of congratulations from the shopping center manager to the tenant on opening day as well as a token gift, such as a plant or flowers, is an especially nice touch. Ideally, the shopping center manager should visit the store in person on opening day. If that is not possible, the shopping center manager should visit the tenant shortly thereafter.

Opening day presents an opportunity for the shopping center manager to review any lease details the leasing agent may not have communicated to the tenant. A separate letter spelling out the lease commencement and ending dates, when and how to make rental payments, and a statement of charges accrued to date may accompany the letter of congratulations or follow a day or so later.

A goodwill gesture on the part of the shopping center owner or manager can go a long way toward setting the tone of the landlord/tenant relationship. An example is an ad in the local newspaper, designed and paid for by the landlord. The same ad can be used for all tenants if it includes a heading such as "Welcoming the Newest Merchant" and closes with the name, address, and logo of the shopping center. The middle section of the ad should be for the tenant's use—an announcement of the tenant's opening or a promotion of a special sale item. Such an ad is a nice welcome for the tenant, and it promotes the shopping center.

MAINTAINING RELATIONS WITH TENANTS

Once the shopping center manager has welcomed a new tenant, i.e., the store owner or manager, every effort must be made to maintain the relationship. The shopping center manager must understand that over the long term he or she is responsible for the relationship with the tenants. The shopping center manager must reach out to the tenant and make the effort to establish and preserve the landlord/tenant relationship.

Creating a sound, well-managed environment in which the retailer can operate and having a management philosophy that recognizes and is responsive to the needs of both the property and the tenants is essential to positive tenant relations. Tenants are more likely to have a positive attitude when the shopping center is well run, and their attitude will create a more pleasant shopping environment for the customers. As a result, both landlord and tenant will benefit.

The keys to successful tenant relations are professional management and marketing of the shopping center as typified by excellent lines of communication and prompt responses to tenants' problems and concerns.

Communicating with Tenants

The nature of tenant relations demands that the shopping center manager possess clear and effective communication and interpersonal skills. The tenants in a shopping center may have differing levels of sophistication and retailing expertise. The perceptions and needs of local entrepreneurs who are starting new businesses are substantially different from those of established retailers; the person hired to manage a store that is part of a franchise or chain differs from a business owner.

The shopping center manager must know not only who the tenant is but also whether the store operator is the owner of the business or an employee of the owner. This chapter addresses the shopping center manager's relationships with those who operate the individual stores in the shopping center.

The use of first names fosters a more personalized relationship, which can be enhanced in each conversation or meeting with the tenant by asking questions that let the tenant know that the shopping center manager is ready to respond to the tenant's problems and wants to help. "How are you today?" "How is business?" "How can I help you?" "What can we do for you?" "Anything I should know about today?"

Such questions may encourage complaints, as discussed in later sections of this chapter. They are also likely to elicit requests from tenants that may be very difficult or impossible to fulfill. When that is the case, instead of just saying no, the shopping center manager can provide some explanation such as "I am really sorry, but we cannot agree to do that because. . . ." and provide a business basis for the decision. Although the result is the same, the shopping center manager has both expressed concern about the tenant's request and explained why it was denied.

The shopping center manager has many opportunities to communicate with individual tenants, and these communications take many different forms. Personal contact is genuinely needed, and that is best done in face-to-face visits. However, the tenants are most likely to use telephone calls, e-mails, and letters—especially if the shopping center manager does not have an on-site office. Perhaps the most important point to emphasize is that the shopping center manager should be responsive to the tenants because their efforts to communicate will most likely relate to their specific problems.

The on-site shopping center manager has many more opportunities to visit with the tenants than does a manager who has a portfolio away from their office. The on-site manager often walks the shopping center and has many opportunities to visit with tenants, compliment them on a good display, discuss sales with them, or just chat about their business in general. In most larger malls and shopping centers, the monthly sales are analyzed and provided to the merchants. Handing the reports out face-to-face and discussing them with the owner or manager at that time is particularly useful.

Personal Visits. Once a tenant has moved in, the shopping center manager should ideally visit the tenant once a month. However, if the shopping center is very new or if there are problems in its start-up, visits every two weeks or more often may be appropriate. The shopping center manager's purpose in these visits is to observe and listen. Tenants are likely to have questions about the status of lease-up and about other tenants' sales.

To answer tenants' questions, the shopping center manager should be prepared with as much positive information as possible. He or she should also be prepared when tenants complain about problems or make suggestions. Each new tenant may want to make the manager aware of things to be done, for example, the installation of additional signage. If such requests are not possible, an explanation—in this instance, that additional signage may be a nice idea, but city ordinances preclude it—will go far in sustaining tenant relations.

The tenant is often aware of problems in the shopping center but does not take the time to call the shopping center manager. The personal visits are the perfect time to gather that information. Every visit to a tenant's store may result in a list of issues that need attention, so the first calls the shopping center manager makes on return to the office should be to take care of the tenant's problems. Telling a tenant when work is in progress helps to put his or her mind at ease. If a problem is big or if it is disruptive to the shopping center's operations, the shopping center manager should make a point of being on-site to show concern and support for the merchants.

Sometimes the tenant will not be in the store when the shopping center manager visits. In that case, the manager should leave a business card with a hand-written note (e.g., "I stopped by to see how things are going."). The card lets the tenant know of the visit, and the note indicates a personal interest.

Telephone Calls. Tenants' telephone calls should always be returned. Even though the shopping center manager is very busy, there is no excuse for not returning a phone call. If the shopping center manager cannot respond directly to the tenant for a few days, the assistant should let the tenant know that the shopping center manager will call as soon as possible and extend an offer to help personally.

In many situations, the management office is located some distance from the retail property, and shop tenants may be reluctant to make a long-distance call. One solution is for the management office to accept collect calls, but that can be very expensive. A better solution is to arrange for off-premises phone extensions in the cities where the remote properties are located. The extension is assigned a local telephone number, and all calls to that number are forwarded to the management office. The tenants make a local phone call that rings at the management office, and the management firm pays for the toll portion of the forwarded call.

Still another option is a custom 800 number. Some 800 numbers cover only the area codes from which the company is willing to accept calls. No additional phone lines are required, and a local 800 number can be comparatively inexpensive. It is also a great convenience for tenants and local contractors who work with the management firm.

Letters and E-mail. From time to time, shopping center managers receive letters or e-mails of complaint from tenants. A letter or e-mail from an irate tenant should not be responded to in kind. The shopping center manager should be sure to have all the facts and understand the situation before responding. The tenant's approach to a problem may not be rational, but a rational response is important.

The shopping center manager should respond to an e-mail as soon as possible and provide as complete an answer as possible. If the response is lengthy or complicated, that response should preferably be made through a telephone call or better yet, a personal visit. Even if the shopping center manager cannot resolve the tenant's problem, a sympathetic approach will go far toward preserving the long-term relationship.

Communication goes both ways, and the shopping center manager must be cautious in using written communications to deal with problems in the shopping center. A letter or e-mail should not be sent to all tenants if only one or two tenants are causing a problem. The tenant who caused the problem should be contacted specifically.

The most likely reason to write to a specific tenant is in regard to something in the lease. A letter related to the lease should show the tenant's proper name, spelled correctly, and it should be sent to the address specified in the lease or requested by the tenant. (Many tenants have offices away from the shopping center, and they do not wish to have their business arrangements known to all store personnel.) When a notice to all tenants is necessary (or appropriate), the letters or e-mail should be addressed to "all merchants" (to avoid the negative connotations inherent in the word tenant).

Support from Management

The landlord (shopping center manager) can also be a source of shopping center industry information that can be helpful to the merchants. The newspaper often prints positive reports on retailing. These can be cut out and mailed to some or all of the tenants—depending on the topic and suitability—with a note saying, "I thought this might be of interest."

Beyond the local newspaper are national resources. The International Council of Shopping Centers (ICSC) publishes *The Retail Challenge,* which is distributed quarterly and provides very specific tips on retailing. Some developers subscribe to multiple copies of this publication for their tenants, at no cost to the tenants.

Reprints of articles are also useful tools. Anything related to retailing that comes to the attention of the landlord or shopping center manager is worth sharing with those tenants who could benefit from the information. Some national and regional chain store operators prefer not to receive such information because they have very strong ideas about how to run their stores. However, most of the tenants in the smaller shop spaces can benefit from timely tips and additional information on retailing, and the landlord or shopping center manager is a logical source for them.

Competition being what it is, the shopping center manager can easily find opportunities to be supportive toward tenants. Every visit to a tenant's store is an opportunity to observe the business in operation. Some points to look for specifically are the physical appearance of the store (neatness, cleanliness, use of the space), merchandise presentation (appropriate displays, inventory levels, pricing), customer relations, store employees, and store management. Over time, the manager can monitor a tenant's advertising and promotions—and levels of sales. All of these observations can provide clues to the ongoing success or potential failure of a particular store.

As indicated in chapter 4, Management Structure, the shopping center manager can foster the tenants' success through education and training in better retailing practices. To be able to recognize potential problems and provide appropriate encouragement and support, the shopping center manager must understand the basics of retailing (see appendix A).

Solving Problems

Common area maintenance is the source of many tenant problems and complaints. The maintenance itself is a management responsibility; the tenants' problems relate predominantly to their prorations for the costs.

One of the quickest ways to lose a tenant's confidence and goodwill is to make charges against the common area costs that are not legitimate. Even though the charges may be reversed upon complaint, the tenants retain the feeling that the landlord tried to take advantage of them. Equally egregious is not crediting taxes, insurance, utilities, and other refunds to the common area charges.

Contractors working on the common areas can pose problems for tenants, and the shopping center manager must work with both parties to resolve them. Other specific sources of difficulty in tenant relations are the maintenance of the tenants' premises and violations of the lease.

Common Area Expense Bills. Many of the shop tenants do not really understand the allocation of CAM expenses, but with a little extra effort, that can be resolved. The first step is a clearly understandable lease provision that sets forth what the tenant will pay, how the amount is computed, and when payment is to be made. In addition, the tenant's bills for CAM expenses should be sufficiently detailed so the tenant can see the total amount of the expense and understand how the proration was determined (see chapter 6, Administration). To expect the tenant to accept whatever is billed, without explanation, is unreasonable, and a bill that shows only the amount the tenant is expected to pay is not appropriate. When a tenant calls with a question, the shopping center manager should take the time to explain the billing computation.

Monthly billings are based on an estimate of the annual costs, and the year-end adjustment statement should provide a comparable level of detail. An accompanying letter should explain any extraordinary expenses. Management may know all the details of a larger-than-budgeted expense, but the tenant cannot be expected to remember it and may not have known about it at all. When a year-end adjustment is much larger than expected, allowing additional time for payment may be appropriate. Some tenants may have difficulty paying a substantial additional amount invoiced. The extra time allowance often overcomes a tenant's need to challenge the billing.

Some national chains and major retailers may require copies of the invoices for common area expenses, and they negotiate that into their leases. In general, however, copies of invoices should not be provided unless it is absolutely necessary. A tenant can use the invoices as a way to delay payment by arguing for more time to review them.

Tenants do have the right to audit the records of common area expenses in the management office, and it is appropriate to provide a copy of an invoice for a single item that is a problem. However, sending copies of all invoices to all tenants becomes very expensive. The cost would have to be borne by the tenants, and most tenants would prefer not to have that expense. The best policy is to permit the inspection of all invoices if that right is in the lease.

Common Area Contractors. Because common area contractors may cause concerns for tenants, contracts for work in the common areas require special attention. First, the shopping center manager's relations with the contractors should be at a distance. Contractors should not be relatives or captive companies unless they are clearly the best and least expensive (or only) providers of a service in the area.

Having all contracted work bid to specifications ensures cost effectiveness and efficiency. All contracts should include a cancellation provision and state a specific period in which the work can occur (e.g., seven days). Contractors should also be required to provide proof of insurance in case claims result from defects in the work or delays in completing it.

Contract workers often do not realize that their activities are disruptive. Some problems, such as having material stacked in a prominent parking space and workers' behavior on the job (listening to loud radios, eating in front of store entrances, etc.) are disruptive for the tenants. They can become big problems for the shopping center manager if they are not resolved quickly. A few words with the contract workers ahead of time can often prevent such occurrences.

Indeed, the contractors who employ those workers must know that the shopping center is an operating entity and that all efforts must be made to do their jobs with minimal disruption of tenants' businesses. This can be stated in the contract itself or in a cover letter, but it must be emphasized. If a contractor's work will be disruptive to one or more tenants, the contractor or the shopping center manager should inform the affected tenants. They should also be assured that the contractor and the shopping center manager will do what they can within reason to minimize the disruption and keep all tenants open for business.

Contractors should be encouraged to be courteous. If work is being done where it cannot be seen (e.g., a roof repair), the contractor should let the tenant know when the work has been started and completed or if the work will be discontinued for a few days. This provides assurance to the tenant that something is in fact being done—perhaps in response to the tenant's complaint. Repairs and other work are often completed out of sight and during off hours, and the tenant who does not see anyone may assume that nothing has been done.

Maintenance of Leased Premises. One difficult area of landlord/tenant relations is the responsibility for the maintenance of the leased premises, especially if the warranty on an item has just expired or if responsibility for the item to be maintained or repaired is questionable (e.g., a sewer pipe that serves only the tenant's premises but is located 20 feet outside the premises). Some leases are very clear on these issues, but many are not. Usually the tenants are responsible for maintaining their premises. However, in questionable situations, the shopping center manager should advise the tenant that management will have a contractor investigate the problem and, if the repair is the tenant's responsibility, the contractor will first notify the tenant of the cost of the repair and then bill the tenant.

While the shopping center manager's first responsibility is to the owner who has retained his or her services, the shopping center manager also has an obligation to be fair and reasonable with the tenants. The owner signs the lease as the landlord and makes a financial decision based on the economics of the deal, however, situations can arise that require an exception to the lease agreement. The shopping center manager must often look beyond the language of the lease in evaluating situations, as the lease may not offer a fair solution to a landlord/tenant problem.

A major tenant, whose employees are sophisticated and understand the ramifications of taking over existing space, is usually in a position to take care of the leased premises. A problem discovered after move-in is not likely to create sympathy for a major tenant or to change the economics of the deal.

The tenant in a small shop space, however, is in a different situation. For example, an interior decorator who has never taken space in a shopping center before may lease an existing store. The space is leased "as is" and, within a month, the water heater fails completely and has to be replaced. This situation may require the shopping center manager to exercise some judgment. Whether the tenant should pay for the replacement under the circumstances may be questionable. If the shopping center manager made a very low rent deal, the "as is" situation was pointed out, and the tenant was made aware of the risks, then replacement should be at the tenant's expense. However, if the deal was for market rent and little attention was paid to the "as is" portion of the lease, for the landlord to pay for the replacement may be more reasonable.

While the landlord should be fair and reasonable regardless of the lease requirements, the lease also represents an economic deal with the tenant, and the basis of that deal will be eroded if the landlord assumes responsibility for what is rightly a tenant's expense. In this situation the shopping center manager has dual responsibilities—furthering the landlord's interest and preserving the landlord/tenant relationship.

Lease Violations. Violations of the lease terms by the tenants require close attention and careful handling. Tenants typically favor a strong lease because it provides a desirable environment for all businesses. However, most tenants also think their individual needs should be more important than the lease requirements. Violation of the lease requires diplomacy and firmness. An explanation of the violation and why it cannot continue is imperative. As with other items in a lease, the lease provision itself should not be the stated reason for the shopping center manager's position. Rather, the reasons behind the lease provision should be explained.

For example, a provision in the lease may state that tenants are prohibited from parking in front of their stores, but it is more effective to indicate the importance of the parking space in terms of customer convenience and what that means to the particular tenant and all the other merchants in the shopping center. (Chapter 4, Management Structure, and chapter 6, Administration, discuss lease administration in more detail.)

POSITIVE TENANT RELATIONS PROGRAMS

Many shopping centers have specific programs to foster good tenant relations. Obviously, the best tenant relations program is a successful, well-run shopping center. However, many shopping center managers take extra steps to strengthen the landlord/tenant relationship.

Although franchise operators and major retailers have their own established systems and procedures, many other retail tenants are comparatively inexperienced and may not understand the complexity of the shopping center environment. Establishing an active program of education and communication directed toward the tenants is an excellent way to bridge the gap on issues about which tenants need to be informed.

The following are suggestions of programs the shopping center manger can provide:

1. A shopping center newsletter that advises the tenants of what is going on in the shopping center, the neighborhood, and the trade area
2. An annual breakfast honoring the best advertising, best window display, highest sales, best increase in sales, etc.
3. Outings such as baseball games or boat rides on the lake or harbor
4. An employee discount card good at all stores in the shopping center
5. Use of the on-site shopping center office for special meetings
6. Retail classes to help merchants improve business, improve window displays, develop a markdown policy, etc.
7. Security classes to address store security, shoplifting, credit card fraud, etc.
8. Advertising classes to educate merchants in the most effective ways to spend their advertising dollars
9. Specialty marketing programs to support categories that may be below average (e.g., restaurants, fashion)
10. Cross-marketing opportunities with other merchants
11. Display merchandise in vacant store windows
12. Use of vacant spaces for temporary storage during peak selling seasons

LEASE RENEWAL AND TENANT RETENTION

Lease renewal is another critical time in the landlord/tenant relationship. The professional shopping center manager keeps abreast of the latest lease terms and conditions. Lease renewals require forethought. Management must first decide whether the tenant should be retained. The tenant's business may no longer be appropriate for the shopping center.

Management must next decide the terms under which the tenant will be retained. An increase in the rental rate is most likely, but other terms of the lease should be reviewed as well. Percentage rents, prorations of pass-through expenses, the need for store remodeling, and the length (duration) of the lease term should be considered carefully.

The shopping center manager should start the renewal process with the tenant approximately six months prior to the expiration date in the lease. This provides the tenant some time to consider the renewal terms and allows the shopping center manager time to inform the tenant about current market conditions. If the renewal discussion is not initiated until close to the lease expiration date, the time may be insufficient to carry out the renewal. If the rent is to be raised dramatically, the shopping center manager should know comparable market rents and be prepared to quote them for comparison. Factors that contributed to specific escalations in rent and other payments required under the lease should be identified and explained.

The shopping center manager may have no choice but to hold out for the new rent and conditions dictated by the market. It the tenant is unable to pay the new rent, the shopping center manager may need to seek a new tenant.

In truth, tenant relations are like the *golden rule:* The shopping center manager should treat the tenants as he or she would like to be treated. Each merchant should be treated every day as though his or her lease were about to expire. The tenant is both a customer and a client to the shopping center manager. This is not to suggest that the shopping center manager should not enforce the lease provisions and strive to make good business decisions, but rather that those actions should be taken with concern and empathy for the tenant's position.

8

Creating the Tenant Mix

The concept of tenant mix is more important for shopping centers than for any other type of commercial property. In shopping centers, one of the criteria for retailers' success is measured in terms of sales volume, and that is expressed in dollars per square foot of gross leasing area (GLA). The best way to generate high levels of sales is by targeting the buyers in the trade area. The more goods and services are tailored to meet the needs of area consumers, the more likely the shopping center (and most of the stores that comprise its tenant mix) is to be shopped by those consumers. Tailoring the tenant mix requires the consideration of many factors.

The tenant mix in each type of shopping center and mall has evolved and will continue to evolve with new retail concepts, new retailers, and changing consumer wants and needs. A good tenant mix must still serve the customers in the shopping center's primary trade area, but a mixing of uses and concepts that was unthinkable twenty years ago is part of the norm today.

Several examples indicate that this change in tenant mixing is more than a trend. For instance, the advent of the lifestyle shopping center has created retail locations for stores that previously only occupied spaces in regional or super regional malls. These tenants are looking for lower occupancy costs and more customer convenience, both of which are offered by the lifestyle shopping center because it has no enclosed mall common area charges and the customer can reach the store quickly and directly.

Off-price and discount stores are locating in shopping centers and malls, which was not common in the past. This trend may well be because fewer department stores exist now than in the 1980s and 1990s, and discount stores such as Wal-Mart and Target are more receptive to leasing existing vacant former anchor store locations.

Fashion retailers are seeking space in neighborhood shopping centers because their customer base—especially working women—needs convenience when shopping for such items as clothing, shoes, jewelry, and accessories. Discount, outlet, and off-price shopping centers have evolved into the big box concept.

Because of all of these changes, the tenant mix for these shopping centers have evolved to serve changing customer wants and needs. Classifying a given shopping center is more difficult, and a broader range of possibilities for creating a strong tenant mix clearly exists.

The mix of retailers at a shopping center—and the types of merchandise and services they provide—is critical to its success. The tenant mix of a shopping center should be the result of careful analysis and planning aimed at providing the broadest range of goods and services consistent with the buying habits and income levels of the people in its trade area. No matter what changes occur in the tenant mix, determination of the nature of the customer and his or her buying power is still essential. This chapter discusses the many aspects of the tenant mix—including the establishment of the tenant mix to re-tenanting a shopping center when an improvement or upgrade in the tenant mix becomes necessary.

ESTABLISHING THE OPTIMUM TENANT MIX

The key elements in establishing an optimum tenant mix are (1) determining the trade area, (2) researching the demographic and psychographic profiles of the trade area population, (3) analyzing the competition already established in the trade area, (4) matching the size and location of individual store spaces in the shopping center to the merchants that occupy them, and (5) evaluating the tenants in the shopping center.

Determining a Realistic Trade Area

Establishing a good tenant mix is as much an art as it is a science. The key is to be realistic in determining the size of the trade area. It is not realistic in most situations to assume that a neighborhood shopping center will draw customers from a 10-mile radius or that customers will drive past two other comparable centers to shop there. The shopping center manager must consider how factors in the trade area affect the tenant mix, and he or she must constantly be aware of changes in the trade area.

Trade Area Factors. The population served by the shopping center and its direct competition are the most important features of the trade area. (The trade area is discussed in the context of market analysis and the development of a management plan in chapter 3, Management Plan and Operations Manual, and the use of a market survey to identify and characterize the competition is discussed in chapter 9, Leasing the Shopping Center.)

The concept of the trade area has geographic limitations. As discussed in chapter 3, the trade area of a given center can be divided into three zones—a *primary zone* from which 70 to 75 percent of its regular customers are derived, a *secondary zone* that represents another 20 to 25 percent of its customers, and a *tertiary zone* that accounts for the remainder. The size of the trade area and its respective zones varies with the size and type of shopping center. (Chapter 1, Shopping Centers: Evolution and Change, describes the types of shopping centers in detail.) The average sizes, trade areas, and minimum populations for many types of shopping centers are discussed below:

- *Convenience (Strip) shopping centers* are comprised of 5,000 to 30,000 square feet of GLA, a convenience market anchor and a few small shops (2 to10 stores). The typical trade area comprises the immediate neighborhood of the site, the traffic on the street, and a minimum population of 1,000 to 2,500.
- *Neighborhood shopping centers* have 30,000 to 150,000 square feet of GLA, a supermarket (plus drugstore) anchor, and 15 to 25 small shops. The typical trade area has a radius of 2 to 4 miles and a minimum population of 5,000 to 40,000.
- *Community shopping centers* have 150,000 to 400,000 square feet of GLA, are anchored by a junior or discount department store (but may include a supermarket and a drugstore), and usually have 25 to 40 small shops. The typical trade area has a radius of 5 to 7 miles and a minimum population of 100,000 to 150,000.
- *Regional malls* range between 400,000 and one million square feet of GLA. They have one to three department store anchors and 50 to 100 small shops. The trade area has a radius of 7 to 10 miles and a minimum population of 150,000 to 300,000.
- *Super regional malls* occupy more than one million and up to three million square feet of GLA. They have four or more department store anchors and 100 to 150 small shops. The trade area has a radius of 10 to 20 miles and a population in excess of 300,000.
- *Specialty shopping centers* vary in size from 25,000 to 70,000 square feet of GLA and usually have no specific anchor tenant. Their main attraction is their specificity and, therefore, their uniqueness. The trade area is defined by the specific use and may extend beyond the radiuses usually associated with centers of this size. Restaurants and entertainment facilities may draw from larger areas than, say, automotive services.

- *Outlet shopping centers* vary in size. They may include off-price and discount merchants, and they attract customers from a radius of 20 miles to as far away as several hundred miles in rural areas. They traditionally require a minimum population of 200,000.
- *Power shopping centers* have between 200,000 and 600,000 square feet of GLA, and several large, strong, high-volume, heavy-advertising retailers occupy most of the space. These shopping centers have very few small shops. The trade area may extend up to 30 miles, depending on local competition; they need a minimum population of 150,000.
- *Lifestyle shopping centers* generally have 250,000 to 500,000 square feet of GLA and have anchor tenants such as Ann Taylor, Barnes and Noble, and Pottery Barn. They have few small shops because they lack the traditional anchor tenants. The trade area may vary quite a bit from one center to another, depending on the local competition.
- *Entertainment shopping centers* are often difficult to distinguish from lifestyle shopping centers, but they are different. Typically, an entertainment shopping center consists of entertainment, dining, and other retail stores. Most entertainment centers have a GLA in the range of 150,000 square feet up to 300,000 square feet, but some are well above those figures. The trade area may vary, depending on the location of any other similar center or competition.

Trade Area Changes. The appropriateness of particular tenants to the tenant mix of a given shopping center varies as the characteristics of the trade area change over time. A new single-family residential development is likely to attract more families with young children. If unmarried professionals living in apartments had dominated the population of the area, the influx of families will be a significant change. If a large manufacturing plant that employed local workers closed, the unemployment would mean reduced income, and that could force people to move out of the area. Construction of new retail space or rehabilitation of an old shopping center can change the character of the competition.

Any or all of these events can occur in an area served by a shopping center. Such changes affect the tenant mix of the shopping center, at least to the extent that individual merchants there are affected.

Conducting Market Research

Once a realistic trade area is identified, the people in it must be counted, and their characteristics must be analyzed. Three key elements must be considered when conducting such market research:

1. The population must be sufficient to support the center.
2. The population must have sufficient income.
3. The competition must be analyzed to ascertain that the market has sufficient capacity to support the type of shopping center and square footage proposed.

To research the three key elements, the shopping center manager must study the demographic and psychographic factors in the trade area population as well as the competition.

A demographic and psychographic profile can yield many different scenarios. For instance, there may not be a large enough population to support a particular type of shopping center at the time it is planned. If the area population is expected to grow substantially over the next few years, it may be appropriate to develop a new shopping center in phases, matching it to the growth of the population and its buying power. On the other hand, sales in the area may be quite strong, but an oversupply of space may mean too many merchants were not serving customer profile in the trade area.

An understanding of the ongoing changes in the demographic and psychographic profile of the trade area will help the shopping center manager, marketing director and leasing agent make the best decisions to keep the shopping center competitive and extend its economic life. The shopping center management team's objective is to create a tenant mix that will best provide the goods and services required and desired by a particular population. In a shopping center located in an affluent community, the shops are more likely to be upscale, with particular emphasis on high-end retailers and aesthetically appealing ambience. On the other hand, in a shopping center serving a lower-income area where shoppers are generally more price-conscious, the tenants are more likely to be offering value-oriented merchandise in a self-service environment. Ambience is always a concern, and all shopping centers should be a clean, pleasant place to shop and an asset to their communities.

The shopping center management team should always strive to provide a tenant mix that offers the broadest range of goods and services consistent with the demographic and psychographic profiles of the area. There is no one "right" tenant mix for a type of shopping center; rather, the tenant mix at a given shopping center must be tailored to the needs and desires of the customers it will serve.

For example, a shopping center located in a retirement community is not likely to include the kinds of shops that appeal primarily to young people (e.g., jeans shops) or an auto supply store. A cafeteria may be more appropriate for that type of location than an expensive sit-down restaurant. A hair salon and a drug store are other likely prospective tenants. The next decade will see continued changes in the demographic profile as America continues to diversify and the population continues to age.

Demographic Factors. In regard to demographic factors, looking in part to growth in the area is appropriate, as long as that growth projection is realistic. Trends in population size, age, and income distribution can be determined from current and prior census data and other sources. (See appendix D, References and Resources.)

Age and family or household composition are critical concerns for some types of retailers. Toy stores or children's clothing stores need families with young children in order to thrive; they cannot expect to do well where the population is predominantly adult professionals.

Family or household income—and the buying power that it indicates—is even more critical. While high-end fashion stores thrive in affluence, discount stores depend on a need to minimize spending. Typically, the former would not be productive in a low- to moderate-income area, while the latter would thrive there. Home improvement stores are more likely to succeed and sales of major appliances and furniture will be higher in areas where home ownership dominates over renting. Stores that sell sporting goods (e.g., skis, golf clubs, and related apparel) do best where the population has ample discretionary (excess) income to support such expensive hobbies.

Income levels of the area population are a very important consideration in planning a tenant mix. In very high income areas, Saks Fifth Avenue, Gucci, and similar shops will do well. In moderate income areas, Macy's and Target are more likely tenants. This does not mean that one tenant is better than another, only that shopping center tenants must serve the trade area if the shopping center is to be successful.

The source of income is also a consideration. To know that a family's income is $65,000 is not enough; how that money is earned becomes a determining factor because blue-collar and white-color workers generally spend their money in different ways. Also key is the amount of disposable income they have. Homeowners have different types of expenses than do apartment renters. People who are in debt often have little money available for niceties (e.g., dining out) after they have paid for the necessities.

Psychographic Factors. Psychographics goes beyond demographics and considers how the population in the trade area lives and spends its money. For example, for young married couples with both the husband and wife working outside the home, price is often a primary consideration. The young upwardly mobile population is accumulating goods but must keep an eye on the family budget. They are also very interested in personal services—they have little time to do things for themselves because they spend so much of their time working. Value-oriented retailers are likely to serve this population.

Tenant mix must also be sensitive to ethnic considerations. In Southern California, for example, a significant portion of the population is Hispanic. The retailer that ignores this fact will miss one-fourth of the potential market for its store. Supermarkets are one type of retailer that evaluates the ethnic composition of an area and then carries specialty foods to serve those segments of the market. Many areas of the United States have diverse ethnic populations, and the shopping center manager should carefully consider the impact of ethnicity on people's wants and needs when planning the tenant and merchandise mix for a shopping center. Retailers (and shopping center managers) may need to hire personnel with language skills that will facilitate accommodation of ethnic diversity—both within the trade area and among visitors to the trade area.

Competition. Once the shopping center manager understands the population in the trade area, he or she must evaluate the competition in the area. The shopping center manager must determine what merchants are already in the area and whether the trade area has sufficient capacity to support additional square footage of the type proposed.

Area Merchants. In particular, the shopping center manager needs to know which merchants are already in the trade area and which of them are especially successful—or unsuccessful—and why. A merchant who is doing poorly may have poor business skills in general or poor retailing skills in particular. That merchant may not be one the shopping center manager would want in the shopping center. However, if a merchant is not doing well in a competing shopping center due to a poor location, that merchant may be successful in another shopping center and may even enhance the shopping center's tenant mix.

Also to be considered are the goods and services that could do well in the trade area but are not there. Often the trade area population changes over time but the merchants do not, and that creates opportunities for the shopping center manager to change or broaden the tenant mix.

Market Factors. The shopping center manager must determine whether the trade area can support additional GLA for specific use. To do that, he or she must first determine the consumer buying power in the area.

Information about *consumer buying power*—how much is spent per capita on specific types of merchandise—is available from many sources. Various government agencies (e.g., the U.S. Department of Commerce, the Bureau of the Census) and numerous private commercial marketing research firms (see appendix D, References and Resources) compile such statistical data for defined geographic areas. The *Sales and Marketing Management's Annual Survey of Buying Power* details how people in every major metropolitan area of the United States spend their money. The *Dollars & Cents of Shopping Centers* includes information on each type of retailer's sales in dollars per square foot. Once the buying power of a given area is established and the sales volumes of specific types of retail tenants are known, an estimate can be made of the square footage of each type of store space that the trade area can support.

As an example, a shopping center manager who is interested in leasing to a drugstore tenant might make the following step-by-step analysis:

> A Retail Trade Potential Report for 2002 indicates that drugstore sales in the shopping center manager's city were $151,747,761. The city population is 223,805, so each consumer in the city spends an average of $678 per year on drugstore items. Analysis of the shopping center's trade area reveals a population of 63,200. Multiplying the population count by the average per capita purchases, potential drugstore sales in the trade area amount to $42,849,600. According to the *Dollars & Cents of Shopping Centers: 2002,* drugstore sales average $381 per square foot per year. Based on these figures, the shopping center manager calculates that the trade area will support approximately 112,500 square feet of drugstore space. If the area already has 84,600 square feet of drugstore space occupied, room is left for approximately 27,900 more. (See the example calculations in exhibit 8.1) If the amount of drugstore space adjacent to the trade area is known to be 40,000 square feet, the impact of that amount of space on the potential expansion in the shopping center manager's county will have to be evaluated. Sales leaving a trade area is known as *leakage.*

Many factors affect the potential for additional drugstore space. If the current drugstores are doing well, strong customer loyalty to them could make it difficult for a new drugstore to enter the market. On the other hand, some of the existing drugstores may be operated very poorly, and that could be an open invitation for a good drugstore operation to enter the market and succeed.

This type of analysis generally can be done for every category of merchandise found in a shopping center. However, there may be exceptions that cannot be analyzed because an item or a potential retail operation cannot be adequately categorized. As an example, per capita spending on hobbies and hobby store sales figures may be available, but these are very broad classifications and a shop specializing in a very narrow hobby (e.g., military models and supplies) may defy adequate analysis for a firm decision.

Managers of regional and super regional malls use this method to determine market support for specific stores, and the results can be very accurate because these shopping centers draw customers from a large trade area population and have predictable market support. For other shopping centers, pinpointing specific tenant types and square footages that can be supported as center size diminishes is increasingly difficult, but the exercise is still worthwhile.

Exhibit 8.1
Buying Power, Store Sales, and Store Size

Given the following information
Drugstore sales in city = $151,747,761
City population = $223,805
Trade area population = $63,200
Drugstores in trade area = $84,600
Average drugstores sales in city = $381 per square foot per year

Calculate per capita purchases

Drugstore sales per year divided by city population = per capita drugstore purchases (per year)

$151,747,761 divided by 223,805 = $678 per person

Calculate potential sales volume

Per capita drugstore purchases times the trade area population = potential drugstore sales volume in trade area per year

$678 × 63,200 = $42,849,600

Calculate square footage of drugstore potential

Potential drugstore sales volume divided by average drugstore sales = potential square footage of drugstore space city will support

$42,849,600 divided by $381 = 112,466 square feet of drugstore space

There is currently 84,600 square feet of drugstore space in the city

112,466 square feet minus 84,600 square feet = 27,800 square feet

There is the potential for an additional 27,800 square feet of drugstore space in the city based on the existing information.

Matching Merchants and Store Spaces

During the development of a new shopping center, consideration of the specific tenant mix precedes construction of the store spaces. The sizes of the spaces to be built and the placement of the retailers in relation to each other in the shopping center are the next issues to resolve.

In an existing shopping center, finding the right use for a particular space and the best merchant to operate within it is essential. The size and configuration of the store space are important considerations. Also important is its location—in the shopping center itself and in relation to other tenants.

A 2,000-square-foot store may be ample for a card or gift store, but it may be too small for a jeans store. A women's shoe store can thrive in less space and will do best if it is near or adjacent to a shop that sells women's apparel or other shoe stores so the customer can comparison shop.

The key objective is to create a synergy among the tenants and to maximize it so the center as a whole generates the type of traffic that benefits most, if not all, of the merchants—i.e., the whole should be greater than the sum of its parts. This often requires the shopping center manager to work with individual merchants to maximize their sales, not only for their own success but also to benefit surrounding merchants and, of course, the shopping center owner. (Working with retailers is discussed in chapter 4, Management Structure, chapter 7, Tenant Relations, and appendix A, Retailing Basics.)

The success of individual tenants is highly desirable from many perspectives. Space in the center can command higher rents if average sales are high—$500 per square foot per year as compared to $250—and successful merchants are candidates for lease renewal and expansion.

Successful tenants are also less likely to be sources of complaints or collection problems. Most shopping center leases include provisions for payment of percentage rent, also known as overage rent, and high sales levels increase the opportunities for collecting percentage rent.

Last but not least, the more traffic and sales that are generated by one store in a shopping center, the greater the likelihood that other stores will benefit from its traffic draw and the potential for cross-shopping activities.

Store Size. Many older shopping centers were built with large store sizes, and that can create a number of leasing problems. As the size (area) of a store increases, it is natural for it to be deeper, and the added depth makes the store more difficult to merchandise. As the store size increases, the number of prospective tenants for a particular space diminishes. Few retailers need (or lease) very large spaces. Smaller spaces command higher rents per square foot, and more prospective tenants generally look for them. The ratio of store frontage to store depth should be approximately 1:3 or 1:4—i.e., one foot of frontage to, at most, three or four feet of depth. Representative store sizes are 15 × 60 (900 square feet), 20 × 80 (1,600 square feet), etc.

Data published in the *Dollars & Cents of Shopping Centers* indicate the ranges of store sizes leased by specific types of merchants in different shopping centers. Indications in recent editions of *Dollars & Cents of Shopping Centers* are that many types of stores are downsizing. With the exceptions of big box category killers (who are known to specialize in and dominate a product line) and discount-type operators, merchants have realized that they do not have to lease very large stores with big storerooms to be successful. Wise merchants lease as small a store as is practical to enhance their likelihood of success. They can later bring in additional merchandise as needed from a much less expensive warehouse location. (Store sizes and related problems are discussed in chapter 2, Development and Rehabilitation of Retail Properties.)

Tenant Placement. In regional and super regional malls, two schools of thought on tenant placement have traditionally existed. The first is to group or cluster similar types of merchandise together to foster cross-shopping activities. The shopper finds dress shops together, shoe stores together, etc. The second school of thought, and the one most popular in the early 1990s, is to spread out the different retailers so the shopper would be exposed to many types of merchandise during a stroll through the shopping center. The early 2000s saw a return to the cluster approach because a large segment of the customer base was concerned with efficient shopping.

The shopping center manager should avoid certain juxtapositions. In particular, a business that generates unpleasant odors (a pet store or a hair salon) should not be adjacent to a food vendor; a noisy business (a video arcade or a music store) should not be next to a quiet one (a bookstore). On the positive side, some scents are very pleasant, and a cookie or a candle store can emit inviting aromas that attract people. To maximize the benefits of such pleasant aromas, these businesses should be placed where their odors will not conflict with each other.

The placement of an individual merchant can be critical to that store's success. Jewelry stores usually seek prominent locations and willingly pay a premium rent to obtain them. Hair salons and other service tenants, on the other hand, normally do not need prime locations; the volume of sales in these types of service businesses generally are not indicative of high rental income for the space. Tenants that are placed between the anchor tenants generally do well because of their exposure to a large volume of traffic.

In some strip shopping centers, certain store spaces do not have front exposure. Businesses in such side locations are not exposed to the traffic generated by an anchor tenant. However, dry cleaners, coin laundries, hair and nail salons, insurance offices, etc., can do well in those spaces. Such *destination services* are specifically sought out by their customers, and heavy pedestrian (or street) traffic is not critical for their success.

An exception to the usual tenant placement rules is the specialty use shopping center in which all tenants are focused on a particular market niche (e.g., an automotive center whose tenants provide a wide range of products and services related to car care).

Controlling the Merchandise Mix

Once the appropriate tenant mix for a shopping center is determined, that plan must be carried out in the actual leasing. The most effective means of controlling the mix of goods and services is the lease document. Of particular importance are use provisions and exclusive use provisions.

Use Provisions. The use provision must be specific as to what the tenant is permitted to sell. An example of such a use provision is "to sell women's shoes and for no other use." Great care should be taken with the wording of the provision. Phraseology such as "and accessories" or "such items as carried in tenant's other locations" allows too much latitude.

An effective use provision allows the tenant to carry the specific merchandise lines necessary to his or her business as an incidental while preventing a broadening of those lines or a total change of merchandise to capitalize on a trend. For example, a restaurant use clause for operation of "a sit-down restaurant" is much too broad. The provision should be more specific: "to operate a sit-down restaurant specializing in Italian foods and selling beer and wine only, and for no other use or purpose." When the use provision is specific, a tenant who wants to change it in the future would have to obtain the landlord's approval. That approval would be subject to consideration and would depend on the other uses in the shopping center at the time and the effect the proposed change by the one tenant might have on the overall tenant mix.

When anchor tenants negotiate their leases, they often seek restrictions on the tenant mix. Sometimes the restrictions are to minimize competition, but they address other concerns as well—e.g., maximizing available parking. Supermarket tenants provide examples of both types of restrictions. To reduce competition, a supermarket lease may prevent the landlord from leasing space to a delicatessen or a liquor store. To protect parking, the same lease might prohibit leasing to a health club or a theater.

Exclusive Use Provisions. Inclusion of an exclusive use provision in the lease is another mechanism prospective tenants seek to use to minimize competition. Landlords should be wary of granting exclusives because they can severely limit future flexibility. If a tenant's use is to operate a shoe store, granting that tenant an exclusive could limit the landlord's ability to lease other spaces if the prospective tenants for them wanted to sell children's shoes or athletic shoes.

To allow an exclusive for a limited time to help a new business get started is reasonable, but that is a rare exception. If an exclusive is granted, the lease should state the conditions under which it applies. An exclusive should be allowed for the initial tenant only and should not be applicable to any assignees or subtenants. It should be in effect only until such time as the tenant's sales reach an agreed level and only so long as the tenant is not in default of the lease. The provision should be worded carefully. The exclusive, as granted, should permit other merchants to carry limited amounts of the protected goods without being in default of the exclusive holder's provision. These issues are addressed more specifically in the discussion of the lease document in chapter 10, Negotiating and Documenting the Lease Terms.

RE-TENANTING A SHOPPING CENTER

One of the most difficult tasks the shopping center manager faces is re-tenanting. If several previously strong tenants have left the shopping center and the center is in significant decline, the best way to turn it around may be to replace some or all of the existing leases as they expire or, if possible, through negotiating a lease buy-out with an existing tenant.

Such change must be approached with caution. In particular, the leases must be carefully controlled. Every new store must enhance the new image of the center, and every reasonable effort must be made to convince the remaining established merchants that they must change their individual images to match that of the renewed center. The services of a retailing consultant can often be helpful.

Sometimes the only incentive for a merchant to make such an image change is a financial one. The landlord may have to convince the merchant that a new image will lead to greater success. The shopping center manager can approach this issue by using demographic and other information the tenant may not have immediately available. Unfortunately, the landlord must sometimes buy out a tenant's existing lease, especially when a store does not fit the new tenant mix. It is always better to have a mutual cancellation or the tenant buy out its lease; however this may not always be possible. (These considerations are presented in more detail in chapter 9, Leasing the Shopping Center.)

Before attempting to re-tenant a shopping center, the shopping center manager must clearly understand why a new tenant mix is necessary and how the existing tenants may or may not fit the intended image. The shopping center manager must also know how flexible the individual tenants may be to remodel or upgrade their store and to bring in merchandise that may be more appropriate for the new tenant mix. All aspects related to the re-tenanting process should be examined before considerable money has been invested.

WATCHING TENANT MIX TRENDS

Shopping center management changes constantly. Whether for establishing a new shopping center or for re-tenanting an existing one, the shopping center manager should keep abreast of trends that indicate changes in what works well in the tenant mix.

The mix of goods and services varies with the type of shopping center, although some types of tenants are found in more than one type of shopping center, and some (e.g., apparel stores and restaurants) are common to all. The *Dollars & Cents of Shopping Centers* provides an analysis of the tenant mixes at all types of shopping centers throughout the United States. The shopping center manager can gain a better understanding of what works in particular shopping centers by studying the analyses of dominant uses and the tabulations of merchandise categories with the highest sales volumes. The specific anchor tenant is another important factor in the analysis because the anchor tenant sets the tone for the whole shopping center in terms of dominant merchandise types, amount of GLA devoted to specific merchandise categories, and pricing.

Dominant Uses

The shopping center manager would do well to study the figures on dominant uses in the *Dollars & Cents of Shopping Centers* reports and to visit other shopping centers to see what works in different situations. By using the figures in the reports as a starting point and then studying the buying habits in a specific market, the shopping center manager can put together an effective tenant mix for a specific location. Summaries of trends in the dominant uses of some types of shopping centers follow. Although each type of shopping center requires special considerations regarding tenant mix, the mix of tenants found in community shopping centers is a good example to use as a starting point in establishing the mix for any shopping center.

Community Shopping Centers. The most common use in community shopping centers as of this writing is restaurants with liquor. In a similar study in 1994, the most common use was women's wear. This change reflects two trends: (1) the working family is eating out more often; and (2) with so many women working outside the home, women's wear has seen fashion tending more toward lifestyle shopping centers and even neighborhood shopping centers for the customers' convenience.

Another interesting trend is in fast food, which previously ranked high as a common use in community shopping centers. While fast food was still doing quite well, the only category to make the top 20 in 2002 was the sandwich shop, which may well have become more popular because many sandwich shops increasingly emphasize healthy foods.

Supermarkets have begun to play a more important role in the community shopping center. In much of the rest of the world, the supermarket is found even in the largest of super regional malls, but in the United States they have traditionally been kept in neighborhood or community shopping centers, as customers generally didn't consider the fashion shopping trip the same as the grocery shopping trip. Recently, having groceries and fashion in the same shopping center fits well with the growing emphasis on the customers' convenience, and that mix is likely to bring customers back for their next trip—regardless of the purpose. Supermarkets have added lines—even drugstores, in an effort to increase profit margins.

The medical/dental use is a newcomer to the shopping center tenant mix; it was not in the top 20 in the earlier report. Shopping centers are excellent locations for medical/dental practices and the exposure to traffic is greater than being located in a medical building. From the shopping center's point of view, they represent a higher rate of rent (even though the lease has no percentage rental clause), and they help the shopping center move toward the goal of offering one-stop service for its customers.

Discount department stores have moved up in the ranks in recent years, which indicates another noteworthy trend in the shopping center tenant mix. Many discount department stores, such as Wal-Mart and Target, preferred to be freestanding in the past, but now they are willing to occupy shopping centers and malls.

Unisex hair salons have replaced women's beauty salons on the top 20 list. Years ago most men would not go to a women's hair salon. Today most beauty salons are unisex, and men and women of all ages frequent them.

Furniture has become much more prominent in the community shopping center tenant mix—probably due to specialty shops, such as mattress shops, leather couch stores, and kitchen furnishings stores. Those stores used to prefer to be freestanding, but over the years they have changed that view and now find the traffic in the shopping center to be worth the higher rents and charges.

Drugstores have seen many changes. More supermarkets are putting in prescription drugs, and more drugstores are looking for freestanding locations rather than locating in shopping centers. The independent drugstore is slowly fading away. As a result, drugstores are getting bigger. They are carrying food items and household items as well as prescription drugs and over-the-counter remedies. A drugstore is unlikely to locate on the same site where a supermarket with a prescription drug operation is located. They often prefer free-standing location because they have drive through windows for picking up prescriptions and have better visibility being adjacent to the street/sidewalk.

Depending on the specific trade area, many other lines of merchandise can be found in a community shopping center. These include liquor and/or wine shops, bicycle shops, optometrists' offices, shoe repairs, pets and pet supplies, computer stores, automotive parts stores, beauty supplies, coin laundries, movie theaters, video rental stores, telephone stores, art galleries, veterinarians, swimming pool supplies, art supplies, athletic goods, electronics stores, etc.

Strip Shopping Centers. The strip shopping center tenant mix is one of a wide variety of tenants such as dry cleaners, video rental, and pizza delivery. One of the focuses of tenanting this center is to secure credit-worthy tenants.

Neighborhood Shopping Centers. The tenant mix at a neighborhood shopping center usually focuses on the population base and the anchor tenant. It is influenced by what is already in the trade area, and it is likely to include numerous services. The tenant mix of a neighborhood shopping

Exhibit 8.2

Highest Volume Tenants in U.S. Community Shopping Centers, 1990 and 2002

1990	$*	2002	$*
Superstore	346.95	Service Station	1,227.80
Telephone store	305.35	Hamburgers	539.16
Supermarket	266.92	Cookie shop	506.91
Jewelry	265.25	Specialty food	499.98
Specialty food	242.45	Aromatherapy store	489.00
Computer/software	233.43	Newspapers/magazines	486.16
Athletic footwear	212.19	Jewelry	452.97
Interior decorator	210.33	Seafood/fish & chips	438.17
Fast food/carry out	200.00	Coffee/tea	430.79
Film processing store	196.08	Steak/roast beef	378.20

*Median sales volume per square foot of gross leasable area (GLA)

Reproduced with permission from Dollars & Cents of Shopping Centers: 1990, 2002 (Washington, D. C. ULI—The Urban Land Institute, 1990, 2002)

center often changes over a period of years as the population in the area around it changes, so the shopping center manager must be up-to-date at all times with the status of the trade area.

Highest Sales Volumes

Like comparing the dominant uses, a comparison of the tenants that have the highest sales volumes can show changes and trends in the tenant mix at the different types of centers. Comparisons of the tenants that had the highest sales volumes in 1990 and in 2002 at community, regional, and neighborhood shopping centers follow. (These comparisons are based on data published in the *Dollars & Cents of Shopping Centers.*)

Community Shopping Centers. In community shopping centers (exhibit 8.2), superstores and supermarkets had among the highest sales volumes per square foot in 1990, but more recently they did not make the list—even though their production increased over that time. The number one producer of high sales volume in recent years is the service station, which was not even on the earlier list. That is most likely the result of the increase in gas prices over the period as well as the decrease in the number of service stations.

The second highest category of sales volumes is hamburgers with median sales of $539.16 per square foot—even though they did not make the top 20 list of most commonly found uses in a community shopping center. Hamburgers are often found freestanding or in the food courts of regional

Exhibit 8.3

Highest Sales Volume Tenants in U.S. Regional Shopping Centers, 1990 and 2002

1990	$*	2002	$*
Cameras	546.58	Jewelry	837.83
Jewelry	452.33	Sunglasses	802.09
Leather Shop	313.75	Computer/software	680.37
Computer/software	302.73	Chicken/turkey	677.09
Film processing store	301.41	Clocks/watches	662.55
Athletic footwear	285.56	Italian fast food	571.30
Telephone store	278.85	Kitchen store	531.76
Tobacco	274.42	Children's shoes	525.45
Candy and nuts	270.74	Luggage and leather	525.16
Fast food/carry out	264.82	Specialty food	517.93

*Median sales volume per square foot of gross leasable areaq (GLA)

Reproduced with permission from Dollars & Cents of Shopping Centers: 1990, 2002 (Washington, D. C. ULI—The Urban Land Institute, 1990, 2002)

and super regional malls and the newer lifestyle and entertainment shopping centers.

Jewelry managed to stay in the top 10 rating for sales per square foot over the years with a very nice increase in production. Aromatherapy stores have become a top producer; they were not on the earlier list.

On the other hand, film processing was previously on the top 10 list but no longer makes the list. That is most likely due to the advent of the digital camera and drugstores, supermarkets, and discount stores having camera departments. Photo processing stores now offer to print digital photos, transfer them to disk, and even e-mail them to the customer's favorite aunt.

Coffee/tea has become one of the top 10 producers. That is most likely due to Starbucks and the designer coffee trend they started. Starbucks is by far the most successful of the coffee chains, but many smaller regional operators do an outstanding job in that area.

On the other hand, computer/software, interior decorating, and athletic footwear were high producers at community shopping centers in the 1990s but not in recent years. That is most likely because those tenants moved to lifestyle shopping centers, regional and super regional malls, and in some, cases, even big box type centers. Those uses are still doing quite well, but they have changed their emphasis on location.

Regional Shopping Centers. A review of regional shopping centers (exhibit 8.3) reveals some changes there as well, but they are less dramatic than those in the community shopping centers.

Exhibit 8.4

Highest Sales Volume Tenants in U.S. Neighborhood Shopping Centers, 1990 and 2002

1990	$*	2002	$*
Superstore	322.75	Service station	1,215.83
Convenience market	302.22	Eyeglasses-optician	494.06
Supermarket	278.48	Coffee/tea	480.89
Meat, poultry, fish	249.08	Hamburgers	468.16
Jewelry	212.29	Women's specialty	448.81
Delicatessen	207.65	Art gallery	435.84
Home accessories	193.70	Jewelry	432.54
Photocopy/fast print	189.68	Drugstore/pharmacy	380.80
Drugs	175.40	Special apparel-unisex	374.82
Super drug	169.44	Women's ready to wear	369.76

*Median sales volume per square foot of gross leasable area (GLA)

Reproduced with permission from Dollars & Cents of Shopping Centers 1990, 2002 (Washington, D. C. ULI—The Urban Land Institute, 1990, 2002)

Cameras were the top producer in sales per square foot in 1990, but jewelry took over that spot in the recent years with an excellent increase in production. With the advent of the digital camera, cameras are more often found in discount stores in big box centers than in regional malls. Computers and computer software are still strong in regional shopping centers and have gained quite well in production. Luggage and leather are still on the top 10 list as they were earlier, and they have shown a good increase in production.

Telephone stores, tobacco stores, and film processing were all in the top 10 in 1990, but they have fallen off the more recent list. Those changes reflect lifestyle and technology changes.

Fast food remains a strong category. Over the years, the reporting has been refined to consider the categories within fast food and make distinctions there. Italian fast food is on the top 10 list, as are chicken and turkey. Candy and nuts are no longer on the list, again reflecting lifestyle changes.

Neighborhood Shopping Centers. Finally, a glance at the high-volume tenants in neighborhood centers (exhibit 8.4) confirms much of what has already been stated. In 1990 three categories of food operation occupied the top three spots on the list of highest sales per square foot: the superstore, the convenience market, and the supermarket. None of them was on the top 10 list for the year 2002. They increased their production over the years, but others increased even faster.

Service stations occupy the first place in high-volume tenants and, as mentioned earlier, that is most likely due to the run-up in gasoline prices. Stores that provide eyewear product and services are the number two producer. As with doctors and dentists, owners of eyewear stores find shopping centers to be a good location because of the amount of traffic they generate.

Probably the most interesting change is that women's specialty and women's ready-to-wear are both on the recent top 10 though earlier they were not even close. The change in women's lifestyles has brought about the need for more convenience, and some of the dress stores are now moving to the neighborhood shopping centers to fill that need. That move is likely to change the overall mix of many small shopping centers because the dress stores will attract shoes, jewelry, accessories, etc.

Anchor Tenants

The tenant mix in a shopping center generally follows the lead of the anchor tenants. If the anchors are value oriented, the pricing in the shops follows the same pattern. For example, if the supermarket in a neighborhood shopping center is a high-end market (such as Whole Foods in the Chicago, Illinois area), the surrounding merchants will most likely be oriented to the higher-end customer. On the other hand if the supermarket is a discount market, the surrounding shops are likely to be more popularly priced to support the customer that is attracted to that type of shop. This holds true for all sizes and types of shopping centers.

Anchor tenants are attracted to a given marketplace by the population, the demographics and psychographics, and the future growth potential. They are sophisticated in their approach to site selection, and they are insistent that their criteria be met.

In the past, developers frequently wanted their centers to be fashion centers, and they tried to attract a high-end, fashion-oriented anchor tenant. Unless the trade area showed a very high income level, no amount of incentives were likely to attract such a tenant if the population did not indicate their success. On the other hand, discount department stores are often attracted to high-end markets because some of their best customers are in the higher income brackets but are interested in saving money on staple items.

The next sections discuss the anchor tenants that tend to locate in certain types of shopping centers and the amount of the GLA allotted to specific merchandise categories in those shopping centers. As previously noted, the anchor tenants have an important impact on the merchandise types and the percentage of the GLA devoted to them.

Community Shopping Centers. The anchor tenant in a community shopping center is usually a junior or discount department store. According to the *Dollars & Cents of Shopping Centers,* 2002, the GLA of community shopping centers was distributed among the various types of tenants as follows: general merchandise 34.2 percent, food 14.7 percent, clothing and accessories (mostly women's apparel) 7.5 percent, food service 6.1 percent, drugstores 6.3 percent, personal services 4.8 percent, and other types of stores less than 3.5 percent each.

Regional and Super Regional Malls. Traditionally, regional and super regional malls have three, four, or more department store anchors. Recently, discount department stores frequently replace full-line department stores in regional malls. Such a change may not change the mix in the entire shopping center, but it surely will make a difference in the tenant mix in that wing.

The tenant mixes in regional and super regional malls are designed not only to meet the needs of the shoppers in their trade areas (i.e., based on the demographic and psychographic profile) but also to provide a reasonably large spectrum of offerings (goods and services) within the designated range.

For example, if the market would support 180,000 square feet of women's wear shops, that amount of GLA will be distributed among a variety of retailers whose merchandise offerings cover a range of prices and styles consistent with the income levels of the population, including a variety of fashion accessories and other related items.

The 2002 edition of the *Dollars & Cents of Shopping Centers* indicated that regional malls had approximately 24.1 percent of their GLA devoted to clothing and accessories, with the remainder of the GLA utilized as follows: general merchandise 23.1 percent, food service 7.4 percent, shoes 7.1 percent, gifts and specialty items 5.3 percent, recreation and community services 4.8 percent, hobby and special interests 5.1 percent, and the remaining tenants occupy less than 4.2 percent each.

Specialty Shopping Centers. Specialty shopping centers have a completely different set of criteria for their tenant mixes, particularly because they may or may not have anchor tenants and they have different subsets. Specialty shopping centers that are tourist oriented are often dominated by entertainment and food services. They usually have several restaurants. For many, such as those located on or near a waterfront (Ghirardelli Square in San Francisco, Navy Pier in Chicago, or Harbor Place and The Gallery in Baltimore, Maryland), the location is part of their overall attraction. For others, the location may be the inspiration for an architectural theme based on the prior use of the site (Trolley Square in Salt Lake City, Utah).

Internally, the restaurants themselves are often the attraction. They draw local people to the center—primarily to eat and secondarily to shop. The tenants in specialty shopping centers often have unique offerings of an exclusive type of merchandise, e.g., teddy bears, music boxes, handblown glass, holiday decorations, left-handed implements, make-your-own wine and beer, movie memorabilia. The shopping center management may try to balance the merchandise mix so it will appeal to local shoppers as well as tourists by including traditional shops and merchandise, but that usually proves to be difficult.

AVOIDING PROBLEMS

While the emphasis throughout this chapter has been on the *do's* of creating a tenant mix, a discussion of a few of the *don'ts* is also appropriate.

The desirability of particular types of tenants and the acquisition of the perfect tenant for a specific space are often wonderful intellectual exercises. However, in the real world, the shopping center manager often has to contend with the owner's objectives or desires, one or more vacant spaces, regular mortgage payments that must be made, and the only prospect for a particular space may be somewhat less than perfect. At times the shopping center manager may be able to hold out for the perfect tenant. However, sometimes that cannot be done. In fact, in times of declining economic conditions, waiting at all may be imprudent. In such cases, the shopping center manager must strive to ensure that the prospective tenant will not be harmful to the tenant mix or to shoppers' perceptions of the shopping center. The prudent shopping center manager will write a lease for a less desirable tenant for the shortest term possible so the tenant mix can be improved as soon as the market will allow.

For example, most managers would not include a dealer in used merchandise (a secondhand store) in a traditional shopping center. The perception of used merchandise is that it is rarely compatible with the typical shopping center mix. Of course there are exceptions—a used bookstore that works well in a traditional center; a used sporting goods store that presents itself just like a traditional sports store (comparable fixtures and merchandising techniques) and provides customer appeal without adversely affecting the other merchants.

Retailers that have poor reputations and poor housekeeping—i.e., those that operate dirty stores or restaurants—will give the shopping center a bad name through guilt by association. Some prospective tenants may prove undesirable once they are evaluated.

Along the same line, the merchant who advertises specials that are not actually specials can affect the reputation of the shopping center as a whole and all the other merchants. The merchant who fails to keep regular store hours in a current location is likely to follow the same pattern in a new one. That unreliable behavior poses a problem for the other merchants in the shopping center because shoppers may come to assume that the merchants are all unreliable, and they will shop elsewhere.

Many factors must be considered when creating the tenant mix for a new shopping center or when re-tenanting an existing shopping center. An evaluation of the population to be served and the competition in the area help the shopping center manager identify the best types of tenants for a particular shopping center. Within the categories of tenants that are desirable, the shopping center manager should approach those that are most likely to lease a space. Marketing the shopping center to acquire the best possible tenants and negotiating satisfactory leases are the subjects of chapter 10, Negotiating and Documenting the Lease Terms.

9

Leasing the Shopping Center

An effective leasing program offers more opportunities to increase the net operating income (NOI) and enhance the value of a property than any other aspect of a shopping center's operations. The leasing plan and the market conditions are two critical factors that affect the property's income stream.

The income stream a property produces, the quality of the tenant mix, and the creditworthiness of the tenants are the typical measures of a property's success. The occupancy of the shopping center, the rental rates, and other charges the tenants pay determine the income.

Reducing the operating expenses of a shopping center will increase its cash flow and enhance its value. However, once a thorough review of the shopping center's operations has been conducted and cost-saving programs have been implemented, few, if any, future opportunities to significantly reduce operating expenses will occur.

On the other hand, an effective program for marketing and leasing the shopping center to prospective tenants offers an endless array of opportunities to enhance the shopping center's income. These opportunities include upgrading retail tenants and the tenant mix; keeping the rental rates at market rates; leasing vacant spaces, dead spaces, and common areas to temporary tenants; finding and leasing storage areas; increasing the opportunities for collecting percentage rents; and negotiating lease buyouts and store splits. The best opportunity to enhance a property's income and value is by maximizing its occupancy, and a good marketing and leasing program does that.

This chapter discusses the components of a successful leasing program as well as the leasing team and its responsibilities.

COMPONENTS OF A SUCCESSFUL LEASING PROGRAM

A successful leasing program for a shopping center has several key components, some of which are unique to shopping centers and other retail properties. When a shopping center's program lacks one of these components, the leasing effort can be difficult; when two or more components are missing, leasing the shopping center will be very challenging.

The first component is the location. Whether it is a shopping center, an industrial building, an office, or a medical building, the location sets a building apart from most or all of its competition. One of the primary criteria in a tenant's selection of a shopping center is its location. A great location may overcome other deficiencies in a shopping center or a leasing plan, but a poor location is a difficult, if not impossible, factor for most retailers to overcome and be successful.

A second component is the shopping center's designs and features. Not all shopping centers are created equal. Tenants look for a shopping center that has specific designs and features that will meet their needs and (for some tenants) the needs of their customers. Chapter 2, Development and Rehabilitation of Retail Properties, discusses shopping center planning and design.

Market conditions are the third component. Property owners, property managers, and leasing agents respond to current as well as anticipated market conditions. Market conditions impact the leasing effort in several ways: (1) they contribute to the negotiating strengths or weaknesses of the property owner or the tenants; (2) they provide the landlord direction as to which categories of tenants and which specific tenants to seek; (3) they are a major factor in establishing rental rates and possible concessions; and (4) they are one of the factors used to establish the criteria to evaluate prospects.

A fourth component is the property owner's understanding of the market conditions. Property owners can make or break a leasing deal, so the shopping center manager or leasing agent must present the most current market conditions to the property owner. When property owners understand the market conditions and their shopping center's position in the market, they are more likely to feel comfortable making new deals. Regular communication with the property owner affords the shopping center manager and the leasing agent opportunities to discuss market conditions, apprise the property owner of leasing deals that are occurring in the market, and present the shopping center's position in the market. Periodic market surveys and articles on market conditions are effective tools the shopping center manager and the leasing agent can use to keep the property owner current on market conditions.

A fifth component is the development and implementation of a marketing and leasing plan that is tailored to the shopping center's unique characteristics and that represents the goals and objectives of the ownership. This plan must be designed specifically for the particular shopping center.

A sixth component involves the tenant mix.[1] As discussed in chapter 8, Creating the Tenant Mix, shopping centers are the only property type in which the tenant mix can impact the business of each tenant. The most important tenants of large shopping malls and strip shopping centers are the anchor tenants. Malls and strip shopping centers that have anchor stores that best meet the demands of their trade areas will draw tenants that want to locate near these anchors. Many retailers have specific criteria as to the cotenancies they want in a shopping center. A poor tenant mix will attract second-tier tenants and, most likely, the wrong mix of products and services for the trade area.

A final critical component is the selection of the right leasing team members. Each member of the leasing team must possess shopping center experience as well as expertise in the type of shopping center (e.g., regional mall, grocery anchored strip shopping center, lifestyle shopping center) being leased. Each leasing team member has an important role in one or several of the components of the marketing and leasing plan.

The remainder of this chapter discusses each component of a successful marketing and leasing plan in more detail.

Selecting the right leasing team is one of the property owner's most important decisions. The leasing team must know the property owner's goals and objectives—which can vary from maximizing the cash flow of the shopping center during the next few years to maximizing long-term appreciation of its value. In the latter situation, a property owner is usually willing to provide lease concessions to attract the best merchants and mutually cancel or buy out the leases of poor performers.

The members of the leasing team must understand the trade area of the shopping center and the characteristics of its population (demographic and psychographic profiles). The team must analyze the shopping center and compare it to competing shopping centers to determine its relative strengths and weaknesses.

The leasing team must also keep abreast of trends in the retailing community and be aware of which established retailers are expanding or closing stores and which new ones are coming into the area. Such understanding and awareness will maximize the results of the leasing team's efforts and minimize the time required to lease a space.

Finally, each member of the leasing team must understand and appreciate of the roles of the other team members. They must work well together and avoid dissension when differences of opinion arise.

Creating the leasing team, determining to what extent the brokerage

1. Alan Alexander and Richard Muhlebach, *Managing and Leasing Commercial Properties,* 3rd ed., vol. 1, John Wiley and Sons, Inc., 2000.

community will be involved, and specifying how members of the leasing team will be compensated are crucial steps in developing the marketing and leasing program.

Members of the Leasing Team

The members of the leasing team vary, depending on several factors. The most important factors are the amount of space and the type of shopping center to be leased. Some property owners and property management firms employ full-time leasing staffs. Such leasing teams may be responsible for leasing multiple properties (i.e., several different shopping centers); for leasing and re-leasing a single major shopping center (e.g., a regional mall); or for the lease-up of a new, rehabbed, or repositioned shopping center. The leasing team may consist of some or all of the following: the shopping center manager, a leasing agent or agents, an architect for a new or rehabbed shopping center, the marketing and promotions director for large shopping centers and malls, members of the brokerage community, and, of course, the property owner.

Shopping Center Manager. The shopping center manager should always be on the leasing team. He or she may lead the team, supervise the leasing agent (as the property owner's representative), have a dual role as the manager and the leasing agent, or support the team's activities.

In the role of team leader, the shopping center manager is responsible for developing the marketing and leasing program and for selecting and directing each team member. When the shopping center manager serves as the property owner's representative and supervises the leasing agent, the leasing agent reports to the shopping center manager, and the shopping center manager is responsible for negotiating the business terms (and possibly the lease provisions) on behalf of the property owner.

As a support member of the leasing team, the shopping center manager advises the leasing agent and actively analyzes and discusses the merits and operational issues of each proposed lease. The shopping center manager may serve as the leasing agent to implement the plan.

Depending on the amount of space to be leased, the shopping center manager may have direct responsibility for leasing some or all of the vacancies. When only a few vacancies exist, the shopping center manager may be able to lease them more effectively than a leasing agent. The shopping center manager can take the time to lease those few spaces while the leasing agent devotes time and energy to properties with numerous vacancies and, therefore, greater commission opportunities.

Leasing Agent. If the shopping center has several vacancies, the shopping center manager is not likely to have sufficient time to prospect for tenants while also fulfilling management responsibilities. In that case, it usually is more effective to assign the leasing responsibilities to a *leasing agent* who is a full-time employee of the property management firm, an employee of the property owner, or an affiliate of a brokerage firm that specializes in the particular type of shopping center.

Some shopping center developers and real estate investment trusts (REIT) have in-house leasing agents. These shopping center owners have large portfolios of shopping centers and/or one or more large malls. A REIT that has several grocery anchored shopping centers in an area usually employs a leasing agent who focuses on leasing those shopping centers. In-house leasing agents usually lease regional malls.

When more than one person is prospecting for tenants, each leasing agent must be assigned specific categories of tenants to pursue. This eliminates duplication of effort or overlooking of prospects—i.e., the same prospects will not be contacted several times and others not at all. For the lease-up of a regional mall, for example, the leasing team may consist of three or four leasing agents. One may be the team captain, but each team member will contact and negotiate leases with specific categories of tenants. The team captain might be assigned food court tenants, if applicable, and other food categories, such as specialty foods and candy stores. Another leasing agent might be responsible for jewelry, gifts, and miscellaneous merchandise categories. The other two might pursue fashion tenants—one assigned to women's wear and accessories and the other to children's and men's clothing and shoe stores. An experienced leasing agent develops working relationships with the real estate representatives of many regional and national retailers.

Marketing Director. The role of the marketing director at malls, lifestyle, outlet, and entertainment shopping centers is essentially advisory. This person is expected to understand the strengths and weaknesses of each tenant and of the shopping center as a whole. The marketing director is expected to be familiar with the competition and to know which tenants are successful and are, therefore, likely prospects for the shopping center or mall. This person should also be active in the retailing community and be aware of new retailers that enter the market.

Brokerage Community. The brokerage community may be involved directly or indirectly. A brokerage firm is often given an exclusive authorization to lease the shopping center. Depending on the amount of space to be leased, one or more leasing agents from the brokerage firm are assigned to lease a particular shopping center, and they report directly to the property owner or the shopping center manager.

Although one brokerage firm may be the exclusive leasing agent, the entire brokerage community should be encouraged to present prospective tenants for the shopping center. The marketing and leasing program should actively work the brokerage community—i.e., all retail leasing agents and their firms should be informed about the shopping center, the space available, and the general parameters of the lease terms. It is a good idea to develop a data bank of the retail leasing agents in the area and their managers and periodically send them e-mail flyers of the vacant or soon-to-be-vacant spaces. Leasing agents from brokerage firms are compensated solely by commissions, so they must also know the commission schedule, the commission split, and how their position in the deal will be protected when they present a prospective tenant.

Property Owner. The final member of the leasing team is the property owner—the person who will ultimately approve or reject each prospective tenant. The property owner must understand the shopping center's position in the market and the market rent for each space. If the property owner has an unrealistic view of the rental value of the spaces, good deals may be rejected, and that can discourage the leasing team and the brokerage community from working the property.

The shopping center manager and the leasing agent are responsible for keeping the property owner informed of the market conditions, rental rates in the area, and market rates for the shopping center. The property owner's understanding of the market will be reflected in his or her ability and willingness to expedite the approval of a proposed lease. Every day that a prospective tenant waits for a lease approval is an opportunity for that prospect to have a change of mind and withdraw the offer. A popular saying among leasing agents is, "Time kills deals."

Leasing Commissions

Leasing agents from brokerage firms receive no salary; they are paid only when a lease is executed, and their compensation is a commission. Though shopping center managers receive a salary, commissions can be a significant source of income for them as well. Leasing agents who are employees of the property owner usually receive a salary; however, the greater part of their compensation may be commissions. Because commissions are the driving force behind all leasing activities, the commission structure should provide more than sufficient incentive for the leasing agent or the shopping center manager who has a leasing responsibility. Commissions are a small price for the property owner to pay for a properly leased shopping center.

Commission rates are always negotiable; no standard commission exists. Commissions are based on a multitude of factors—the difficulty of the assignment, the value of the income stream to the landlord, the size of each space, the amount of space to lease, the brokerage firm's or shopping center management company's cost to do business, how important the leasing

Exhibit 9.1

Commissions Based on a Percentage of the Rent

A commission will be earned for all executed leases based on 6% of the base rent for the first 5 years, 3% for the next 5 years, and no commission for any term beyond 10 years.

Store Size: 1,200 sq ft
Term: 7 years
Rent: $15 for 2 yrs; $16 for 3 yrs; $17 for 2 yrs

Year	Sq. Ft. × Rate	Rent	Commission Percentage Rate	Commission
1	1,200 × $15	$18,000	6%	$1,080
2	1,200 × $15	$18,000	6%	$1,080
3	1,200 × $16	$19,200	6%	$1,152
4	1,200 × $16	$19,200	6%	$1,152
5	1,200 × $16	$19,200	6%	$1,152
6	1,200 × $17	$20,400	3%	$ 612
7	1,200 × $17	$20,400	3%	$ 612
			Total Commission	$6,840

assignment is to them, and what the property owner is willing to offer. Commissions are usually calculated either as a percentage of the income during all or part of the lease term or as a rate-per-square-foot dollar amount.

Percentage of Income. Commissions based on the income may be a percentage of the gross income (i.e., base rent and pass-through charges), or a percentage of base rent only. Once the income basis is agreed, the percentage rate must be determined. The rate may be a fixed percentage that is applied to the income for the entire lease or for only a portion of the lease term. In other words, a 6-percent commission may apply to all 20 years of a lease or, say, only the first 10. Alternatively, the percentage rate may decline over the life of the lease: A 10-year lease may be commissioned at 7 percent of the first year's income, 6 percent the second year, 5 percent the third year, 4 percent the fourth year, 3 percent the fifth year, and 2 percent for each of the remaining 5 years. A common approach is a flat rate, say 5 percent, for the first 5 years of the lease and 3 percent for the remaining term of the lease, not to exceed 5 years. Another approach to a declining percentage commission is shown in exhibit 9.1.

Rate Per Square Foot. The other method of calculating commissions is based on a rate per square foot. The commission schedule may be $4 or more per square foot for all leases in excess of three years (exhibit 9.2), with the rate prorated for a lease term of less than three years. Some property

Exhibit 9.2

Commissions Based on a Rate Per Square Foot

A commission will be earned for all executed leases based on $4.00 per square foot for all lease terms 3 years or longer. How much commission would be earned on a 1,850 square foot space leased at $17.25 per square foot for 3 years?

Term:	3 years
Store Size:	1,850 sq ft
Commission Rate:	$4.00/sq ft
Commission Amount:	$7,400 (1,850 sq ft x $4)

owners prefer to use a rate per square foot because they prefer shorter lease terms, and they believe the leasing agent may encourage a longer lease term if the commission is based on a percentage of the rent received over the entire term of the lease.

Additional Incentives. An additional commission may be offered as an incentive for leasing a problem shopping center, to encourage extra effort on the part of the leasing agent, to get the attention of the brokerage community, or to achieve a specific leasing goal. Because a leasing agent may not negotiate the best terms if the incentive is based on just one factor (e.g., percentage of space leased within a specific period), the incentive may be based on multiple factors. The additional incentive might be stated: "An additional incentive for the shopping center's leasing agent of $1.00 per square foot of leased space will be paid if 30,000 square feet are leased within nine months at an average effective rate of $20 per square foot per year." An incentive for the brokerage community might be 150% of the commission offered to lease any space or a specific space.

Commission Payment Schedule. After the commission rate is negotiated, the commission payment schedule must be negotiated. The size of the payments and their timing can vary substantially. Half the commission may be paid when the lease is executed and half when the tenant opens for business or when the tenant opens for business and minimum rent commences. Alternatively, commissions may be paid over the term of the lease—if the commission rate is 5 percent of the collected income, 5 percent of the rent collected is paid each month during the term of the lease. Multiple payments help the property owner regulate cash flow. Sometimes the property owner or the leasing agent will negotiate an early payoff of the commission based on discounting the total commission earned.

Lease Renewals. A commission may also be negotiated for lease renewals. These, too, may be approached in several ways—a full commission, a partial (say, one-half) commission on a new lease, a percentage of the increased rent, or a fixed fee. Because commissions are an important incentive to those who do the leasing, the commission schedule should be commensurate with the assignment and the competition in the market.

LEASING TEAM RESPONSIBILITIES

The leasing team has many responsibilities, including meetings and reports; analyzing the trade area, the competition, and the shopping center; determining rental rates; prospecting for and evaluating tenants; and developing creative leasing solutions for the shopping center and its tenants.

Leasing Meetings and Reports

Leasing meetings are held to report on the status of each prospective tenant, identify new prospects to be contacted, and review the ongoing publicity and advertising campaigns. At each leasing meeting, the leasing agent or the captain of the leasing team submits a report that tabulates the status of the leasing activity with specific prospects (exhibit 9.3). Leasing reports are necessary to track the progress of the marketing and leasing program. Regular leasing meetings and reports can accomplish several objectives:

1. Inform the property owner about the leasing team's activities.
2. Make the property owner aware of changes in rental rates in the market.
3. Allow the property owner and members of the leasing team to adjust rental rates and make concessions to reflect changes in the market.
4. Review marketing and leasing progress since the previous leasing meeting.
5. Review prospects listed in the leasing report.
6. Review proposals and counterproposals (negotiations).

Leasing meetings are usually scheduled every two to four weeks. If meetings are held too frequently, they take up time that can be better used pursuing prospective tenants. Less frequent meetings can lead to communication breakdowns. Whether the leasing agents are diligently pursuing the marketing plan and actively prospecting for tenants should be readily apparent at these meetings.

Ideally, the property owner should attend each meeting. When the owner's attendance at leasing meetings is unlikely, leasing conference calls can be arranged. This is appropriate in the case of an absentee property owner or when an asset manager who visits the shopping center infrequently represents the property owner. The shopping center manager

Exhibit 9.3

Example Leasing Prospects Report Form

Project Name ________________ Date Prepared ________

Month ________________ Prepared by ________

Space No.	Usable Sq Ft	Date Shown Space	Prospective Tenant (Co.)	Type of Business	Name of Contact	Current Location	Phone No.	E-Mail Address	Term Yrs	Rent Quoted	TI Allowance (est)	Broker Comm	Status/Remarks

Status Legend
6 = Lease completed
5 = Lease out for signatures
4 = Lease under negotiation
3 = General terms discussion
2 = Preliminary project talks
1 = Problem in talks
0 = Dead deal

Source Legend
(How prospect found out about building)
A = Drive-by
B = Newspaper advertising
C = Cold call by property staff
D = Direct mailing
E = Broker
F = Other

Reprinted with permission from Alexander, Alan A., and Muhlebach, Richard F.: *Managing and Leasing Commercial Properties* (New York: John Wiley & Sons, Inc., 2000).

should include a thorough leasing report in the monthly management report to ensure that the property owner is appropriately informed.

The activity of the leasing team should be monitored not only to measure its success but also to determine when changes are necessary. Leasing the shopping center as quickly as possible on the most favorable rental terms to the best tenants should be the common goal of every member of the team.

However, leasing agents from brokerage firms that are leasing several shopping centers commonly devote more time to the properties with the most numerous or most lucrative opportunities to make deals. Because they are paid only when a lease is executed, leasing agents must constantly seek opportunities to make deals happen. They often try to maintain a listing even after the leasing slows at a particular location because they do not want to give up or because they will earn at least a partial commission if a leasing agent from another firm presents a prospective tenant.

When the leasing agents have exhausted all their contacts and leasing activity slows, the shopping center manager should suggest to the property owner that another firm be given the leasing responsibility. Even in the absence of any suggestion of change, the property owner will soon detect the lack of activity, terminate the leasing agreement, and hire another leasing agent.

Analyzing the Trade Area

Members of the leasing team must be aware of prospective tenants' concerns. The primary concerns of a prospective tenant are (1) whether his or her customer base is represented in the shopping center's trade area and (2) whether the location will assist in attracting those customers. Those concerns must be addressed before the prospect will be willing to make a deal and lease a space in the shopping center.

When opening a store in a shopping center, a retailer must be confident that the demographic and psychographic profile of the trade area is representative of its typical customer and that consumers will patronize the new store in sufficient numbers for it to be successful. Department stores, supermarkets, super drugstores, box stores and other potential anchor tenants conduct extensive surveys of an area before they commit millions of dollars to a location. National retailers that lease shop spaces also survey a market before penetrating it. However, local retailers usually do not conduct sophisticated surveys but rely on basic demographic and psychographic information provided by the leasing agent.

The leasing agent must understand the shopping center's trade area before approaching prospective tenants. Understanding the trade area enables the leasing agent to identify retailers that are likely candidates for the shopping center and to contact only those that have a high probability of leasing space in the shopping center and being successful there. The knowledgeable leasing agent does not waste time pursuing a prospect whose customer base is not represented in the shopping center's trade area or whose store in the shopping center would be likely to fail.

Defining the Trade Area. To understand the shopping center's trade area, the leasing agent must determine its boundaries and analyze the characteristics of the population and the competition within the area. This information is used to determine which categories of merchants are over- and under-represented in the trade area. It also assists in positioning the shopping center in the marketplace. From this information base, the leasing agent can determine a tenant mix, solicit categories of retailers, and identify specific prospective tenants.

A shopping center's *trade area* is the geographic area in which most of its customers live, work, commute, or play. The customers for a video rental store live in the immediate neighborhood. The trade area of a delicatessen in a downtown office building may be within a radius of a few blocks because its primary customers work there and walk to the deli during lunch and after work. The customers of an ice cream store in a specialty shopping center or in a resort community are tourists and visitors to the area. The majority of the customers in the trade area of a typical suburban shopping center live in that area.

A rule of thumb for determining the trade area is to draw a circle around the shopping center. The radius of the circle for a neighborhood shopping center is typically 2 to 5 miles, while the radius for a regional mall in an urban area is typically 8 to 10 miles. This is only a guideline, however; the actual boundaries of the trade area for a particular shopping center must be determined from a specific investigation, and they are not shaped like a circle.

Barriers. Natural and manmade barriers that may prevent, hinder, discourage, or delay a person from traveling to the shopping center define the boundaries of a trade area. An example of a *natural barrier* is a river that can only be crossed at a bridge several miles from the shopping center. That distant crossing may discourage people on the other side of the river from patronizing most grocery anchored strip shopping centers, but it may not be a barrier for a regional mall or for a lifestyle, outlet, or power shopping center. *Manmade barriers,* on the other hand, may be more difficult to pinpoint—for example, a change of property types. A large industrial development two miles from the shopping center may be a detriment because consumers living on the other side of the industrial park may not want to drive through a busy industrial area to get to a shopping center.

The primary barrier that defines a trade area, however, is the location of the competition. If two shopping centers that have similar anchor and shop tenants are located four miles apart, one boundary of their respective trade areas will be approximately midway between the two shopping centers. A neighborhood shopping center anchored by a supermarket and a drugstore in a heavily populated suburb may have a trade area of 2 to 3 miles in all directions. The trade area for a similar shopping center in a small rural community may extend 10 to 20 miles. The trade area for a regional mall in Orange County, California, may extend less than 5 miles in some directions because of overlapping trade areas due to the proliferation of malls in the county. A regional mall in a rural location in the Midwest may have a trade area that extends more than 100 miles.

Multiple Trade Areas. A shopping center may have different trade areas, especially if it has different types of anchors. A supermarket that has multiple competitors in the area may draw customers from an area within only a few miles of the shopping center. The trade area of a home improvement center that has fewer competitors may extend several miles from the same shopping center. Small shop tenants will have different trade areas, too. A dry cleaner's trade area may extend 3 miles, while the trade area for a sporting goods store may have a radius of 10 miles.

The trade area can also be defined by the drive time to the shopping center. As mentioned in other chapters, the trade area of a shopping center can be divided into three zones. The primary zone accounts for 70 to 75 percent of the center's sales, the secondary zone for 20 to 25 percent; the tertiary zone, which is the most difficult to define, accounts for the remaining sales.

Creating a Demographic Profile. A demographic analysis of the primary, secondary, and tertiary trade area zones usually includes the following data:

- *Population size* and a projection of future growth or decline. Changes over the preceding 20 years may indicate future trends that need to be studied.
- *Family or household composition* including its size and the ages of its members. The racial and ethnic composition of the area are also included.
- *Home ownership* as compared to rental housing. The number of owners versus the number of renters is an important consideration for many retailers, especially those that deal in furniture and housewares (e.g., carpets and draperies). The cost of housing may be an indicator of relative affluence and the availability of disposable income.
- *Household income* is a critical consideration because most retailers market to a specific income level. Household income is the primary indicator of disposable income.

- *Employment data,* including types of employment and specific employers. Buying habits can be related to type of employment, which is also related to income. The primary source of employment and the kinds of jobs available are important, as is dominance by a single company or a single industry.
- *Education* is a factor in purchasing decisions, such as preferences in reading materials, restaurant choices, and food purchases. Psychographic information describes people's shopping preferences. People can have the same or very similar demographics but shop at different stores in the same neighborhood. For instance a high school teacher who has a graduate degree is likely to have different interests and shopping preferences than a neighbor who is a blue-collar worker and did not attend college. These two individuals may have similar incomes and the same family makeup, but they may have different interests in reading materials, entertainment, specialty foods, etc.

Specific demographic and psychographic information for very small geographic areas can be obtained from commercial sources (see appendix D, References and Resources). The data on population size, income, etc., may support a particular size or type of shopping center, but the numbers mean nothing if most of the potential customers will not shop at the new shopping center because of its location, design, layout, or tenant mix. Chapter 3, Management Plan and Operations Manual, discusses trade area analysis in relationship to the management plan. Chapter 8, Creating the Tenant Mix reviews trade area analysis from the perspective of creating the most suitable tenant mix.

Analyzing the Competition

An analysis of the competition can provide additional direction to the leasing plan. First the design, layout, and size of competing shopping centers can be indicators of which shopping centers can accommodate expansion and possibly an additional pad, anchor tenant, or shop tenant. By visiting and touring the competition, the shopping center manager or leasing agent will know which shopping centers have design problems, such as poor visibility, spaces that are too large or too deep, or inadequate parking. This analysis will provide insight into which shopping centers would meet the location, tenant mix, co-tenancy, and space requirements of specific national and regional shop tenants.

Often the most important analysis is of the competitions' tenant mix. Who are the anchor and shop tenants? This analysis indicates several important issues, including which tenants are represented in the market and whether they want to increase their market share by opening a store at the subject shopping center. By reviewing the tenants in all of the competitions' other locations, the leasing agent can discover which uses are over-, under-, or not represented in the trade area. This provides invaluable information as to which uses and which prospective tenants the leasing agent should aggressively seek and which to avoid contacting. This allows the leasing agent to market the shopping center efficiently using a targeted, well thought-out approach in which contacts are made with the prospects that are most likely to lease space rather than losing valuable time by approaching every possible business.

After getting to know the competition, the leasing agent or the shopping center manager should develop a list of the vacancies in each of the competition's shopping centers. This information tells the leasing agent which shopping centers have space available that will be in direct competition for specific prospects. The information is needed to determine the relative negotiating strengths and weaknesses of the landlord and each prospect. Of course, the rental information on the competition's vacant spaces and their sizes, configurations, and locations within each shopping center is important in determining the market rental rates for each vacancy at the subject property.

Analyzing the Shopping Center

Understanding the strengths and weaknesses of the shopping center is critical to the development and successful execution of the marketing and leasing plan. The shopping center manager and the leasing agent must know how the shopping center measures up to its competition. They must also understand which features of the shopping center meet the needs of prospective tenants, which areas are deficient, and which of those deficiencies can be corrected. The analysis should include a review of the location and design of the shopping center, traffic counts, an assessment of the desirability of each space, the tenant mix, the tenants' sales, and lease renewals. This analysis is necessary to sell the advantages of the shopping center to prospects.

Location and Design. A well-known axiom is that the three most important things in real estate are location, location, and location. This applies directly to the success of shopping centers and retail properties. A good shopping center location has several key components—demographic and psychographic profiles, which have been discussed, and visibility, and accessibility. Visibility and accessibility are design criteria.

Accessibility: Traffic Counts. Traffic counts are a measure of the viability of a location; they are a factor that permits the comparison of shopping centers. They are also related to visibility and access.

Traffic counts are estimated in two ways: (1) from the number of vehicles that drive by the shopping center and (2) from the number of people who visit the shopping center. Strip shopping centers usually rely primarily on the number of vehicles that pass the shopping center each day. Comparison figures should be available from a local governmental agency. Most municipalities regularly count traffic on their main thoroughfares. At some shopping centers, the number of vehicles entering the parking lot is counted each day. If the average number of people in a vehicle entering the parking lot is known, the number of people visiting the shopping center each day, each week, and each month can be calculated. When the numbers of vehicles passing by the shopping center and its competition are known, the shopping center can be compared to the competition.

Another variable related to traffic is ease of entry into the parking lot. If traffic is passing at high speed or if left turns are not allowed, entering the parking lot from that street or expressway may not be convenient.

Visibility. Layout and design for visibility are considered next. In a strip shopping center, visibility from the street, from cars in the parking lot, and to pedestrians walking the property is critical. A high traffic count may be meaningless if the stores are not visible from the street. When a shopping center is built on sloping land, the parking lot may be on higher ground than the buildings in the back. If the buildings are set back several feet below street level, they may not be visible from the street. Visibility is also restricted when a shopping center is built perpendicular to the street. The ideal layout for a strip shopping center is to have all of the stores facing the street. The layout and design of the shopping center must not impede the visibility of or access to the tenants' spaces.

Enclosed shopping centers are usually adjacent to or near an expressway for easy access and as a constant reminder of the shopping center to the people who pass on the expressway. Proximity to an expressway may expand the trade area of the shopping center.

Visibility within an enclosed mall is related to the mall walkways or corridors and any setbacks or obstacles that are present. Temporary or permanent retail merchandising units (RMUs), carts or kiosks, oversized mall furniture, landscaping elements, and mall directories can reduce visibility of the individual shop spaces.

Signage is an important part of visibility. The shopping center's sign criteria must provide for tenants to display signs that are easily seen from both the parking lot and the street in strip shopping centers or from the walkway in a mall. The shopping center itself should have an identification sign that is easy to read and that creates an image for the whole.

Desirability of Store Spaces. Just as the shopping center itself is evaluated, all store spaces, especially those that are vacant, should be evaluated for their location. In addition to location, the size, frontage, and depth of each space are evaluated to determine which categories of tenants are probable candidates to lease the space.

Store Location. The first consideration with respect to the desirability of a store location is visibility—from the street, from the parking lot, from the mall corridor, from wherever the majority of the shopping center's customers spend most of their time while at the shopping center. The next consideration is the amount of traffic that walks by the space—whether the space is next to an anchor tenant (a major traffic draw) a center court, an end cap space), or in a low traffic area. The third consideration, accessibility, involves the presence of any actual or perceived barriers, e.g., no left turn on the street fronting the shopping center is a classic access barrier.

Store Size. Store size is one of the primary criteria of leasability from a tenant's perspective. Each type of retail business has a size range in which it can operate profitably. In community shopping centers, the coffee and tea shops usually average 1,350 feet of GLA in a range from 799 to 2,070 square feet. The typical card and gift shop may have 4,000 square feet of GLA and range from 1,495 to 9,640 square feet, while the typical barbershop has 790 square feet of GLA and ranges from 480 to 1,274 square feet. The average size of specific uses, provided in the Urban Land Institute's publication, *Dollars & Cents of Shopping Centers,* is the best indicator of which uses are likely candidates for specific spaces. The size of a space indicates which types of tenants can occupy it and which cannot.

Store Frontage. The next consideration is store frontage. Tenants want as much frontage as possible—for visibility. As a rule of thumb, the ratio of the frontage (width) to the depth of the store should be one to three (1:3); a store 20 feet wide should have a depth of 60 feet (20:60 = 1:3). This ratio has been reduced continually since the 1980s, when the ideal store depth was thought to be 80 feet—a ratio of one to four (1:4). The change in the ratio of width to depth over the years has resulted from many categories of retailers downsizing their stores. These merchants discovered that they could generate equivalent or greater levels of sales in smaller-sized stores. Such downsizing results in a lower occupancy cost and a more efficient store operation. Part of the reduction in size comes from the fact that merchants no longer need large storage rooms; most, if not all, of their merchandise is displayed on the sales floor, and computerized control of store inventories allows for frequent deliveries of merchandise as needed.

In downsizing, retailers want the same amount of frontage but less depth. In strip shopping centers, stores that are more than 75 feet deep have a limited number of prospective tenants. The ideal store size in a strip shopping center is 20 to 25 feet wide and 55 to 70 feet deep. Most tenants in those shopping centers occupy less than 2,400 square feet of GLA.

A few categories of stores have increased in size, however, including supermarket and movie rental stores. Any state-of-the-art supermarket today occupies more than 50,000 square feet. Movie rental stores continue to evolve and increase in size—to as large as 7,500 square feet. They have changed from simply providing rentals of movies on video or DVD formats to selling the movies and other electronic games, toys, etc.

Store Configuration. Store configuration is another major consideration for attracting a particular retailer. The ideal shape is a rectangle; other configurations can create problems in store layout and merchandising. In particular, the pie-shaped shops found in the middle of an L-shaped strip shopping center and T and L-shaped stores have limited tenant prospects. Because of their less-desirable configurations, the rent for such spaces is usually discounted. See chapter 2 for an in-depth discussion on store design issues.

When evaluating the size and configuration of store spaces, the shopping center manager should seek opportunities to change undesirable spaces. In particular, larger spaces can be subdivided. For example, a 4,200-square-foot space may be leased more easily if it can be divided into two smaller spaces, an 1,800- and a 2,400-square-foot space. If a fabric store operator in a 10,000-square-foot space wants to downsize to 6,500 square feet, the remainder may be more easily leased as two spaces (one 1,500- and one 2,000-square-foot store) depending on the depth of the space for each.

Tenant Mix. The last item to evaluate is the shopping center's tenant mix. Each shopping center's tenant mix must be analyzed based on how the shopping center serves the community. This analysis indicates the shopping center's weaknesses—which tenants or categories of tenants no longer fit—and which areas or portions of the shopping center are having problems.

Shopping center marketing and leasing is unlike the marketing and leasing of any other type of real estate. The leasing of all other types of real estate is primarily concerned with filling a rent roll. Which space is leased to which particular tenant is of little importance. In a shopping center, however, every tenant has an impact on the tenant mix. Not only the type of merchandise (athletic versus dress shoes) but also its price range (discount or popular price versus designer) will affect the tenant mix. Changing customer preferences in fashion, dining, and entertainment venues as well as changing merchandising techniques affect consumers, merchants, and, ultimately, the shopping center. The shopping center manager and the leasing agent must consider what impact each prospective tenant will have on the other tenants and the tenant mix.

A major concern in leasing to a tenant is whether the community will accept the tenant. In any other type of property, selecting the wrong tenant may result in a defaulted lease and the probability of lost rent and remodeling expenses, but that defaulted lease will not particularly affect any of the other tenants in the building. Community awareness of specific tenant failures in offices, medical buildings, and industrial properties is usually minimal; awareness of residential lease defaults may be nonexistent. However, the failure of a shopping center tenant has broad implications. Loss of a tenant and vacant stores in a shopping center weakens the tenant mix—assuming the store was appropriate to the tenant mix in the first place—because it eliminates a product or service and thus reduces the synergy of the mix. Tenants in adjacent spaces suffer from the loss of the traffic that the former tenant generated. The community has one less choice of merchandise or service.

Of course a tenant may be wrong for a shopping center—even though the business may be successful there. Specifically, a tenant whose merchandise or pricing is inappropriate for the trade area or the specific shopping center can be detrimental to the tenant mix. For these reasons, tenant selection is critical. Chapter 8, Creating the Tenant Mix, discusses this topic in detail, including the importance of a tenant's compatibility with the other tenants and with the shopping center's image.

Analysis of the tenant mix occurs for many reasons. If one or two vacancies exist or a tenant will not be renewing, the shopping center manager or leasing agent must analyze the tenant mix to determine which categories of merchandise or services will strengthen the overall mix. Sometimes the analysis is done to re-tenant or remerchandise the shopping center. That may be necessary due to new competition, new retail concepts, or changes in the demographics and psychographics of the trade area. This often happens when an enclosed mall is de-malled or when a large strip shopping center loses its anchor tenant and the tenant is replaced with a different use.

Tenant Sales. A useful approach to evaluating individual tenants is to analyze their sales per square foot. Each tenant's sales should be compared to the national averages, to the sales levels of other tenants in the same retailing category for the type of center, and to their sales ranking within their chain. A good source for this information is the *Dollars & Cents of Shopping Centers,* which is issued every two years by the Urban Land Institute (ULI). It provides data on sales per square foot for hundreds of categories of tenants that lease space in neighborhood and community shopping centers and in regional and super regional malls as well as data on other specific types of tenant information. Separate reports are included for both the United States and Canada. Other ULI publications that compile data on specialty shopping centers are listed in appendix D, References and Resources. See chapter 8 for more discussion of the comparison of sales volumes.

When each tenant's sales are compared to the national average for the category, sales that are significantly below the national averages may be interpreted in several ways. Too many similar stores may be located in the shopping center—or in the area generally—or a sustained demand for the particular merchandise may not be present. The economy in the area may be weak or the tenant's customer base is not represented in the trade area. Another possibility is that the tenant may not be reporting its sales accurately. However, a reasonable explanation is that the tenant is a poor merchant.

When a shopping center has several tenants in a category, each tenant's sales should be compared to those of similar tenants in the shopping center. From this information, a ranking based on sales per square foot can be developed, and the total sales per square foot for the category can be determined. This is another indicator of which tenants are performing well and which are not. If all the tenants' sales are substantially above the national average, this may indicate the potential for one or more additional tenants in this category. For instance, if sales for the three jewelers in a regional mall range far in excess of the national average per square foot, there is probably sufficient sales potential to support an additional jewelry store. Conversely, if the furniture store sales in a community shopping center are less than the national sales per square foot, the demand for furniture may be limited, the merchandise may be wrong for the market, or the tenant may be a poor merchant. When the sales analysis indicates limited or no demand for specific merchandise or when too many similar stores are located in the shopping center or area, the shopping center manager or leasing agent should not approach retailers in those categories as part of the prospecting.

An analysis of tenants' sales in different portions of the shopping center indicates areas where traffic may be limited, merchants may not be competent in selling their merchandise, or the wrong types of merchants are in place. If a mall has an unanchored wing that receives considerably less traffic than the other areas of the mall, most retail tenants located there will not do well unless they are destination tenants, e.g., formal wear rentals, specialty restaurants, travel agents.

Lease Renewals. The strengths and weaknesses in the tenant mix are important factors when the shopping center manager evaluates lease renewals. Lease renewals should be planned, and to do so, each tenant's lease term must be reviewed in advance.

A plot plan of the shopping center that has a list of each tenant's lease expiration date and options next to the individual space can be a helpful tool. Notes on the plot plan should also indicate those spaces where tenants are not expected to renew, the landlord will not offer a lease renewal, or vacancies exist.

The shopping center manager can approach tenants whose sales are poor can be approached for an early lease termination or buyout, provided their spaces are readily leasable. Certainly, each shop tenant whose lease is expiring within a year should be contacted. (Lease renewals and buyouts are discussed in more detail later in this chapter.)

To further assist in the evaluation, a plot plan that color codes each use can indicate where specific uses are located and possibly clustered and where to best place future tenants. This also highlights the amount of space devoted to each category of merchandise. Another color-coded plan can show each tenant's sales per square foot. This plan indicates the level of sales in specific areas of the shopping center. It is especially helpful for leasing and remerchandising large shopping centers and malls.

Determining Market Rental Rates

Correctly pricing vacancies is a critical component of a successful leasing program. If above-market rents are published, vacant space will not be leased until the market catches up to the asking rates. If space is priced below market, the vacancies will lease, but the below-market rents will negatively impact cash flow and the value of the property. Since retail leases are usually for a term of 3 to 10 years with some tenants' leases running up to 20 years, an error in underpricing space will have a long-term effect on the shopping center's cash flow and value.

Real estate is typically leased at a *market rental rate,* which is the most probable rent a property owner can expect to receive for a vacant space exposed to the open market. Market rent is similar to fair market value. The shopping center manager or leasing agent must determine the range of market rental rates for the shopping center. Once the range of rates is determined, each space is priced based on its location within the shopping center and its size, depth, configuration, and visibility. Other factors to consider are adjacent merchants and design-related features that may enhance or detract from the perceived value of a particular space.

Conducting a Market Survey. The market rental rate range is determined by conducting a market survey to compare the shopping center to its competition. The shopping center manager or leasing agent should visit each competitive shopping center and compile a list of its features. See chapter 8, Creating the Tenant Mix, for a discussion of researching the competition.

Use of a survey form expedites the collection of the necessary comparison data (exhibit 9.4). The form used should provide spaces for information on the size of the shopping center, a list of the anchor tenants, the number of shop spaces, existing vacancies, asking and deal-making rental rates, pass-through charges (e.g., common area maintenance, taxes, insurance), the condition of the shopping center, and its location. The location of each shopping center in the survey should also be indicated on a map of the area and the map should be attached to the survey form. This not only provides a good perspective of the shopping center's location in relationship to its competition but it can also be used in subsequent surveys to locate the competition.

Some data can be gathered easily, merely by observation. The person conducting the survey should drive through the shopping center's trade area

Exhibit 9.4

Example Shopping Center Survey Form

	Center Data				Majors	Rental Information										Condition					
Center	Age	Number Shops	Sq Ft	PK Lot	Majors	Vacancy	Asking Rts	Deal-making Rts	%	Tax	Ins	CAM	CPI	HVAC	Other	P/L	Bldg	Area	Access	Tenants	Comments

Reprinted with permission from Alexander, Alan A., and Muhlebach, Richard F.: *Managing and Leasing Commercial Properties* (New York: John Wiley & Sons, Inc., 1990).

looking for competing shopping centers. Once located, each competing center should be inspected from marketing and leasing perspectives. The sizes of vacant stores can be estimated by pacing off the front of the store (width) and counting the rows of ceiling tiles (depth) or pacing off the side of the building. If there is no "For Lease" sign or the name of the property management company is not shown, the person conducting the survey can visit one of the tenants and request the information. While touring the area, the shopping center manager or leasing agent should note all "For Lease" signs with "Shopping Center Coming Soon" messages. The shopping center manager can also inquire at the local building department whether any shopping center plans have been submitted for approval in the trade area.

The leasing agent or the shopping center manager at each property on the survey list and each proposed shopping center should be contacted by telephone or visited personally. The best way to obtain the desired information about the competitor is to introduce oneself, state the purpose of the call or visit, and then share rental information on the subject property.

For example, the leasing agent or shopping center manager might say, "The asking rate at my shopping center is $25 per square foot; we're making deals between $23.50 and $24.50 per square foot; we've been giving up to two months free rent for a five-year lease; and we have an annual Consumer Price Index adjustment, a percentage lease provision, and tenant charges of $5.00 per square foot per year. What are the asking and deal-making rates for your vacancies?" Because no two shopping centers are exactly alike, this type of dialog would not lead to any price-fixing; it is simply sharing information that is available to anyone who inquires about space at the shopping center.

Asking and deal-making rents, standard concessions, and other specifics—examples of the information being sought—should be readily available to those who inquire. When information is provided up front, the other person is more likely to share similar information. In this context, distinguishing between asking and deal-making rates is important. If only one rate is stated, it is usually the asking rate. Learning the sizes of the spaces to which the quoted rates apply is also important. The shopping center manager should inquire about specific vacancies when visiting a particular shopping center and before calling the leasing agent or shopping center manager.

Analyzing the Survey Information. When the survey is completed, the information should be analyzed, and the subject property should be compared to the competition. Two of the most important features to compare are the locations and the anchor tenants. Analysis of comparable rents is an art, not a science. Many variables can affect rental rates—e.g., access to the shopping center, visibility of small shops, overall condition (maintenance), and the location, size, and configuration of each vacancy—and these can only be discovered by visiting the shopping center. Conducting a market survey for the first time could take several days. Once the locations and leasing agents of all the competing shopping centers are known, subsequent surveys can usually be conducted in less than a day.

Pricing Each Store. After the shopping center has been compared to the competition, a range of market rental rates should be apparent. Each space in the subject center is then priced within the market rental rate range based on its location, visibility, size, depth, and configuration.

Presenting the Results to the Owner. The final step in determining the market rental rates for a shopping center is to present the survey and then recommend rental rates to the property owner for final approval to lease space at these rates. A property owner often perceives a higher value in the vacancies than the market will accept. Rental surveys and, if possible, the lease terms of recent deals at competing properties and the subject shopping center are valuable data that will assist the property owner in understanding the market rates for the shopping center.

Prospecting for Tenants

The main responsibility of the marketing and leasing program is prospecting for tenants. Prospecting consumes more of the leasing agent's time than any other activity. It is a critical element in determining the success of the marketing and leasing program. It includes the development of marketing materials and the understanding and use of many techniques for finding tenants.

Developing Marketing Materials. *Marketing materials* assist the leasing agent in selling a prospective tenant on the shopping center. When developing these materials, the shopping center manager or leasing agent should adopt the point of view of the prospect in order to decide what information the prospect needs to know about the shopping center—such as its tenant mix and trade area. The information that will be included in the marketing materials is readily available at a reasonable cost. All the materials should be professionally prepared in a manner that reflects the quality of the shopping center and the professionalism of the shopping center manager or leasing agent.

Leasing Package. Items to consider for a leasing package follow. Not every shopping center requires all of them.

- Transmittal letter
- Brochure
- Layout
- Tenant list
- Aerial photo
- Photos of the shopping center and the vacant space
- Renderings of the shopping center

- Map of the area
- Accessibility and transportation
- Demographic and psychographic profiles
- Traffic counts
- General sales information
- Calendar of marketing and promotional events
- Unique features
- Disclaimer

Transmittal Letter. A letter that is tailored to the prospect is more likely to receive the prospect's attention than a standard letter about the shopping center. The transmittal letter should be tailored to the prospect's business. It should focus on the issues that are important to the prospect. For example, letters sent to all the ice cream parlors in the area might focus on the proximity of the shopping center to schools and emphasize the numbers of children and young families in the trade area. The letter may be an announcement of space availability or a more specific invitation to visit the shopping center. Using today's office technology, letters can be personalized and focused specifically for a given tenant use.

Brochure. A brochure can be elaborate, have several pages including photographs, and be printed in color, or it can be a simple one-page flyer printed in two colors. Usually only large malls or lifestyle shopping centers need elaborate brochures; a one-page handout is adequate for most strip shopping centers. The brochure or flyer should include a rendering (for a new shopping center) or photograph of the shopping center, along with demographic and traffic count information, a list of current tenants, and a layout of the shopping center highlighting the anchor tenant(s)and the vacant spaces. A small locator map is also a nice touch. The shopping center manager or leasing agent's name, company name, phone number, and e-mail address should be in a prominent place on the front of the flyer.

Layout. Regional malls, lifestyle shopping centers, and large specialty, outlet, and entertainment shopping centers need a separate one-page layout of the shopping center. Such layouts include the names of existing tenants, spaces leased but still unoccupied, and the size of each vacant space.

Tenant List. A separate list of current tenants is appropriate if the list is not included in the brochure.

Aerial Photo. An aerial photo is a great leasing tool because it vividly shows the access to the shopping center and the relationship of the shopping center to major roads and expressways. It also shows the density of houses and apartment buildings in the immediate area. If the shopping center is in a strong retailing area, the aerial photo will show the adjacent shopping centers. If the photo is scanned, the names of the major tenants can be inserted on the map. If the shopping center is across the street from a regional mall or another large shopping center, such as a power shopping center, the aerial photo will indicate the collective drawing power of all the shopping centers in the area and their anchor tenants.

Photos or Renderings. Photos of the shopping center or renderings of a proposed shopping center under construction provide a prospect an idea of the architectural style and the features of the shopping center.

Map of the Area. Geographic information systems (GIS) is a software program that analyzes and displays data for a particular area. The data include demographic information that can be displayed graphically on a map. For instance, household income for a city may be displayed using different colors for each income level for each neighborhood or zip code in a particular area. For prospective tenants who are not familiar with the location of the shopping center, a map showing expressways, major streets, and other major buildings in the area can be extremely helpful.

Accessibility and Transportation. If the area has good public transportation, as do Washington, D.C., Chicago, and San Francisco, information about the mass transit system provides alternative forms of transportation to the shopping center.

Demographic and psychographic profiles. These are among the most critical pieces of information to aid in a prospective tenant's decision to lease space at a shopping center. Typically, information is provided on the residents within a one-, three-, five-, and (for larger shopping centers) ten-mile radius of the shopping center. The information includes the total population of the area (broken down statistically into age, sex, and ethnic groups); the average family or household size and income level; and the percentage of single-family home ownership. Demographic and psychographic information can be purchased from research firms, and the source should be included with the information in the leasing package.

Psychographic data indicate the lifestyle and purchasing preferences of the people in the area. The type of shopping center, the location of its competition, its anchor tenants, and the geographic area determine the radius from the shopping center to use in the materials in the leasing package. A regional mall in an urban area may only need data from a 10- to 20-mile radius, while a regional mall in a more rural area may collect data for the entire county or a good portion of the state. A grocery anchored strip shopping center may need data for up to a 5-mile radius. This information will assist a prospect in estimating his or her sales potential. Demographics and psychographics are also discussed in chapter 8.

Traffic Counts. The number of vehicles that pass by and the number of people who visit the shopping center are important indicators of business (retail sales) potential. Local governmental agencies periodically conduct vehicle traffic counts in specific sections of the area—often in front of shopping centers. Regional malls and large shopping centers often have traffic counters at the entrances of their parking lots. To arrive at the hourly shopping center traffic, the number of cars entering each hour is multiplied by the estimated number of people in each vehicle for that time of the day. Shopping centers in dense urban areas that have good public transportation factor in the number of people who arrive by public transportation. (Traffic counts are also discussed earlier in this chapter in the context of shopping center analysis.)

General Sales Information. Retailers consider a location based on the potential sales that can be generated there. They want to know the performance of the shopping center, and they often use their own resources to find out how specific merchants in the shopping center and in the area are performing. Mall and lifestyle shopping center retailers especially look at the sales of specific retailers to gauge their sales potential at the shopping center. If the shopping center's sales are strong, the leasing package should include that fact. Figures should be listed for the entire shopping center and for specific categories of tenants that are present in multiples (e.g., five shoe stores in a regional mall), but individual tenant's sales should never be indicated—that information is confidential. However, the manager of an anchor or national shop tenant may give permission to disclose some positive sales information, such as that the store is in the top 10 percent of store sales in its region or within the entire chain.

Calendar of Marketing and Promotional Events. If the shopping center or mall has a coordinated marketing and advertising program, the calendar of any promotional activities should be included in the leasing package. Photos of successful merchandising, sales, and promotional events show that the landlord is interested in aggressively marketing the shopping center. Copies of newspaper ads and articles about the shopping center or its events, especially those containing endorsements by prominent citizens or community officials, are good additions, too.

Unique Features. Identifying specific benefits of locating in the shopping center is also a good selling point. Any unique features—such as a major transit stop in front of the property, a major employer, a school within walking distance of the shopping center, or a major regional mall in close proximity—should be included in the leasing information package.

Disclaimer. Individual components of the leasing package will vary in how long they will be accurate and, therefore, useful. For some protection against liability for information and data that may change in the future, such as the list of tenants occupying the shopping center and possible expansion and remodeling of the shopping center, it is wise to include a disclaimer on such items in the brochures, layouts, tenant lists, etc. A simple statement—i.e., information, list of tenants, layout and design of the shopping center is subject to change—may be adequate. Legal counsel can advise on the need for specific disclaimers and provide appropriate language.

Presenting the Leasing Package. The shopping center manager and the leasing agent should also consider how to package this leasing information. A marketing package for the lease-up of a new lifestyle shopping center and regional mall may warrant special design and packaging by an advertising or marketing firm. For a less-intensive program (e.g., limited turnover in an established shopping center of any size), a folder with pockets or an envelope may be appropriate. The packaging will depend on the number of component items and their size—and the funds available to spend on them. The shopping center manager may want to provide only some basic information on the first visit to a prospective tenant, and then if the prospect is interested, present the remainder as a follow-up package. This allows the shopping center manager or leasing agent to better tailor the leasing information to the prospect's needs. Of course the leasing agent's business card should be provided to all prospects, regardless of whether they receive a comprehensive leasing package.

Techniques for Finding Tenants. The shopping center manager or leasing agent can use several techniques for finding tenants. Different techniques will be effective depending on the type of shopping center. The most effective leasing programs include several prospecting techniques. The shopping center manager or leasing agent must first determine which techniques to use and then decide which to emphasize. *Prospecting*—generating interest on the part of prospective tenants—may take several forms, including canvassing or cold calling, advertising, public relations, and signage as well as attending deal-making sessions, working the brokerage community, and using various leasing directories. A direct approach can be used once a specific prospect has been identified; however, identifying prospects may require indirect approaches.

Canvassing and Cold Calling. Direct contact with prospective tenants is called canvassing or cold calling. These terms are often used interchangeably but there is a difference between them. *Canvassing* is contacting all the tenants in a building, a shopping center, or an area. *Cold calling* is contacting specific tenants in a building, a shopping center, or in the surrounding area. Each technique is time-consuming but often very effective. Not every retail business in the community is a prospective tenant; the leasing agent should cold call only those categories of tenants that are needed in the shopping center and are likely prospects. Although more people can be contacted by phone, telephone canvassing is generally not as effective as a personal contact, but it is often used as follow-up to a direct-mail campaign. From a practical viewpoint, many cold calling efforts start with telephone calls and then proceed to in-person visits. An effective cold calling technique is to establish a daily goal for telephone cold calls and a weekly goal for personal cold calls. Prospects should be cold called more than once because their need to relocate or to add an additional store may change from the time they are first contacted.

A rule of thumb for the number of cold calls to reach a deal follows: 10 calls generate a suspect, 5 suspects generate a prospect, 4 prospects generate one deal. According to those figures, 200 calls will generate a deal. Obviously several variables determine how many calls are required to generate a deal for each shopping center, but this example demonstrates that cold calling is a time-consuming, but ultimately productive, leasing technique.

Current tenants in the shopping center should be contacted first. One or more may be interested in expanding or opening another type of business. They or their associates and colleagues may know other merchants who want to expand their businesses or start new businesses. Competing shopping centers are always cold calling each other's tenants; leasing agents should not forget to canvass these properties.

Advertising. Advertising is an indirect approach to prospecting because it reaches a wide range of audiences, not all of which include prospective tenants. However, successful advertising brings prospects to the shopping center. In reaching out to all retailers, it has the potential to connect with specific merchants who might not have been anticipated as prospects. Advertising may take many different forms.

Classified Ads. Leasing agents report mixed results from classified ads in newspapers. When they are used, the ads should be very specific about the location of the shopping center and the size of the space available.

An ad in the local newspaper's space available section indicating the size of the vacancy and potential uses may attract interest for a small strip shopping center. Placing an ad in the newsletter or directory of professional associations, such as the local or state chiropractic, dental, or medical association's newsletter may attract a medical professional for a strip shopping center. Other businesses have similar newsletters and directories that may be cost-effective means to reach an entire industry. The likely tenants for a strip shopping center include local businesses. Lifestyle, entertainment and power shopping centers as well as regional malls often advertise in national shopping center and retailer's trade journals in order to reach the high-end and big box retailers.

Display Advertising. A display ad in a trade magazine may be effective for targeting a specific merchandise category. Just about every category in retailing has a trade or professional organization, and most of those organizations publish magazines. The local public library may have copies of the resources used by advertising agencies; retailers may be willing to share copies of their trade publications for examination.

Internet Web Sites. The Internet also provides an abundance of outlets for marketing available retail space, and since the early 2000s shopping centers have found Web sites essential.

Internet Marketing. National Internet commercial real estate hosting sites list properties for lease by brokerage firms around the country and in other countries. For example, sites such as http://www.cityfeet.com and http://www.loopnet.com list over two billion square feet of available commercial space. In addition, regional Web sites post vacancies for the local area only. Such sites allow potential tenants to search for available space using geographic parameters, square footage requirements, and rental rates, among other qualifiers. Search results include photographs, plans, detailed property information, and leasing contact information. Listing space on these Web sites is relatively inexpensive, and they reach a wide audience. For an additional fee, some Web sites offer the opportunity to promote a shopping center as a featured listing on the homepage and other high profile areas of the site. Vacancies can be placed on these listing services, and prospects and brokers can view them.

Brokerage firms and shopping center management firms have their own Web sites where they list their properties for lease; if they represent tenants, they also list their clients' site requirements. Some of these Web sites have demographic information on the trade area of the properties along with general information on the property and the area.

Finally, the Internet can be used to post advertisements on Web sites that are visited by the shopping center's target market. This may include commercial property listing sites as well as trade association Web sites. Internet advertising is typically purchased in the form of a banner ad or a small box containing text and images that appears at the top or side of the Web page. A banner campaign can often be tailored to specific messaging needs.

Web Site Development. As mentioned, Web sites have become essential, so each shopping center manager must explore the creation of a Web site if the shopping center does not already have one. For Web site development, a number of options are available, depending on the shopping center's scope and budget:

- Outsource to a vendor who develops Web sites, preferably for other real estate entities.

- Hire an internal webmaster to develop and maintain the site.
- Create the site with shopping center management staff using Web site development software such as Microsoft FrontPage (www.microsoft.com/frontpage) or Dreamweaver from Macromedia (www.macromedia.com).

In each case, the shopping center manager must purchase a domain name and sign up with a Web site hosting service. If shopping center management staff creates the site, they should keep in mind the "7Cs" of Web site design:

- *Context:* the layout and design of the site should be user-friendly and attractive
- *Content:* content should be interesting and constantly updated to maintain currency
- *Customization:* the user should be able to tailor the site to their needs
- *Communication:* the site should include e-mail addresses, phone numbers, and other contact information
- *Connection:* the site should provide links to other relevant sites
- *Commerce:* the site should enable or prompt commercial transactions
- *Community:* users should be able to communicate with one another[2]

(The last "C" may not be applicable to shopping center Web sites.)

After the Web site is developed, the site must draw shoppers to it. Being listed on major search engines, such as Yahoo! and Google, can give the shopping center's Web site a significant traffic boost. Several online search engine sites will submit the shopping center's Web site information to search engines. Some firms manage the entire search engine submission process for a fee.

Public Relations and Publicity. A very cost-effective means to promote the shopping center is to send a message or press release about the shopping center to the local media. This message should be targeted to the community at large and to local businesses. During the development and the ongoing operations of a shopping center, several activities are of interest to the community.

For a new shopping center, these events include the announcement of the development of the shopping center, anchor tenants executing their leases, ground breaking, other tenants executing their leases, construction completion, grand opening, and the success of the grand opening.

Similar press releases can be sent to the media for a shopping center that is being remodeled or rehabbed or one that is undergoing a change of

2. Jeffrey F. Rayport and Bernard J. Jaworski, *e-commerce,* McGraw-Hill, 2001, p. 116.

use. Additional press releases include new tenants, new store managers, marketing, special promotions, and community activities.

Signage. One of the most effective leasing tools for small and large strip shopping centers and street retail buildings is signage. Thousands of people pass by these properties each day, and some of them are retailers, service providers, and leasing agents.

Signs. On-site leasing signs should be prominently displayed near the street. Large paper or poster board "For Lease" signs can be placed in the window of each vacancy. The name, phone number, and e-mail address of the shopping center manager or leasing agent is the most important information on these signs. Some leasing agents include the square footage of the vacancy to prequalify prospects.

Billboards. Very large signs or billboards are used for leasing purposes only for large new shopping centers or for those soon to be under construction. A simple presentation that focuses on the shopping center's identification and includes the leasing agent's name, phone number, and e-mail address is best.

Project Signs. These large signs are often placed on-site prior to and during construction; they may be incorporated in the materials that form the protective enclosure. Such signage usually includes a rendering of the shopping center, a list of the anchor tenants, and the names of the project participants—lender, developer, architect, general contractor—as well as the leasing agent's name, phone number, and e-mail address prominently displayed.

Tenants' Advertising. The shopping center manager and leasing agent should also monitor retailers' advertisements in the newspaper, on the radio, on television, or on the Internet. Monitoring advertising is one way the shopping center manager and the leasing agent can become aware of prospective tenants in the area. Aggressive local advertisers may be looking for additional locations; others may be seeking opportunities to expand into the area.

Deal-Making Sessions. The International Council of Shopping Centers conducts deal-making and educational sessions regionally and nationally. At a deal-making session, retailers, developers, and brokerage firms have booths to promote their products or services. Usually 25,000 to over 35,000 shopping center professionals attend the annual deal-making sessions held in May of each year. Most of the attendees do not operate from booths but schedule meetings with prospects and visit the retailers in their booths. Each regional meeting has an annual two-to-three day deal-making and educational session. These events are great places to meet prospects, network, and exchange ideas with other shopping center managers and leasing agents.

Brokerage Community's Support. The shopping center manager and leasing agent should keep the brokerage community aware of the shopping center and encourage brokers to bring prospective tenants to the shopping center. Many retailers are exclusively represented by leasing agents, and they rely on their brokers to provide them market information; collect demographic, psychographic, and traffic data; and provide rental rates for properties in the area and locate sites. The shopping center manager and the leasing agent should network regularly with retail brokers to discuss the shopping center and the leasing activities in the market. Periodically mailing or e-mailing a flyer to brokers keeps them informed about vacancies, new tenants, marketing activities, and tenants' success stories.

Leasing Publications. Several directories of retail tenants are excellent resources for direct-mail campaigns or telephone cold calls. The retailers are commonly listed by category, and the listings include a variety of information—e.g., the tenant's name, address, and telephone number; the number of locations already established; the type of shopping center preferred and geographic areas sought; and the name of the leasing representative. These mailings can be followed up with a phone call, and when practical, a personal visit. Several directories are listed in appendix D, References and Resources.

Other Resources. Locally, telephone directory Yellow Pages and the chamber of commerce should be useful sources. Retail trade suppliers (e.g., coin laundry and restaurant equipment vendors; merchandise wholesalers) are other possible resources. In particular, they are likely to know which businesses are successful and which ones are interested in expanding.

Successful merchants often want to establish additional locations. Personal networking with shopping center managers and leasing agents from other shopping centers can be a source for such leads.

Shopping center managers and leasing agents should maintain a contact list of tenant prospects, preferably organized by merchandise categories. Even though a prospect may not be interested in locating at a particular shopping center or may not be appropriate for the shopping center's tenant mix when initially approached, that merchant may be an ideal prospect for a different shopping center or even for the same shopping center at a later time.

Evaluating Prospective Tenants

The objective of prospecting is to identify and negotiate leases with merchants who will succeed in the shopping center. One way to help ensure any tenant's success is to be selective in the initial qualification process. Prospective tenants for any type of property are evaluated to determine their ability to fulfill the terms of the lease, especially the payment of rent and other charges. Retail tenants are also evaluated on their ability as merchants, their sales potential, their compatibility with the shopping center's tenant mix, and their anticipated benefit to the shopping center.

Usually when a tenant moves out during a lease term, it is because the business has failed. The failure may be due to insufficient capital, inadequate business experience, or an inappropriate use for the shopping center or the area. Sometimes the consumers no longer accept the concept. The tenant that fails usually owes back rent. A tenant's failure is costly to the landlord, not only because of the rent lost on the broken lease but also because of the rental income lost while the space is vacant and the extra expenses incurred for re-leasing. *Downtime*—the period a space is vacant until another tenant takes occupancy and commences paying rent—can range from a few weeks to many months or even years. Re-leasing expenses include commissions in addition to the cost to clean the premises. Sometimes they include the costs to demolish the prior tenant's improvements or to construct new ones and possibly the costs to bring the space up to the new building codes.

In order to evaluate prospective tenants properly, the shopping center manager or the leasing agent must understand the fundamentals of retailing. (Key considerations for judging a prospective tenant's potential to succeed are addressed in appendix A, Retailing Basics.)

Intended Use. The first concern in the evaluation of a prospective tenant is its intended use for the premises. The shopping center manager or leasing agent should meet with the prospect and discuss the business and how it operates. If the prospect is a first-time retailer, the shopping center manager should inquire into the prospect's experience in the intended line of business and request a business plan with financial statements.

A visit to the prospect's present store (multiple stores if the prospect is a chain) should yield answers to other questions about the prospect's business. In a shopping center, each store's appearance reflects on the shopping center as a whole. The shopping center manager should observe how merchandise is displayed and how the store fixtures are arranged. An important consideration is the efficiency of the operation because that is a measure of success. In the case of a new business, the prospect's design plans for the store should be reviewed. (If the prospect is not sure how the store should be designed, visits to similar stores that are successful should be encouraged.)

Few retailers have poor reputations; those that acquire negative images usually do not stay in business long. However, some stores have a specific reputation for service, quality, or value. For example, Nordstrom, a Seattle-based specialty department store, is nationally known for its customer service and the quality of its merchandise. Wal-Mart and Target stores are known for value pricing. The reputation of the store will be reflected on the reputation of the shopping center.

When the shopping center manager reviews the prospect's business plan, he or she should fully assess the proposed inventory levels, sales policies, sales projections, operating expenses, staffing, advertising schedule, and budget. This review should reveal whether the merchant understands the proposed business and has realistic expectations for its success.

Effectiveness. Next, the prospect's efficacy as a merchant is evaluated. This assessment should be based on such considerations as merchandise type and price; sales figures (total volume, sales per square foot, trends); and present operation (store appearance, efficiency, and reputation; management procedures; and advertising plan).

A tenant's sales volume indicates its ability to draw traffic to the shopping center, operate successfully, and pay rent—and whether it will pay percentage rent. The sales volume at the prospect's current store should be evaluated; if the prospect operates other stores, the sales volumes from those stores should be reviewed, too.

However, sales volumes alone can be misleading. Sales should also be evaluated based on dollars per square foot. Eight hundred thousand dollars in sales volume may be good or poor, depending on the size and the type of the store. In a 2,000-square-foot store in a strip shopping center, annual sales of $800,000 is typically an acceptable level equal to $400 per square foot for many tenants. In a 20,000-square-foot store, the same annual sales volume would be very weak at $40 per square foot.

The prospect's sales should be compared to the sales of similar stores in the shopping center or centers in which it is located. The shopping center managers of those properties can be asked to share how the prospect's sales rank compared to similar stores in those shopping centers.

A new business has no sales volume to evaluate, so the shopping center manager should request the prospect to provide a sales projection. The prospect's projected annual sales volume should be calculated as dollars per square foot and should be compared to the national averages in the *Dollars & Cents of Shopping Centers*. If the projected sales are significantly below the national average for the category, the prospect has little chance to succeed; if the projected sales are significantly above the national average, they may reflect unrealistic expectations.

Financial Strength. The prospect's financial strength must be evaluated. The shopping center manager must be assured that the prospect has sufficient capital to start business at a new location. This includes proper inventory levels, funds for advertising and promotions, and a reserve to carry the business until it is profitable. If the prospect is part of a chain or a franchise, additional resources may be available. However, many novice retailers believe their stores will be successful from the day they open for business, and that is often not realistic. In fact, it can take between one and three years for a new business to become successful. The owner of a new business is often unable to draw a salary during the first year of operation. If the prospect is a new business, the owner must have sufficient capital to support both personal needs and business operations until the business is profitable.

The shopping center manager should ask the prospect to submit a financial statement for the business and for each of the other stores owned, if any. If the company is new or has a weak financial statement, the shopping center manager should request a personal financial statement from the owner or owners. Two important items on a financial statement are liquid assets and monthly obligations. A personal financial statement may show a fairly strong net worth, but the assets may consist solely of the value of a residence and selected items of personal property, neither of which is easily convertible to cash. A prospect must have sufficient liquid assets (e.g., bank savings accounts, stocks, bonds, etc.) to adequately support the business.

The shopping center manager should obtain a credit report on the company from Dun and Bradstreet. In the case of a new business, a credit report should be obtained on the owner as well. Credit references listed by the prospect should always be checked.

From a pragmatic viewpoint, the strength of the landlord's negotiating position and the occupancy level of the shopping center may influence the criteria used to evaluate a prospective tenant. Shopping centers that have strong tenants' sales seldom have a vacancy and can therefore establish high standards for evaluating prospects; a problem shopping center may need to lower its standards for some prospects until the property is almost fully leased.

Anchor Tenants. The anchor tenants set the tone for the tenant mix of the shopping center, and they are the first prospects a leasing agent or team pursues. Leasing deals with anchor tenants can become very complex, but they are critical to the success of the shopping center. Chapter 2, Development and Rehabilitation of Retail Properties, provides prospecting information for determining the anchor tenants of new or rehabilitated shopping centers and discusses the importance of the anchor tenants to the shopping center. Full discussion of negotiating the anchor tenant deal follows in chapter 10, Negotiating and Documenting the Lease Terms.

As an example of a particular anchor tenant's influence on the shopping center as a whole, consider a shopping center that has an anchor supermarket or drugstore. In this example, the supermarket or drugstore establishes a shopping center of destination tenants. Supermarket and drugstore customers know what they want, and they shop for predetermined items at the centers anchored by such stores. They are not looking for a leisurely shopping experience, and they are not as likely to shop impulsively. With either or both as anchors, other tenants that leasing agents should pursue would include services (e.g., dry cleaning and shoe repair) as well as food vendors (e.g., fast food, quick service and table service restaurants, delis, and bakeries).

Chapter 8, Creating the Tenant Mix, lists common types of shopping centers, their typical sizes, and their usual anchor tenants. That chapter also discusses the importance of the anchor tenant to the tenant mix as well as recent trends toward different mixes of anchor tenants and other stores than were previously possible.

Pad and Outlot Spaces. A *pad* or *outlot* is a parcel of land in a high-visibility, high-traffic area of the shopping center parking lot. Pad and outlot buildings can generate high rents, add to the draw of the shopping center, and provide a unique product or service to the tenant mix. The arrangements with the tenant are sometimes similar to those negotiated with anchor tenants.

Types of Pad Deals. There are three types of pad deals: ground leases, built-to-suit, and the sale of the parcel.

Ground Leases. The ground lease is the pad deal most preferred by landlords because their expenses may then be limited to the cost to legally create a separate parcel of land and (possibly) the cost to bring in the utilities. The two most common pad or outlot uses are restaurants and banks, both of which require long-term leases (typically 10 to 20 years, with two to six 5- to 10-year options). Some credit tenants prefer to build their own buildings because they can obtain more favorable financing than the landlord can, thus lowering their occupancy cost.

Build-to-Suit Leases. With the *build-to-suit lease,* the property owner invests in and constructs a building to the specifications of the tenant. However, if the original tenant fails, the building may require major modifications to suit a replacement tenant. Because build-to-suit leases are risky ventures, they are usually not offered to prospects that are not triple-A rated (AAA credit rating, as from Dun & Bradstreet).

Selling the Parcel. The third option—to sell the parcel to a user who will construct a building—is the least preferable of all, due to the complexity of the construction and the timing of the completion of the pad with other shopping center activities

Feasibility of a New Pad or Outlot. If a shopping center does not presently include a pad or an outlot parcel—or if additional space is desirable—the shopping center manager should investigate whether creating a new pad or an outlot space is permissible and feasible. The primary considerations are the shopping center parking ratio and whether the property will still meet municipal requirements if some parking stalls are eliminated while additional gross leasable area is added for the pad or outlot building. (The municipal parking ratio is discussed in chapter 2, Development and Rehabilitation of Retail Properties.)

A review of established leases and common area agreements will reveal any other prohibitions. Anchor tenants are concerned that a building in the parking lot will block their visibility or view corridor and take away a convenient customer parking area, so their leases often contain a required parking ratio or prohibit a pad or an outlot building in specific areas of the shopping center. The restriction may limit the location, size, and height of a pad building. Some shop tenants' leases and existing common area agreements may include similar restrictions.

Prospecting for Pad Tenants. When prospecting for pad tenants, two critical tenant issues need to be determined. First, what size building can the pad accommodate? Pad users often have prototype buildings, and if the pad is too small they will not be able to set the building on the pad. When creating a pad, the shopping center manager should survey pad users for their space requirements. The second issue is whether the pad building can have a drive-up window. This is a requirement for many fast food pad users.

Restaurants and banks are logical users for a pad. Before cold calling these users, the shopping center manager or the leasing agent should determine which restaurants and banks are not in the immediate area and call them first. Next they should contact restaurants and banks that are in the area and inquire if they are interested in another location or would prefer to relocate to the subject site.

Adding a pad tenant to a shopping center is a great way to enhance the value of the property. For instance, if the pad annual ground rent is $65,000 and the property is valued using a 10 percent cap rate, the value of the property increased by $650,000. The shopping center manager must be prudent when adding pads to a shopping center, however. Too many pad buildings will block the visibility of strip shopping centers and reduce the value of the in-line shop spaces.

Food Court Tenants. Food courts have been popular components of malls and shopping centers for many years. A food court will not reach its full potential if it is placed in a secondary location; it should always be prominent. Some of the best locations are adjacent to movie theaters or other entertainment facilities (e.g., an ice skating rink).

Food courts normally have two customer bases—shoppers and store employees. If office buildings are nearby, lunchtime business from office workers can be significant on weekdays. Food choices change with trends and the promotion of health consciousness, so the tenant mix of a food court must be adjusted periodically to accommodate consumers' changing eating habits.

Food court spaces may be leased individually, or the food court may be operated as a concession, in which case the concessionaire (as the lessee) negotiates arrangements with individual food vendors. As with any food service operation, special care must be taken in locating the food court area and the individual vendors. Food courts thrive on a tenant mix that includes both national and local vendors.

When evaluating potential food court tenants, the shopping center manager or the leasing agent should pay careful attention to the cleanliness of the prospective tenant's operation. The lease document for food court tenants should follow the requirements imposed on any other type of food vendor with respect to operations and compliance with local health codes.

According to statistics published in the 2002 *Dollars & Cents of Shopping Centers,* food court tenants operate in spaces ranging from less than 300 to a little more than 1,000 square feet of GLA, and most of those tenants' sales exceed $500 per square foot due to the small square footage of their shops. Total rent per square foot tends to be substantially higher than the rent other tenants pay, although food court tenants may not pay specific percentage rent (because the sales breakpoint is so high). Many also pay prorated pass-through operating expenses (including property taxes and insurance), and many pay special common area maintenance (CAM) charges that encompass common areas of both the food court and the shopping center as a whole.

Specialty Leasing. *Specialty leasing,* previously known as temporary leasing, has become an integral part of the leasing, marketing, and merchandising strategies of many retail properties. A specialty leasing program with its temporary tenants diversifies a shopping center's tenant mix and enhances its drawing power. A specialty leasing program may provide a shopping center the unique opportunity to utilize otherwise nonproductive space.

Temporary tenants provide additional income and amenities to the shopping center, and most shopping centers have several possibilities for locating them. The obvious place in all types of shopping centers is vacant space. In a strip shopping center, temporary tenants may be located in the parking lot or on the sidewalk; in a mall, they may be placed in the mall corridor, against a vacant space (or inside it), underneath the stairs or escalator to the second level, or along a blank wall.

The landlord provides most temporary spaces, such as carts or kiosks, to ensure they conform to the architecture of the shopping center. Occasionally the tenant wants to use its own kiosk or cart or offers to build one to the landlord's specifications. (This often occurs when a tenant offers to lease space and place its kiosk in the parking lot.)

Advantages of Specialty Leasing. The advantages of a specialty leasing program are numerous. First, temporary tenants are an additional source of revenue that can range from a few hundred dollars a year from Christmas tree sales in the parking lot of a strip shopping center to more than a million dollars from a year-round temporary tenant program in a regional mall. Short-term, small-space tenancies can provide an opportunity for entrepreneurs to test new products and concepts. They add a sense of newness that attracts shoppers. Temporary tenancies offer landlords opportunities to evaluate new merchants without committing to a long-term lease, and some temporary tenants may become permanent occupants of in-line spaces as a result.

Types of Specialty Leasing. Shopping centers can use a variety of specialty leasing possibilities, such as carts, kiosks, retail merchandising units, and even vacant in-line stores, to great advantage.

Kiosks. Mall space is ideal for kiosks. They are also found in lifestyle and entertainment shopping centers. Kiosks can be leased for one month, one year, or several years, depending on whether they are temporary or permanent. The temporary kiosk rental agreement is for one to six weeks. Most permanent kiosk tenancies are under short-term leases or license agreements, usually for one year.

The specific advantage of a kiosk is that the tenant can merchandise and sell from all four of its sides, a feature that is attractive to merchants who sell impulse items such as prepackaged food (candy, nuts, dry fruit, popcorn, and specialty cheeses and jellies) or food prepared on-site (pretzels, cookies, etc.). Sales of handcrafted items (leather goods, rubber stamps, keys, stuffed animals, dolls, artwork, calendars, jewelry) and mobile phone service providers are other typical uses.

Residential real estate sales companies have leased mall kiosks to display listings and generate walk-in traffic. One of the first kiosks was Photomat—drop-off and pick-up photo processing—which was located in shopping center parking lots near the street. In the early 1990s and continuing into the 2000s, drive-through espresso kiosks became common in parking lots in many areas of the country.

Carts. Carts can turn small amounts of previously unused space into money-making opportunities, and they offer many advantages over kiosks because they are more attractive and provide a unique charm. Carts also take up less space than kiosks, and they can be moved easily to accommodate shopping center promotions or to be positioned in front of a vacancy or a blank wall. They can be quickly removed and stored when not in use.

The term of the agreement between the landlord and the tenant is often as short as one week or one month. When a mall has several carts, weekly rotation of merchants from one cart location to another provides each merchant the opportunity to have selling time in the best location. The types of merchandise sold from carts are typically impulse items that are sold at low to medium prices.

Retail Merchandising Units. A *retail merchandising unit (RMU)* is similar to and larger than a cart but smaller than a kiosk. RMUs have display areas, storage, and lighting, and they have more area to display merchandise. They are often owned by the shopping center and leased to a tenant. They are leased and operated like a cart. They are the display unit of choice for many shopping centers.

Wall Shops. Department stores in shopping centers often have blank walls between their entrances and their display windows. Building wall shops 8 to 10 feet deep in front of these walls provides space for both temporary and permanent tenants. Wall shops also eliminate the barren appearance of a blank wall and create an area filled with merchandise and activity, drawing traffic to the entrances of the department stores.

In-Line Spaces. When temporary tenants occupy in-line spaces, they may merchandise the entire space or only the front portion (one-fourth to one-half) of the premises. If they occupy only part of the space, it may be necessary to build a temporary partial back wall (backing). Usually the tenant paints the walls. In-line spaces are good locations for service tenants or those who sell bulky or large items or offer several types of goods. A tax preparation service is a common use during the early months of the year; a photo studio is a good seasonal use for the December and Easter holidays and the weeks preceding Mother's Day and Father's Day. Furniture stores, spas, bookstores, and liquidators are good uses for large vacant spaces. A costume store is an excellent use the week or two before Halloween and Christmas decorations stores are popular from early November until the day before Christmas.

Incubator Tenants. Incubator tenants or users typically lease the front portion of in-line spaces. They are usually local businesses trying out a concept on a short-term lease or license agreement. The intent of the landlord and the tenant is that the business will grow into the entire space and become a permanent tenant.

Parking Lots. Parking lots were locations for temporary tenants long before there was such a concept. Three of the most common uses are fireworks stands the week before Independence Day (July 4), pumpkin patches the last week of October, and Christmas tree lots from mid-November through Christmas Eve. Other popular uses are a weekend car, boat, or recreational vehicle (RV) sale. These sales are especially popular in shopping centers that are adjacent to and that have good visibility from a highway or expressway. These temporary uses not only generate additional revenue but they can be a major draw to the shopping center. A car dealership will advertise extensively for a weekend blowout sale. Areas for such uses may need to be roped off, and safety walkways may need to be clearly marked. State and local laws may limit specific uses (e.g., sales of fireworks are prohibited in some states).

Dead Spaces. Older shopping centers and malls may have some spaces that are too deep, and most tenants do not need the back 20 to 40 feet. That space can be demised for the tenant and chain link storage spaces can be installed in the back unused space. The storage spaces can be leased to other shopping center tenants.

Identifying Specialty Leasing Prospects. Many regional malls have a full-time, on-site person who is responsible for leasing to temporary tenants. An owner of several shopping centers in an area that has space for temporary tenants usually has one leasing person devoted full-time to the specialty leasing program for all the shopping centers in the area. If that person is responsible for only one shopping center or mall, he or she may also administer the specialty leasing program, including the management activities associated with the tenants (e.g., rent collection, ensuring all rental agreement terms are honored, etc.). Shopping center managers who occasionally have specialty leasing opportunities in their properties usually handle the leasing themselves.

Before looking for prospects, the shopping center manager or leasing agent should consider the types of specialty spaces that are available in the subject shopping center. Enclosed malls provide a weather-protected environment, after-hours security, and high-volume pedestrian traffic for carts, RMUs, and kiosks. Open malls and other types of shopping centers need additional security devices or enclosures. Carts, RMUs, and kiosks are added to malls and shopping centers during peak selling periods and some are permanent. Kiosks, carts, and wall shops can be found at airports, train stations, and specialty shopping centers, and they can be used for temporary or permanent tenants.

The first place to look for temporary tenants is among the existing permanent tenants. Many of these merchants can expand their concept or create a new concept for the peak selling seasons. Asking these tenants if they would be interested in leasing temporary space creates goodwill because the shopping center manager is giving them the first opportunity to lease the temporary space, kiosks, carts, and RMUs. Some temporary tenants may have two or three temporary spaces in a shopping center.

Some of the best places to find temporary tenants are at other malls and shopping centers, flea markets, or craft and gift shows. If none of the tenants in those places is interested in the shopping center, the leasing agent can note the best concepts and suggest to its temporary tenants the opportunity for one of them to operate that concept at the shopping center. Vending machine businesses are another source of specialty leasing.

Some prospects for temporary space may walk into the office or call the shopping center manager. Most of these individuals have a creative idea, however, the leasing agent must carefully qualify them as temporary tenants. He or she must gauge their ability to operate a business and the likely success of their concept.

Working with Temporary Tenants. Some temporary tenants are national retailers, such as candy stores, who have permanent locations and operate temporary locations during specific selling periods. Some national tenants only operate out of temporary locations. These tenants are usually knowledgeable retailers.

Many local retailers, and in particular novice retailers, are not knowledgeable or sophisticated retailers, and they may need guidance from the specialty leasing agent. Such retailers are usually given a short rental agreement—usually three days to a month. They may be given the name of a person who specializes in assisting small local retailers in operating their businesses—especially in the area of visual displays.

Specialty Leasing Package. The prospects are provided a leasing package that includes the rental agreement and the rules and regulations, which should be explained. Many prospects may not realize that they must stay open for business all the hours the shopping center is open. Additional information may include photos of the visual displays of successful temporary tenants, information on how to obtain a city permit to do business, insurance requirements, the shopping center's calendar of events, and the advertising plan for the remainder of the year. Novice temporary tenants initially require a lot of handholding. The book, *Ultimate Guide to Specialty Retail* by Patricia Norins, is written for the temporary tenant, especially the novice tenant.

Specialty Leasing Problems. Leasing to temporary tenants is not without problems. Two potential problems that must be resolved before a temporary tenant program can be established are existing restrictions and future conflicts.

Common area agreements may include restrictions against leasing any portion of the common areas or using the common areas to sell merchandise. Established leases may include similar restrictions. If such restrictions exist, they are most likely to be found in the leases of anchor tenants and strong national shop tenants. The other shop tenants' leases should also be checked. Anchor leases may restrict the use of the common areas within a specified distance from their premises or within a defined area of the shopping center. The lease for a department store may restrict placement of RMUs, kiosks, and carts within a specific distance of its entrance; that for a supermarket may prohibit displays in the area of the parking lot in front of its premises. Another restriction that must be honored is that imposed by a tenant's exclusive use provisions. The merchandise sold by any temporary tenant must not violate any other tenant's exclusive.

Conflict may arise between the landlord and the permanent tenants regarding direct competition from temporary tenants. The shopping center manager must be sensitive to the concerns of the permanent tenants. Because permanent tenants pay rent 12 months a year, including the months with slow sales, and have a large capital investment in their stores, they may rightly object to merchants occupying space only during the best selling periods and taking business away from them. For this reason, temporary tenants should complement the existing tenants and not compete directly with them. To be more readily accepted, temporary tenants should sell merchandise (handcrafted items such as dolls and bears as well as specialty foods and calendars) or provide a service (key duplication, engraving) that is not the primary merchandise or a substantially similar merchandise or service found in the other stores. It is often possible, and even necessary, to include in the temporary tenant's license agreement or lease the landlord's right to relocate the temporary tenant if the location assigned or the type of merchandise sold is problematic to an in-line permanent tenant.

Rental Agreements. The rental arrangements with a temporary tenant may take the form of a lease or a license agreement. Because temporary tenants use space for a short time—typically one week to three months—many landlords prefer to use a license agreement that does not offer the tenant the same rights as those found in a lease. A *license agreement* provides the tenant with a right to use the space but does not create a landlord-tenant relationship. The user of the space does not have all the protection of landlord-tenant laws.

Whichever form is used, the rental agreement should include very specific use restrictions. In addition to use restrictions, the agreement should state the term (duration), rental rate, frequency of rent payment, and other specific provisions.

Use Restriction. Because a temporary tenant may be tempted to sell different types of merchandise during the holiday season (approximately Thanksgiving to New Year's Day) in an effort to find the one item that will be a best seller, the tenant's lease or license agreement must contain a very specific use restriction. As an example, if the agreement states that the use of the space is "to sell handmade wooden toys only," sale of any other item would be a violation.

Term. The length of time of the temporary tenancy should be stated, and it should include specific opening and closing dates. If the agreement is for the holiday season, the commencement date and the date the tenant opens for business should be between November 1 and one week before Thanksgiving. This will provide sufficient time for the tenant to organize and set up. In addition, the tenant should be required to remain open through December 31 to accommodate returns and refunds.

Rent. The rent charged temporary tenants is seldom based on dollars per square foot. Rent is determined by the amount of traffic that will be in the shopping center during the time the tenant occupies the space and is directly related to its potential sales volume. Higher rent can be charged for a kiosk or a 1,000-square-foot vacancy during the holiday season than at any other time of the year. Kiosks and carts should be located in high traffic areas. A kiosk, which typically ranges from 75 to 150 square feet, or an RMU, which is smaller, can command several thousands of dollars per month in base (or minimum) rent during the peak selling seasons. Rent may be collected weekly or all in advance.

Percentage Rent. In addition to base rent, temporary tenants should be required to pay percentage rent. Typically, the percentage rate is higher than that for a similar tenant in a permanent location. For instance, if a permanent gift shop pays 5 percent, the percentage rate for a temporary gift shop may be 10 percent. Temporary tenants pay a premium base rent and percentage rate because they are usually brought into the shopping center only during the best selling periods, and they do not experience the slow sales periods. In addition, they do not have the significant build-out cost of a permanent tenant.

Sometimes escalating rates can be negotiated for a holiday season (e.g., 10 percent on sales up to $20,000, then 12 percent up to $30,000, and 15 percent thereafter) to encourage the landlord to provide the best possible location and the least possible competition while the tenant has basically the same overhead at any volume of sales. However, auditing the reported sales volumes of temporary tenants is often difficult, and it is therefore appropriate for the shopping center manager to remind temporary tenants that participation in future programs will depend heavily on their reported sales as well as their compliance with other provisions of the lease or license.

Rent Payment. Temporary tenants can be in one day and gone the next, so it is important that they pay rent often and on time. Percentage rent should be paid for the same period that minimum rent is paid, and sales reports that support it should be submitted at least monthly. Collecting a security deposit is also prudent; it serves as a guarantee of the performance of the agreement. The schedule for payment of minimum rent may be once a week, every two weeks, or once a month.

Other provisions. The temporary tenant should be required to pay marketing fund or merchants' association dues. Because the tenancy is short-term and the space may be very small, the dues should be a fixed amount rather than being prorated based on square footage. Temporary tenants should be required to advertise in the vehicle used by the shopping center for distribution to shoppers on-site. This may be an advertising section in a newspaper or tabloid or a weekly flyer (newspaper stuffer). Some temporary tenants may group together and take one large ad. Each temporary tenant then pays its prorated share of the ad cost.

Other important provisions of the agreement relate to the temporary tenant's operations. Stringent guidelines, including required landlord approval, should be in place for the design of the space; design and use of signage (specific signage criteria must be developed for temporary tenants); and the manner in which merchandise is displayed (merchandise that is not professionally displayed creates a flea-market image). How merchandise is displayed in RMUs, carts, and kiosks may be limited. For instance, merchandise cannot be displayed above a specific height, and it cannot extend beyond the RMU, cart, or kiosk. The users should be required to maintain shopping center hours. The landlord must maintain the right to relocate the user. If an in-line space is occupied, the utilities should be billed in the tenant's name.

Renewing Leases

Lease renewals can be the easiest or the most difficult deals to negotiate. If the tenant is doing well and understands the current rental market, renewal negotiation can be easy. However, if a tenant's rent is significantly below the market rate, the tenant is unaware of market rates, and/or the shopping center has several vacancies with no replacement tenants available, lease renewal can be difficult.

Renewal Considerations. Regardless of the situation, the shopping center manager or the leasing agent must consider several factors when a tenant's lease is expiring:

1. Should the lease be renewed?
2. How successful is the tenant?
3. How well does the tenant fit the current and anticipated tenant mix?

4. Does the tenant benefit the shopping center?
5. What is the current market situation?
6. Does the tenant have a pattern of late rental payment or other lease violations?
7. Does the tenant generate traffic?
8. Is the tenant the best merchant in its category available for this shopping center?
9. What is the financial strength of the tenant or parent company?

Lease renewal time may be an opportunity to upgrade the shopping center's tenant mix. Does the tenant still fit the tenant mix? If not, the availability of a replacement tenant should be explored. There may be an equivalent or better prospect for the location.

Another consideration is whether the tenant has contributed to the success of the shopping center or been a chronic problem. Regular advertising in the shopping center's advertising flyers and participation in merchandising events and promotions are measures of a tenant's contribution. Difficulties with rent collection or late submission of sales reports and percentage rent payments, especially on a recurrent basis, signal problems that may caution against renewal.

Finally, market conditions and the number of vacancies, if any, in the shopping center must be taken into account. The shopping center manager or leasing agent must calculate the cost to replace the tenant. This cost may include the loss of rent and tenant charges, tenant improvement allowances, concessions, a lease commission, and an intangible—the impact of a vacancy on the other tenants and the shopping center. A marginal tenant may be offered a lease renewal because no other prospective tenant is available for the space.

Renewal Negotiations. Lease renewal negotiations for shop tenants should begin no later than six months before the lease expires; those for anchor tenants should begin at least two years before the lease expires. If a tenant has regularly violated one or more lease provisions, the new lease should address those particular issues. As an example, if a tenant routinely submits its sales reports after the due date, the new lease may provide for the payment of a penalty (e.g., $200 every time the sales report is late or $10 for each day it is late). If a tenant has been a chronic problem, its renewal lease may be for a shorter term than is usually offered. If a shop tenant has not agreed to a lease renewal 90 days before the current one expires, the shopping center manager or leasing agent should start to market the store.

Renewal Documentation. The easiest way to document a lease renewal is by drafting an addendum to the lease that includes the new terms and is signed by the landlord and the tenant. However, this often has drawbacks.

If the original lease is more than a few years old, it probably does not have the latest shopping center lease provisions. A common and possibly costly mistake when using an addendum to renew a tenant is including the phrase, "all terms and conditions remain the same except the lease is extended for X period and the monthly rent is $XX." If the original lease included tenant allowances or other landlord concessions, the tenant may insist that they be offered again since the addendum states all the same terms will apply to the lease renewal. The best way to avoid this potential problem and include the latest lease provisions is to use a new lease form when renewing a tenant.

Most lease renewals are cost-effective. They have no downtime, and they seldom involve any tenant improvement or concession costs. Also, the commission is typically less than would be paid for a replacement tenant. However, this may be an opportunity to upgrade the use of the premises and improve the overall tenant mix. Successful regional and super regional malls commonly replace 5 to 10 percent of the shop tenants every year. The mall operators are always looking to increase the mall's draw by adding popular merchants that best serve its current and expanded customer base.

Leasing a Shopping Center That Has No Vacancies

An effective leasing program does not stop when the shopping center is fully leased. A store may close unexpectedly due to poor sales, a bankruptcy, or a serious illness or death of a local merchant. Opportunities may arise to replace or downsize a struggling tenant.

The shopping center manager and the leasing agent should always be looking for opportunities to add seasonal temporary tenants and to create additional gross leasable area. They should monitor new retailers who enter the market and existing retailers who expand their market presence. They should periodically visit the competition's shopping centers to look for leads for prospects, and they should encourage retail brokers to make them aware of the tenants the brokers represent.

The shopping center manager and/or the leasing agent should maintain a list of tenants to call when an existing tenant decides to vacate or a tenant's lease will not be renewed. They should remember to stay in touch with the tenants at the shopping center. The tenants may be aware of a tenant who is planning to close a store before the lease expires. Tenants can usually provide good prospect leads. The shopping center manager and the leasing agent should maintain a list of businesses that have shown interest in the shopping center along with a list of likely prospects for when spaces become available.

Lease buyouts and store splits are creative, proactive ways to increase the shopping center's productivity and to upgrade the tenant mix.

Lease Buyout. Shopping center managers should always be looking for opportunities to improve the tenant mix and to increase the net operating income. Replacing a retail store that no longer contributes to the success of the shopping center is a way to enhance the shopping center's image, its potential sales performance, its cash flow, and its value. There are three opportunities to replace a tenant: (1) when the lease expires (nonrenewal), (2) when a tenant fails and moves out (replacement as necessity), and (3) when a tenant's problems would be solved by a lease buyout or mutual cancellation.

Every month, the shopping center manager should analyze each tenant's sales and the timing of the rent payment. A tenant is a possible candidate for a lease buyout if any of the following is true:

1. Its sales are significantly below the national average.
2. Its sales volume has been regularly declining.
3. It has trouble paying rent on time.
4. It has a rental rate below the current market rate.
5. It provides a product or service that is no longer in demand.
6. The ratio of occupancy cost to sales is too high.

Of course a buyout should be considered if the tenant no longer fits the shopping center's tenant mix.

The landlord does not always pay the tenant to buy out the lease. The lease may be canceled by mutual agreement, or the tenant may pay the landlord to terminate the lease early. An example occurred in a regional mall on the West Coast that was being converted from an open to an enclosed mall. A shoe store occupied a prime center court space the landlord wanted to recapture and divide into two spaces. Prior to offering the tenant a $100,000 buyout, the shopping center manager asked the tenant if he would be willing to pay a fee to terminate the lease. The tenant offered—and the manager accepted—a $50,000 fee for an early termination.

There is no rule of thumb on how much either party should pay to terminate a lease. However, some factors can guide a shopping center manager in deciding the amount of a buyout. First and foremost is the amount of additional rent another tenant will pay and how much additional value will be created. This assumption is based on the probability that the space can be leased at a higher rental rate in a relatively short time. Many sophisticated tenants know this and will negotiate for a favorable buyout; other tenants are happy to be paid to close a marginal or unsuccessful business. A supermarket that is closing its store and opening a larger state-of-the-art store a few blocks away is aware of the value of its leasehold estate based on its current rent and the amount of rent for which the landlord can re-lease the space at the current market rent. The supermarket may offer to terminate its lease for a substantial fee, and if the landlord refuses, the supermarket will sublease its space. Since the landlord wants to control the replacement anchor tenant and earn the increased rent, it usually buys out the remaining term, which includes multiple options, from the supermarket.

Improving the tenant mix is a major consideration in a lease buyout. An existing tenant's ability to operate successfully is another. If a tenant is likely to struggle with its rent payment for the remainder of its lease term, negotiating a lease buyout or mutual cancellation may be better. The time remaining in the lease term determines whether to offer a buyout and how much to offer. A tenant whose lease term has several years remaining may be able to negotiate a higher buyout payment than one who has only a short lease term remaining.

Once the amount of the buyout has been determined, the next decision is how payment will be made. The buyout can be paid in a lump sum when the lease is terminated or in installments. The latter may be paid monthly over the remaining term of the cancelled lease or over the term of the replacement tenant's lease.

Before negotiating a buyout, the shopping center manager should approach several prospective replacement tenants and identify one or two who are interested in leasing the space when it becomes available. However, telling prospective tenants that a particular tenant will be approached for a mutual lease termination or buyout is not advisable (or necessary) because that would place the replacement prospect in a stronger negotiating position.

Store Split. Sometimes a tenant that can generate an equivalent sales volume in less space would be happy to give up part of its leased space in order to reduce its occupancy expenses. As an example, a 10,000-square-foot dollar or fabric store may be able to do the same level of business in a 7,500-square-foot store. The 2,500 square feet that the tenant gives up may be divisible into two 1,250-square-foot spaces. If so, the rent for the 2,500-square-foot space or the two smaller spaces is likely to be twice the rate per square foot that the larger user paid for the area, and one or two new merchants will be added to the shopping center's tenant mix. A reduction in the amount of space leased may or may not be specifically compensated.

Such a store split may be negotiated as part of a lease renewal, with the large tenant paying a higher rent per square foot for the space retained. However, if the store split is arranged during an ongoing lease term, the exchange of funds (from landlord to tenant or vice versa) may amount to a partial lease buyout.

The cost of splitting the store and creating one or two new stores can be considerable. The new space or spaces will need new store fronts, entrance doors, possibly back doors, and separate restrooms. In addition, the utilities (e.g., electricity, gas) must be separated. New heating, ventilating, and air conditioning units (HVAC) may need to be installed for each of the new spaces. The increased cash flow and value usually more than justify the cost of splitting the stores and the possible buyout fee.

Lease buyouts and store splits are unique opportunities for shopping centers to increase NOI, cash flow, and the value of the property. The shopping center manager and the leasing agent have endless opportunities to improve the shopping center by improving the tenant mix, upgrading tenants, negotiating lease buyouts and splits, establishing temporary leasing. Maintaining an aggressive and proactive leasing plan when a property is 100 percent leased will minimize the number of vacancies and the amount of lost rent over the life of the shopping center.

Leasing Problem Shopping Centers

Leasing shopping centers that have excessive vacancies requires all the analysis discussed above. The most important component of a leasing plan for a troubled shopping center is the selection of the right leasing agent. The leasing agent must have sufficient time to devote to leasing the problem shopping center.

The leasing agent must also have a compensation package that encourages the person to devote most or all of his or her time to accomplishing the task of leasing the excessive space. This usually requires a salary or monthly fee in addition to the opportunity to earn commissions. The salary or monthly fee, which is not applied against the commission earned, is necessary because the chances of making deals on a problem shopping center are much less likely than on a typical shopping center. The salary or monthly fee enables the leasing agent to focus on leasing the problem shopping center and not worry about having an income stream to pay personal expenses.

A compensation structure that was successful in shopping centers managed by one of the authors is payment of $5,000 to $8,000 a month plus a market rate commission for a leasing agent working full-time on the problem shopping center. The agreement with the leasing agent is for 6 to 12 months. After that period, the leasing results are evaluated and a decision is made whether to continue the arrangement. The cost for this arrangement is nominal considering the monthly loss of rent and other charges from several vacancies and the significant impact the vacancies have on the value of the shopping center. The leasing agent is given an on-site office. One of the more visible vacant spaces is converted into a temporary office with attractive, but minimal, office furniture and equipment.

Being on-site, the leasing agent can get to know the tenants, talk to shoppers about what types of merchants they would like to have at the shopping center, easily canvass or cold call the area, and generate walk-in prospects. When the leasing agent operates from an on-site office he or she is not distracted by other activities and can focus 100 percent of the time on leasing the problem shopping center.

If the leasing agent is from out-of-town, housing should be located close to the shopping center. This allows the leasing agent to quickly become knowledgeable about the shopping center's trade area and to get to know other retailers and restaurant operators in the area through daily shopping and eating out. In this situation, the leasing agent is provided a housing allowance.

After meeting with the tenants, studying the trade area and the competition, and completing the other steps necessary to leasing a retail property that are discussed in this chapter, the leasing agent must analyze the shopping center's positioning in the market. This analysis concludes with a review of whether the shopping center should be remodeled, redesigned, or changed to another retail or other use.

For instance, a small, distressed, enclosed community mall anchored by a supermarket and a super drugstore was de-malled and converted to a large grocery anchored strip shopping center. Strip shopping centers in which smaller anchor spaces were vacated have combined adjacent spaces with the anchor space to create a larger anchor space to accommodate a state-of-the-art supermarket.

When leasing a problem shopping center, the leasing agent must develop a new story based on realistic goals and facts about the shopping center. This story could be of the remodeling or repositioning of the property, a new anchor tenant, or more aggressive lease terms. Marketing materials must be developed to support the new story. The final components to the leasing plan must include extensive cold calling because problem shopping centers have a reputation among retailers as being a difficult place to earn a profit. The leasing agent must spend considerable time conveying the new story of the shopping center so prospective tenants can reanalyze their potential success at the shopping center.

The lease negotiations must reflect the current conditions of the shopping center. The leasing agent—and especially the property owner—must be flexible in negotiating the rental and other lease terms. Lease concessions may include one of a combination of the following: free rent, percentage rent only for a specific period or the entire lease term, lower starting rent, cancellation rights, caps on tenant charges, and other concessions. (These provisions are discussed in detail in chapter 10, Negotiating and Documenting the Lease Terms.) The landlord may need to offer the better tenants lease provisions that seldom are granted, such as co-tenancies and cancellation rights. Leasing a shopping center that is experiencing difficulties requires lease concessions, but the analysis discussed above provides a clear indication of the extent of the concessions that must be provided to "do the deal."

An effective marketing and leasing program can increase the net operating income and enhance the value of a shopping center more than any other aspect of its operations. A successful program begins with the selection of the right leasing team. Every member of the leasing team must fully understand and faithfully perform the team's many responsibilities—from attending leasing meetings through leasing problem shopping centers.

10

Negotiating and Documenting the Lease Terms

The successful negotiation of leases is one of the most important responsibilities the shopping center manager and the leasing agent have. The outcomes of lease negotiations have long-term effects on the shopping center in many ways.

First, they impact the shopping center's value. An investor's primary criterion for purchasing a property is for its income stream and the resultant net operating income (NOI). Most lease provisions impact the property's NOI and value—either directly or indirectly.

The lease also establishes the shopping center's tenant mix. The use provision grants each tenant the right to sell specific products or services while an exclusive provision prohibits other tenants from selling specific products or services—thereby eliminating many potential tenants. The skillful negotiation of these provisions is critical to developing the best tenant mix for the shopping center and the trade area and one that complements the anchor tenants.

Nonmonetary lease provisions provide parameters within which the tenants operate their businesses. These provisions include establishing the hours the tenants must operate, whether they must join a coordinated advertising program, where their employees can park, and many other issues necessary for the successful operation of the shopping center.

Finally, the lease provides for remedies for monetary and nonmonetary defaults. These provisions include penalties (such as charges for late rent payment), and provide remedies for curing the defaults.

The person responsible for negotiating the lease must understand how each lease provision impacts the cash flow and value of the shopping center as well as its tenant mix and daily operations. Most shopping center leases are several pages long and may include lengthy, complicated documents, e.g., Reciprocal Easement Agreements (REAs) or Common Area Agreements. These leases can be intimidating.

To be prepared for lease negotiations, shopping center professionals must understand every lease provision and know how each one affects the shopping center's value and/or operations. With a thorough understanding of the lease document, the shopping center manager or leasing agent can negotiate each provision to achieve the best possible deal for the landlord and at the same time help the tenants succeed in the shopping center.

This chapter is designed as a reference for landlords, shopping center managers, leasing agents, and anyone else who negotiates shopping center leases. It begins by considering the preparation necessary for negotiations. Next, it covers the types of shopping center leases and the components that are required for a lease to be valid. Each of the essential lease components is then individually detailed. Because of the many unique facets of the anchor tenant lease and its negotiation, the chapter ends with an in-depth look at negotiating the anchor tenant lease.

PREPARING FOR NEGOTIATIONS

A thorough understanding of the lease, coupled with the ability to compromise through negotiation, distinguishes the deal maker from the deal breaker. The ultimate goal is not just to make the deal but also to make a good deal for both the landlord and the tenant. That is accomplished through careful preparation and skillful negotiations.

Preparation

The person who negotiates the lease must thoroughly understand the owner's goals and objectives for leasing the shopping center space. He or she must evaluate the prospective tenant and determine how well that prospect will fit in the current or projected tenant mix. The negotiator must also assess the relative strength of each party's negotiating position.

Evaluation of the Prospective Tenant. First, the negotiator evaluates the desirability of the prospective tenant and determines that tenant's motivation for renting the space. Then the negotiator reviews the prospective tenant's financial statement and assesses the prospect's merchandising abilities. What are the merchant's sales in other stores? What reputation does the prospective tenant have among consumers and other shopping center landlords? What are the merchant's business plan and three- to five-year budget projections? What percentage of budgeted sales does the rent for the subject store represent?

Tenant Mix Considerations. Next, the negotiator studies the shopping center's tenant mix. How well does the prospective tenant fit with the current tenant mix? What is the current and projected occupancy? Will this prospect be a customer draw or depend on the traffic of the other tenants? How important is this tenant to the shopping center's success? Will the tenant attract other tenants to the shopping center?

Alternative Locations. The negotiator also evaluates potential alternative locations for the prospect in the shopping center's trade area. What other locations are available that would meet the prospect's requirements? What other shopping centers in the area might be competing for the tenant? How do those shopping centers compare to the shopping center the leasing agent or shopping center manager is leasing? This information helps assess how strongly motivated the prospect will be to acquire the space and how strong the shopping center's negotiating position is.

Negotiations

Some landlords have attorneys negotiate their leases, but most have their shopping center managers or their leasing agents negotiate leases. The person who negotiates the lease should have a clear understanding and appreciation of his or her negotiating strengths.

The specifics of a lease are generally negotiable, and negotiations should result in a compromise between the landlord and the tenant that protects the landlord's position in the property and affords the tenant the opportunity to operate a successful business without unnecessary encumbrances. Each party must compromise on some issues to arrive at a win-win situation. Only then will both parties be satisfied with the outcome of the negotiations; only then can a deal can be completed. Once these areas of evaluation are completed, lease negotiations can begin.

THE LEASE FORM

The first area of negotiations involves the form of the lease to be used. Several types of lease forms exist, and the negotiator must understand the differences among them to make an informed negotiation. Both parties frequently have lease forms they prefer because both would like the lease to represent their ideal position on each provision. Whatever lease is ultimately chosen, it must contain six required components to be valid. This chapter details those components.

Types of Leases

When negotiating with tenants, different types of leases can be used. The differences among them are based on the kinds of operating expenses that are passed through to the shopping center tenant on a pro rata basis. The most common lease types follow:

- In a *gross lease,* the tenant pays base rent only. No charges are passed on to the tenants for reimbursement; in theory, those charges are included in the base rent.
- In a *net* (or *single-net*) *lease,* the tenant pays base rent plus real estate taxes.
- In a *net-net* (or *double-net*) *lease,* the tenant pays base rent plus real estate taxes and building insurance.
- In a *net-net-net* (or *triple-net*) *lease,* the tenant pays base rent plus real estate taxes, building insurance, and maintenance costs.
- A *fully net lease* is a type of triple-net lease that requires the tenant to pay capital and/or replacement costs.

The letters T I M (or the name) provide a useful mnemonic device for remembering the degrees of "net-ness": T = taxes, TI = taxes and insurance, TIM = taxes, insurance, and maintenance.

The foregoing are textbook definitions of gross and net leases. In the real estate industry, some people refer to a triple-net lease as a net lease, while others use the textbook definition. To avoid confusion when the terms "net" or "triple-net" are used, the negotiator should always confirm the intended definition of the term with the other party beforehand—especially if it is not spelled out in the lease.

Most shopping center leases are *modified triple-net leases* under which the landlord may have some maintenance obligations that are not billed back to the tenants (e.g., maintaining the vacant spaces and possibly the building exterior and the roof). However, since the late 1980s, the shopping center industry has moved in the direction of true triple-net leases, and by the beginning of the 1990s, many developers and property owners included roof maintenance, exterior building maintenance, and the management fee as common area expenses in shop tenants' leases. Those expenses are now common pass-through or common area maintenance (CAM) expenses. Anchor tenants often negotiate not to be charged for these expenses. (The last section of this chapter discusses the anchor tenant lease in detail.) Tenants in most shopping centers that were built over fifteen years ago are likely to have several different lease forms—many of which may have exceptions to a true triple-net lease.

Choice of the Lease Form

Both the landlord and the prospective tenant may have lease forms they prefer. If two documents are proposed, both sides must carefully read the documents and then agree on one. Regardless of whose lease form is used, both parties will attempt to negotiate the best deal for themselves. The party whose lease form is chosen starts the negotiations by presenting that party's side of each issue. The other party proposes alternatives to the provisions that might be detrimental to the deal from its viewpoint.

Landlord's Lease Form. The landlord's lease form is generally used when negotiating with local tenants and national shop tenants. Some national tenants will request to use their lease forms, but most will concede to the shopping center manager's insistence to use the landlord's lease. Anchor tenants usually require the use of their lease forms.

A landlord is usually willing to negotiate and compromise on numerous lease points with a strong regional or national tenant but will negotiate only a few items with a local merchant. Numerous lease questions are commonly raised for discussion or negotiation in a lease with a national shop tenant (e.g., Payless Shoes, Radio Shack), while a local merchant may be granted only a few changes to the lease. That occurs for several reasons.

National shop tenants usually have good credit ratings, are strong advertisers, and have established identities in the community. They have excellent reputations and appeal to the public. They are in high demand as tenants because of the volume of traffic they draw. National tenants rarely violate any lease provisions, and consequently, landlords tend to have fewer disputes with them. National tenants usually pay their rent and other occupancy expenses on time. In addition, their approach to merchandising and the business aspects of their operations is normally very professional.

Other Lease Form. When the tenant's lease form is used or the tenant agrees to the landlord's lease form but requests several changes, the shopping center negotiator must carefully review the tenant's lease or the tenant's requested changes to the landlord's lease. Each provision the shopping center negotiator wants to change from the tenant's lease or will not accept from the tenant's request should be listed with the reason why it is not acceptable and with a proposed alternative. This system provides the other party a clear understanding of the shopping center negotiator's position and thus expedites the lease negotiations.

Required Components of a Valid Lease

No matter which lease form is used, to be valid, it must include six required components, and they must be described and defined in very specific language. The required components are (1) the parties to the lease, (2) a description of the leased premises, (3) the term (duration) of the lease, (4) the consideration to be paid to the landlord, (5) a description of the tenant's use of the premises, and (6) the rights and obligations of both parties. These components may appear in a different order, but the six components must be present for the lease to be valid. The first five components are typically found on the first page or two, and the sixth requirement is covered throughout the rest of the lease. The next section of this chapter details each of the required components as well as information that may precede the body of the lease (a table of contents) and lease exhibits that may follow the lease.

SPECIFIC CONTENTS OF THE LEASE

The initial pages of the lease provide a summary of the basic lease terms and a listing of the parties to the lease. They also include a description of the permitted uses, the duration of the lease term with its commencement and expiration dates, the amount of minimum rent as well as rent escalations or increases, and when the first payment is to be made (rent commencement date), the percentage rent rate, the proration basis for pass-through tenant charges (itemized for operating expenses and common area maintenance), and the amount of the security deposit. If the lease requires a *guarantor*—i.e., another individual (or organization) who promises to assume the tenant's obligations in case of default—the name and address of that party are also included. Most of the information on the initial pages of the lease will be recorded on the lease summary used by the management firm to track variations among individual leases. (See chapter 6, Administration.) The remainder of the lease gives a detailed description of the rights and obligations of each party.

The descriptions that follow are intended to indicate the range of provisions in a retail lease, but their presentation is not always representative of the sequence in which they would appear. Many other provisions may apply in particular situations, and specific legal requirements vary in different areas of the United States.

Table of Contents

Because of the length and complexity of the retail lease, a table of contents usually precedes the lease itself, and those pages are numbered with lowercase Roman numerals. The table of contents is included with, but is not actually a part of, the lease. Its purpose is to identify the lease provisions and indicate the page numbers where they can be found in the lease document.

Parties to the Lease

This section includes the business name and address of the landlord. Also to be listed are the name and address of the tenant—in this case, the address of the leased space—and the tenant's home office, when that is appropriate. When the business operated by the tenant is a sole proprietorship, the tenant's home address should be included. When the tenant is a corporation, the address of the corporate headquarters is listed. This section also has spaces to list the tenant's *trade name*—the assumed (legal) business name.

Legal Competence. The lease must include the correct names and signatures of legally competent parties. If a minor signs a lease, it is voidable. The age of majority (usually between 18 and 21 years) varies from state to state, and an underage signatory may void the lease. Mental capacity is another criterion of legal competence. If a signatory of a lease is senile or insane, the lease is also voidable by the tenant.

Authority of Signatory. Establishing the authority of the individual who represents a business entity is essential. An entrepreneur signs the lease for a business as its owner. In the case of a corporation, an officer of the company may be a signatory on behalf of the corporation. However, the authority of that officer to commit the corporation to the lease should be officially documented. In fact, the landlord should require a corporate resolution authorizing the corporate officer to sign the lease. The corporate resolution should be appended to the lease as an exhibit. Lease exhibits are discussed at the end of this section.

Lease Guaranty. A lease guaranty is generally attached as a separate document (exhibit) to the lease. In some instances, the lease guarantor is different than the named tenant on the lease. Many states require that the signature of the parties to the lease be notarized. The notarial seal is typically placed on the bottom of the signature page.

Description of the Leased Premises

The lease must include a readily identifiable description of the leased premises. This takes several different forms—e.g., a street address, a description of the space covered by the lease, the legal description of the property.

Site Plan. A site plan showing the layout of the building is usually attached to the lease as an exhibit. The leased premises, including its dimensions, are identified on the site plan (cross-hatched, outlined in red, or otherwise delineated). A ground lease may include a *metes and bounds* (boundary) description of the land parcel.

Disclaimer. A disclaimer should be included on the site plan and in the body of the lease stating that the site plan is not drawn to scale and that the landlord has the sole right to alter the site plan without the tenant's approval. This disclaimer is very important in case the landlord wants to expand the shopping center by extending or adding a building, create a separate parcel in the parking lot for a pad or outlot tenant, or remodel or rehabilitate the property.

Landlord's Reserved Rights. In addition, the lease states the landlord's reserved rights with regard to the property as a whole:

1. The landlord has the right to change the size, layout, and dimensions of the shopping center and the parking areas and to modify the number and location of the buildings on the property.
2. The landlord makes no representation or warranty with respect to the occupancy of any tenant or tenants (including anchor tenants). This is intended to prevent a tenant from claiming the right to cancel the lease or sue for monetary damages if a particular tenant moves out or never takes possession of its premises.
3. The landlord has the right to lease space in the shopping center to any tenant for any purpose including retail, office, medical, governmental, and nonretail uses. Most shopping centers, regardless of their size, have some service and/or office tenants. This provision is to prevent the tenant from claiming the right to cancel the lease or seeking monetary damages if the shopping center is not occupied entirely by retail tenants. Sometimes a tenant may consider suing the landlord as a last resort to solve its financial problems. In that case, the tenant may claim that the landlord breached either a written covenant or an oral agreement. To ensure that there is no cause for such a claim, the shopping center's brochure should also refer to "retail, service, and office space" being available for lease rather than "retail space" only.
4. The landlord reserves to itself the exterior walls, the roof, and any installations in or on them.

Term or Duration of the Lease

A lease must have a finite term with fixed starting (commencement) and ending (termination) dates—e.g., "The term of this lease shall be five years, beginning on November 1, 2004, and ending on October 31, 2009." The lease should not have an open expiration date—e.g., a date "to be agreed upon in the future." To control occupancy levels, all of the leases in a shopping center should not expire on the same date; the expiration dates should be staggered over several months and several years.

Typical Duration. National shop tenants typically negotiate for a lease term of approximately 10 years; most local tenants negotiate for a lease term of 3 to 5 years. Landlords usually prefer a short lease term so the rent can be adjusted upward more frequently. Also, if a tenant's sales are poor, the landlord can replace the tenant with a stronger merchant sooner than would be possible under a longer-term lease.

An exception to this is a tenant whose build-out costs are high (e.g., a restaurant). Such a tenant needs a longer lease term to amortize the cost of the tenant improvements and fixtures; additionally, the loan to finance the purchase of the equipment may be for a period longer than 5 years. To accommodate these factors, this type of tenant may also be granted a short-term option to extend the lease. In that case, the lease term might be 10 to 20 years with one 5- to 10-year option. Leases for pad, parcel, and outlot tenants are typically for terms of 20 to 30 years—with options.

Tenants are usually the only ones who benefit from options, so granting them generally is not in the landlord's interest. Options provide tenants a right to extend their leases and place an obligation on the landlord to honor the tenants' decisions. Options are discussed in detail later in this chapter.

Holiday Term Extension. Regardless of the number of years involved, many landlords and tenants prefer a lease to be extended through the December holiday season. The extension gives the tenant an additional selling period and provides a greater opportunity for the tenant to pay percentage rent during the last year of the lease. (Most retailers do 20 to 30 percent of their annual sales volumes between the Thanksgiving and Christmas holidays.) A five-year lease that commences on September 1 and would normally expire on August 31 may be written for a term of five years and four months so it will expire on December 31.

Uncertain Commencement Date. When a lease is entered into before or during the construction of a shopping center, or if the tenant is to reconstruct an existing space, determining the exact commencement date may not be possible until the shopping center is complete. In that case, the lease may state: "The commencement date shall be 60 days after the landlord turns the premises over to the tenant, or the date the tenant opens for business, whichever occurs first." (A lease with an uncertain commencement date should also provide that the landlord and the tenant will sign a *lease commencement letter* that ratifies the actual commencement date.)

After Turnover of Premises. A retailer who enters into a lease will need time to build out the premises (or remodel a previously occupied space), move in fixtures and inventory, and set up merchandise displays. The tenant is typically given 30 to 60 days after turnover of the premises to ready the store to open for business; however, the tenant may be able to accomplish that in less time.

On a Specific Date. As another alternative, the lease may state that the commencement date will be the day the tenant opens for business, or a specific date, whichever occurs first. If the lease states a date of April 1 and the tenant opens for business *after* April 1, the lease term and payment of rent would commence on April 1. If the lease commences on a date other than April 1, the shopping center manager should send the tenant a letter (written notice) that states the actual commencement date and the expiration date. To avoid any dispute over this date, the lease commencement letter should provide a space for the tenant to sign (in acknowledgment); the letter should be sent to the tenant in duplicate; and the return of a signed copy should be requested.

Rent Abatement. A third option is not to charge tenants rent if they open before a specific date, such as in the above example that uses April 1 as the commencement date. This encourages tenants to open early and benefits the shopping center and the other tenants by having another operating business open sooner.

Landlord's Failure to Deliver Premises. In rare instances, the landlord may not be able to deliver the premises to the tenant on the agreed lease commencement date due to a delay in the construction of a new shopping center, the move-out of the existing tenant in the premises, or force majeure. Because the landlord does not want to lose the new tenant, in case of the landlord's failure to deliver the premises the lease should provide the following: (1) the lease remains in force, (2) the landlord cannot be held liable for any loss or damage, and (3) the minimum rent and all tenant charges are waived until such time as the landlord delivers possession of the premises to the tenant and the tenant has utilized the allotted time for start-up of the business (usually 60 days).

In negotiating the lease term, the tenant may request that any delay in possession should extend the term of the lease an amount of time equal to the period of delay. In fact, the tenant may insist that, if the delay extends beyond a certain number of months, the tenant has the right to cancel the lease.

Some retailers will only open a new store during specific periods of the year; they typically will not open one during what are considered *blackout periods* (e.g., November, December, or January). If a window of opportunity is missed, the retailer may not open for three or more months. These practices are not unreasonable. Regardless of when the tenant actually occupies the leased space, rent should be paid from the scheduled commencement date unless other arrangements have been made.

Monetary Lease Provisions

Because economic issues are of the utmost importance, most lease negotiations are focused on the monetary provisions. The provisions in the "rent" or "considerations to be paid to the landlord" sections in the initial lease pages detail many lease provisions that directly affect the property's NOI: minimum rent, percentage rent, Consumer Price Index (CPI) adjustments to rent, and pass-through operating expenses. Other monetary provisions that also directly affect the shopping center's NOI and value, such as expressly defined maintenance responsibilities of the landlord and the tenant, are found within provisions throughout the lease.

Minimum Rent. This provision states that the tenant will pay to the landlord, without notice or demand and without any deductions, a fixed annual minimum rent to be paid in monthly installments, in advance, on or before the first day of each month of the lease term. If the lease commences on a date other than the first of the month, the monthly minimum rent is prorated for the first month, based on a 30-day month.

If free rent is given to the tenant, the lease must be very specific whether or not all other charges (e.g., CAM, taxes, insurance) are also free during the free minimum or base rent period. The best way to prevent any misunderstanding is to state the date each of these charges will commence.

All rents and tenant charges, except percentage rent, are due and payable monthly concurrent with the payment of minimum rent. Percentage rent is usually paid at the end of the month based on the prior month's, quarter's, or year's sales. (Percentage rent is detailed below.) Collectively, these payments comprise the tenant's *occupancy costs.*

Minimum Rent Adjustment. This is one of the most negotiated lease provisions. The two issues to negotiate are the amount of each increase and the frequency of the increases. The landlord will want the rent adjusted annually. The tenant may initially asked for a flat rent during the term of the lease but will often agree to a periodic rent increase that will be adjusted annually or every few years.

Rent Adjustment Documentation. The increases may be stated as part of the minimum rent provision or in a separate provision. Regardless of its presentation, the provision for increased rent includes several blanks for listing the adjusted (stepped-up) annual and monthly rental rates and the periods they cover. The specific increases may be an agreed fixed amount (e.g., $1.00 per square foot per year) or a percentage increase.

Cost of Living Adjustment *(COLA).* Another approach—one that both landlords and tenants believe to be fair—is based on the rise in the cost of living (i.e., the inflation rate measured in the Consumer Price Index or CPI). The increase in minimum rent is based on the percentage increase in the CPI from one period to another.

Landlords generally believe that an annual CPI rent adjustment protects the property's value from increased operating expenses that are not reimbursed by the tenants and from inflation. However, tenants are usually concerned that the CPI increase may exceed the increase in their sales. For those reasons, minimum rent adjustment based on the CPI is negotiable.

In the early 1980s, the CPI increased more than 10 percent each year. To prevent a double-digit percentage increase in the minimum rent, tenants attempted to negotiate a ceiling or cap on the CPI increase—a tenant might agree to an annual CPI adjustment not to exceed 5 percent. In conceding to a CPI cap, the landlord will want to be assured of receiving no less than an agreed minimum increase and therefore will negotiate for a floor to the CPI. Thus, if the tenant requests a 5 percent ceiling, the landlord may insist on a 3 percent floor. The lease in this situation may state, "The annual rental increase shall be based on the CPI but will be no greater than 5 percent and no less than 3 percent."

When the parties agree that the minimum rent adjustment is to be based on the CPI, several specific issues must be resolved and stated in the lease. Those issues are detailed in the following sections.

Base Year. The first is a definition of the *base year*—i.e., the year from which the CPI increases will be measured. Usually it is the year the tenant takes occupancy or the first full calendar year during which the tenant occupies the premises. A tenant that takes occupancy in November will want the base year to be the following year, but the tenant that assumes possession in February should accept the year in which the tenant first occupied the premises as the base year.

Effective Date. Along the same line, the next issue to resolve is the date the CPI rent increase is to become effective. CPI increases may commence on the anniversary of the rent commencement date or on January 1 following the rent commencement date. Thus, if a lease commenced July 1, 2005, the base period for rent adjustment would be the first year of the lease—July 1, 2005 to June 30, 2006. However, if the lease stated the CPI adjustment would commence "on January 1 after the lease commencement" (base year as defined above), the first lease adjustment would be for the period January 1, 2006, to December 31, 2006.

Geographic Price Index. A third issue to resolve is which geographic price index will be used. The CPI—published monthly by the U.S. Department of Labor, Bureau of Labor Statistics—includes the national (U.S. city) average as well as the averages for many (but not all) major metropolitan areas. (The CPI for a few cities is published bi-monthly—some in even-numbered months, others in the odd months—or semiannually.)

The landlord will not know how to compute the tenant's CPI-related rental increase until the CPI is published. The U.S. city average and the CPIs for those cities that are reported monthly is normally available three to four weeks after the adjusted month—i.e., the CPI for January is published around the end of February. For those metropolitan areas whose CPIs are published semiannually, the report may not be released until three or four months after the period ends. In a major metropolitan area whose CPI is not reported monthly, the landlord may prefer to use the U.S. city average to expedite the adjustment of tenants' minimum rents. For CPI increases, the landlord may prefer to use "All U.S. cities and U.S. averages" while the tenant may prefer "specific U.S. city and specific U.S. average."

Adjustment Frequency. The frequency of minimum rent adjustment is another issue to negotiate and resolve. Landlords prefer annual adjustments, while tenants usually negotiate for less-frequent adjustments (e.g., every three years). Anchor tenants often negotiate for a fixed rental increase every five years.

Full or Partial Adjustment. Also to be decided is whether the increase will be based on the full CPI (100 percent) or a part of it. In a partial adjustment, the agreement may be to increase the minimum rent based on a particular percentage of the CPI increase (e.g., .67 percent). Thus, if the CPI increase were 6 percent, the rent would be increased 4 percent (6 percent × .67 percent = 4 percent). However, if the change in the CPI were negative—i.e., a decrease from the prior period—the minimum rent would not be reduced.

Percentage Rent. As mentioned earlier, tenants in shopping centers typically pay minimum (base) rent and, if sales exceed the breakeven point, they pay percentage rent—a pro rata share of real estate taxes, insurance, CAM expenses, and possibly other charges, e.g., marketing fund dues, heating, ventilation, and air-conditioning (HVAC) maintenance, etc. The typical retail lease provides for payment of the greater of the minimum rent or a percentage of the tenant's sales. The percentage rent provision states the percentage rate that applies. (The percentage rate varies with the type of business, as noted in chapter 9, Leasing the Shopping Center.) Most tenants will accept a fixed percentage rate for the entire term of the lease. Negotiating percentage rent with an anchor tenant is discussed in the anchor tenant section at the end of this chapter.

Note that percentage rent is one of the shopping center's income components and can have a significant impact on the property's NOI and value. Negotiating the percentage rate determines the landlord's opportunity to collect percentage rent and the amount of percentage rent that will be collected. *Dollars & Cents of Shopping Centers,* published by the Urban Land Institute, lists the median percentage rate and the lower and upper decile percentage rates (the typical range) for each tenant category.

Establishing Breakpoints. The lease establishes the tenant's annual and monthly breakpoints. When sales exceed the breakpoint, the tenant owes percentage rent. The breakpoint can be natural or artificial. A *natural breakpoint* is derived using a simple mathematical formula:

Rent ÷ Percentage Rate = Breakpoint

An *artificial breakpoint* is one that has been negotiated. When tenant improvements are very expensive or a tenant's store is being remodeled, the tenant may negotiate to set an artificial breakpoint *above* the natural breakpoint. This allows the tenant to offset the cost of the improvements with some of the percentage rent that would otherwise be owed if a natural breakpoint applied. If the shopping center's sales are substantially higher than average, the landlord may insist on an artificial breakpoint *below* the natural breakpoint so percentage rent is greater and becomes due earlier. In this situation, the landlord is in a strong negotiating position and can command an advantageous artificial breakpoint. Similarly, the landlord who contributes to the tenant's improvements and wishes to be expeditiously reimbursed for that contribution may insist on an artificial breakpoint *lower* than the natural breakpoint. (Appendix C, Math Basics for Shopping Center Managers, provides additional information regarding breakpoint and other financial calculations.)

Decreasing Percentage Rate. Some tenants, usually the anchor tenants, will negotiate for a declining percentage rate. For instance, a supermarket may agree to a specific rate to determine the breakpoint and want the rate to decline as its sales increase. The supermarket may agree to a percentage rate of 2 percent to determine the breakpoint and then 1.5 percent for the next $5,000,000 of sales and 1.25 percent on all additional sales. Exhibit 10.1 shows the calculation of the declining percentage rent for the supermarket.

Exhibit 10.1

Decreasing Percentage Rate Example: Supermarket

LEASE TERMS		
Store size	50,000 square feet	
Rent	$12 per square foot	
Minimum rent	$600,000	
Percentage rent	2% to breakpoint 1.5% next $5,000,000 1.25% all additional sales	
Sales breakpoint ($600,000 ÷ 2%)	$30,000,000	
SALES		
Tenant sales		$37,000,000
Less sales breakpoint		−$30,000,000
Sales above breakpoint		$ 7,000,000
Less next $5,000,000		−$ 5,000,000
All additional		$ 2,000,000
PERCENTAGE RENT CALCULATION		
Next $5,000,000 after breakpoint × 1.5%		$ 75,000
Plus all additional $2,000,000 × 1.25%		$ 25,000
Total percentage rent		$100,000
TOTAL RENT		
Minimum annual rent		$600,000
Total percentage rent		$100,000
Total rent owed		$700,000
Total rent per square foot		$14.00

Increasing Percentage Rate. A landlord may negotiate for an increasing percentage rate after the tenant's sales exceed a specific amount. One percentage rate is used to determine the breakpoint and a higher percentage rate is applied to all sales above the breakpoint. The calculation of the increasing percentage rent for the restaurant is shown in exhibit 10.2.

Percentage Rent Payments. Though percentage rent owed is based on annual sales, landlords prefer to receive percentage rent payments on a monthly basis. In fact, shop tenants are usually required to submit sales reports monthly, typically by the twentieth day of the following month—i.e., January sales figures and percentage rent owed are due no later than February 20th—but anchor tenants usually submit sales reports and pay percentage rent annually.

Because collecting sales reports and percentage rent can be more diffi-

Exhibit 10.2
Increasing Percentage Rate Example: Restaurant

LEASE TERMS		
Store Size	3,000 square feet	
Rent	$20 per square foot	
Minimum rent	$60,000	
Percentage rent	5% to breakpoint 6% all additional sales	
Sales breakpoint ($60,000 ÷ 5%)	$1,200,000	
SALES		
Tenant sales		$1,750,000
Less sales breakpoint		−$1,200,000
Sales above breakpoint		$ 550,000
PERCENTAGE RENT CALCULATION		
All additional **$550,000 × 6%**		$27,500
TOTAL RENT		
Minimum annual rent		$60,000
Total percentage rent		$27,500
Total rent		$87,500
Total rent per square foot		$29.17

cult than collecting minimum rent, many leases provide for a monetary penalty or fee if tenants do not submit sales reports on time.

Percentage Rent Refunds. If the tenant pays percentage rent for some months based on monthly calculations, but annual sales ultimately are not sufficient to mandate payment of percentage rent, the landlord is obliged to refund the excess percentage rent to the tenant after the first of the year.

One type of tenant whose sales fluctuate greatly from month to month is a candy store. Sales may be high during five months of the year because of specific holidays—e.g., Valentine's Day in February, Easter in March or April, Mother's Day in May, Father's Day in June, and Christmas in December—and the store may owe percentage rent for some or all of those five months but not for the other months of the year. If this tenant's annual sales do not exceed its annual breakpoint, then the percentage rent paid during the months that sales exceeded the monthly breakpoint is typically refunded to the tenant by the end of February of the following year. Ultimately, and unless the lease states otherwise, annual sales determine whether or not a tenant pays percentage rent or receives a refund of percentage rent paid during the year.

Gross Sales Definition. The percentage rent provision also defines the gross sales to which the percentage rate will be applied and lists which items, if any, may be excluded from gross sales. Sales tax is one exclusion; refunds and returns may also be deducted. Tenants often seek to exclude discounted sales to their employees, and landlords may be willing to grant this but with limitations—i.e., the lease may refer to "sales to employees at a discount, not to exceed 2 percent of Tenant's total gross sales." Landlords want to include as many items as possible in the definition of gross sales to maximize the opportunity to collect percentage rent. Obviously, tenants prefer the opposite.

Key Money. A seldom-used lease provision that benefits the landlord is the *key money provision.* The tenant pays the landlord a fee, usually a substantial amount, for the right to lease space in a retail property. This provision might be used for a new retail property that everyone expects to be a great success or an existing retail property that is extremely successful. Landlords are rarely able to charge this fee.

Tenant's Pro Rata Share. The tenant's proportionate share of the pass-through expenses is calculated as a percentage based on the relationship between the square footage of the tenant's premises and the leasable area (also known as *built and ready for leasing*) or the leased areas (also known as *open and occupied*) of the shopping center. The distinction here is between potential and actual leased square footage, and the difference in the resulting payment can be substantial. The *leasable area* includes the square footage of all the buildings in the shopping center, whereas the *leased areas* comprise those spaces in the shopping center that are actually under lease.

Leasable Area Formula. Shopping center leases typically base the tenants' pro rata shares on the leasable area, which includes all occupied and vacant spaces in the shopping center. Each tenant's pro rata share is computed by multiplying the specific expense (e.g., insurance, taxes, CAM) by a fraction, the numerator of which is the GLA of the tenant's premises and the denominator of which is the GLA of the shopping center:

GLA of Tenant's Space ÷ GLA of Shopping Center = Tenant's Pro Rata Share

Leased Space Formula. When the formula is based on leased space, the numerator is still the GLA of the tenant's premises, but the denominator is the GLA of the leased spaces only:

Exhibit 10.3

Example Lease Clause—Tenant's Pro Rata Share

For the purposes of this Lease with respect to allocations of each Tenant's share of taxes, insurance, common area maintenance expenses and other Tenant charges, the term "Tenant's Pro Rata Share" shall be a fraction, the numerator of which is the gross leasable area of the Premises and the denominator of which is the gross leasable floor area of the buildings constructed within the Shopping Center from time to time. Provided, however, that if any tenants in said buildings have obtained written approval from Landlord to pay their taxes directly to any taxing authority, or to carry their own insurance, or to maintain part of the common area at their own expense, their square footage shall not be deemed a part of the floor area for the purposes of prorating said taxes, or said insurance, or said common area maintenance expenses.

GLA of Tenant's Space ÷ GLA of Leased Spaces = Tenant's Pro Rata Share

As a result, the denominator changes every time a space is vacated or leased. Also, as the denominator gets smaller, the tenant's pro rata share gets larger.

Pro Rata Formulas Compared. For example, a tenant in a 2,000-square-foot space in a shopping center that has 100,000 square feet of GLA has a pro rata share of 2 percent based on leasable square footage (2,000 ÷ 100,000 = .02). However, if the shopping center is only 80 percent occupied, that tenant's pro rata share becomes 2.5 percent when based on the leased space (2,000 ÷ 80,000 = .025). That one-half percent difference becomes more meaningful when applied specifically. If the pass-through tenant charges (CAM, taxes, and insurance) total $300,000, the tenant in the example pays $6,000 based on the leasable area ($300,000 × .02) but the same tenant would have to pay $7,500 based on the leased area ($300,000 × .025).

The above example plainly demonstrates why tenants believe they are being unfairly penalized by having to pay a higher percentage of tenant charges because the landlord is unable to lease the vacant spaces in the shopping center. The landlord's argument for using leased space as the denominator is that the current tenants and their visitors are the only ones using the whole of the common areas of the shopping center.

Most sophisticated tenants will not accept a pro rata formula based on the leased area, and most shopping center leases use the leasable square footage in the denominator. (An example of a definition of "tenant's pro rata share" based on the leasable area appears in exhibit 10.3.)

Pro Rata Payments. Most shopping center leases require tenants to pay their pro rata shares of tenants' charges (pass-through expenses) each month based on the landlord's estimated budget. After the end of the year, the actual costs are reconciled with the budget. If the total paid out exceeds the budget, the tenants will be billed for their shares of the difference. However, if the budget exceeds the actual costs, the overpayment is returned to the tenants, either as an outright refund or as a credit toward the next month's rent. (See also the discussion of lease administration in chapter 6.)

Common Area Maintenance. CAM charges are a major component of pass-through expenses. They include several expense categories—e.g., maintenance, utilities, insurance, security, and administration.

Lease Language. The lease should not limit the expenses included in the CAM charges by stating that the tenant will pay "the following list of expenses." The tenant may interpret this to mean that any expenses incurred but not listed are not CAM expenses. The landlord should have the right to pass through to the tenant all the legitimate expenses of maintaining and operating the common areas of the shopping center.

The lease should state the basic CAM expenses and allow for additional CAM items. Representative lease language would be "the common area maintenance expenses shall include but are not limited to the following list," and the provision would include an itemized list of specific components of the CAM charge "and such other related expenses as may be incurred."

Unanticipated and Major Expenses. The provision should allow for unanticipated expenditures such as a need for temporary or permanent security. Many landlords also pass through as CAM expenses such items as roof repairs, painting of the building exterior, and funding (development of capital reserves) for future maintenance for such items as parking lot resurfacing or replacing the flooring in an enclosed mall. Alternatively, separate provisions may define those expenses and state how the tenant's pro rata share is determined.

Management Fee or Administrative Fee. In the late 1980s, some landlords began including the management fee as a CAM expense. (An example of a CAM provision that includes the management fee is shown in exhibit 10.4 on page 293.)

If the management fee is not included as a CAM expense, common practice is to add an administrative fee for supervision of the common areas. This fee may be 10 to 15 percent of the actual common area expenses. When the CAM charges include the management fee, charging an additional administrative fee is inappropriate because both charges are for the same services.

Anchor tenants are generally the only tenants that object to the management fee as a CAM expense. However, they will agree to an administrative fee. Typically, the management fee, which is usually based on a percentage of the property's collected income, is much greater than an administrative fee, which is a percentage of the common area maintenance.

CAM Accounting. The CAM provision gives the landlord the right to give the tenant an estimate of the CAM charges for the coming year. It also obligates the landlord to provide the tenant a year-end adjustment of the estimate to the actual CAM expense by a specific date.

Some landlords charge tenants a flat CAM charge and do not adjust the charge based on the actual CAM expenses. This gives the tenants a known cost for CAM charges. It is risky for the landlord because the expenses may exceed the flat charge.

Open and Enclosed Mall CAM. A mall has two CAM budgets—one for the parking lot and exterior areas and one for the mall common areas. This permits separation of these pass-through expenses for tenant billings. Tenants who do not front on the mall, such as pad or outlot tenants, pay their pro rata shares of the parking lot and exterior CAM expenses, but they are not billed for the mall CAM expenses. Anchor tenants often negotiate exemptions from paying enclosed mall CAM expenses. In such cases, the anchor tenant pays only a pro rata share of parking lot and exterior CAM expenses.

When the anchor is exempted from paying mall CAM expenses, the landlord usually wants the shop tenants to pay the entire cost of the mall CAM. Each shop tenant's proration is then based on the square footage of its premises divided by the total square footage occupied by shop tenants whose stores front on the mall. (Store areas of shops in a satellite building and/or pad tenants are not included.) That produces an equation that is a variation of the leased space formula discussed in the section on the tenant's pro rata share above:

GLA of Tenant's Space ÷ GLA of Shop Tenants with Mall Frontage
= Tenant's Pro Rata Share

Thus, if a mall has 800,000 square feet of GLA of which shop tenants occupy 200,000 square feet, anchor tenants have 575,000 square feet, and pad tenants occupy 25,000 square feet, the denominator for the shop tenants' proration formula would be 200,000 square feet. A shop tenant in a 2,000-square-foot space would pay 1 percent of the mall CAM costs (2,000 square feet ÷ 200,000 square feet = .01). However, the denominator for parking lot and exterior CAM for all tenants would be 800,000 square feet, and the same shop would pay one-fourth of one percent as its share of those costs (2,000 square feet ÷ 800,000 square feet = .0025).

An example of a provision that provides for the exclusion of the anchor tenant's square footage in determining a shop tenant's pro rata share of mall CAM expenses is shown in exhibit 10.5 The sample provision also includes an administrative fee.

Exhibit 10.4
Example Lease Clause—Common Area Maintenance

1. The term "common areas" refers to all areas within the exterior boundaries of the Shopping Center which are now or hereafter made available for general use, convenience and benefit of Landlord and other persons entitled to occupy space in the Shopping Center, which areas shall include but not be limited to parking areas, driveways, open or enclosed malls, sidewalks, landscaped and planted areas, and roofs.
2. The Landlord shall keep or cause to be kept the common areas in a neat, clean, and orderly condition, properly lighted and landscaped, and shall repair any damage to the facilities thereof, but all expense in connection with the common areas shall be charged and prorated in the manner hereinafter set forth. It is understood and agreed that the terms "common area maintenance charge" and "expenses in connection with the common areas" as used herein shall be construed to include, but not be limited to, all sums expended in connection with the common areas for all general maintenance and repairs, relocation of facilities; resurfacing; painting; striping; restriping; cleaning; snow removal; sweeping and janitorial services; maintenance and repair of sidewalks, curbs and Shopping Center signs, landscaping, irrigation or sprinkling systems; planting and landscaping; lighting and other utilities; directional signs and other markers and bumpers; all roof repairs and maintenance including but not limited to patching, resurfacing and preventive maintenance and painting or renovation of the exterior portion of all or any part of the improvements constructed on the Shopping Center; maintenance and repair of any fire protection systems, lighting systems, storm draining systems and any; other utility systems; all cost or expense incurred by reason of any repairs or modifications to the Shopping Center and/or its improvements and/or repair or installation of equipment for energy or safety purposes; personnel to implement such services including, if Landlord deems necessary, the cost of a maintenance supervisor and/or the cost of security guards; all costs and expenses pertaining to a security alarm system for the tenants and/or Shopping Center; reserves for future maintenance and repair work and reserves for replacement of existing capital improvements in the common areas which Tenant hereby authorizes Landlord to use as Landlord deems necessary; personal property taxes on the improvements located on the common areas; fees incurred in managing the Shopping Center and in the performance, management and supervision of the common area maintenance services and obligations and/or administering the accounting, bookkeeping and collection of the expenses in connection with the common areas and Shopping Center; and public liability and property damage insurance covering the common areas in amounts as required by Landlord. Landlord may cause any or all of said services to be provided by an independent contractor or contractors.
3. Should Landlord acquire or make available land not shown as part of the Shopping Center on the Site Plan Exhibit and make the same available for parking or other common area purposes, then said expenses in connection with the common areas shall also include all of the aforementioned expenses incurred and paid in connection with said additional land.

CAM Insurance. Note that the sample provision in exhibit 10.4 refers specifically to insurance coverage. In the absence of an itemized list, the reference can be inferred in exhibit 10.5. The insurance included in CAM charges is for property damage to the common areas and for liability coverage if someone is injured in those areas. This portion of the insurance premiums

Exhibit 10.5

Example Lease Clause—Enclosed Mall Common Area Maintenance

Shop tenants having storefronts on the enclosed mall shall pay their Pro Rata Share of the enclosed mall operation and maintenance expense; Tenant shall pay to Landlord a monthly enclosed mall maintenance charge to defray the enclosed mall operation and maintenance expenses; provided, however, that it is understood and agreed that the area leased by major tenants having storefronts on the mall shall not be included within the formula used to determine Tenant's Pro Rata Share of mall operation and maintenance expenses. In addition, Tenant shall pay a monthly sum to Landlord for the accounting, bookkeeping and collection of the enclosed mall operation and maintenance expenses in an amount equal to fifteen percent (15%) of the total of Tenant's Pro Rata Share of the aforementioned expenses for such year. The amount of the monthly enclosed mall maintenance charge shall be equal to Tenant's Pro Rata Share of the mall operation and maintenance expense. The share shall be determined by multiplying such expense amounts (less the sums, if any, contributed by major tenants for such expenses, under their leases) by the Tenant's percentage of enclosed mall operation and maintenance expenses, which percentage is computed by obtaining a fraction, the numerator of which is the leasable area of the Premises and the denominator of which is the gross leasable floor area of shops and services located in and fronting on the enclosed mall area.

is excluded from the building insurance expense that is billed separately to the tenants. (That insurance expense is discussed below.) The insurance premiums are divided this way because some tenants—i.e., those in freestanding buildings and sometimes the anchor tenants—are responsible for providing their own fire, extended coverage, and liability insurance.

For example, the landlord would not include a freestanding restaurant in the insurance coverage for the shopping center, and the restaurant's square footage would be excluded from the denominator used in calculating the other tenants' pro rata shares of the building insurance expense. However, the restaurant tenant would still be obligated to pay a pro rata share of the common area maintenance expenses, including the liability and property damage insurance coverage on the common areas as already mentioned. By allocating part of the premium for the insurance on the whole shopping center as a CAM expense, the landlord ensures that those tenants who pay for maintenance of the common area also pay to insure it. The same situation prevails when an anchor tenant owns and insures its building but pays a pro rata share of CAM expenses.

Security Deposit. A *security deposit* is an amount paid by the tenant to the landlord to be used as recourse if the tenant were in default of the lease. It is not intended to be the last month's rent.

Anchor tenants and national shop tenants typically have established credit ratings, and they will negotiate to omit the provision for a security deposit. On the other hand, local and regional merchants will agree to pay a security deposit. In lieu of a specific deposit, the lease can require the tenant to provide a letter of credit valued at a certain amount.

Amount of the Security Deposit. The amount of the security deposit is typically one month's rent. However, if the tenant's business is new or financially weak, the equivalent of two or even three months' rent as a security deposit may be appropriate or necessary.

Landlord's Use of the Security Deposit. If the tenant does not pay the monetary obligations under the terms of the lease, the security deposit may be used to cure the nonpayment. The security deposit may also be used to undertake repairs or maintenance as required of the tenant under the lease but that the tenant refuses to perform. The security deposit provision should require the tenant to reimburse (or restore) the full amount of the security deposit held by the landlord if the deposit is used to cure a default by the tenant.

Early Refund of the Security Deposit. A financially strong local or regional tenant with a successful business may negotiate for an early refund of the security deposit. For example, the landlord may agree to credit the security deposit to the rent for the twenty-fifth month if the tenant's rent has always been paid every month by the first of the month and the tenant was never in default of the lease during the first two years. If a tenant paid a larger-than-usual security deposit because of a weak financial statement and faithfully performs all of the lease obligations for two years, the excessive portion of the security deposit may also be refunded early—on the twenty-fifth month of the lease.

Another approach is to make an early refund contingent on the tenant's sales exceeding an agreed dollar volume or the payment of percentage rent. This provision might read, "If Tenant's sales exceed $350 per square foot during the second calendar year of the lease, and if Tenant's rent has always been paid on or before the first of each month, and if Tenant was never in default of the lease, the security deposit will be credited to the twenty-fifth month's rent."

A reverse approach requires no security deposit unless the tenant's net worth falls below an agreed amount; however, this approach is more difficult to monitor. The best policy is not to refund the security deposit prior to the expiration of the lease.

Return after Lease Expiration. The security deposit provision usually concludes with a statement that the landlord will return the security deposit to the tenant without interest and within a set number of days after the ex-

Exhibit 10.6

Example Lease Clause—Real Estate Taxes

The term "real estate taxes" shall include all real estate taxes and assessments, whether special or general, and including any road improvement districts, water improvement district, if any, and any other utility installation hookup, tie in, or similar charges or assessments that are levied upon and/or assessed against the Premises or the Shopping Center and/or payable during or with respect to the Lease Term, and the costs of professional consultants and/or counsel to analyze tax bills and prosecute any protests, refunds, and appeals, provided that all such payments shall be paid on a cash basis without regard to whether such real estate taxes apply to a period before or after the Lease Term and without regard to whether the Tenant was in possession of the Premises during the time covered by the particular tax statement.

piration of the lease term, depending on local laws, and if the tenant has faithfully performed each provision of the lease.

Taxes. The tenants usually pay the real estate taxes and assessments levied by local governments against the shopping center or other retail properties. The landlord usually estimates the amount of the taxes and other assessments, bills the tenants monthly for the charge, and adjusts the estimated payments to the actual cost early the following year.

A prudent shopping center manager analyzes each successive assessment when it is received. If the analysis reveals that the assessment is incorrect, the shopping center manager may hire a consultant to appeal it. If the appeal is successful, the savings will be passed on to the tenants—their pro rata shares of the taxes will be lowered. Because the tenants will be the beneficiaries of any tax savings, it is appropriate that the lease require the tenant to pay for the analysis and appeal of the assessment. An example of a typical "real estate taxes" lease provision is shown in exhibit 10.6.

Insurance. The tenant is responsible for reimbursing the landlord's cost to insure the property. This provision should not limit the type or amount of insurance coverage that may be necessary. The lease may state that "insurance shall include all insurance premiums for fire, liability, rent loss, flood, earthquake, and any other insurance and endorsement, which may include an 'all risk' endorsement or any other insurance that the Landlord or Landlord's lender deems necessary." Some anchor tenants may attempt to have specific coverage, such as earthquake and loss of rent insurance, excluded from their pro rata insurance cost.

Anchor and freestanding pad tenants usually insure their buildings. The shopping center manager should separate the cost of the building's insurance from the common area insurance. The building insurance is billed to all the tenants whose premises are covered by the landlord's insurance, and the cost of the insurance for the common area is included in the common area billings to all tenants, as discussed above.

A landlord should carry "Loss of Rents" insurance to protect itself when a tenant cannot pay rent due to destruction of the premises or the shopping center. A tenant should carry "Loss of Business Interruption" insurance to cover its expenses in case of destruction. (See chapter 6, Administration, for further discussion on insurance.)

Late Charge. The lease gives the landlord the right to assess a late charge if the tenant does not pay the rent by a predetermined date. If a tenant does not pay the rent on time, the landlord has two primary means of recourse—to give the tenant formal notice of default or to assess a late charge.

The provision may require the landlord to give the tenant written notice that the rent has not been received and to grant a grace period before the late charge is assessed. Alternatively, the lease may state that if the rent is not received on the date it is due, the landlord may automatically assess a late charge. Because most commercial tenants pay their rent by mail, the landlord should give a three- to five-day grace period before the late charge is assessed.

The amount of the late charge should be stated (e.g., 12 percent of the amount past due); in no event should the percentage rate be more than the legal maximum allowed. If the landlord uses the services of an attorney to collect delinquent rent, the attorney's fees should be a tenant expense in accordance with the terms of the lease.

Holdover. This provision has important economic implications for both parties. Any holdover by the tenant after the expiration or termination of the lease is construed to be a month-to-month tenancy subject to all the terms and conditions set forth in the lease. However, the minimum rent is increased for the holdover period—usually in an amount equal to one and one-half to four times the minimum rent due for the last month of the lease term. The greater the rent increase during the holdover period, the greater the likelihood that the tenant will agree to a lease renewal or vacate the premises. A large rental increase can motivate the departure of a tenant that is considering a delay in vacating the premises (past the lease termination date). This is especially helpful when the premises are already leased to another tenant that expects to take occupancy by a specific date.

Maintenance of Tenant's Premises. This provision states that the tenant is responsible for all repairs and maintenance to the leased premises. It also states which repair and maintenance items are the landlord's responsibility. The tenant is usually responsible for all maintenance inside the leased premises, and the landlord performs all maintenance outside the tenant's premises. Typically, the landlord maintains the exterior walls, roof, foundation, and structural portions of the building. The cost of repairing and maintaining some or all of those areas may be included in the CAM charges.

If the tenant fails to maintain the premises, the landlord, after written notice, has the option of performing the maintenance or repairs and charging the cost to the tenant. The tenant is expected to repay the landlord promptly for any such maintenance or repairs or the tenant may be placed in default.

Landlord's and Tenant's Work. The lease usually includes a provision that states the condition of the premises when the landlord delivers them to the tenant, and that the tenant agrees to accept the premises subject to completion of any landlord's work, which is to be described in the landlord's and tenant's work exhibit (discussed later in this chapter). The exhibit also specifies what work the tenant will provide in its premises.

Existing Shopping Center Space. Typically, when space in an existing shopping center or other retail property is leased, the tenant assumes the premises to be in "as is" condition. That usually means that the prior tenant's fixtures have been removed and the space is broom clean. In general, any painting and replacement of the prior tenant's improvements by the landlord would be wasted because the new tenant usually redesigns the premises for its specific business.

Most retailers and service tenants have their own unique store designs and layouts. Regional and national tenants usually have contractors who do all their tenant improvements in a specific area. They can build out a space more efficiently, at a better price, and often faster than if the landlord were to contract for the work.

When a tenant successfully negotiates with the landlord for tenant improvements, the landlord usually provides a monetary allowance and the tenant does the build-out. The allowance is paid *after* the tenant completes the improvements and provides the shopping center manager copies of the paid invoices for the work, lien releases, and a copy of the certificate of occupancy issued by the municipality's building department.

New Shopping Center Space. New shopping center space is usually leased in shell condition to be completed by the tenant. In a strip shopping center, the landlord may provide a concrete floor, unfinished demising walls, a drop ceiling, an HVAC unit, light fixtures, a restroom, and a storefront. In other types of shopping centers and in different areas of the United States, what is provided as shell space can vary substantially. A new regional mall may provide the tenants just a dirt floor and the rear exterior wall and the tenants must provide all the rest of the build outs. (See also the discussion of tenant improvements in chapter 5, Maintenance and Operations.) In these circumstances, the landlord provides a monetary allowance toward the tenant's build-out expense (e.g., $5 per square foot), or the landlord agrees to provide (build out) some or all of the improvements to the tenant's premises.

Tenant's Use of the Premises

The landlord's control over the shopping center's tenant mix is based on the allowable use or uses in each tenant's lease. The lease must state the tenant's use of the premises, and the use provision should be very specific about what business the tenant can conduct in the leased premises. Landlords often want to avoid unnecessary duplication of uses in order to enable each tenant to maximize its sales potential, which increases the possibility of percentage rent payment. In particular, a shopping center is likely to have only one dry cleaner, shoe repair, barber shop, or drugstore.

In some situations, having more than one tenant with the same use may be desirable. Regional malls as well as lifestyle, specialty, and outlet shopping centers include several clothing, shoe, gift, and jewelry stores to provide consumers a wide selection of merchandise and opportunities for comparison shopping. All types of shopping centers often have multiple restaurants.

The use provision should limit the type of business the tenant may operate and the products or services that can be sold, without being so restrictive that the tenant cannot operate successfully. Examples of tightly controlled uses are restaurants and shoe stores. If a shopping center has three restaurants, the landlord will not want all three to serve the same type of food. To do so would dilute the sales of each restaurant, limit the variety of selections available to customers, and reduce or eliminate the potential for percentage rent. The likely result would be that one or all of them could go out of business.

The use provision in a restaurant lease states the type of food, whether alcoholic beverages (liquor) may be served, and whether the food is eaten in the premises or not (i.e., carryout or drive-through). Such lease provisions might be phrased as follows: "Mexican restaurant with beer and wine for on-site consumption and takeout" or "Chinese restaurant with on-site consumption, takeout and delivery, and no liquor served." It is the exception to restrict carryout food.

Similarly, a landlord will not want every shoe store to sell the same types of shoes. A shoe store's use may be specified as retail sales of a particular type of shoes—women's, men's, children's, athletic, family.

Limit GLA for a Particular Use. When a tenant has a broad array of merchandise and the landlord does not want that tenant to dominate a particular product line, the use provision may limit the amount of gross leasable area (GLA) that can be devoted to a particular—perhaps subsidiary—use.

As an example, a bookstore may be allowed to use only 20 square feet of its premises for the display of greeting cards.

Limit Percentage of Sales for a Particular Use. Another way of limiting the use is to state what percentage of the store's entire sales a particular product may represent. A landlord who believes that only one candy store can be successful at the shopping center will be rightly concerned when a lease proposal is received from a card and gift store chain whose national format includes incidental sales of candy. In order to allow the card and gift store to operate its standard store and still protect the sales and potential percentage rent of a candy store, the use provision could limit the card and gift store's square footage of candy display or limit its percentage of candy sales. For instance, "Sales of candy may not exceed six square feet of display area." The other alternative is "Candy sales can not exceed 15 percent of the tenant's total annual sales volume." It is easier to monitor and enforce a restriction based on square footage than one based on sales. Another approach would be to state that the sales of candy are incidental to the sales of cards and gifts. (Exclusive use provisions are discussed later in this chapter.)

Legal Use. An additional requirement for tenant uses in general is that *the tenant's use must be legal.* If the tenant's use of the premises is illegal—i.e., gambling in a state where gambling is against the law—the lease is voidable, and the landlord may cancel it.

Rights and Obligations of the Parties

The last requirement of a valid lease are provisions regarding the rights and obligations of each party. These lease provisions include some of the monetary provisions already discussed that directly affect the shopping center's NOI and value as well as other provisions that indirectly affect the property's NOI. Several lease provisions can be detrimental to the landlord, and the shopping center negotiator should try to avoid them. If such provisions must be included, they should be negotiated with great care. Finally, these provisions cover management and operations issues that affect the operation of the tenant's business. Although these are generally nonmonetary issues, they can potentially affect the shopping center's profitability.

Provisions That Indirectly Affect NOI. While these provisions do not have the direct impact on the shopping center's net operating income and value that the monetary provisions have, they do indirectly affect the bottom line. Lease provisions that indirectly affect the property's NOI include sales reporting and landlord's auditing rights, merchants' association or marketing fund dues, assignment and subletting, radius restrictions, and exclusives.

Sales Reports. When tenants' rents are at or close to market rent, their sales typically do not exceed their breakpoint. The exceptions are in shopping centers and other retail properties in which most of the tenants produce exceptionally high sales; some categories of tenants, such as jewelry stores, trendy fashion stores, and restaurants may produce high sales wherever they are located. If the tenants' minimum rents are low, they are likely to pay percentage rent. This often occurs when a tenant is in the latter years of a long-term lease that has few rental increases.

The lease should require the tenant to submit sales reports to the landlord whether the lease contains a percentage provision or not. The best way for the landlord to know how the tenant is performing is to receive a monthly sales report. Even if the tenant is not required to pay percentage rent, the landlord and the shopping center manager need this information to determine whether to renew the tenant's lease. Monthly sales reports also provide the landlord with advance warning if the tenant is having financial problems. The sales reports from all the tenants enable the shopping center manager to better analyze the performance of the shopping center and each of its tenant categories.

Landlord's Auditing Rights. The percentage rent provision requires the tenant to submit monthly sales reports and an annual statement of sales signed by an officer of the company. The provision should also state that the payment of percentage rent does not constitute a partnership or joint venture relationship between the landlord and the tenant. The provision also requires tenants to maintain sales records for a minimum of three to five years and grants the landlord the right to audit the tenant's sales. The landlord is responsible for the cost of the audit unless the tenant's reported sales are inaccurate by a certain percentage or more. Some leases permit the landlord to cancel the lease if the tenant deliberately understates its sales.

Store Hours. This provision protects the landlord's opportunity to collect percentage rent. Landlords want all tenants to maintain necessary and reasonable hours to maximize their sales. Tenants have the best chance to maximize their sales if all tenants maintain the same core hours of operations. This provision is also for the convenience of the shopper. It assures shoppers that all the stores will be open during the shopping center's stated hours.

This lease provision is unique to retail properties and has evolved over many years. Originally, the retail lease stated that shop tenants would maintain the same hours as the anchor tenant. When anchor tenants—namely supermarkets—extended their hours, requiring shop tenants to maintain the same hours as the anchor tenants became impractical. Another approach was to require the tenant to maintain the hours of similar businesses in the community. That allowed an outside influence to determine the merchant's hours of operation.

Days Closed. A store hours provision may also state which days, if any, the shopping center will be closed—usually for specific holidays: New Year's Day, Easter, Independence Day (July 4), Thanksgiving, and Christmas. This particular stipulation is only needed in leases for enclosed malls. Landlords do not want to open a mall if only a few tenants will be open. In an open mall or a strip shopping center, tenants may be open on those days. If the lease states the days the mall will be closed, it should also provide for the landlord to change those days.

Core Hours. The most effective approach to store hours is to state the basic daily hours of operation in the lease and to allow the landlord to change them when necessary or appropriate. The typical core hours for strip shopping centers and other nonenclosed shopping centers are Monday through Friday from 10:00 a.m. to 9:00 p.m., Saturday and holidays from 10:00 a.m. to 6:00 or 7:00 p.m., and Sundays from noon to 5:00 or 6:00 p.m.

Individual tenants may open earlier and stay open later than the core hours. Supermarkets and restaurants usually have more extended hours—both earlier and later than the core hours for the rest of the shopping center. Pad and outlot tenants may also stay open for extended hours, as may tenants located in entertainment shopping centers. A few nonretail tenants, such as medical, office, and government tenants, are usually granted the right to maintain negotiated hours.

Continuous Operation. An element related to store hours and critical to the synergy of a shopping center is uniform hours of operation in all the stores. The continuous operation provision requires the tenant to maintain store hours as designated by the landlord. It also requires the tenant to keep in stock, on the premises, a full and ample line of merchandise and to maintain an adequate sales force.

The shopping center and other retail properties are the only property types that require a continuous operation provision in most, if not all, leases. The landlord requires tenants to remain open because of each tenant's importance to the synergy of the property's tenant mix. The more tenants that are open, the greater choices for the shoppers. (Anchor tenants and the continuous operation provision are discussed later in this chapter.)

Marketing Fund or Merchants' Association. Most malls as well as lifestyle, specialty, and outlet shopping centers and some large strip shopping centers have a marketing fund or a merchants' association. The merchants' association was the marketing and advertising vehicle for shopping centers until the early 1980s. Most shopping centers built since then use a marketing fund to promote and market the shopping center. However, some older shopping centers and malls continue to operate with a merchants' association.

Participation Requirement. This lease provision requires the tenant to participate in funding the marketing fund or the merchant's association, whichever exists at the shopping center. The provision states the minimum payment (per square foot) and provides for an annual increase in funding. The requirement to contribute to a marketing fund or membership in and the requirement to pay dues to a merchants' association should not be contingent on a percentage of all the tenants belonging to or paying for either organization. Older shopping center leases stated that the tenant was required to join the merchants' association only if a specific percentage (usually 75 or 80 percent) of the merchants belonged. If the landlord believes that a marketing fund or merchants' association will benefit the shopping center and the tenants, the tenants' participation should be mandatory. As noted elsewhere, anchor tenants seldom agree to mandatory membership in a merchants' association; however, they will often agree to contribute to the funding of a merchants' association or a marketing fund.

Dues and Contributions. Marketing fund or merchants' association dues are a flat rate per square foot for shop tenants; they are negotiated with the larger tenants. Anchor tenants' contributions may be based on a fixed annual amount or on a formula that makes dues less per square foot than those of a shop tenant. All dues are paid monthly. Because inflation will erode the buying power of the marketing fund or merchants' association if dues are fixed for the term of the lease, the provision may call for an annual increase in dues based on a CPI adjustment.

In a new shopping center, the tenants are required to pay an additional grand opening assessment, which is usually a set dollar amount per square foot. Tenants who open for business within a year of the grand opening are also assessed grand opening dues to offset the initial marketing of the shopping center.

Landlord's Contributions. The landlord may agree to pay 25 percent of the annual funds collected from the tenants, which is 20 percent of the marketing fund or merchants' association budget. The landlord also makes a major contribution toward the grand opening event. The grand opening event funds are usually budgeted in the development's pro forma.

Assignment and Subletting. Over the years, the courts have ruled both for and against the landlord's right to deny a tenant's request to assign the lease. Early shopping center leases gave the landlord the right to approve or deny a tenant's request to assign the lease or sublet the premises. Some states have ruled that the landlord must be reasonable in any decision to deny the tenant's request.

Landlord's Reasonable Business Judgment. One version of the assignment provision allows the landlord the right to refuse to consent to an assignment or sublease if, in the landlord's reasonable business judgment, the merchandising experience or financial worth of the proposed new tenant (assignee or sublessee) is not of the same caliber as the primary tenant or that tenant's guarantor. The assignment provision may allow the landlord to charge the tenant a fee, usually a few hundred dollars, for processing the request for assignment or sublease. The lease should not be silent on this issue.

Assignment with or without Release. If the landlord approves an assignment, it should be characterized as an *assignment without release*—i.e., the *assignor* (the tenant assigning its lease) must fulfill the obligations of the lease if the assignee defaults. Under an assignment without release, the landlord can collect from the assignor if the assignee stops paying rent. An *assignment with release* frees the assignor from all future obligations of the lease. If the assignee defaults, the landlord cannot look to the assignor to cure the default.

Assignor Guarantee. If the issues of an assignment with or without release must be negotiated, an alternative would be to require the assignor to guarantee the performance of the assignee for the first few years of the remaining terms of the lease. If the assignee has not defaulted in any obligations, then the assignor can be released of the guarantee. Default of a lease is usually nonpayment of rent.

Radius. To protect the landlord's opportunity to collect percentage rent, the tenant is prohibited from diverting sales from the shopping center by opening another store nearby. The radius provision prohibits the tenant from opening a similar store within a specified distance, i.e., three to five miles from the shopping center, or requires the tenant to add the sales from any other similar store it operates within a certain distance of the shopping center to the sales of its store in the shopping center when calculating percentage rent.

Provisions That Are Detrimental to the Landlord. Several provisions are detrimental to the landlord, specifically: exclusive use, co-tenancy, most favored tenant, and options. These provisions place restrictions on the landlord and the shopping center management.

Exclusive Use. A tenant may seek to negotiate an exclusive use provision that grants the tenant the sole right to sell a specific product or provide a specific service. Because such an exclusive prevents the landlord from bringing in other tenants whose product lines are the same or similar to those of the first tenant, landlords are understandably reluctant to grant a tenant an exclusive.

Exclusives place a limitation on the landlord's ability to lease the shopping center by excluding additional tenants who provide the same merchandise or services. Exclusives also put an administrative burden on the landlord and the management company, and if violated, exclusives create a liability. Even if the landlord does not intend to duplicate a use, it is best not to grant an exclusive. The exclusive could be detrimental to the landlord's effort to create the best tenant mix for the shopping center.

In a mall as well as a lifestyle or an outlet shopping center, most uses can and must be duplicated to provide the consumer a wide variety of merchandise and opportunities for comparison shopping. In neighborhood, community, and specialty shopping centers, many uses can be duplicated without harm to any of the merchants.

Exemptions to an Exclusive. The landlord may be able to grant an exclusive that, while it may not fully satisfy the tenant, will be less burdensome for the landlord. If an exclusive must be granted in a lease for a shop tenant, the following restrictions (exemptions) should be considered:

1. *It should not apply to the anchor tenant, its assignees, or sublessees.* Anchor tenant use provisions have few, if any, restrictions. The anchor tenant will add new lines of merchandise during its lease term, and some of that merchandise may conflict with a shop tenant's exclusive.

2. *It should not apply to any existing tenants.* One or more existing tenants' use provisions may not prohibit them from selling a product that a new tenant has an exclusive right to sell. (An exclusive can apply to future time and subsequent tenants but not to current or prior tenants.)

3. *It should not apply to the tenant's assignee or sublessee.* (The tenant that is granted an exclusive should not be allowed to transfer the exclusive to others.)

4. *It should be very limited.* For example, an exclusive use to operate a hair salon should not include the exclusive right to sell beauty products because several other types of stores sell such products.

5. *It should exclude the incidental sale of the product by other tenants.*

6. *It may be limited to a particular area.* For example, it might apply only to the north wing of the shopping center.

7. *It may be contingent on payment of percentage rent.* For instance, if the tenant does not pay percentage rent by the second or third calendar year of the lease, it loses the right to the exclusive.
8. *It may be offered for a specific period.* It might be apply only to the first year of operations. This provides the tenant a chance to start the business without direct competition in the shopping center.
9. *It must definitely provide for specific damages if the exclusive is violated.* This is very important to the landlord. If specific damages are not included in the lease, the tenant may claim loss of business and loss of the value of the business in the millions of dollars. As an example, the damages might give the tenant the right to cancel the lease or have the minimum rent eliminated; the tenant would then pay percentage rent only along with the other tenant charges.

Monitoring for an Exclusive. When an exclusive is granted, the shopping center manager must monitor the items sold by the other tenants and take the exclusive into account whenever new tenants are considered. The purpose of an exclusive is to prevent others from operating the same type of business or selling the same product within the shopping center. Seldom, if ever, should a landlord give a tenant an exclusive.

Co-tenancy. A *co-tenancy provision* provides a right to one tenant based on another tenant's ceasing operation at the shopping center. Such provisions should be avoided. National shop tenants commonly sign leases for space in a shopping center because of the presence and traffic draw of a specific major tenant or combination of tenants. That tenant may ask for a lease provision that allows it to pay percentage rent only or, worse yet, cancel the lease, if a major tenant leaves or the occupancy of the shopping center's shop space falls below a specific percentage.

Most shopping center managers hope to avoid tenants *going dark* (ceasing operations because another tenant leaves or the shopping center's occupancy drops) by including a continuous operation provision in the lease. Store closings and other efforts by tenants to terminate leases can have a disastrous effect on the shopping center. Seldom are co-tenancy rights included in a tenant's lease—not even an anchor tenant's lease. However, if an important tenant is in the balance, the landlord and the shopping center manager may not have a choice.

If a co-tenancy is granted, the provision should allow the landlord six months to one year to replace the vacating tenant before that tenant may cancel its lease. An alternative to allowing the tenant to close the store and cancel the lease is to allow the tenant to pay reduced rent or percentage rent and tenant charges only until the space is re-leased.

Most Favored Tenant. The *most favored tenant provision*—also known as a *favored nation provision*—derives its name and function from the favored nation trade advantages that one country gives another. Such a provision grants a tenant all the concessions that other tenants are or have been granted.

For example, if one tenant has a cap on real estate taxes and another does not pay CAM charges, a tenant whose lease includes a most favored tenant provision is granted those same privileges. Tenants whose leases are negotiated early in the lease-up period of a new shopping center may seek this provision. The first tenant to lease space may be told it is receiving the best deal any tenant will be offered. To assure itself that it is getting the best deal, that tenant asks for a most favored tenant provision.

This lease provision should be avoided. It is likely to appear in a lease form generated by a tenant. Occasionally a national shop tenant will include this provision in its standard lease form, usually toward the end of the lease. However, at the landlord's insistence, the tenant will usually delete it.

Options. Several options can be incorporated into a retail lease, and they are usually granted by the landlord as specific concessions. The option or options granted in a particular lease may relate to the lease term (extension or renewal of the lease), the premises (expansion of the tenant's space), or the lease itself (cancellation by the tenant). Because options favor the tenant at the landlord's expense, landlords are understandably reluctant to grant them.

Option to Extend. An option to extend grants the tenant the right to extend the lease term without interruption. This provides a benefit to the tenant and creates an obligation for the landlord. Most landlords prefer not to grant this option because many factors can work to the landlord's detriment during the term of the lease—e.g., a tenant's sales may be low, rent may not be paid on time, or a tenant may be a poor merchant. Seldom should a landlord agree to an option to extend, but some situations call for it, as noted earlier. If an option to extend the lease must be provided, it should be contingent on several criteria, including those listed below:

1. The tenant must not be in default of the lease on the date the option is exercised and the lease is extended.
2. The tenant must provide notice of its intention to exercise the option within a specific time frame in relation to a lease termination—e.g., no later than 120 days and no sooner than 180 days before the lease expires.
3. The option right should be canceled if the tenant is in default, assigns the lease, or subleases the premises. This is a difficult restric-

tion to achieve since it can restrict the tenant's ability to sell the business.

4. If possible, the option should be contingent on the tenant paying percentage rent or exceeding a specific sales volume during the last two years of the lease.

The rent for the option period can be stated as a predetermined amount, as the market rate, or as an increase based on the CPI. However, it should be no less than the rate paid during the last month of the prior lease term, and that requirement should be specifically stated. If the rent is to be based on the current market rate and that market rate is less than what the tenant is already paying, setting such a minimum will protect the landlord from undue financial loss. If the rent in the option period is based on "market rent," this provision should describe other comparable shopping centers and the size and location of spaces that will be used to determine market rent.

Option to Expand. An option to expand the tenant's leased space may be stated as such and related to specific space designated on a plan of the shopping center. However, a landlord is more likely to grant a *right of first refusal* to lease additional (usually contiguous) space, based on the lease terms the landlord would offer to another prospective tenant for that space, and the tenant is given a limited time (usually three to five days) to accept the landlord's offer. Alternatively, some landlords offer a *first right to negotiate,* which gives the tenant the opportunity to negotiate for additional space before the landlord negotiates with any other prospective tenant. When this provision is used, it should state that if the landlord and tenant are unable to agree on the terms of the lease for the additional space within a specific time period (e.g., 10 days), the landlord may negotiate and enter into a lease with another tenant. Neither of these "first rights" provisions is common in shopping center leases.

Option to Cancel. Occasionally, a tenant may request an option (right) to cancel its lease. The landlord should avoid granting this, but such an option may be a necessary concession in order to have a lease with a good tenant in a distressed shopping center. If an option to cancel is granted, the lease should be very clear on the conditions under which it can be exercised:

1. The right or option to cancel should be contingent on the tenant's failure to achieve a predetermined sales volume within a specified period. (The tenant must have had sufficient time to achieve the stated sales volume.)
2. The option should be granted as a one-time right and should require the tenant to provide sufficient advance notice (a specific period of

notice may be stated). "If, in the second calendar year of the lease term, Tenant's sales volume does not exceed $500,000, Tenant may cancel this lease by providing Landlord with written notice of cancellation during the month of January following the second calendar lease year. Tenant's lease shall be canceled 90 days after Landlord has received written notice from Tenant."

3. Whenever possible, the landlord should attempt to obtain a cancellation fee, and the right to cancel should be a mutual right of the tenant and the landlord.

Option Favoring the Landlord. It may be appropriate for a lease to include options that favor the landlord. The landlord may have the right to terminate the lease if the tenant does not achieve agreed sales objectives, which may be stated as total dollars or dollars per square foot, within a certain period. The lease may also be cancelable if the tenant has not generated overage (percentage rent) within a prescribed period. Seldom will a tenant agree to this provision.

Management and Operations Provisions. Many nonmonetary lease provisions address issues that affect the daily management and operations of the shopping center. These issues also affect how tenants operate their businesses, and many indirectly impact the property's cash flow and value.

Signs. Tenants want identity and exposure to people walking or driving by the shopping center or their stores, and the landlord wants to control the appearance of the shopping center and prevent it from being gaudy or offensive. To address both parties' desires and concerns, the landlord should develop signage criteria that limit the types and sizes of tenants' signs, while still allowing them to have signage that is representative of their business, easy to read, and visible. Sign criteria should take into account any local laws that may govern the issues of size, materials, and positioning for display.

A signage provision requires tenants to submit plans for their exterior signs for the landlord's approval. The plans must be based on the shopping center's sign criteria, which are included as an exhibit appended to the lease, and the sign must be installed and maintained by the tenant. The municipality must also approve the signage.

The tenant usually arranges for a sign contractor to prepare a drawing of the proposed sign—showing the details of dimensions, colors, and materials to be used—and submits it to the shopping center manager, who is responsible for approving or denying proposed signs based on the sign criteria.

When a sign is denied, the shopping center manager should tell the tenant why. The most common reasons for denial are excessive size and use of unsatisfactory or inappropriate colors or materials. This provision also addresses which, if any, types of signs may be attached to the storefront windows.

Advertising. The landlord wants all the tenants to advertise and promote their businesses to maximize their sales potential. An advertising provision is seldom used in the typical strip shopping center lease, but it is often used in leases for regional malls as well as for lifestyle, entertainment, specialty, and other types of shopping centers.

Originally this provision required tenants to spend a minimum percentage of their gross sales on advertising (usually 2 percent) and to provide evidence of that expenditure. Monitoring the amount a tenant spends on advertising is difficult for the landlord, and a dispute can arise over what constitutes advertising.

As an alternative, the advertising provision may require the tenant to advertise in a minimum number of the shopping center's advertising tabloids. If the tenant does not advertise a minimum number of times, the landlord may place an ad giving the tenant's name and address, and the tenant will be responsible for reimbursing the landlord for the cost of the ad. Alternatively, the tenant may be required, or have the option, to pay into a marketing fund.

Floor Area—Definition of Measurement. Unlike the office building industry, the shopping center industry does not have a standard method for measuring the tenants' premises. This provision of the lease states the method to be used in measuring the tenant's premises. Typically, measurements are made from the centers of *demising walls* (the walls or partitions that separate tenants) and from either the inside or outside of exterior walls. No deductions from the square footage of the floor area are made for columns, shafts, or any penetrations of the floor. Mezzanine areas are usually measured and included in the tenant's GLA.

Tenant Alterations. A shopping center is one of the few property types in which the tenants are responsible for coordinating and contracting for the improvements to their premises. The lease should state that the tenant cannot construct any improvement to the premises until the landlord reviews—and approves in writing—the plans for any alterations, additions, or other improvements in or to the premises.

This provision should state that the tenant must abide by any regulations the landlord imposes, such as providing its own container for construction debris, requiring the contractor to maintain specific insurance coverage and name the landlord and the property management company as additional insureds, etc.

Tenants are usually prohibited from doing work on the roof without the landlord's prior written approval and supervision by the landlord's representative, and many landlords prohibit tenants from core drilling or other construction activities during normal business hours because of the likelihood those activities will be disruptive to the other tenants and their customers. In a newly constructed shopping center where store spaces are leased as shells, improvements to tenant spaces may be arranged as part of construction "finishing," and the lease provision regarding tenant alterations would reflect this.

Some tenants negotiate the right to make nonstructural changes and improvements—up to a certain dollar amount—without the landlord's approval. These improvements may include replacing the flooring, installing lighting, etc. At the landlord's request, the leased premises must be restored to its original condition (except for real property improvements) at the tenant's sole expense when the premises are vacated or the lease expires.

Tenant's Insurance. The landlord wants to be certain that if any of the tenant's inventory, fixtures, or equipment is damaged, stolen, or destroyed, the tenant will have the funds to replace those items and to continue to operate the business. The insurance provision states that the tenant must carry insurance on the furniture, fixtures, equipment, and inventory of the business in addition to plate glass coverage and liability insurance in a required minimum amount.

The tenant is required to provide the landlord with evidence of such insurance and to include the landlord and the landlord's property management company as named insured parties on the policies. Some anchor tenants negotiate for the right to self-insure. The landlord often agrees to this provision if the tenant's net worth remains above a specific amount.

Tenant's Employee Parking. Convenient parking is an important criterion for a successful shopping center. The parking stalls that are closest to the stores turn over six to eight times a day—i.e., six to eight customers may use each of those convenient stalls each day. When a tenant's employee parks all day in one of those stalls, one of the most convenient stalls has been taken away from six to eight customers.

This provision requires tenants' employees to park in a designated area of the parking lot. It prohibits their use of prime customer parking areas and may grant the landlord the right to fine tenants and/or to tow the employee's car each time an employee parks in a nonemployee parking area. The fine (usually $25 to $100 per violation) is assessed against the tenant, not the employee, because the tenant is the party to the lease. A tenant may negotiate to receive a warning the first time one of its employees parks in a nonemployee parking area and for the fine to apply to subsequent violations.

Auction and Sale. Because "going-out-of-business" signs, sales, or auctions can give the impression that the shopping center itself is failing, landlords include in the lease a provision stating that the tenant may not conduct a bankruptcy or going-out-business sale or auction—or post signs announcing such activities—without the prior written consent of the landlord.

HVAC Maintenance. Tenants were originally responsible for maintaining the HVAC units in their premises, but improper maintenance during occupancy and costly repairs after the premises were vacated led to a requirement that tenants submit copies of their maintenance contracts to the landlord. Use of different contractors, inconsistencies in the quality of service and specifications in the maintenance contracts, and the added problem of damage to the roof made the situation worse. (HVAC maintenance is discussed in detail in chapter 5, Maintenance and Operations.)

The updated HVAC maintenance provision gives the landlord the right to maintain the HVAC unit and makes the tenant responsible for the cost of preventive maintenance, repairs, and replacements. Because all work is contracted to one company, the shopping center manager is usually able to negotiate a discounted service price. This ensures that HVAC units will be serviced properly and in good condition at the expiration of the tenants' leases. An efficiently run HVAC unit and a discounted service fee also result in direct savings for the tenant, and the life of the equipment is prolonged.

In addition, only one service contractor has access to the roof. HVAC units are usually located on the roof. If several contractors were allowed to perform maintenance on them, the likelihood would increase that the maintenance contractors would damage the roof due to excessive foot traffic.

Utilities. This provision requires the tenant to pay, in a timely manner, all utilities that are billed directly to the tenant for its premises. The provision also grants the landlord the right to bill the tenant for a pro rata share of any utility that is not separately metered for each of the premises. Electricity and gas are commonly provided by private utility companies and metered directly to each tenant, but other arrangements may exist. Municipal or other governmental authorities often provide water, and charges for sewage disposal are usually based on water consumption.

The lease should specify the sources of utility services for the shopping center and spell out the formula for allocating costs for the shopping center as a whole. All shopping center tenants will have electricity expenses and, unless their store spaces do not include restrooms, they will all have some water (and sewer) expenses.

Determining Utility Use. Sometimes an incoming utility is on a master meter for the shopping center as a whole. In that situation, submeters can be installed for each tenant, and when a tenant uses more than its pro rata share, the landlord will have the right to charge the tenant for the excess utility usage. Water is a typical example of a master-metered utility for which the landlord bills each tenant on a pro rata basis. However, some tenants (e.g., restaurants, laundromats, and hair salons) use large volumes of water—excessive amounts in comparison to a typical tenant's usage. Because of that, the shopping center manager should estimate the percentage of the total water bill each tenant should pay based on use rather than any other proration formula. A representative from the water company can provide typical water usage data for each tenant category.

Waste Disposal. Garbage pickup (trash disposal) may be considered as a utility, or it may be addressed separately in the lease. Disposal service may be contracted for the entire center and charged in the CAM expenses, or individual tenants may contract for disposal service and pay the charges directly to the waste pickup service.

If the expense is charged to CAM and the anchor tenants pay directly for their pickup service, an adjustment must be made to the CAM billings so the anchor tenants are not charged for this service—except for the portion of the charge that is for disposing of debris in the common areas of the shopping center. One of the best ways to handle this issue is to create a separate charge to those tenants that use the common pickup services and to exclude this charge from CAM. A small portion of the expense is charged to the CAM expense for emptying the common area trash from the trash cans.

Tenants whose garbage can pose disposal problems—e.g., food wastes from restaurants, animal excrement and other materials from pet stores—may be required to have special water-tight containers. Some waste materials are potentially hazardous (e.g., medical wastes, dry cleaning chemicals, photo processing agents) and this provision must address the disposal of such hazardous waste.

Relocation. A provision granting the landlord the right to relocate the tenant's premises is not often found in shopping center leases. It is usually omitted for several reasons: the importance of location in a shopping center, the differences in the rental rates for particular locations, and the costs of relocation. However, relocation may be an important consideration in a lease with a temporary or seasonal tenant. (See chapter 11, Marketing the Shopping Center.)

Most experienced retail tenants will not accept a relocation provision. However, when this provision is acceptable to a tenant, it has benefits for the landlord. The shopping center manager may have to protect a location for future expansion of a valuable tenant, for combining spaces to attract a large tenant, or to allow the flexibility to recapture a space to expand or remodel the shopping center. In any of these situations, the lease should have a relocation provision.

If the tenant agrees to such a provision, the relocation will probably be limited to a particular area in the shopping center and to premises of approximately the same size as those the tenant presently occupies. The landlord is responsible for the tenant's moving expenses and improvements to the relocation space, and rent is usually abated during the time the tenant's business is interrupted.

Rules and Regulations. The landlord is responsible for operating the shopping center in a manner that is generally beneficial to both tenants and shoppers. To achieve this, the landlord usually sets rules for tenants and their operations that address issues of conformity and safety. Typically, rules and regulations may specify constraints on such activities as loading and unloading, shipping and deliveries, accumulation of garbage, maintenance of the shopping environment (store temperature, use of loudspeakers, etc.), employee parking, and general housekeeping.

The provision requires the tenant to comply with the rules and regulations that the landlord may promulgate or modify. It also states that the landlord is not responsible to the tenant for the nonperformance of any rules and regulations by any other tenant and that the rules and regulations will apply and be enforced uniformly. Some leases include a set of rules and regulations as an addendum or an exhibit to the lease; other leases include the rules and regulations in specific provisions throughout the lease.

Liens and Encumbrances. If the tenant does not pay its contractor for tenant improvements or maintenance, that contractor may place a lien on the leased premises or on the shopping center itself. Such an encumbrance can delay or prevent the sale or refinancing of the shopping center. To protect the landlord's interests, this provision requires the tenant to keep the premises and the shopping center free from any liens arising out of any work performed or contracted by the tenant. It also gives the landlord the right to require the tenant to obtain payment and performance bonds in an amount equal to one and one-half times the estimated cost of such work, materials, labor, and supplies.

Broker's Commission. Occasionally, more than one broker or leasing agent claims to represent the same tenant. A dispute can arise if it is unclear who represents the tenant, and the landlord may be forced to pay a double commission or incur legal expenses, or both. To protect against that possibility, the lease provides a blank space for the name of the tenant's broker and requires the tenant to represent and warrant that no other broker is authorized to represent the tenant. Some states require leasing agents and shopping center managers to inform the parties to the lease which entity they represent. Such a statement can be included in this provision.

Estoppel Certificate. The lease includes a provision that requires the tenant to execute an *estoppel certificate*—a statement by the tenant of the status of the lease—at the landlord's request (usually within 10 days of the request). If a tenant does not respond to the landlord's request, the landlord is empowered to act as the tenant's attorney-in-fact in executing the estoppel certificate.

A prospective buyer of income-producing property or a lender who is financing or refinancing the shopping center will want to know the status of each tenant's lease and to verify the information provided by the landlord. An estoppel certificate includes the following information: the term of the lease, the rental charges, the amount of the security deposit, whether any rent is delinquent or prepaid, whether any option exists, and whether the tenant or the landlord is in default of the lease. It also states that the lease is in full force and effect, and it should include the date to which rents and other charges have been paid.

Condemnation and Eminent Domain. This provision addresses the government's right to take property for public use upon the payment of just compensation. Such a provision cancels the lease if all the premises are taken by eminent domain. In case of a partial taking, the landlord and the tenant have a right to cancel the lease if more than a specific percentage (e.g., 20 percent of the premises or common area) is taken by eminent domain.

The provision reserves to the landlord all rights to the entire damages awarded or the total payment for any taking by eminent domain. The tenant is allowed to claim from the condemning authority all compensation that may be recoverable because of any loss incurred by the tenant in removing its merchandise, furniture, trade fixtures, and equipment or damage to the tenant's business.

Force Majeure. This provision relieves the landlord of liability or responsibility if the landlord is delayed or hindered in, or prevented from, performing any act or obligation required by the lease because of strikes, lockouts, acts of God, riots, failure of power, governmental laws or regulations, war, or other causes beyond the landlord's reasonable control. Any obligation so delayed is extended for a period equivalent to the period of the delay. The most likely delay on the landlord's part is during construction of the shopping center or the tenant's improvements. Tenants usually negotiate for the same right.

Hazardous Substances. Cleaning up a hazardous spill is very costly. In addition, a buyer may delay or cancel the purchase of a shopping center or a lender may delay or cancel the financing or refinancing of a property until the hazardous substance is removed. However, some tenants must use hazardous materials in the operation of their businesses—photo processors, dry cleaners, and service stations are obvious examples—and their activities must be monitored. The landlord's main concerns are illegal use and disposal of hazardous materials.

Beginning in the 1980s, a hazardous substances provision was added to commercial leases to prohibit tenants from illegally using or disposing of hazardous substances in or on the premises or the common areas of the shopping center. The tenant is required to (1) comply with all governmental regulations regarding hazardous substances, (2) allow the landlord to inspect the premises, and (3) pay for all cleanup costs, fees, and penalties imposed by any governmental authority.

Tenant's Right to Audit Tenant Charges. The tenant is given the right to audit the CAM and other charges. Because the landlord incurs expenses on behalf of the tenants, it is only fair that they have the right to audit the landlord's common area maintenance and other charges and review the invoices. The landlord should place the following restrictions on that right:

1. The audit must commence within 90 days of the date the tenant receives the year-end adjustments.
2. The tenant can only audit the period of the most recent year-end adjustment.
3. The audit will be conducted in the place where the landlord maintains the financial records.
4. The results of the audit will be kept confidential.

To avoid delays or costs related to audits, some landlords and tenants agree to fixed CAM charges with no reconciliation. This eliminates the need for an audit.

Arbitration. If the landlord and the tenant do not agree on certain issues, such as the market rent for an option period (if the lease specifies renewal at "market rent"), they submit the issue to arbitration.

Typical Arbitration. The typical arbitration provision states that each party will choose an arbitrator, the two arbitrators will chose a third arbitrator, and the three will decide the issue. The lease should state the minimum qualifications of the arbitrators, such as five years' experience in commercial real estate in the area in which the shopping center is located.

Baseball Arbitration. Another approach is referred to as the *baseball arbitration* method. The landlord and the tenant select what they believe should be the market rental adjustment, and the arbitrators must decide which rate is the closest to the market rate. This encourages each party to study the market and submit a rate close to or at the market rental rate.

Quiet Enjoyment. This is one of the few lease provisions that directly benefits the tenant. "Tenant shall have and quietly enjoy the premises during the term of the lease, provided that Tenant fully complies with and promptly performs all of the terms, covenants, and conditions of the lease."

Final Considerations. Numerous other issues are covered in a lease form, usually in standardized language and as part of the "standard form." In particular, the landlord should be able to access the leased premises under specific circumstances (e.g., in an emergency) as well as to show the premises to prospective replacement tenants when the lease nears expiration. Provision for notification of the parties is commonly included, and a separate section may include definitions of terminology used in the lease.

Signatures. The document concludes by renaming the parties and providing spaces for signatures of the authorized representatives. (Because the management firm and the tenant are usually companies, the authority of those signing should be indicated as well.) If the document was not dated at its beginning, it should be dated at the time of signing. Including signatures of witnesses may also be appropriate.

Lease Exhibits

Attached to and incorporated in the lease are several exhibits. They are usually appended in the order in which they are referenced in the body of the lease, and they are identified as Exhibit A, Exhibit B, etc. These attachments usually augment or clarify specific aspects of the lease or spell out details that are relevant to that lease alone. The most common lease exhibits are listed below:

- *Site Plan of the Shopping Center.* This exhibit depicts the layout of all the buildings and the boundaries of the shopping center. It is likely that there will be changes to the site plan in the future, the most common being changes to the parking lot to accommodate expansion of the main building, addition of a pad or outlot building, or changes in configuration when the shopping center is remodeled or rehabilitated. The site plan should include a disclaimer that allows the landlord to make changes to it. (An example of such a disclaimer appears in exhibit 10.7.) The same statement or one similar to it should be considered for inclusion in the shopping center's brochures if they include a site plan.

Exhibit 10.7

Example Disclaimer for a Site Plan

Landlord does not make any representation or warranty with respect to any matter shown in this site plan, which is not drawn to scale, and reserves the right to modify this site plan, in whole or in part, to change, add, relocate, eliminate, modify the size, shape, nature or identity of any improvements, buildings or common areas shown herein and/or to modify, add or eliminate the name, nature, or use of any tenancy shown herein.

Landlord shall also have the right to convey its ownership of all or any part of the shopping center to one or more third parties and thereafter the third party shall have the right to remove said conveyed portion from the definition of "shopping center" set forth in this lease.

- *Demising Plan of Tenant's Premises.* The tenant's premises (store) are marked on a layout of the building where the tenant's leased space is located. It may be outlined in colored ink or cross-hatched in red or blue. The same disclaimer that appears in the Site Plan exhibit should be included in this exhibit.
- *Description of Landlord's and Tenant's Work.* This exhibit, usually a standard form, lists the improvements to the premises that will be provided by the landlord and by the tenant. Usually this document also includes specifications for particular work—e.g., storefronts.
- *Corporate Resolution of Tenant.* If the tenant is a corporation, a corporate resolution authorizing one or more individuals to sign the lease should be appended to the lease. The resolution, which should be signed by two officers of the corporation, states that the officers who signed the lease on behalf of the tenant have the authority to bind the corporation to the lease.
- *Guaranty of Lease.* If the landlord thinks that the tenant may not be able to perform its lease obligations, especially those related to rent, the landlord will require one or more individuals to guarantee the lease. If the tenant is an individual who has a limited net worth, a friend or relative may guarantee the lease. If a corporation has a limited net worth, the landlord will require the owner (the officers or principal stockholders) or key employees of the corporation to personally guarantee the tenant's performance of the lease.

The tenant may counteroffer a limited guaranty, which may be for a specific period (e.g., two years) or limit the amount of money that is guaranteed. The guaranty may be terminated after the tenant's sales exceed a certain volume during any calendar period, after the tenant has paid percentage rent, or after the tenant has paid its rent on time for a specific period, e.g., two years. The assumption in this situation is that the tenant's business is prospering and a guarantee is no longer needed.

- *Sign Criteria.* The sign criteria restrict the size, location, and materials used for fabricating the tenant's sign. All tenants' exterior signs must comply with the sign criteria in order for the shopping center to maintain its image.
- *Letter of Credit.* A letter of credit may be agreed to in lieu of a security deposit (or to assure availability of funds for tenant's improvement expenses or other use). The bank issuing such credit writes a letter stating the amount of credit allowed and the terms under which such credit is obtainable.

NEGOTIATING THE ANCHOR TENANT LEASE

Leasing negotiations with an anchor tenant can be one of the most rewarding as well as one of the most difficult and frustrating experiences for a shopping center manager or a leasing agent. In lease negotiations with a prospective anchor tenant, all parties need to know each other's strengths and weaknesses. They must also know the concerns of major retailers in general because these may become issues in a lease negotiation. An anchor tenant makes a long-term investment in its location and its store space, and consequently its representatives want every possible assurance that nothing will be done to the shopping center that will be detrimental to its sales and profitability.

Types of Anchor Tenant Leases

The real estate deal with an anchor tenant may take one of several forms:

1. In a *build-to-suit* arrangement, the landlord builds the store to the tenant's specifications, and the store and the land beneath it are leased to the tenant on a long-term lease with multiple options.
2. Another approach is a *ground lease* in which a parcel of land is leased to the anchor tenant for its building and required parking, and the tenant builds and owns its building.
3. A third option is *outright sale*—the anchor tenant buys a portion of the site, builds its own building, and owns its building and the land underneath it, plus the land for its required parking.

A ground lease or land sale option usually results when the anchor tenant is able to obtain better financing terms than the developer can, or if the anchor tenant wants to own its own building. To raise capital, the anchor tenant that owns its own building may package several of its holdings into a *sale-leaseback* (sell its buildings to an investor and lease them back).

The land may be sold at *par value* (the developer's cost), and par value may be used to determine the anchor tenant's leasehold rent. The rental rate is stepped up periodically—usually every five years.

Whichever type of real estate deal is negotiated, it is usually on very favorable terms for the anchor tenant and is often considered a "sweetheart" deal. The type of deal—build-to-suit or ground lease—in large part determines the specific terms of any lease that is negotiated.

A lease always covers occupancy of the premises and the financial arrangements related to occupancy. Other considerations that are important to the prospective tenant (visibility, access, etc.) may be negotiated and stated in the lease, but not necessarily in a direct manner. For example, issues related to visibility may take the form of limitations on other tenants—to be stated in their leases as well—such as, no pad tenant in specific areas of the parking lot or no kiosk within a specific distance from the anchor tenant's entrance.

Occupancy Issues. Among the anchor tenant's concerns are its occupancy costs—specifically, base rent, percentage rent, pass-through charges, and any upward adjustments to them. All shopping center tenants are expected to pay their full pro rata share of the real estate taxes and the insurance for their premises and the common areas. Other expenses that are passed through to tenants include management and administrative fees and contributions to common promotional funds.

Base Rent. Major retailers know that few prospects are available to anchor a proposed shopping center and that anchor tenants are indispensable to the development. Consequently, they are able to negotiate a very favorable base or minimum rental rate. Because many major retailers build and own their own buildings, they know the developer's approximate land cost and the cost to build and finance their store areas in a new shopping center. With this information, they can easily calculate the developer's cost to amortize the loan for their portions of the shopping center site and building, and they use that information in negotiating base rent. The rental rate an anchor pays for the initial term of its lease, or the first five years of a longer-term lease, is seldom more than the cost to service the developer's loan for the anchor's building and site.

Percentage Rent. One element in the landlord's favor is the possibility of collecting percentage rent from the anchor tenant. When anchor tenants agree to a percentage rent clause in their leases, the typical percentage rate for a department store is 2 percent; the range is from 1.5 to 3 percent. The typical percentage rate for a supermarket is 1 to 1.25 percent with a range from 1 to 1.5 percent. Anchor tenants often negotiate a declining percentage rate. For example, the percentage rate for a supermarket may be 1.5 percent on the first $15 million of annual sales, 1.25 percent on the next $7.5 million of sales, and 1 percent on all remaining sales.

Increases. The anchor tenant will want a long lease term because it is investing millions of dollars into its store. The typical lease with a supermarket or department store is 20 to 30 years with multiple (often up to six to eight) 5-year options. The developer is usually able to negotiate several increases in the rental rate during the initial term of the lease—for instance, a fixed rental increase every 5 years and at the beginning of each option.

Expense Provisions. Anchor tenants usually agree to pay their pro rata share of most of the shopping center's common area maintenance (CAM) expenses, although they sometimes attempt to negotiate a cap or lid on the expenses. An *expense cap* limits the amount of one or more of the charges passed through to the tenant and can be a fixed dollar amount. For example, the supermarket lease may state: "The Tenant will pay its pro rata share of CAM expenses not to exceed $4.00 per square foot per year." Alternatively, the cap may be based on the tenant's sales: "The pro rata share of CAM expenses shall not exceed one-fourth of one percent of the tenant's sales."

Parking Lot Costs. A well-maintained and adequate-sized parking lot is also important, and anchor tenants usually agree to pay their pro rata shares of the parking lot CAM costs. Parking lot expenses include maintenance, lighting, and insurance. On the other hand, the anchor tenant may attempt to negotiate not paying for a particular parking lot expense such as security.

Enclosed Mall CAM Costs. While anchor tenants in enclosed malls may agree to pay their pro rata share of parking lot CAM expenses, they often negotiate *not* to pay any CAM expenses for the enclosed mall in which they will reside. Their rationale is that the parking lot is needed for their customers, but they can operate freestanding and without the benefit of the enclosed mall area. Many anchor tenants negotiate to pay either a nominal charge—far less than their pro rata share—or to pay no enclosed mall CAM expenses. Mall developers and owners frequently succumb to this request. In shopping centers where anchor tenants own their stores—and sometimes the land beneath them as well—payment of CAM charges must be negotiated carefully on both sides.

When an anchor tenant does not pay enclosed mall CAM expenses, the leases with the other tenants usually state that the denominator for calculating their pro rata shares of enclosed mall CAM expenses will *exclude* the GLA of the anchor tenants. As a result, the small shop tenants pay the anchor tenant's share of the enclosed mall CAM expenses. Conversely, if the leases for the shop tenants state that the denominator will include the GLA of all tenants in the mall (thus including anchor tenants), the anchor tenant's share is borne by the landlord. This is a significant expense for the landlord and should be avoided.

CAM Administrative Fee. One part of the CAM charge that becomes a negotiable issue with anchor tenants is the CAM administrative fee. Most shopping center leases allow the landlord to add to the common area expenses a 10 to 15 percent fee for administration of the common areas. While tenants in the smaller shops may accept this charge, anchor tenants usually negotiate to pay no CAM administrative fee or to pay only a nominal fee (e.g., 5 percent). In recent years, however, landlords have been successful in negotiating a CAM administrative fee from many anchor tenants, though it is seldom as high as the fee paid by the shop tenants.

Since the late 1980s, developers have replaced the administrative fee with the shopping center's management fee in the CAM expenses to bring the shopping center lease closer to a pure triple-net lease. Although shop tenants have accepted this change, anchor tenants inevitably negotiate the management fee out of their CAM charges. However, they may pay a CAM administrative fee of 5 to 10 percent of the actual CAM expenses. Most shopping center owners do not charge both an administrative fee and a management fee because those fees are for the same service.

Taxes and Insurance. Other specific expense items that are negotiated with anchors are real estate taxes and insurance. In some shopping centers, anchor tenants pay their pro rata shares of these charges when the charges are due; in others, anchor tenants pay after the landlord provides evidence that the charges have been paid. In the second case, the lease should require the tenant to reimburse the landlord within a short time, say 10 days, after receiving evidence that the landlord has paid the charges.

Anchor tenants may negotiate to exclude reimbursing the landlord for specific insurance coverage such as earthquake and loss of rent insurance.

Marketing Fund Dues. The final expense item to negotiate is marketing fund or merchants' association dues, if applicable. Historically, the landlord has not been successful in negotiating this issue with anchor prospects. The anchor tenant's position is that it is spending millions of dollars to promote its store; it does not need the marketing, promotions, and advertising of the marketing fund. The usual outcome is that the anchor tenant either does not contribute at all or makes only a nominal monthly contribution.

Other Lease Considerations. The negotiations between a shopping center owner and an anchor tenant include negotiating an agreement that establishes how the common areas will be maintained and who will be responsible for their management. The anchor tenant is making a major financial commitment by entering into a long-term lease with the developer, and it wants assurance that the shopping center will not be operated in a manner that could have a negative impact on its business. The form and documentation of the agreement depend on the ownership (leasing) arrangements between the developer and the anchor tenant.

Common Area Agreement. A *common area agreement* conveys rights and obligations to both parties. It sets the standard for maintenance, states how each party will be billed for the CAM expenses, and indicates the method for removing the common area manager for nonperformance. The agreement may prohibit the landlord from making changes to the common areas—relocating entrances, adding a pad or outlot building—without the written approval of each signatory to the agreement.

Reciprocal Easement Agreement. When the shopping center is not under one ownership, a *reciprocal easement agreement (REA)* is often used to state parking rights. The REA is a cross-easement in which each party has the right to use the other party's parking area for customer parking. If anchor tenants own their buildings and land—or if different entities own separate buildings in the shopping center—an agreement must provide for mutual access to each owner's portion of the parking lot and for maintenance of the parking areas. Usually one of the parties to the REA is assigned as the manager of the entire parking area. The REA may include several of the issues found in a common area agreement.

When changes to a shopping center are being considered—especially expansion or remodeling, as they result in changes to the parking areas—the shopping center manager must review these operating agreements. If the anchor tenants have approval rights, the approvals must be obtained before work commences. Violating an anchor tenant's rights can be very costly to the property owner and possibly to the property management firm.

Continuous Operating Covenant and Right of Assignment. Two major issues to be negotiated with anchor tenants are a *continuous operating covenant* and a *right of assignment.* For many years, anchor retailers have not been willing to sign a continuous operating covenant; they have wanted the sole right to close their stores and cease operations at will. When an anchor tenant goes dark, it may close all its stores in an area or only the unprofitable ones. An example is the supermarket chain that closes one of its smaller stores and opens a larger state-of-the-art store just a few blocks away.

An anchor tenant that closes or goes dark may sublease its premises. Often the rent received from the subtenant is greater than the rent it paid to the landlord, and the anchor tenant makes a profit on the sublease. If it is operating another store in the immediate area, however, it usually will not sublease to its same use. In other words, a supermarket is not likely to sublease to another supermarket; it is more likely to sublease to a large space user that is not a competitor—e.g., an auto supply store, a furniture store, or a fabric store.

The results of an anchor tenant subleasing its space can be devastating to a shopping center. Seldom does the sublessee have the customer drawing power of the original anchor tenant, and the traffic to the shopping center will be significantly reduced. Retailers in the small shops may fail, rental rates for existing vacancies may be reduced, and renewal rents may be reduced or only slightly increased. As a result, the shopping center's net operating income will be reduced, and there will be a corresponding reduction in its value. The values of many shopping centers around the country dropped radically when major tenants vacated in the past.

Since the 1980s, however, landlords have attempted to negotiate a provision that would prevent that from occurring. Rarely will an anchor tenant agree to a continuous operating covenant, but many shopping center owners have negotiated the right to cancel the anchor tenant's lease if it vacates its premises or proposes to sublease its space or assign its lease to another business. If the landlord cannot negotiate such a right to cancel the anchor tenant's lease, the right to approve any sublease or assignment by the anchor or an agreement that limits any sublease or assignment to the same use as that of the original tenant should be sought. If the anchor's customer draw is lost to the shopping center, the landlord will be burdened with an unfavorable lease with a replacement tenant that is not equal to the original tenant.

A FINAL WORD

The foregoing discussions highlight many of the specific provisions that are commonly found in retail leases and present a sense of their respective importance to both landlord and tenant. The final contents and the terms and conditions of a specific lease depend not only on the parties to it (i.e., the landlord and the tenant) and their negotiating positions and skills but also on the type and complexity of the property and the premises being leased.

11

Marketing the Shopping Center

Marketing, advertising, and promotional activities have always been important means of attracting customers to shopping centers. Marketing programs have evolved as different types of shopping centers have been developed. Competition from new shopping center formats and new entertainment venues has caused marketing directors to change the direction and emphasis of their marketing plans. This chapter gives an overview of important changes in the marketing of shopping centers that have lead up to the coordinated marketing programs that are common today. It examines the benefits and types of coordinated marketing programs as well as the roles and responsibilities of those who participate in them. Finally, the chapter details the components of a successful marketing program.

MARKETING OVERVIEW

Early shopping centers staged frequent promotions to draw nearby residents. As the shopping center industry matured, comprehensive marketing plans were developed to address the more complex shopping center environments. In *comprehensive marketing programs,* the shopping center management and the tenants participate in a marketing program that promotes the individual stores as well as the shopping center as a whole.

The first comprehensive marketing programs were called *merchants' associations.* In those associations, the landlord and a committee of merchants participated in developing and implementing the marketing program.

Later, many developers replaced the merchants' associations with *marketing funds,* which are marketing plans that are developed and implemented solely under the landlord's authority. (Merchants' associations and marketing funds are discussed in more detail later in this chapter.)

Further changes that affected shopping center marketing and promotions were the advent of big box stores, the increase in the size of supermarkets, and the expansion of their product lines. For instance, as anchor tenants grew larger and more big box stores were created, less room was available to build smaller, individual shop spaces in neighborhood and community shopping centers. Shopping centers that have such large anchors rely primarily on the advertising and presence of the anchor tenants to draw shoppers. When the number of shop tenants decreased as the anchor tenants grew, sustaining a coordinated marketing program became difficult in many grocery or big box anchored shopping centers. At the same time, the malls, as well as the specialty, outlet, and lifestyle shopping centers continued to fine-tune their marketing plans to compete with the new retail venues.

Not only do shopping centers compete with each other but they also compete with catalog shopping, home shopping on cable networks, and shopping on the Internet. The competition for the shoppers' dollars is fierce and ever increasing. Because of the escalating competition, every shopping center needs an excellent marketing plan, and coordinated marketing plans are generally the most successful.

COORDINATED MARKETING PROGRAMS

A coordinated marketing program has been an integral component of the operations of many shopping centers since they were first developed. Shopping centers that have coordinated marketing programs are the only property types for which the landlord provides funds to promote the tenants' businesses. The most important reason for that is the bottom line. The key to a shopping center's success is *sales volume*—the volume of sales generated by each tenant and by the center as a whole, measured in total dollars and in dollars per square foot of gross leasable area (GLA). A high sales volume typically translates into overage (percentage rent) that is paid to the landlord. Thus, promoting sales in order to improve net operating income (NOI) and enhance the value of the shopping center is in the ownership's interest.

The success of a property is directly related to the coordinated marketing efforts of the shopping center management team. A comprehensive marketing campaign with clearly defined tactics is essential. Periodically measuring the effectiveness of the various efforts will highlight which tactics have been successful and which may need modification. Coordinated marketing programs have many benefits.

Benefits of a Coordinated Program

A coordinated marketing program, with its advertising and promotions, benefits everyone involved in the shopping center—the landlord, the tenants, the shopping center manager, the leasing agent, and the community at large.

Landlord. For the landlord, coordinated marketing results in increased tenants' sales, which means more successful tenants, higher base rents, and greater opportunities for percentage rent as well as less tenant turnover and faster lease-up of vacant spaces. All of these are reflected in the shopping center's cash flow and, from that, the property value increases.

Tenant. For the tenant, a coordinated program provides opportunities for more sales and, therefore, greater success. Specific tenant benefits include:

- A location where most (if not all) of the other merchants are coordinating some of their advertising. This means one tenant can capitalize on a major promotion by another tenant. For example, if a department store anchor is having a seasonal sale, other merchants can plan similar sales for the same period. Department stores do extensive advertising for such events, and if the other tenants use the same media, they can maximize the impact of their ads by association with the department store's ad. Thus, the department store will draw more customer traffic, and shoppers will be looking for additional bargains at the other stores' sales.
- The opportunity to participate in the shopping center's regular advertising pieces—e.g., flyers for on-site distribution, tabloid sections inserted in the local newspaper, direct mailings, and the shopping center's Web site. The individual tenant's ad has more impact if it is included with other tenants' ads than if it is run by itself in the newspaper. When tenants advertise jointly, they can often negotiate a lower ad rate for each participating tenant.
- Increased traffic flow. Promotional events at the shopping center attract additional visitors—each one a potential customer.

Shopping Center Manager. For the shopping center manager, coordinating promotional activities provides an opportunity to develop a rapport with the tenants. The resulting goodwill can carry well into the future, meaning likely lease renewals, positive tenant activities to increase the success of their shops, and consequently greater income for the shopping center.

Leasing Team. Additionally, the job of the leasing team is easier when a shopping center's tenants are successful. Nothing sells as well as success, and retail tenants are attracted to shopping centers where the tenants—individually and by categories—have high sales volumes. In fact, such shopping centers become known throughout the retailing community. Consequently, the annual marketing plan, the specific advertising campaigns, and the promotional events become effective tools in the leasing agent's discussions with prospective tenants. Prospects can be shown how the shopping center works for its tenants—advertising and promotions bring customers to the center.

Community. Finally, the community as a whole benefits from a shopping center's marketing, advertising, and promotions in several ways:

- Being made aware of new fashions and products—coordinated merchandising programs (e.g., back-to-school and spring fashions) address consumer's needs on a seasonal basis.
- Saving money—periodic center-wide sales events (e.g., Presidents' Day sale, mid-year anniversary sales, and post-holiday sales) provide a wide array of merchandise at lower prices.
- Being entertained—promotional events (e.g., arts and crafts festivals, boat shows, authors' book signings) are repeated annually at many shopping centers, often becoming traditions for local shoppers.
- Participating in community-focused activities—use of the shopping center for fundraisers, membership drives, educational displays, etc., benefits particular groups (Girl Scouts, Little League, charitable organizations) as well as the individual shopper.

When a shopping center has a coordinated marketing program, the landlord and the tenants are investing in the success of their businesses.

Types of Coordinated Marketing Programs

The management team can take several approaches to marketing a shopping center. The most commonly used approaches are establishing a merchants' association, making joint or single efforts, and establishing a marketing fund.

Merchants' Association. A once common approach that is now usually only found in older regional or super regional malls is the merchants' association, which was a joint effort by the landlord and the tenants (with a lease obligation) to promote the shopping center. The merchants' association was the first attempt at organizing tenants at a shopping center to promote both the shopping center and the tenants, and it was widely used for that purpose until the early 1980s. Although few shopping centers use merchants' associations today, understanding their structure and history can help shopping center management avoid the pitfalls that were the downfall of many merchants' associations.

Initially, merchants' associations were voluntary organizations. However, as their benefits became apparent, a merchants' association provision was incorporated into the shopping center lease. Early lease provisions stated that when a percentage of the tenants (usually 75 to 80 percent) agreed to form a merchants' association, all tenants had to become members. Ultimately, the lease provision made membership in the merchants' association mandatory.

Originally, dues were based on *frontage* (the number of front feet of the tenant's premises) or *area* (the square footage of the tenant's store). Eventually, the latter system prevailed, and dues were calculated as a rate per square foot. This can be a flat rate (e.g., one dollar per square foot per year) or a declining rate (e.g., one dollar per square foot for 1,200 square feet, 75¢ for each additional 1,200 square feet, and 50¢ each for all square footage in excess of 2,400). Dues are computed annually but paid monthly or quarterly. The merchants' association has the right to increase the dues.

A major disadvantage of a merchants' association and a reason for its lack of popularity today, is friction among the merchants regarding the types and frequency of promotions and which media to use. Another potential problem is that some tenants attempt to use the merchants' association as a forum to complain to the landlord about the cost of common area maintenance, the level of maintenance, vacancies in the shopping center, etc.

Joint or Single Efforts. Some other approaches include the landlord and tenants periodically jointly advertising their stores and the shopping center. In some cases, the landlord and the shopping center tenants share the costs of quarterly advertising in a local newspaper. Such arrangements have no lease obligations.

In another approach, the merchants in a shopping center may come together to create joint advertising without the landlord's participation. In still other cases, tenants from around the local area jointly advertise their shops in a local paper.

Sometimes the landlord markets the shopping center without any participation from the merchants. In the case of a shopping center grand opening, the landlord may promote the shopping center using his or her own funds.

Marketing Fund. The *marketing fund,* formerly known as a promotions fund or advertising fund, is a landlord-controlled method of marketing the shopping center in which the tenants may have an advisory role. Today it is the most common and most successful way to handle the marketing programs for the shopping center.

The marketing fund is covered by a specific lease provision that requires the tenant to contribute to the marketing fund. It also provides for an

Exhibit 11.1

Example Lease Clause—Advertising and Promotional Service; Marketing Fund

Advertising and Promotional Service. Landlord may, at its option, establish an Advertising and Promotional Service (the "Service") to furnish and maintain professional advertising and sales promotions to benefit all merchants of the Shopping Center. In conjunction with said Service, Landlord shall, in its discretion, hire and supervise all necessary personnel, including but not limited to a marketing director and sufficient secretarial and support services. The salaries, office rent, utilities, supplies, telephone systems, and all other administrative expenses necessary for efficient day-to-day operation of the Service shall be paid from the Marketing Fund, as described below. A committee, composed of a representative of Landlord, the anchor tenants, and two representatives of the shop tenants in the Shopping Center, will be formed to annually review and make recommendations regarding the annual advertising and promotional activities sponsored by the Service. Decisions as to the advertising and promotional activities will be the sole responsibility of Landlord.

Marketing Fund. In the event Landlord elects to establish a promotional service as described above, Tenant agrees to pay Landlord an annual amount equal to *[specify rate]* per square foot of floor area of the Premises per year, or a minimum annual fee of *[specify dollar amount]* per year, whichever is greater ("Tenant's Marketing Fee"), as Tenant's contribution toward the costs of operating the Service. Tenant's Marketing Fee shall be payable by Tenant in twelve (12) equal monthly installments due on the same day as Minimum Rent is due under this Lease. Tenant's Marketing Fee, together with similar fees paid by other tenants of the Shopping Center, shall be collectively referred to as the "Marketing Fund." All monies received by Landlord under this Section shall be used solely for the purpose of conducting advertising and promotional services of the Shopping Center, for payment of the personnel, operational, and administrative expenses of the Service, and for related purposes. Tenant's Marketing Fee shall be increased at the end of each Lease Year in the same proportion that the revised Consumer Price Index—All Urban Consumers—All Items (1982–84 = 100) for the U.S. City Average as published by the United States Department of Labor, Bureau of Labor Statistics, published at the end of each Lease Year, is increased over the same index for the prior Lease Year. Landlord hereby agrees to contribute to the Marketing Fund an annual amount equal to twenty-five percent (25%) of the total amount of the Marketing Fund contributions by Shopping Center tenants for such year. Landlord shall not be obligated to expend more than twenty-five percent (25%) of the Marketing Fund actually collected from Tenants for each such year. In addition to the foregoing, Tenant also agrees to pay Landlord, within ten (10) days of execution of this Lease, an initial assessment of *[specify rate]* per square foot of the floor area of the Premises, or *[specify dollar amount]*, whichever is greater, for pre-opening advertising and promotional activities.

annual increase in funding and for the appointment of an advisory board consisting of representatives of each anchor tenant and the shop tenants (usually only two of the latter). Finally, the lease provision gives the landlord sole responsibility for the development and implementation of the marketing program. (Exhibit 11.1 shows an example.)

In order to gain the tenants' support, the landlord must have good communication with them. That is largely achieved through the efforts of the marketing director and the shopping center manager. The most effective means of communication is one-on-one meetings with the tenants.

The advisory board meets regularly (usually quarterly or semiannually) with the marketing director and the shopping center manager. The board has no control over the activities of the marketing fund; rather, its purpose is to suggest programs, assess proposed plans, and evaluate past events. Each month a newsletter is usually sent to all the tenants informing them of upcoming promotions.

Since the marketing fund is currently the most popular and successful type of coordinated marketing program in shopping centers, the rest of this chapter focuses on that marketing approach.

Roles and Responsibilities of the Participants

The success of a coordinated marketing program and, ultimately, the success of the shopping center depend on the landlord, the shopping center manager, the marketing director, and the tenants and how they fulfill their respective roles.

Landlord. An effective program begins with the right attitude on the part of the landlord. The landlord must understand how coordinated marketing, advertising, and promotions benefit the landlord's investment, the shopping center as an entity, the individual tenants, the leasing effort, and the community at large.

The landlord's support of the program must be evidenced by a specific commitment to the marketing fund. That usually means contributing a portion of the funds. It also means providing personnel to coordinate the program. The costs of the coordinated marketing program are reimbursed from the dues paid by the tenants and the landlord. The landlord should set an example for the tenants. Without the landlord's active support, the probability of the program's success is greatly diminished. The scale of the landlord's commitment will depend on the type and size of the shopping center.

The astute shopping center owner actively supports and participates in a coordinated program to market, advertise, and promote the shopping center. Providing funds to promote the shopping center and thus the tenants' businesses is not for altruistic reasons—shopping center owners regard their financial contributions to a marketing fund as an investment from which they expect a return in the form of increased cash flow and enhanced property value.

Shopping Center Manager. First and foremost, the shopping center manager provides leadership. He or she represents the landlord in developing and/or supervising the implementation of the marketing program and interacting with the tenants. Working with the marketing director, the shopping center manager is responsible for starting the marketing fund. The shopping center manager and the marketing director are responsible for meeting with each tenant to explain the purpose, goals, and benefits of a coordinated marketing program.

The shopping center manager is responsible for supervising the activities of the marketing director and approving the annual budget and calendar of activities. He or she should also periodically review the financial reports. The shopping center manager may be one of several signatories for the entity's checking account.

The shopping center manager's duties include managing the common areas, which includes reviewing and approving how the common areas will be used for promotional activities. (See chapter 4, Management Structure, for a detailed discussion of the shopping center manager's duties.) If the shopping center manager believes a promotional activity may cause damage to the property or injuries to customers or tenants' employees, he or she can veto the activity. As an example, a hot-air balloon ride promotion might be vetoed because it presents too great a liability.

The shopping center manager, along with the marketing director, is responsible for maintaining the tenants' interest and active participation in the marketing program. Though the shopping center manager is a major player in developing the marketing program, the day-to-day operations of the marketing fund are usually the responsibility of the marketing director.

Marketing Director. This individual is directly responsible for developing and executing the marketing program and for the operation of the marketing fund. He or she must be creative in developing an effective marketing strategy and successfully executing the advertising and promotional programs. A marketing director must have good communication and interpersonal skills to gain tenants' confidence and cooperation and to motivate them to active participation in a coordinated marketing program.

Each year, the marketing director must determine the marketing budget. The anticipated funding determines the specific programs that can be accomplished. Next, a marketing strategy is developed and from that is developed a calendar of merchandising, community and promotional events, and advertising and public relations support. This plan is typically developed in September or October and before the December holiday season so the marketing staff can devote their full time and effort to implementing and monitoring the critical holiday season events starting in mid-November and continuing through December.

Under a marketing fund, the program is submitted to the shopping center manager for approval, and then it is presented to the merchants. The marketing director prepares the meeting agenda, sends out the notices and reminders, and conducts the marketing fund meetings. Implementation of the marketing program includes creating, planning, and coordinating ad-

Exhibit 11.2
Example Lease Clause—Tenant Advertising

The Marketing Fund shall schedule and offer regular promotional and advertising events ("Advertising Events") during each calendar year through the local newspaper, direct mail, radio and/or television media to promote the business of tenants in the Shopping Center. Tenant shall, at its own expense, contribute at least six (6) print advertisements for its business during each year. The Marketing Fund shall provide Tenant with a schedule for the Advertising Events. Tenant's advertisements must be submitted to the Marketing Fund or its newspaper advertising representative no later than thirty (30) days prior to the publishing deadline for the advertising events, which deadlines shall be set forth in the schedule. (All advertisements shall be subject to approval of the Marketing Fund.) In the event that Tenant fails to submit six (6) approved advertisements from among the first nine (9) advertising events of each calendar year, the Marketing Fund shall be authorized to include advertisements for Tenant of the Marketing Fund's own choosing and design, in any or all of the last three (3) advertising events of each year, provided that (a) Tenant does not submit approved advertisements bringing to six (6) the number submitted each calendar year by the deadlines stated for those last three (3) advertising events, (b) the Marketing Fund shall not be authorized to require Tenant to have more than six (6) advertisements in any one calendar year, and (c) the cost for any such advertisements added by the Marketing Fund on Tenant's behalf shall be charged to Tenant and shall be due and payable by Tenant upon receipt of a written invoice from the Marketing Fund or the newspaper or other media advertising representative.

vertising, publicity, and promotional events. (See chapter 4, Management Structure, for further discussion of the role of the marketing director.)

Tenants. In a marketing fund, tenants may be appointed to an advisory board. In the ideal situation, the lease will require all tenants to belong to and contribute funding for a marketing fund. To ensure tenant participation, many landlords include a mandatory tenant advertising provision in the lease (exhibit 11.2). This provision requires the tenant to participate in a minimum number of advertising events. If the tenant fails to do so, the landlord may submit an ad on behalf of the tenant and bill the cost to the tenant. Lease requirements for mandatory tenant advertising are most common in regional and super regional shopping centers and in lifestyle, specialty, or theme shopping centers. The tenants collectively provide the bulk of the funds to market, advertise, and promote the shopping center.

The effectiveness of specific advertising is directly related to the number of tenants that participate in it and the selection and price of the merchandise advertised. The greater the number of tenants who participate in a shopping center's tabloid section or other print or electronic advertising vehicle, the greater its impact, and the greater the sales for each store. Tenants must also participate in merchandising events, such as fashion shows and sales events, and they should be encouraged to coordinate store windows (and perhaps even apparel that store employees wear) with the theme events, such as western days or a Halloween activity. The benefits the tenants derive from the marketing program are directly related to their levels of active participation.

CREATING A SUCCESSFUL MARKETING PROGRAM

Shopping center marketing programs are complex. They begin with the development of an annual marketing plan that is based on anticipated funding. Media advertising and promotional events comprise most of the budgeted items, and they are important components of a successful program. For a new shopping center, a grand opening event is funded separately; it is planned while the shopping center is under construction.

Annual Marketing Budget

The first step in preparing the annual marketing plan is to propose a specific budget or develop the budget from the tenants' and the landlord's anticipated dues. This requires an analysis of the available income and an evaluation of how it can best be spent.

Analysis of Available Income. The major sources of income are the respective contributions from the tenants and the landlord. Other sources of ancillary income should also be included in the budget.

Sources of Income. Merchants' contributions are based on their square footage, so the larger the shopping center, the bigger the budget. If contributions are not mandatory for the anchor tenants, voluntary contributions should be solicited. While they may agree to monthly or annual cash contributions, the anchors may prefer to participate in other ways—e.g., contributing merchandise as prizes for promotional drawings or contributing funds for holiday decorations.

The bulk of the funding comes from the shop tenants as mandated in their leases. However, other variables affect the amount collected. These include the rate per square foot, the anchor tenants' contributions, if any (and their rate), and the landlord's percentage contribution. Some leases commit the landlord to a specific financial contribution. Sometimes the marketing fund provision states a formula for the landlord's contribution. Typically, the landlord's contribution is equal to 25 percent of the amount collected from the tenants, which amounts to 20 percent of the total funding. This makes the landlord the largest contributor. Thus, for a super regional mall, if the tenants contribute \$800,000, the landlord's contribution would be \$200,000 (\$800,000 × .25 = \$200,000). The total funding available would be

$1,000,000 ($800,000 + $200,000 = $1,000,000). Thus, the landlord's share would be 20 percent of the total ($200,000 ÷ $1,000,000 = .20).

In addition to a specific cash contribution, the landlord may pay the marketing director's salary and contribute office space, equipment, and supplies. In large shopping centers and malls, the marketing fund reimburses the landlord for the marketing director's salary, payroll costs, and benefits. The landlord provides the office space free of charge, and the marketing fund pays for all other office expenses. In smaller shopping centers, this service is often contracted and the fees are paid from the marketing fund dues.

Other Sources of Funding. Other sources of funding the marketing efforts should also be explored. These include sponsorship programs and other ancillary sources of income.

Sponsorship Programs. Sponsorship programs became popular in the 1990s. In these programs, companies contribute dollars, equipment, amenities, or major prizes for an event to gain name recognition and create goodwill in the community. Some regional malls have a goal of receiving 25 to 30 percent of their annual marketing budget, which can range from $400,000 to $1,000,000, from sponsorship programs. Sponsor companies contribute cash or in-kind services to participate in a program or event or to receive the naming rights for an area of the shopping center. In-kind services defray all or a portion of the cost of an event.

In the first sponsorship programs, companies provided directories for malls in return for the right to the advertisement on the back of the mall directories. In other instances, a company may pay for seating or for a children's play area in a shopping center court for the area's naming rights. If a car or an all-expenses-paid vacation is the prize for a drawing, the car dealership or travel agency that donates the prize usually receives recognition by having its name and logo included with all the advertising prior to and during the event. The car may also be on display at the mall with the dealer's name and related information; the travel agency may provide a display with photos of the vacation to win.

A hospital or retirement center may sponsor a mall walker program. A bookstore in a shopping center may sponsor a children's reading program. Companies will pay for the naming rights to an area of the shopping center or mall, such as the center court or other open spaces. Some shopping centers have sold advertisements on barricades that cover areas of the interior and exterior shopping center that are under construction. Some of the major malls owned by REITs and developers have staffs devoted exclusively to selling sponsorships for their malls.

Ancillary Income. The opportunities for *ancillary income*—vendor fees, cooperative advertising, etc.—occur primarily in larger shopping centers.

Occasionally, merchants located near a shopping center contribute to its marketing fund so they can participate in the joint advertising and promotions (e.g., an adjacent strip shopping center may join with a larger shopping center). Significant income can also result from vendor fees. Many malls and shopping centers charge dealers to display their cars, RVs, or boats during shows. Income from such events (often exceeding $20,000 each) can be used to defray the costs of advertising and promoting the event. Another possibility is cooperative advertising with a manufacturer—a cookie company may donate money or goods for a tie-in to a cookie promotion.

Analysis of Expenses. The amount of money available for advertising and promotions determines the magnitude of a center's marketing plan. In general, the larger the shopping center, the more extensive the marketing program can be. The funding available for marketing a neighborhood strip shopping center over the course of a year is likely to be between $20,000 and $40,000, while that for a regional mall may range from $400,000 to over $1,000,000.

The size of the marketing budget also determines the size of the marketing staff. The primary expenses of a marketing program are administration, advertising, promotions, and decorations. Administration includes the salary and employee benefits for the marketing director (and other marketing personnel) plus office and general administrative expenses. Advertising expenses have two components—ad costs and agency fees. The agency's fee includes the cost of producing the ad. The costs to implement most promotional events are usually limited to the expenses to coordinate them—rented equipment (tables, chairs, podium, microphone), decorations, and supplies. Some traveling promotions may charge shopping centers a fee. The budget should include reserves for unexpected expenses and donations.

Advertising

The purpose of advertising is to appeal to a specific audience—in this instance, so they will visit the shopping center and shop there. Many large shopping centers hire ad agencies to assist in planning ad campaigns, recommend media and negotiate contracts, create and produce the ads, place the ads with the media, and handle the accounting and record keeping. Smaller shopping centers may rely on services provided by the media (their sales representatives or production departments). Advertising for strip shopping centers is often scheduled on a regular basis (e.g., a monthly or quarterly joint advertising section in the local newspaper and a monthly coupon promotion).

The marketing director is responsible for determining the right media mix for the advertising program. The media mix depends on the location of the shopping center, the size of its trade area, the specific audience each medium reaches, and the advertising budget. Though numerous advertising media are available, the ones used most often for shopping centers are newspapers, direct mail, the Internet, radio, television, transit signs, and billboards.

Newspapers. The cost of newspaper ads makes them available to any shopping center, regardless of size. Compared to other vehicles, newspaper ads are a relatively inexpensive means of obtaining broad market coverage. Rates are usually quoted by the column inch, and volume rates or discounts are offered. When tenants group their ads together, they can achieve a volume rate considerably lower than the *open rate* that they would pay to advertise alone.

The marketing director can select the size, placement, and design of an ad as well as when it will be published. Newspapers that serve major metropolitan areas usually have zoned editions that allow the advertiser to target a specific neighborhood or suburb. For example, if the marketing director at a mall located in Orange County, California, does not want to pay for the entire distribution area of the *Los Angeles Times,* ads can be placed in a zoned edition for Orange County.

Direct Mail. Flexibility is one of the main advantages of direct mail advertising. Direct mail has no broadcast schedules or publication deadlines. For the best results, direct mailings should be planned, periodical mailings so the recipients are reminded of the shopping center and its tenants on a consistent basis. In recent years, the marketing director can choose between traditional (hard copy) direct mail and direct e-mail.

Traditional Direct Mail. With traditional direct mail, the marketing pieces can vary in size, shape, color, and texture. They can be inserted in newspapers or mailed separately or with other direct mail advertisements. Direct mailings can be targeted to specific segments of the market based on postal zip codes, occupations, membership in specific organizations, etc. Mailing lists can be purchased from organizations, created from directories, or compiled from customer information taken at the time of purchase. Stores that issue their own credit cards have ready-made mailing lists. Names and addresses can be collected during contests or at promotional drawings held at the shopping center.

The marketing director must take some special considerations into account when he or she creates direct mail advertising campaigns. Postal regulations define dimensions, weights, and degrees of presorting required to qualify for the most economical bulk mailing postage rates. These rules should be studied beforehand. Delivery of third-class mail is often not expedited, so extra time must be allowed. Also, while printing costs on a per-piece basis decrease as the number of printed pieces increases, such items as specialty papers, specified ink color matches, die cutting, and special folds add to the costs.

Direct E-mail. As a lower-cost option, broadcast e-mails can be sent to attract prospects to the shopping center. The marketing director and the shopping center manager should be aware that legislation restricts some direct mail campaigns via e-mail. In December 2003, legislation was passed to control unsolicited commercial e-mails. The legislation responded to marketers, retailers, and Internet account providers who sought a single set of rules that would apply nationwide. The bill does *not* ban unsolicited commercial e-mails, but it does establish requirements that senders of commercial e-mails must follow:

- Include a legitimate return e-mail and physical postal address.
- Include a functioning opt-out mechanism and a clear and conspicuous notice of the opportunity to opt out.
- Honor any opt-out request.
- Include a clear and conspicuous notice that the message is an a dvertisement or solicitation.
- Clearly identify messages that contain pornographic or sexual content.

In addition, the legislation prohibits senders from falsifying or disguising their true identities and from using incorrect, misleading, or fraudulent subject lines.[1]

Coupons. As a mailing—either through e-mail or regular mail—a collection of coupons from a variety of stores within the shopping center provides an array of savings opportunities for the consumer. This can lead to multiple purchases, cross-shopping, and repeated shopping trips—all traceable to the one promotional mailing. As with traditional direct marketing pieces, e-mail campaigns from individual retailers may include a redeemable coupon—to be used by providing the promotion code at the retailer's online store or by printing it out and redeeming it in the store.

The Internet. It has become essential that every shopping center, and even each tenant within the shopping center, create an Internet presence with a Web site. At the very least, a shopping center can develop a Web site that has a directory of tenants, including their phone numbers and addresses as well as the shopping center's hours. The Web site should also include a directory by merchandise types and should be updated regularly for new tenants and to communicate about upcoming events. (See chapter 8, Leas-

1. Adapted from IREM® education course, **Marketing and Leasing: Retail Properties**, 2004.

ing the Shopping Center, for details on setting up a Web site and using the Internet to assist in leasing efforts.)

An indirect but potentially very successful way for retailers to draw in traffic is through the retailer's own Web site. The frenzy of dot-com businesses in the late 1990s attempted to persuade consumers to change their shopping habits and buy online. Savvy retailers have since learned that rather than drawing the consumers to their Web sites to purchase something, they can use the site to offer a variety of services to their potential customers, e.g., discount coupons, information about special promotions, customer care contact information. Each merchant may wish to have a link from the individual store's Web site to the shopping center's Web site.

A common method retailers use to build their online customer bases is to have the salesperson or cashier ask the customer at checkout if they would like to be on the retailer's e-mail list. Successful retailers use the customer's e-mail addresses strictly for store information and do not disclose or share the e-mail addresses with any other businesses.

Radio. This medium continues to reach a vast audience within U.S. households. Radio is flexible advertising in which ads can be changed on short notice. Every major market has a wide range of local radio stations, almost all of which accept advertising. The stations in large metropolitan areas often serve suburban communities and adjacent rural areas as well. Stations that are part of a national network also accept advertising for the local market. This multiplicity of choices allows the marketing director to target a specific audience. Based on the station's format (all news, all talk, sports) or programming (including broadcasts in foreign languages) and the type of music played (pop, new age, classical), the message can be targeted to a specific audience by age, income, type of work or profession, gender, ethnic group, etc.

Radio is one of the least expensive electronic media, and radio advertising is affordable for most shopping centers. Ad rates depend on the number of *spots* (commercials), the time period specified, and the radio station's share of the total audience. In major metropolitan areas, the advertising day is commonly divided into five time periods or segments:

Morning drive—6:00 a.m. to 10:00 a.m.
Daytime—10:00 a.m. to 4:00 p.m.
Evening drive—4:00 p.m. to 7:00 p.m.
Evening—7:00 p.m. to midnight
Nighttime—midnight to 6:00 a.m.

Radio advertising works especially well in smaller communities where the shopping center's trade area encompasses most of the broadcast area and few stations exist. In major metropolitan areas, ads cost more because a station's broadcast range is wider and the audience is much larger. Regional and super regional malls use this medium to attract shoppers from outside their normal trade areas. For a strip shopping center, on the other hand, radio advertising may not be the most cost-effective medium. The cost of advertising beyond the shopping center's trade area must be weighed against the number of people within the trade area who will receive the message.

Television. Prior to cable television, only enclosed malls and very large shopping centers advertised on television—once again, because of the cost. Cable television is more affordable than the main networks, and most shopping centers can afford to use this electronic medium. While radio spots can be read by staff announcers (rather than prerecorded), TV ads must have visual impact to be effective, and therefore the production cost is high compared to such costs for other media. The rate for a television spot ad is based on the time of day, the size of the audience, and the length of the spot. Television time is sold in 10-, 20-, 30-, and 60-second increments. Discounts may apply for multiple spots or extended advertising periods (over days, weeks, or months), and the advertiser may have to contract for a minimum number of spots.

Television advertising is more costly than other advertising methods, but it can be very effective. Television reaches a large and varied audience. As with radio advertising, specific audiences can be targeted based on the time of day and type of show (morning cartoons, afternoon soaps and talk shows, evening news, prime time, sitcoms, adventure series, late-night talk shows and movies, and scores of cable channels targeted to specific audiences such as sports, cooking, and classic movies). In some markets, cable television advertising may be more affordable than spots on local commercial stations. Both types of television stations should be able to characterize their markets so advertisers can choose spots that will optimize the audiences they reach.

Transit Advertising. Advertising on mass transit (buses, elevated and subway trains, streetcars, or trolleys) allows the shopping center's message to be seen over a wide area. Advertising space is available on the exteriors and interiors of most such vehicles, including taxis. Some rapid transit districts can ensure that an ad will be on a specific route. The cost is relatively low, and such programs offer flexibility in ad design, use of color, and frequency of message changes.

Billboards. Billboards can be used to direct people to a shopping center or to promote a major event such as a grand opening. They mainly provide repeated exposure to the message, and the cost per view is measurably lower than for any other medium. However, billboards are seldom used for shopping center advertising because of their limited effectiveness. Though the message can be changed frequently, the changes themselves can be expensive. Billboard ads are typically prepared as painted or printed panels, and their showing locations are rented for a minimum of three to six months. The time frame makes them less useful for advertising a specific short-term event. In the early 2000s though, some large shopping centers began using electronic billboards or reader boards on the site adjacent to the main street on which they front.

Publicity

Publicity is information that is published or aired by the media at no charge to the shopping center. Shopping centers have countless events that an editor of a newspaper or the manager of a radio station might consider reporting, especially if press releases or announcements are received in advance. Stories that feature local residents (prize winners, new local merchants, store or shopping center personnel changes, such as promotions and appointments) are of interest to the community at large. Community activities at the shopping center (a Girl Scout exhibit, a health fair, Little League signup) and major activities or unusual promotional events, such as a carnival in the parking lot or a bridal fair, may bring media people to the shopping center so they can report personally.

The marketing director should always notify the media well in advance of events that are newsworthy. However, there is no guarantee that such information will be published or aired. Selection for publication is based first on space or time available and then on the interest to the community. Copies of press releases should be kept together in a file along with notes or records of their publication. A useful exercise is to calculate what they would have cost if they had been purchased ads. An ongoing publicity program can augment purchased advertising and help promotional dollars go farther.

Promotional Events

To be successful, promotions must be well thought out, and they must be planned well in advance. The marketing director's annual marketing plan includes promotional events that will be supported by advertising and publicity. The number of promotions a shopping center can conduct is directly related to its marketing budget and the amount of time the marketing staff has to plan and implement the events.

The marketing director should check the dates of major activities planned by local authorities, community organizations, and the shopping center's anchor tenants to be certain that no other event will detract from promotions planned for the shopping center. A shopping center's promotion can often be coordinated with an anchor tenant's promotion (e.g., a sidewalk sale the same weekend as the anchor's midsummer clearance sale or a supermarket's western days sale).

Most promotions require three to six months of preplanning. There are four basic types of promotions:

1. *Sales events* are among the most successful promotions, and they offer endless possibilities tied to seasons or particular holidays (e.g., Presidents' Day sale, after-Christmas sale, the shopping center's anniversary sale). Sales provide the merchants opportunities to mark down and sell items that are not selling well at their regular prices or that are left over from the recent season. For example, summer merchandise can be placed on sale during the end of summer or early fall. These clearance sales provide the merchants with cash to purchase new merchandise and keep their stores looking fresh.
2. *Entertainment activities* are popular promotions. Traditional examples include arts and crafts, boat, RV, auto, bridal, fashion, and antique shows. Some events may compete with the merchants for the consumer dollar, but the increase in traffic to the shopping center usually more than offsets this potential competition. Auto and boat dealers usually pay to display their vehicles and boats during the show. The funds collected from the dealers are used to advertise the event.
3. *Educational events* can be coordinated with local agencies and community organizations. The shopping center can cosponsor a safety fair with local police and fire departments or a health fair with the local hospital.
4. *Community events* allow local groups opportunities to promote their organizations. Several groups might sell handcrafted items or baked goods at a charity bazaar, or a local college might exhibit its new semester's curriculum and provide class registration.

Whenever possible, merchandising should be related to the promotion. If a shopping center has a boat show, clothing stores should be encouraged to display summer and beach wear or nautical styles, and sporting goods stores should feature swimming, fishing, and boating equipment.

After each promotion, the marketing director should poll the merchants for their opinions of the event and their sales figures during it. Not every promotion will directly benefit every merchant. A sporting goods store will benefit directly from a boat show but not from a bridal show; however, a bridal show can provide exposure and recognition that will result in sales of sporting goods later.

Grand Opening of a Shopping Center

The grand opening of a shopping center is a major one-time event in a shopping center's life. The only similar event likely to occur is a grand reopening after major remodeling, rehabilitation, a change of use, or an expansion. A grand opening takes months of planning because every aspect of the event must be as professional—but exciting—as possible. The grand opening should have a theme to help focus the advertising, publicity, and promotional events. Planning and creativity are the keys to a successful grand opening event. Its objectives are also important. From preopening publicity through the grand opening celebration, every detail must be carefully planned.

Objectives. The objectives of a shopping center's grand opening vary somewhat with the particular needs of the shopping center. However, they usually include the following specific goals:

- To build awareness of the shopping center in the community
- To position the shopping center as a valuable asset in the community
- To gain community support
- To introduce new merchants to the community
- To capture a share of the retail sales in the community
- To assist the center's leasing program

The adage, "you never get a second chance to make a first impression," certainly applies to the objectives of the grand opening. The effort to make that first impression begins long before the actual event. The steps necessary for making the grand opening a success are the same regardless of the type of shopping center, although a larger shopping center will have a larger budget, more people involved in the planning, more tenants to work with, and larger crowds of visitors. A well-executed, creative event will draw many customers to the shopping center and establish the standard for the ongoing marketing program.

Preopening Publicity. Even before the grand opening of a shopping center is planned, a comprehensive publicity program should be developed. In particular, press releases should be sent out announcing specific milestones leading up to the opening:

- Development of the shopping center
- Lease commitments by anchor tenants
- Ground breaking
- Construction progress
- A list of tenants who have signed leases
- The grand opening events

Once the shopping center is open, periodic press releases should continue. Announcements of new tenants and special promotional events are possibilities.

Budget. The grand opening budget may equal or exceed the budget for a year of advertising and promotions. The amount of money available for the event must be determined well in advance. Review of the leases will indicate each tenant's grand opening assessment and ensure accurate billing. Tenants' grand opening assessments typically range from 50¢ to $1.00 per square foot or more. The anchor tenants may not be obligated to participate; in which case, they should be asked to make a donation.

When a shopping center is not fully leased by the grand opening date, the landlord often contributes the amount that would have been collected if the vacancies were occupied. This ensures that sufficient funds will be available for all the grand opening activities. As vacant spaces are leased, new tenants may be billed their share of the grand opening expenses up to one year after the event. Even though they were not open at the time, they benefit from the grand opening.

Schedule. The next step is to create a schedule of specific deadlines for accomplishing different phases of the grand opening program; this may be developed with an advertising agency. A timetable of grand opening events must also be planned. The grand opening itself will be the culmination of a series of events that have already been publicized.

Traditionally, a grand opening begins with a ribbon-cutting ceremony. Promotional activities and, possibly, giveaways are included. The benefits of the grand opening can be maximized by extending it over three to four days (e.g., beginning on a Thursday and continuing through Sunday).

As grand opening planning begins, many stores will not have managers appointed yet, or appointed managers may be busy preparing the stores for opening. As a result, tenants rarely are available to participate in the planning. Regular communication with the merchants is essential so they will be kept up-to-date with the plans and the schedule of events. A meeting should be held with the merchants to present the program and solicit their support. The merchants will need to know the advertising plans and specific ad deadlines.

If some of the tenants are part of a national chain, those merchants should be encouraged to send broadcast e-mails to their marketing customer base within a specific distance of the new shopping center to advertise the grand opening of their store in the new center. Click-through coupons can be included, and mention of the shopping center entertainment and other special activities can all be a part of the e-mail message.

Numerous other details must be addressed well in advance. Some specific examples are noted here:

- Develop an advertising schedule that includes preopening, opening, and post-opening advertisements—a comprehensive program should consider using newspapers, radio, TV, billboards, and direct mail as well as creating a Web site.
- Develop a press kit for media representatives.
- Schedule a press conference before the charitable event or before or during the grand opening proper.
- Select decorations and arrange for their installation and removal.
- Prepare an agenda for the ribbon-cutting ceremony.
- Send invitations to community leaders.
- Invite two or three VIPs to speak and cut the ribbon.
- Select and purchase promotional giveaways—e.g., balloons, refrigerator magnets, shopping bags—imprinted with the shopping center name and logo.
- Hire extra personnel and select costumes or special apparel for those who will hand out promotional items.
- Design and print a consumer brochure showing the layout of the shopping center and a list of the tenants; arrange to install holders for the brochures near the mall entrances or directories.
- Interview, hire, and schedule entertainers.
- Arrange for catering, music, equipment rentals, etc.
- Hire a photographer to take publicity photos—include dignitaries, entertainers, the ribbon-cutting ceremony, crowds, and the full parking lot—for a follow-up press release and for inclusion in the leasing package.
- Send flowers and a welcoming card to each tenant.
- Schedule the cleanup of the mall and parking lot.
- Hire additional maintenance personnel and security guards.
- Develop a contingency plan in case anything goes wrong.

Operations Issues. In addition, several operational issues must be thoroughly analyzed, planned, and implemented. First, everyone on the management and marketing teams must be briefed on the event and assigned their particular duties. The shopping center manager, the marketing director, and the director of operations or maintenance supervisor should arrive at the shopping center several hours before each event is scheduled.

Maintenance. Items such as trash cans, ash urns, planters, and benches must be installed in their proper places. Extra maintenance personnel must be scheduled to work in the shopping center and in the parking lot. Elevator and escalator service personnel should be on call or at the shopping center during the beginning of the events.

Security and Crowd Control. Security and crowd control are especially important. Additional security personnel should be hired and assigned to the shopping center itself as well as the entrances and the parking lot. Security can also monitor activities in the parking lot from the roof. The local police department should be asked to direct traffic in front of the shopping center as well as several miles away at highway exits if the event is expected to draw people from surrounding communities. Security personnel should direct traffic inside the parking lot. All security personnel should have a form of two-way communications and be in direct communication with the shopping center manager, marketing director, and security director or operations manager. Levels of traffic control and shopping center patrols should be coordinated with scheduled events.

Emergency Communications. The marketing director or the shopping center manager must develop a plan to communicate with the media during a crisis, such as a storm, an arson, a terrorist attack, or a medical emergency. One person should be the spokesperson for all media contact. The designated spokesperson is usually the marketing director, the shopping center manager, or a public relations firm representative. All other staff members and on-site contractors' employees, such as security guards and maintenance personnel, should direct all questions to the designated spokesperson. The spokesperson should treat the media courteously and should provide them with accurate and timely information to prevent rumors and unintentional false statements. The staff should be trained on their roles in dealing with the media. (Chapter 5, Maintenance and Operations, details the handling of all facets of emergency procedures.)

12

The Retail Component in Multi-Use and Mixed-Use Developments

Retail has become an integral and profitable component of most property types. Significant retailing—defined as either the amount or the quality of retail tenants—has been included in airports, train stations, hotels, resorts, amusement parks, waterfront developments, multistory office and residential buildings, and ground-floor space in small neighborhood buildings. The retail component in these multi-use and mixed-use buildings provides many benefits:

- Space leased for retail use typically commands higher rent and has the possibility of collecting percentage rent.
- A retail component provides a service to the building's occupants and visitors, which can add value to the other space in the building.
- An office tenant may be willing to pay higher rent if the building has banking and stock brokerage services, quality restaurants, branded and upscale retailers, and other services.
- Residents prefer to have services in or near their buildings.
- A strong retail core downtown or in a neighborhood adds value to the buildings in those areas. Shopping is an activity that attracts people to an area or a building, and it provides a form of entertainment for those who need to wait for a plane or a train.

MULTI-USE VERSUS MIXED-USE

"Multi-use" describes several types of developments. Mixed-use developments are one type of multi-use development. Understanding the mixed-use concept helps explain the other multi-use types.

Multi-use developments encompass three broad categories: (1) densely configured developments that achieve physical and functional integration but include only two uses; (2) mixed-use developments as described below; and (3) developments with two or more uses that lack physical and functional integration, usually because of their large scale, low density, or lack of a coherent plan.

The Urban Land Institute defines a *mixed-use development (MXD)* as a large-scale real estate project that has three principal characteristics. The first is incorporation of three or more significant revenue-producing uses (e.g., retail, office, residential, hotel, recreation). In well-planned projects, the uses are all mutually supporting. Most include substantial areas devoted to parking, and in urban MXDs in particular, parking can be an additional source of revenue.

The second characteristic of an MXD is a significant physical and functional integration of project components and, thus, an intensive use of land. Although this integration can take many physical forms, its main objective, interconnection of the uses, is often achieved via uninterrupted pedestrian walkways. Integration can be achieved by the following:

- Vertical mixing of project components into a single tower that occupies only one city block.
- Careful positioning of key project components around centrally located focal points (e.g., arrangement of retailers in a shopping gallery; a hotel containing a larger central court; a central open-air plaza; a park or water feature within the MXD).
- Interconnection of project components through an elaborate pedestrian circulation network, such as subterranean concourses, walkways and plazas at grade level, or aerial bridges between buildings.
- Extensive use of escalators, elevators, moving sidewalks, and other mechanical means of facilitating horizontal and vertical movement of pedestrians.
- The third characteristic of an MXD is conformance of the development to a coherent plan. Minimally, this plan sets forth the type and scale of uses, permitted densities, and related items. Exhibit 12.1 compares the three categories of multi-use developments.

The other two types of multi-use developments can be defined in contrast to the mixed-use development. An example is Newport Center, a 622-acre development in the affluent coastal community of Newport Beach, CA.

Exhibit 12.1
Categories of Multi-Use Developments and Their Characteristics

	Category 1 (Multi-Use Only)	**Category 2 (Multi-Use and Mixed-Use)**	**Category 3 (Multi-Use Only)**
Number of uses	2	3+	2+
Configuration	Dense	Dense	May or may not be dense
Achieves physical and functional integration	Yes	Yes (significant integration includes interconnection of uses; intensive use of land)	No
Large-scale project	Sometimes	Yes	Frequently
Development conforms to a coherent plan	Sometimes	Yes	Sometimes

In the center of this development is Fashion Island, a super regional mall that contains primarily high-end department and specialty stores. For years this mall did not reach its full potential. The mall underwent major redesign—space was added for several additional shop tenants and the retail tenant mix was upgraded. The mall has since become one of the more successful malls in southern California. A six-lane ring road encircles the mall and its self-contained surface parking. Office and medical buildings, freestanding restaurants, two multiscreen theaters, hotels, and residential complexes are located outside the ring road. Though this project has numerous uses, it lacks physical integration because it is spread over such a large area. Therefore, it does not conform to the definition of an MXD, and it is classified as a multi-use development.

Much of this chapter refers to MXDs because they are similar to shopping centers in many respects. The chapter also discusses aspects of the other multi-use developments that are similar to shopping centers.

THE MIXED-USE DEVELOPMENT

Mixed use of a site is not a new idea. The Agora, a medieval market square in ancient Greece, and residential-commercial blocks throughout Europe also had multiple uses. What *is* new is the intentional development of an entity with a singular identity that includes several different types of specific uses on a large scale.

Evolution of the Mixed-Use Development

The first mixed-use developments in the United States were large, almost monolithic office towers that included some retailing on the lower floors. A good example is Rockefeller Center, a New York City landmark since the 1930s. Rockefeller Center is dominated by office buildings and includes a multitude of uses, though it does not have three or more major revenue-producing uses. (In particular, there is no residential component.) In the 1960s, the typical MXD was gigantic, averaging 2.2 million square feet. As the number of MXDs grew, however, the structures were made smaller. By the end of the 1980s, MXDs averaged only 1.1 million square feet, and the retail, hotel, and entertainment components were expanded at the expense of office space. The office building height, especially the large high-rise building, can act as a visual focus for the entire MXD, creating prestige and identity from long distances.

Uses Frequently Found in MXDs

Offices are the most frequently found use in MXDs. However, retail can be a significant component in mixed-use developments, and it can provide ancillary services to the other uses. Office buildings serve their own tenants and visitors; out-of-town guests primarily use hotels; and apartments and condominiums are oriented toward their residents. But retail and entertainment uses open the MXD to the public. An Urban Land Institute survey found that 98 percent of MXDs include retail uses. Though merchants can derive many benefits from locating in an MXD, if the primary customer base is not the people who live and work in the MXD, the retail component will need to draw customers from the public to be successful.

Retail businesses add vitality and appeal to a mixed-use development. Managing, leasing, and marketing the retail component is complex, and the individual who assumes these responsibilities must have specialized knowledge and experience. The manager's expertise is key to maximizing the benefits to retailers who locate in an MXD. Simply being present in a mixed-use development will not ensure the success of the retail component. The location of the MXD and the design and integration of the retail component into it, coupled with the right tenants for the trade area, are essential criteria for a successful retail component in an MXD.

Locations of MXDs

Mixed-use developments are found in both urban and suburban locations. Downtown areas have always been the center of commerce; until the development of regional malls, the downtown was the retail center of every community. In large cities especially, the downtown area has typically served as the primary location for the finest hotels, live-performance theaters and entertainment, and the community's nightlife. Not surprisingly, the first MXDs were developed in downtown areas.

Urban MXDs. Urban MXDs consist of one or more vertical structures developed on a relatively small parcel of land. Many urban MXDs are dominated by one use, whereas others have a relatively equal distribution of space among uses. One of the first urban MXDs, Penn Center in Philadelphia, with its rapid transit system below ground has three uses: offices, retail space, and a hotel. Chicago has several MXDs in its extended downtown area, each of which originally created a separate identity that emphasized its different uses. Several MXDs that were developed in the 1970s and 1980s have replaced some of their uses to stay competitive as the market changed. These changes often impact the retail component, regardless of whether it is the dominant use in the development.

The following three mixed-use developments, located in Chicago along or near Michigan Avenue, represent MXDs with three different dominant uses. The John Hancock Center is predominantly an office building, Marina City is primarily a residential building, and Water Tower Place focuses mainly on retail. The first two were built in the 1960s and have undergone major redevelopment and changes in some of their uses.

- *Marina City,* a 1.6-million-square-foot MXD situated along the Chicago River, is dominated by two circular 65-story, 896-unit residential towers, with adjacent structures originally enclosing 16 floors of office space (180,000 square feet) and three movie theaters, all rising above two levels of retail and service shops. As built, the project included a marina, a health club, a bowling alley, and a skating rink, plus parking for 900 automobiles. The residential use is dominant. Originally rental apartments, the twin towers were converted to condominium apartments in 1977. The office component was converted to a hotel, and the entertainment area was expanded with the addition of an entertainment venue, House of Blues, and several restaurants. The relatively small retail component includes a grocery store and service tenants.
- *John Hancock Center,* on North Michigan Avenue, is a 100-story, 2.8-million-square-foot office and residential project with more than 800,000 square feet of office space, 705 condominiums, and parking for 650 automobiles. It was developed in 1969. The retail component on one level below grade originally comprised mostly small shops and services. (Bonwit Teller, a department store, originally occupied space on the first five floors.) In 1995, a $22 million renovation over a 4-year period included converting the retail compo-

nent to a two-level garden plaza. Restaurants and fashion stores anchor the plaza, which also includes gift, specialty food, and service tenants. The complex has an observation deck on the 94th floor.

- *Water Tower Place,* across the street from the John Hancock Center, is internationally known for its vertical regional mall. The eight-level, 613,700-square-foot retail component is anchored by two high-end department stores: Marshall Field's and Lord & Taylor. T}his MXD includes a 450-room Ritz Carlton Hotel on 20 floors, approximately 200,000 square feet of office space, and 260 luxury condominiums—along with parking for more than 650 automobiles—and entertainment facilities. Its dominant feature is the grand atrium leading to the vertical mall.

In each of these three urban MXDs, retailing plays a significant, but distinctly different, role. Marina City is known primarily as a residential project, the John Hancock Center as an office building, and Water Tower Place as a shopping center. Each, however, has other uses that are a significant part of the success of these projects. Two of these large MXDs—Marina City and the John Hancock Building—had their ancillary but important components redeveloped and re-tenanted.

An example of an MXD that has been successful since its development and has retained its original use structure is Copley Place in Boston. Developed in 1982, it has 100 retail stores, 800,000 square feet of office space, two world-class hotels, and a 1,400-car parking garage. It is an example of how the correct integration of various uses can stand the test of time. The retail component consistently generates sales per square foot in excess of national averages.

Suburban MXDs. Suburban MXDs are large-scale projects that cover many acres and are located away from the downtown area. They often are developed on a tract of land in excess of 100 acres. They usually have several buildings ranging from small, low-rise office or retail buildings to large, high-rise office or residential towers. Each use may occupy its own building, or buildings may be connected to the other buildings in the MXD by pedestrian walkways.

The Houston Galleria is one of the earliest suburban MXDs. Developed in stages beginning in 1967, it originally had a fairly equal distribution of office, retail, and hotel space. Though this MXD was best identified by its 1.6-million-square-foot super regional mall, it also included 1 million square feet of space in high-rise office buildings and a 22-story, 405-room luxury hotel (800,000 square feet). The mall has been expanded to 2.4 million square feet with six department stores and a newly added second hotel.

Two other suburban master-planned developments that broke ground on the first phases of their developments in the late 1960s are The City and

Newport Center, both in Orange County, California. The City occupies 175 acres at the junction of three expressways in the center of Orange County. The heart of this MXD originally was a 700,000-square-foot regional mall that was developed as an open-air center, which was never successful and was converted to an enclosed mall in 1978. In the 1990s the mall was demolished and replaced with a retail and entertainment development called The Block at Orange. This 811,000-square-foot lifestyle entertainment center with 80 tenants has 70 percent of its space dedicated to entertainment and restaurant uses. Adjacent to the mall are a low-rise office building and a high-rise office tower. A four-lane ring road encircles the interior buildings. Outside the ring is surface parking. Additional office buildings, a 441-unit garden apartment complex, and a high-rise hotel are located on the perimeter of the project. The development has entertainment facilities, a 30-screen theater, and several restaurants in freestanding buildings located throughout. This MXD was developed over 30 years ago and has had two major redevelopments of its retail component.

ADVANTAGES AND CHALLENGES OF THE MIXED-USE DEVELOPMENT

The MXD presents unique management, marketing, and leasing advantages. Along with these advantages are the challenges related to its variety of uses. Because retail businesses create a focal point in the community, provide services to adjacent businesses, often pay higher rents than other uses, and are successful in a variety of locations, they are an important component in the success of many MXDs. The concept that "the whole is greater than the sum of its parts" aptly describes an MXD and the benefits to retailers of locating there.

The MXD offers unique advantages that cannot be found in single-use buildings. Each separate use has a built-in customer base, so each component benefits the others and, in particular, all the other components benefit the retailers. Office, hotel, and entertainment uses draw people to the MXD from beyond the retailers' primary and secondary trade areas. Hotels attract out-of-town customers, such as tourists, conventioneers, and business travelers. Office buildings provide a base of professional and white-collar workers who patronize retailers during two periods when store sales are normally slow—lunchtime and immediately after work—and few of these workers live nearby. A residential component (condominium or rental apartments) usually houses people in the middle- to upper-middle-income brackets who will patronize the retailers.

If the development is a landmark in the community and has an atmosphere of prestige and success, a retailer's image and identity will benefit from being located in the MXD. Retailers must remember, however, that locating in an MXD does not guarantee success. The criteria retailers use to analyze a shopping center location must be applied to a location in an MXD.

The retail component adds vitality to an MXD and extends its active life into the evenings and weekends. Without the retail and entertainment components, the MXD would be primarily a residential development or an office park that would appeal only to a small segment of the population. Retailers broaden its appeal to the entire community.

Specific Advantages

A well-conceived mixed-use development offers many advantages over a single-use development.

Each use provides an amenity to the other uses:

- Large size makes it a landmark.
- A luxury hotel adds to its prestige.
- Retail, restaurant, and entertainment uses create community awareness and add an array of services.
- High-end specialty department stores add a mystique to the development.
- Moderate-price merchants provide convenient shopping for office workers and residents.
- Office workers and condominium or apartment residents provide a stable customer base for the other uses.
- Mixed uses provide for higher density.
- Multiple uses are an added benefit in marketing and leasing each individual use.
- Management operations can be more cost-effective.
- Shared use of parking reduces the area devoted to parking and allows more area for buildings.
- Large suburban sites can be developed more rapidly as MXDs. Because each building in the MXD shares the infrastructure of the project, multiple uses can be developed simultaneously.
- Rents are typically higher for office buildings and apartments that are in an MXD.

Specific Challenges

Each component in the MXD—office, retail, residential, hotel, entertainment—must be able to succeed on its own without the benefit of the other uses. A use that by itself at this location would be a failure will not thrive in an MXD even if other uses in the project are successful. If a site is not a good location for an office building, creating an MXD with a major office building as a component use will not make the office building successful. Similarly, a poor retail site cannot be made successful as a shopping center by massing office buildings around it.

People who work in an office building shop primarily for convenience items and food during their lunch breaks, and they do not make enough major retail purchases to support most of the merchants. If the shopping center must rely on office workers for its primary customers, it will fail. Though office workers, hotel visitors, and residents in an MXD are a captive market for retailers and restaurants, they will only improve an already successful business. Few, if any, retailers can survive on a customer base limited to these groups.

The massiveness of the MXD can be a drawback for shoppers. Though the retail component in a downtown vertical MXD may be located on the lower floors with easy access from the street, the retail component in a suburban MXD may be in the middle of a sprawling complex or even hidden behind rows of office buildings. Entrances to the retail component in a suburban MXD, whether for pedestrian or vehicular traffic, must be prominently identified by signage and must be easily accessed. Metered parking with a time-use fee may be a hindrance to retail shoppers.

LEASING THE RETAIL COMPONENT IN MIXED-USE AND MULTI-USE DEVELOPMENTS

The retail tenant mix for each of the different property types described above is determined by several factors. First, where is the property located? Ground-floor retail space in a multistory building will have a different tenant mix depending on whether the building is in the heart of the city's retail core or in an urban neighborhood. A building in the retail core is likely to be tenanted by national and regional fashion, jewelry, gift, and specialty food tenants. Ground-floor space in an urban neighborhood is likely to have more local merchants and restaurants, with some national retailers. If the retail space is in a building in an upscale neighborhood, it will have national and boutique children, teen, and adult fashion stores, along with local merchants, restaurants, and convenience stores. Retailing in airports and major train stations has evolved from offering limited overpriced and off-brand merchandise to a mini-mall with national retailers and popular specialty food and restaurants with street pricing.

Leasing Issues

Adding a retail component to buildings requires a different set of leasing and management skills that property managers and leasing agents who specialize in managing and leasing nonretail buildings have not had the opportunity to develop. If a team is used to recruit retail and service tenants, the areas of responsibility can be divided by merchandise categories to maximize each team member's efforts and avoid contacting the same prospects. For example, one member may be assigned to clothing and shoes, while another is assigned to accessories, gifts, and jewelry, and a third to food services and miscellaneous merchandise. The retail leasing team must coordinate its efforts with those who are leasing the other property uses. First, the leasing agent needs to understand the customer base of the building. This may require studying the demographics and psychographics of the residents living in the area; analyzing the makeup of the people working in the area; and studying the profile of the guests at hotels, resorts, or other property types. Office employees and residents represent captive customers, so demographic and psychographic studies of these groups should be conducted. A well-structured study will reveal the size of each group and the distribution by age and gender, and, possibly, income level.

Information can be gathered in several ways. Questionnaires can be distributed to every resident and office worker. A resident profile can be determined from a summary of applications for rental apartments. The number of visitors can be estimated by counting the people who enter the office building between the hours when most of the people employed there arrive for work and go home (excluding lunch hours). When members of the leasing team approach prospective tenants, they should be able to characterize the unique aspects of the MXD and the specific benefits of locating there.

After learning who the shoppers are and their needs and wants, the leasing team can develop the right tenant mix for the building. Before the retail leasing agent or property manager contacts the targeted retailers, specialty food merchants, restaurants, and service tenants, a story must be developed as to why those businesses should locate in the building. The story tells the targeted prospects that the profile of the building's shoppers and visitors represents their customer base and that they should be able to operate a profitable store at this location. With this analysis, the leasing agent or property manager is ready to contact the prospects. When prospects are convinced—through the information provided by the leasing agent and their own analysis—to lease space in the building, the leasing agent must understand which retail lease provisions must be added to the building's lease or develop a new lease for the retail component of the building. Often a retail leasing agent is hired to lease the retail and service components of the building.

Management Issues

The manager responsible for operating the retail components in office and residential buildings and mixed-use properties must understand how they are similar to and different from traditional shopping centers. A retail component adds new management and operational issues not common with the primary uses of the building. These can include hours of operations, signage, deliveries, trash removal, and security issues. A large mixed-use development may have a property manager for each major use, such as a hotel manager, an apartment manager, an office building manager, and a retail or mall manager. Separate leasing agents may also handle the leasing of these components. Airports, train stations, amusement parks, and similar sites have property managers for their retail components.

The leasing and marketing staff must use special leasing tools in working with prospective retail tenants. In addition to the leasing strategies commonly used for shopping centers, the MXD offers the leasing agent additional selling points and opportunities.

Some prospective tenants may have difficulty grasping the concept of an MXD. The flow of traffic within the MXD, how each component relates to the others, and the demographic profiles of the people living and working at the MXD all require explanation. Though a model of the project as a whole can be used to highlight the location and features of the retail section, a video or PowerPoint presentation may be necessary to explain the magnitude of the MXD. Photographs (including aerial photos of the surrounding area), a rendering, and descriptions of the adjacent buildings and the general area are essential components of the leasing package, along with demographic and psychographic profiles of the trade area that include the people who live and work in the MXD.

Retail Lease Provisions

If the standard lease is an office building lease format, rather than amending a retail lease, the manager or leasing agent must add several retail lease provisions to the office building lease. These provisions, which are discussed in chapter 9, Negotiating and Documenting the Lease Terms, include percentage rent, sales reporting, sales audit, hours of operations, maintenance of the premises, signage, over-standard utility usage, and a radius provision.

Internal Promotion of the Retail Component

The MXD provides a unique opportunity for marketing and promotion. Typically, the thousands of people who work and live in the MXD and the hundreds of people who visit it daily are a captive customer base for the retail and service tenants. Following are several inexpensive ways to reach that captive customer base:

- *Newsletters* can be mailed, e-mailed, or delivered by the security guard to residents and office tenants each month. Upcoming promotions, new merchants, and stores that are adding new merchandise can be featured, along with profiles of established merchants and general information on the management and operations of the mall and the MXD.

- *Promotional flyers* can be placed in a brochure rack, distributed to tenants and residents, or posted on bulletin boards in the recreation rooms of residential buildings or in lunchrooms or mailrooms in office buildings. Merchants should be encouraged to provide the property manager with flyers promoting their sales or new merchandise.
- *Elevator signs* can be used to promote a different tenant or category of merchandise each week. Merchandising and promotional events can also be announced in this manner. A glass-enclosed frame can be mounted inside each elevator to hold professionally designed signs. If several elevators serve each floor, each elevator can carry a different sign. This will increase the promotional impact because workers will use different elevators during the week.
- *Posters* promoting upcoming events can be displayed throughout the MXD.
- *Mall brochures or directories* can be placed in the lobby of every building. These should be pocket sized, list every merchant, and include a layout of the mall.

Many shopping centers provide a community room for use by nonprofit groups and organizations, and an MXD can do the same. Flyers, brochures, and signs—even photos of past promotions—can be displayed in the community room. A small brochure or flyer that focuses on the retailers and restaurants can be provided to hotels in the area.

Special Programs. The marketing director of the retail component can coordinate entertainment and educational programs for people who live and work in the MXD. Fashion shows, merchandise displays, and lectures—even seminars on financial planning—can be presented in the evenings in the recreation room of a residential building or in the community room of the MXD. Programs for people who work in the office buildings can be presented at lunchtime. A tenant's conference room, the conference room of the building, or a vacant office may be the right size. Another possible site is a theater in the complex.

Special Promotions. Sidewalk sales, arts and crafts shows, and entertainment, which normally occur on the weekends, can be started on Thursday or Friday morning. That permits workers in the office buildings to participate in such events. Special noontime events can also target office workers (e.g., special fashion shows on business clothing and accessories). Frequent shopper discounts can be granted to residents and office workers in the MXD by issuing special identification cards that the retail and service tenants honor.

Only the imaginations of the property manager and the marketing director of the shopping center or the retail component limit the number and type of activities to promote the retail component to the other buildings in the MXD.

A final point about marketing the MXD: Promotional activities for one use can also benefit the other uses (e.g., a merchandising event on the mall will increase the traffic to the MXD), and the other restaurants and entertainment facilities can capitalize on the increased traffic. The entire spectrum of marketing activities outlined here can be used throughout the MXD. Coordination of the marketing of each property type using a unified logo and theme will establish the identity of the project as a whole and promote the relationship of the component uses to each other.

MANAGEMENT

Mixed-use developments typically are large projects that exceed one million square feet of gross leasable area (GLA). The synergy created by the multiple uses is nurtured by cooperative management and marketing of each property type. One challenge to coordinating the management and marketing is that individual buildings or portions of buildings may be under different ownership. In a large suburban MXD, the regional mall may have been built by one developer, the office buildings by a second developer, and the residential component by a third. A convention center or other public facility in an MXD may be owned by the city or one of its agencies. The size and scope of MXDs reduces the likelihood of single ownership. A development company may sell some or all of its buildings to one or more investment groups.

In such multiple ownership situations, the individual owners are likely to be responsible for managing their own buildings, or they may contract separately for property management services. However, the owners usually will agree on central management of the common areas, especially if some facilities, e.g., mechanical and heating, ventilation, and air conditioning equipment (HVAC), are shared, as is often the case if the entire MXD is located in one or two high-rise buildings. To accomplish this, the owners may enter into a formal management and maintenance agreement among themselves. Management of the common areas and facilities may be assigned to one party and include responsibility for security, maintenance, design approval, HVAC and utilities services, and financial accounting. The agreement among the owners of the MXD should address several important issues as noted below. (Note that the management agreement between ownership and a property manager or a property management firm is a separate document, as described in chapter 4, Management Structure.)

- Effective management of common areas and internal boundaries between two uses and allocation of expenses between owners.
- Uniform standards for maintenance, operations, and use—regardless of ownership.
- Mutual protection for all owners against deterioration and adverse use of surrounding property.
- Promotional mechanisms and responsibilities, with fair representation of diverse interests.
- Equitable sharing of financing by the project's beneficiaries.
- Continuity in public participation, where appropriate, despite policy or organizational changes in the public agency's participants.
- Mechanisms for change and flexibility, as appropriate, to deal with unforeseeable circumstances and events.

From a property management perspective, the ideal arrangement is to have the entire MXD under one management. An exception to this would be the management of a hotel, which is likely to be autonomous in its operating hours, parking requirements, and provision of security. The success of most major hotels depends on the national reservation network of a hotel chain. In addition, hotel management is a specialized field of property management and is often contracted to a major hotel chain operator.

The reality is that each property type in a large MXD typically has a property manager for each use. Each use requires specific knowledge and skills, and few property managers have extensive experience and expertise in the management, marketing, and leasing of multiple property uses. An exception may be made if one property use is comparatively small (i.e., if the retail component consists of only 50,000 square feet of GLA, the property manager of the office building is likely to also be responsible for the retail sector).

OPERATIONS

Operating differences can have an adverse effect on the management of each property type as well as on the entire MXD. The property manager for each component of the MXD must recognize and appreciate the varying needs of the other property types. Each component should have a coordinated management plan that maximizes the benefits of being a part of an MXD and resolves any conflicts that occur. Effective property managers understand that in terms of overall operation, the good of the entire MXD must take precedence over that of any one component.

Hours

Hours of operation provide a good example of the differences in operational requirements. An office building is operated primarily between 7:00 or 8:00 a.m. and 6:00 p.m. on weekdays. Shopping centers and their retail tenants are typically open from 9:00 or 10:00 a.m. to 9:00 p.m. on weekdays and 9:00 or 10:00 a.m. to 6:00 to 9:00 p.m. on Saturdays and 11:00 a.m. or noon to 5:00 to 7:00 p.m. on Sundays, with extended hours during the holidays. Entertainment facilities usually operate from 11:00 a.m. or noon to midnight seven days a week, although some cinemas have only evening screenings except on weekends. The residential component, whatever its nature (e.g., rental apartments, condominium, or hotel) is a round-the-clock operation.

The differing hours of operation vary the demands for maintenance and security. Maintenance of residential projects is generally performed during business hours on weekdays. In office buildings, maintenance and repairs may be done during the day, but janitorial work is done in the evening and early morning hours. Most maintenance in a shopping center is done on weekdays—general cleaning and policing of the grounds seven days a week during shopping hours; heavy janitorial work after the shopping center is closed. The parking lot is swept in the early morning hours, while litter is picked up throughout the day.

Parking

The parking demands of each commercial use parallel the hours the tenants are open for business. Office building tenants require long-term parking on weekdays, while retail customer parking is needed through the evening hours on weekdays and in the afternoon on weekends. Special selling hours may periodically extend those times. The parking required for customers of entertainment facilities may extend past midnight.

Availability of ample and convenient parking for their customers is a major concern of retail tenants. In a suburban MXD with acres of surface parking for the entire complex, employees of the office tenants may park in the prime areas for retail customer parking. To reduce this problem, property managers must designate customer parking, notify the office building workers where *not* to park, and possibly use chains to close off some of the retail parking areas 30 minutes before the merchants open for business. During the lunch break, these areas may have to be patrolled to discourage office workers from parking there. The entrances and exits of the different parking areas must be clearly delineated and have good directional signage. In general, the directional signs in an MXD must be easy to read and provide clear directions on how to move about the project and how to locate tenants.

Special Retail Concerns

Several management issues need to be addressed when a retail component is included in a multi-use or mixed-use development. When the retailer's store is planned, HVAC requirements must be reviewed. The retailer may need a supplemental HVAC unit. This is especially important if the tenant (e.g., a restaurant) has equipment that generates excessive heat.

Will the retailer's utilities be separately metered or will a submeter be installed? Office building tenants are provided with janitorial service, but retailers prefer to contract for their own janitorial service or have their employees provide the service. One of the reasons for this is their concern for the security of their merchandise. When the retailer does not receive janitorial service from the landlord or is separately metered for utilities, these expenses must not be included in the operating expenses billed to the tenant.

A retail tenant needs good signage that is easily readable and identifies their location. Separate sign criteria must be developed for the retail component of the development.

Restaurants and some retailers have daily deliveries. The building may limit deliveries to specific times during the day. The removal of trash, especially wet trash, may also be limited to specific hours during the day and this trash may require special containers. Restaurants and specialty food merchants may be required to contract for additional pest control service in addition to the service that the landlord provides. Another issue is the possible odor from restaurants or hair and nail salons.

Emergency Procedures

Emergency procedures must be coordinated among all the buildings in the MXD. All security and maintenance personnel should be able to communicate with one another to warn of potential problems and to request assistance in emergencies.

Operating Expense Accounting

The complex nature of the MXD makes it essential to account for operating expenses accurately and to bill each building and its tenants correctly. As is usual in commercial properties, the landlord passes most or all of the operating expenses through to the commercial tenants. However, in an MXD, some expenses may be charged to each building separately, whereas other expenses must be allocated among all of the buildings. Common area expenses, taxes, and insurance premiums are among the most difficult to allocate fairly. Utilities can be separately metered to each building and submetered to each tenant.

Allocation of operating expenses should be based on a master plan that utilizes a formula to prorate each building's share. The basis may be the leasable area of the building, proportionate use of the service, or the comparative value of one building in relation to the values of the other buildings. Whatever the basis for the master formula, allocation of common area and joint expenses must be fair and defensible. Once a formula is developed, it should not be changed unless the size of the MXD changes or a formula error is discovered. Accurate accounting of operating expenses and proper allocation of the cost to each building or use is in everyone's best interests.

RETAIL AREAS IN AN OFFICE BUILDING

Frequently, high-rise office building developments include a retail component. Retail and service businesses can expand the base of potential users for office space. They also add amenities to the building that make it more marketable to office tenants, and they generate additional income for the building owners. If specific areas in the building are more valuable to a retail or service tenant, the base rent charged for those areas can be increased above the rate an office user would pay. Ground-floor space in an office building located in the retail core of a downtown often commands substantially higher rent than the office space in the building. That is especially true of class B office buildings located in good retail areas. In addition, the leases for retail tenants and for many service tenants can include a percentage rent provision that requires them to pay percentage or overage rent in addition to their base or minimum rent if their sales exceed a predetermined volume.

Spaces for retail and service tenants are usually located on the ground floor of an office building, although a restaurant or business club may occupy the top floor of the building. Sometimes, less-desirable space in an office building can be leased to health clubs or daycare facilities. Some major office building developments include multiple floors for retail and service tenants, starting at the ground floor.

Ground-Floor Retail Space

A ground-floor location provides maximum visibility to and access by potential customers walking past the building. Placement of ground-floor retail and service space may be planned in four different ways, and any one or all four methods may be used for a particular building.

Street Access. The first method is to have all of the ground-floor retail and service space in the front of the building, with direct access to the street.

Street access often has more value to a retail or service tenant than to the typical office user because these tenants usually prefer a prominent and easily accessible location. The value of this space to a retailer or service tenant depends primarily on the sales volume the tenant can expect to achieve. The anticipated sales volume is directly related to the size and demographic profiles of two discrete populations—the people who work and live in the immediate area and the people who walk by the office building every day. Suburban office building locations usually do not have sufficient numbers of either group to support substantial ground-floor retail or service operations.

Less-Desirable Location. The second method of designing space for retail or service tenants in an office building is to provide significant space in less-desirable locations at a lower rental rate than the rest of the building. For example, basement areas may be leased to large destination uses such as a health club or a printer.

Lobby Shop. The third method is to develop one or two small shops in the lobby area, usually near the office building entrance or next to the elevators. Once called "smoke shops," these spaces are suitable for merchants whose merchandise is mostly convenience items and whose sales are totally dependent on the captive population of building employees and visitors. These shops are usually open early in the morning before the office tenants open for business, and they may close in the afternoon or shortly after the office tenants close. They are not open on weekends. Since the 1990s, coffee and espresso shops have leased space on the ground floor of office buildings with an entrance from the street and, if the design of the office lobby allows, a second entrance from the lobby.

Concourse. The fourth method is to design a concourse area, which can be likened to a small enclosed mall with no anchor tenant. A concourse area is usually located on the ground floor of an office building, but occasionally it is one level below or above the ground floor. A concourse consists of several retail or service tenants located along a single corridor. It can be *single-loaded* (tenants on one side only) or *double-loaded* (tenants on both sides). Because most, if not all, of the spaces in the concourse area have no direct access to the street, these tenants' sales are dependent on people who work in and visit the building. Concourse tenants are usually destination uses (e.g., a travel agent, an office supply store, a mini-convenience store, a florist, or a coin shop).

A variation of the concourse shopping area may be developed if several office buildings are joined together by an underground passage. This provides an opportunity to merchandise the sides of the passageway. Generally, the building must have a large office population and high traffic to be successful.

Top-Floor Retail Space

A retail or service business may occupy the top floor or penthouse in an office building. Usually this is a quality, full-service restaurant with a lounge or a private business club. Some developers lease top-floor or penthouse space at a rate below that an office user would pay because these types of tenants add prestige and identity to the building. In addition, the restaurant or private club may provide unique amenities, which can be a plus in the building's marketing and leasing program.

Multilevel Retail Space

Another approach to developing an office building project is to create multiple levels for the retail and service component. The dedicated area usually comprises the first two to four levels of the building, and its development is similar to that of a multiple-level enclosed mall. However, most of these areas are developed without anchor tenants. Depending on the location of the building, the ground-floor space may be fashion, and the upper floor food and service tenants. Again, this property would need to have a large office population and high traffic for the retailers to be successful.

THE OFFICE BUILDING'S RETAIL TENANT MIX AND CUSTOMER BASE

A retail component adds to the amenities and identity of an office building and broadens the market from which prospective tenants can be sought. However, caution must be exercised when adding this component to an office building. The process of selecting retailers and service businesses to be tenants in an office building is no different than the one used to select tenants for a shopping center. In other words, consideration should be given to the location of the building, the trade area, the demographic and psychographic profile of the customer base, the volume of traffic that passes the building, the compatibility of the retail uses with the existing tenants and the building's location, and the physical needs of the tenant. Part of the analysis of the design phase of an office building should include consideration of space for retail and service tenants.

Tenant Mix

The proposed tenant mix for a multilevel retail component of an office building must be carefully analyzed. In the absence of a retail anchor tenant such as a department store, it may be difficult for fashion retailers to be successful above the ground floor in such a project. (Most fashion retailers need the synergy created by other fashion stores and the traffic draw of one or more department stores in the immediate area to be successful.) If fashion is on the second floor, the stores are often two-level stores with their primary displays on the ground floor. A major retailer who takes a two-level space may attract other retailers to the second level. Without fashion stores, the project will have service, food, and nonfashion retailers as tenants. This might include a bookstore or a card and gift store.

The first consideration is the location of the building. A high-rise building located in the center of the retail core of the central business district will have a different retail and service tenant mix than a similar building located just a few blocks away outside the retail core. The retail core is likely to have department stores, national fashion retailers, upscale and trendy restaurants, jewelry stores, and unique gift stores. These stores help determine the likely users for the ground-floor and possibly the upper-floor retail space in office buildings in this retail core.

Customer Base

The next issues to consider are who the customers are, and where they come from. If the building is outside the retail core and is without a fashion element, the customer base for the project will be drawn largely from two sources: the employees of the office tenants in the building and people who work in adjacent buildings. The fact that the primary customers will be employees in the building raises two concerns: First, if the building is outside the retail core, it must be of sufficient size to have tenants with enough employees to support the service and retail component of the building, or it must have other large buildings within a short walk. Second, the office component of the building may lease up slowly, in which case, the sales of the service, food, and retail tenants will be significantly affected. Depending on the size of the building, the service and retail components may not be successful until the office space is almost fully occupied.

The secondary customers for the retail and service tenants—people working in adjacent and nearby buildings—are most likely to shop the retail areas of the building during their lunch breaks. The boundaries of the trade area—the buildings from which people will come to shop this project—can be determined fairly easily. Most of the shoppers who work in nearby buildings will be within a short, easy-to-walk distance of the building, probably no more than 10 to 15 minutes away. It is important to note that weather can affect customer traffic as office workers will not want to walk to shops in bad weather, and they may want to eat and shop in good weather. Their time to shop will be limited, and most of their purchases will be preplanned (e.g., lunch, a greeting card, a book). A suburbanite working in a downtown office building has a completely different buying orientation than other shoppers. The normal percentage distribution of sales or merchandise categories becomes heavily skewed toward consumables and services, with an emphasis on specialty foods, although cosmetics, hair styling, shoe repairs, banking, and travel agencies are also popular. The opportunities for gift and jewelry merchants improve as the number of people working in the area increases and if the building is in the retail core.

A third potential customer base is people who are visiting the city—tourists, convention delegates, and business travelers. These people are likely shoppers in the retail core and will shop for convenience items and food when visiting buildings outside the retail core.

The fourth potential customer base is the residents in the metropolitan area who shop the retail core of the central business district. Major cities such as New York, Chicago, and San Francisco have maintained strong, vibrant downtown retail districts for over a hundred years. Some mid-sized cities, such as Seattle, have revitalized a struggling retail core.

RETAILING AT AIRPORTS

Airport managers can generate additional revenue and provide travelers with a variety of restaurant and shopping choices by expanding and upgrading their retail areas throughout their airports. Many of the airports in the United States and Europe have created the equivalent of a minimall within the airport. Their retail component includes fashion, gift, and specialty food stores. The airport in Amsterdam has a minimart with groceries for the return travelers who do not have the time or the inclination to stop and shop at a supermarket before arriving at their homes. These retail areas or malls have a captive audience that is waiting 60 to 90 minutes for a domestic flight and two hours or more for an international flight. Some airports that have over 15 million travelers have as many travelers as the best malls have shoppers. These airports have transformed their small retail areas that had limited, mostly off-brand merchandise at high prices to areas that resemble neighborhood retailing or shopping centers with street pricing. The tenants consist of three categories of retailers: food and beverage, specialty retailing, and convenience retailing. National retailers and chain restaurants as well as specialty food operators have located in airports because of the daily traffic the airports generate. Merchants and restaurant sales per square foot at some airports are greater than the sales per square foot at many regional and super regional malls.

Retail Plan

Developing a retail plan for an airport has many similarities to developing a shopping center. The anchor tenants for shopping centers are the department stores, whereas the anchors for the airports are the airlines. Just as major retailers attract a different customer base (e.g., Target and Nordstrom's), the airlines attract travelers with different profiles. Commuter airlines have more business travelers, and their stay at the airport is relatively short. The travelers on international airlines arrive at least two hours before their flights and have more time to eat and shop at the airport. Each of these travelers needs and wants different things at the airport. The purpose of the trip will determine the amount of time the traveler is at the airport, the time they have to eat at a restaurant, and the merchandise they may be interested in purchasing. Airport managers survey their travelers and know how long they stay at the airport and their needs and wants. These surveys and the airline serving each concourse enable the airport managers to develop a travel profile for each concourse. This profile enables the person responsible for retail leasing to develop the tenant mix that will best serve the traveler at or near each concourse.

Leasing Methods

Airports use one of three methods to lease their retail areas: (1) They may have a retail leasing specialist on staff who leases all the shop and restaurant spaces. (2) They may lease all or some of the retail areas to a master concessionaire. The concessionaire in turn may sublease some of the areas to merchants and restaurants. In other situations, the concessionaire may operate some stores and restaurants and enter into license agreements to operate other stores, specialty food shops, and restaurants. For instance, a national coffee shop might license the right to operate its business to the master concessionaire. (3) The airport may contract with a developer to not only lease all the retail areas but also to design and develop those areas. Airports generally require that the merchants and restaurants offer street pricing.

Tenants' spaces in airports are usually smaller than their counterpart stores in shopping centers, but the rent per square foot is the same as or higher than they would pay at shopping centers. The tenants usually pay a minimum rent versus a percentage of sales. They usually do not pay common area maintenance (CAM) charges, except for some food courts, but their percentage rate may be higher than is typical for a shopping center. The lease terms are similar to those at traditional shopping centers. Shop tenant leases range from 3 to 7 years. Restaurant leases are typically in excess of 12 years. Leases for freestanding kiosks and carts range from 90 days to 1 year.

WATERFRONT RETAILING

Many cities have created vibrant and entertaining areas along their waterfronts. For over 100 years, San Francisco's Fisherman's Wharf has been one the most popular places to visit in one of the best tourist cities in the world.

San Antonio turned a run-down area along a neglected river into one of the most popular attractions in Texas—the River Walk. Baltimore's Inner Harbor has been developed into one of the most exiting entertainment, educational, and shopping areas on the East Coast. Portland's River Place, Seattle's Lake Union, and Cleveland's The Flats were once industrial areas that have become popular entertainment areas. Common elements in each of these waterfront areas are entertainment and restaurants. A multilevel mall anchors Baltimore's Inner Harbor. San Francisco's Fisherman's Wharf has popular restaurants that have been owned and operated by the same families for decades, and in 1978, Pier 39, a specialty shopping center, was developed two blocks east of Fisherman's Wharf. Pier 39 has 110 stores and 11 restaurants on two levels. The pier is also home to an aquarium and a fleet of tour boats. A few blocks from Pier 39 is the old Ferry Building, built in 1898. For many years it was a transportation hub for trains and ferries. Its 240-foot-tall clock tower, designed after a bell tower in Seville, Spain, has served as a waterfront landmark. When the building was no longer needed for its intended use, it stood vacant for many years. The building was redeveloped in 2000 with 175,000 square feet of office space and a 65,000-square-foot farmer's marketplace with 100 farmers and 25 artisans and food vendors.

Restaurants with great water views are traditional waterfront uses. Entertainment uses are also common on the waterfront. Tour boats, fishing charters, boat moorage, museums, aquariums, conference centers, and hotels are major waterfront attractions.

Retailing can be the most difficult use to design, lease, and operate along a waterfront, and it is not appropriate for all locations. Retailing on the waterfront is usually specialty retailing, but it may include traditional retailing. Some of the waterfront may be a working waterfront and other areas will have little tourist traffic. For retailing to be successful, it must not be forced into a development or area but should rather be a response to the needs and wants of the visitors to the area. The main issue to consider when developing a retail component in a waterfront development is, "Who are the primary shoppers?" The tenant selection will vary if the visitors to the area are mostly tourists or locals. Tourist retailers need a steady flow of traffic that changes constantly. The tourist season for many waterfront developments is from April through September and the December holiday season. The retailers must realize and plan for the likelihood that for five months during the year their business will be slow.

Waterfront developments are expensive to build, maintain, and operate. If they are in a strong tourist area, they can generate more traffic than most malls and shopping centers. The weather and wind increase their operating expenses and influence customer traffic and sales. If the pier's pilings are wood, they are expensive to maintain and costly to replace. Workers' compensation for people who work over water is an added cost. Sprinkler systems may be required above and below the deck. Because of limited parking in most waterfront areas, validated parking may need to be offered. Even though waterfront developments and areas are inherently more management intense and require knowledge of specialty leasing, they are among a city's treasures.

Appendices

Appendix A

Retailing Basics by Robert Bearson

The evolution of the shopping center as described in the Introduction to this book is an extension of the history of retailing. Retailing in the United States began with Yankee peddlers selling door-to-door and progressed through a variety of distribution forms, all of which can be seen today.

General stores
Single-line stores
Department stores
Variety stores
Mail-order houses
Chain stores
Discount stores
Catalog stores
Supermarkets
Shopping centers
Automated Retailing
Convenience stores
Warehouse "stores"
Home shopping networks (TV)
Internet shopping (e-tailing)

Almost every new retailing "method" has been sold to consumers as a way to save money. Each innovation has been based on reduction or elimination of some expense, benefits of bulk purchasing, or savings associated with more-professional management. What the shopping center offers is (1) variety in a wide assortment of merchandise at one location, (2) breadth of selection based on competing stores,

(3) convenience of common and long shopping hours, (4) ready access through proximity of stores, and (5) parking that is convenient—and usually free. However, this also saves the consumer money—one-stop shopping reduces the time invested in shopping and saves the time and expense of traveling among several stores at different locations while providing opportunities for comparison shopping for the best prices.

Shopping center managers should keep in mind that selection and convenience are what make shopping centers successful and invest their efforts in further improving those elements. Also desirable from the viewpoint of the present-day shopper is saving money. This can be met by encouraging off-price or discount operations to locate close to or become tenants in the shopping center.

Evaluating Prospective Tenants

The most desirable prospects are those who have proven themselves in other retailing environments. The merchant who has done well in one location usually will do equally well in another; if a new location is more favorable, a successful merchant will do even better. Current sales volumes can be used to predict future success in a new location, provided the locations are comparable. A successful strip shopping center merchant may not be as successful in a regional mall or a lifestyle center due to higher costs and a different anchor, or no anchor at all.

Because a shopping center usually includes other complementary shops, it provides an optimum environment for sales growth. In fact, analysis of various locations relating occupancy costs to sales potential and profit projections yields the following order of preference: super regional shopping center > regional shopping center > specialty shopping center > community shopping center > strip shopping center > free-standing store. On the other hand, development of large regional malls has been curtailed, and the many chain retailers still intending to expand will have to consider locating in smaller shopping centers, lifestyle centers, or centers they would have passed over previously. As occupancy costs increase at regional and super regional malls, the profit potential will improve at smaller shopping centers—notwithstanding lower sales volumes.

In evaluating prospective tenants, the primary concern is usually the prospect's financial strength—the ability to pay rent and meet other lease obligations. However, the prospect's retailing expertise should also be a consideration, especially if a prospect is starting a new business. This can be addressed by seeking answers to the following questions which address the six essentials for successful specialty store retailing.

1. Is the planned mix of merchandise adequately specialized?
2. Is the store likely to be as good as or better than any in its trade area?
3. Will the merchandise include adequate representation of higher-priced items?
4. Does the retailer's operating plan permit the store to be fully price competitive on identical merchandise?
5. Does the retailer's plan include a specific program to rid the store of past-season, slower-selling merchandise?

6. Will top management (or ownership) of the store be personally involved in daily operations?

Other important considerations are whether the store appeals to women, how its customers are treated, and what efforts are made to promote the store.

Only if the mix of merchandise is narrow can the specialty store be truly outstanding. The smart merchant will have chosen a merchandise category in which the shop can be the very best in the trade area. In a large community with a heterogeneous population, interested customers will find the specialty shop and patronize it.

While competitive pricing is important, the shopping center manager must understand that specialty retailers cannot always compete effectively. In highly competitive areas, large-scale discounters have essentially eliminated the opportunity for independent specialty retailers to sell identical brand-name merchandise. The large discounter has a tremendous advantage in buying power, continuous market presence, management expertise, and financial strength. It is just not practical for the single store or small chain operator to maintain a comparable selection and offer the same low prices. Successful discounting requires volume sales. More items must be sold at a lower price to break even—i.e., to recoup the cost of merchandise and operating expenses such as rent, utilities, salaries, etc. Initial pricing (markup) must be adequate for a specialty retailer to break even, let alone make a profit.

As mentioned above, a key point to be considered is whether a store appeals to women shoppers. Because women typically shop for themselves, their homes, *and* their families, it is reasonable to assume that women account for most of the purchases in a shopping center. It is therefore important for retailers and shopping center managers to recognize that women are their predominant customers and that stores and promotions should be designed primarily to appeal to women.

However, because such a large population of women are now part of the work force, they have less and less time to shop. Shopping is no longer recreation; it has become a necessity. This is borne out by responses to customer surveys conducted at shopping centers. The surveys indicate that most visitors to a shopping center are shopping for a particular item or at a particular store. The stores most frequently shopped are women's apparel stores and department or specialty stores. Most shoppers visit a shopping center twice a month or more and spend one to two hours there. High percentages of shoppers indicate weekends as most convenient days for shopping, and actual sales levels at shopping centers support this: Sunday has the most sales hour for hour and Saturday is the best full day of the week. While evenings are not clearly rated the most convenient time to shop, evening shopping hours contribute more business per hour to shopping centers than do daytime hours. Clearly, shoppers' preferences must be addressed in creating a tenant mix for a shopping center and in establishing centerwide store hours.

Once a customer enters a store, it is important for the customer to feel welcome and important. Customer policies are a major factor in customer satisfaction. Many independent retailers drive customers out of their stores and into their competitors' larger stores because they are unwilling to offer the same liberal customer policies. It is good business practice to follow the adage, "the customer is always right." It is rare that an exception to this has to be made, and the payback is enormous. Liberal policies on acceptance of merchandise returns, cash refunds, exchanges, etc., foster customer goodwill and bring in more business. If a customer can return an item and receive a refund, the store will sell more merchandise. Liberal policies also make sales staff and supervisors more comfortable in their roles.

An unhappy customer, on the other hand, can have tremendous negative impact. This is confirmed by information from Technical Assistance Research Programs, a consulting firm in Washington, D.C. They found that most customers will not complain to management if something goes wrong with a purchase. However, "depending on the severity of the problem, an average customer will tell between 9 and 16 friends and acquaintances of the bad experience. Some 13 percent will tell more than 20 people. More than two out of three customers who received poor service will never buy from the store again and, worse, management will never know why."

Customers are easily discouraged. Many merchants are sensitive to pilferage and react to this by reducing merchandise on open display or preventing handling altogether by locking it in display cases. Preventing merchandise handling is more likely to reduce sales than to preclude pilferage. A reduction in sales of less than 1 percent is approximately equivalent in gross margin dollar loss to a stock shortage in excess of 2 percent.

It is more productive to bring customers into the store and encourage shopping and buying. A store's advertising and promotion should be evaluated. A recommended pattern is for small specialty stores to allocate between 3 percent and 5 percent of projected annual sales to advertising and promotion. First priority should be direct mail advertising to the store's own mailing list. Second priority should be cooperative promotion with other merchants in the center. (If there is a merchants' association or marketing fund, the latter will usually be required by the lease.) Any leftover funds should be used to experiment with other forms of promotion.

Cooperative promotions are effectively limited to seven times during the year.

January—clearance
February/March—sidewalk sale
May—Mother's Day specials
June/July—clearance, Father's Day specials, graduation gifts
September—sidewalk sale
October/November—clearance
December—Holiday specials

Advertising and promotion of the shopping center itself generally are not very important in attracting shoppers. The exceptions to this are announcements of grand opening or grand re-opening. It is the cooperative promotion of all the retailers in the center that is most effective. People come to a shopping center in response to specific merchandise being offered. To effectively stimulate business, a center will do well to schedule sales events in which all merchants offer significant savings.

Retailers should be encouraged to experiment with having something on sale at all times and having a sign at the door announcing it. Placement of a sign may be limited by center policies; if it cannot be outside the door, then it should be just inside. Giveaways, contests, and drawings can be used to attract customers. Names can be drawn from the store's customer mailing list, or business cards can be collected in a fishbowl or forms filled out in the store. The "prizes" need not be expensive to be effective (e.g., a free cup of coffee, a merchandise item, free gift wrapping).

Helping Tenants Succeed

In a shopping center, it is the first-time retailers that are most likely to have problems and need assistance and encouragement. Failures of "new" businesses can result in vacancies that are difficult to fill. Many small shops in retailing centers struggle with a number of issues. In particular, they have difficulty recruiting salespeople. Sales jobs are relatively low paying, so they do not always attract highly motivated, formally trained personnel, especially during strong economic period. Retail selling is often sought as an interim job or a means of supplementing a regular income, and large numbers of teenagers are hired for part-time and seasonal jobs. Management personnel in retail stores may be so occupied with buying and administrative activities that they have little time for training and supervision of sales workers.

Given the shopping center manager's role in making the shopping center successful, it is both practical and appropriate for the manager to offer assistance and promote sales training and professionalism to the managers of tenant stores. Store owners and managers who are new to retailing can benefit from seminars and workshops relating to internal business operations, merchandise presentation, and motivation. Sales techniques are another important area for training. Newsletters can be an economical means of reminding all tenants of merchandising opportunities and fostering good retailing practices.

Helping tenants succeed does not mean the shopping center manager has to be better at retailing than the tenants. It does mean the manager must be a keen observer of what makes retailers successful and have the ability to communicate those observations to other retailers effectively and in a manner that will earn the retailers' respect. In situations where the shopping center manager observes a problem but is unable to communicate it effectively (or with authority), it may be more appropriate to bring in a consultant (i.e., a respected retailing expert) with whom the merchant can work directly.

Merchandise Presentation

One of the things a shopping center manager should evaluate is the retailer's merchandise presentation. This can be accomplished by answering some specific questions regarding the store.

- *Initial impact*—Do the windows, entrance area, approach to the store, and area immediately inside the entrance help the customer quickly identify what the shop is all about?
- *Merchandise suggestions*—Are merchandise displays shown at every opportunity (in the aisles, hanging from the ceiling, on the walls, on the ends of fixtures)?
- *Idea presentation*—Does each display and display area convey only one idea?
- *Use of color*—Is the impact of single-color families carried throughout the store (e.g., windows, wall displays, area displays, each merchandise presentation)?

- *Vertical stocking*—Is merchandise stocked vertically to allow more categories to be represented at eye level (using available sources such as shelving, wall areas, etc.)?
- *Categorization*—Is merchandise categorized by use, product, sex, age, interest?
- *Service desk*—Is the service desk being used to sell? Does it call attention to items that (1) deserve to be talked about; (2) are new, timely, or higher priced; (3) can be pointed out to a customer; (4) can be demonstrated?
- *Sampling or demonstration*—Is merchandise shown voluntarily or on request?
- *Price marking*—Is the price easily available to the customer for each item and each price-reduced item?
- *Gift suggestion*—Is gift giving suggested by presenting reminders such as wrapped packages, bows, gift certificates, signs announcing gift-giving occasions (e.g., graduations in June, weddings, birthdays and anniversaries all year round, and less-traditional but often promoted occasions such as Secretary's Day or Sweetest Day in October)?
- *Signage*—Do signs appropriately announce such things as sales, specials, pricing, price guarantees, store policies, and store hours?

The shopping center manager is in a unique position to evaluate the effectiveness of merchandising techniques. The manager can help a struggling retailer understand the importance of merchandising by pointing out examples of successful presentations by other stores in the center and suggesting things the retailer can do to achieve comparable results.

Sales Training

In a shopping center environment, the shopping center manager can play a key role in encouraging store managers to train their sales personnel to give more personal service. By observing sales transactions, the shopping center manager can identify areas that can be improved by application of professional selling techniques.

A retail sales transaction can be divided into the following elements.

- *Preplanning*—The salesperson should know the merchandise and the store's policies and procedures so that he or she can provide accurate information to customers.
- *Greeting*—Customers should be greeted warmly as soon after entering the store as possible—within one minute—to assure them that the salesperson is ready to be of help.
- *Identification of customer's interest*—Often it is possible to establish an area of customer interest by observation (an item the customer looks at or touches, comments to a companion, etc.).
- *Approach*—Personal selling means the salesperson engages the customer in conversation, commenting about a merchandise item on display or an expressed need that was overheard, etc. (Assistance may be offered, but not with the words, "May I help you?")

- *Merchandise presentation*—The customer should be encouraged to handle merchandise, to try on clothing. This is an opportune time to present information about the item (features, special care required) and demonstrate its use if appropriate. Observing what the customer takes into the fitting room provides opportunities to bring additional items to the customer's attention.
- *Countering objections*—The salesperson should listen to what the customer is saying and be prepared to counter a customer's stated objections with facts about the merchandise—or alternatives to consider. Having presented an item's features (preceding step), it is appropriate to describe its benefits (i.e., how those features will help the customer personally). In the ideal situation, the customer will be choosing between two items to buy rather than deciding whether or not to buy only one.
- *Closing*—The salesperson should encourage the customer to finalize the transaction by asking how it will be paid for or if it is a gift. This is the step in which store policies regarding guaranteed pricing, merchandise returns, and layaways can be explained.

A shopper entering a store is interested in the merchandise and may be looking for a specific item. The customer entering a specialty store is most likely looking for whatever is that store's unique offering. The decision to buy is usually made while in the store, and the customer will generally do the "selling." What is needed is help in locating merchandise. While it is important to point out items that are on sale, it is a disservice to show only those with low prices—the merchandise that is unique to a store is likely to be higher priced. For the customer, having found and bought a particular item provides more satisfaction than savings alone.

The role of the salesperson should be that of a helper. It is more important to show merchandise to the customer than to sell it. Interaction with the customer is key. Salespeople who become involved with their customers derive greater satisfaction from their work. When customers are engaged in conversation, they are likely to remain in the store longer. Such interactions provide the salesperson opportunities to respond to questions and to counter objections. By demonstrating competence, knowledge, and professionalism, the salesperson can inspire customer confidence. The longer the customer stays, the more items the customer can be shown and the more items that will be considered and bought.

By applying the guidelines outlined in this appendix, store management can anticipate a significant increase in customer satisfaction, dramatic improvement in staff feelings of professionalism, and a substantial percentage increase in sales.

Retailing Fundamentals

The key to helping retailers succeed is understanding, and that means the shopping center manager must learn some of the fundamentals of retailing. The following discussions of basic arithmetic related to retail pricing and inventory and definitions of retailing terms are not intended to be comprehensive.

Retailing Arithmetic

Achievement of adequate sales volumes depends on appropriate pricing, which, in turn, depends on merchandise costs and other factors. It is also important to have sufficient merchandise in stock. This means not only replenishing inventory as needed but selling off out-of-season merchandise and replacing it with new. Merchandise is marked up initially to cover operating expenses and achieve a profit. It is marked down later on to make way for new stock.

The terms markup, mark-on, and margin are often used interchangeably to identify the difference between the cost of an item (plus inbound freight) and its selling price. An item that sells for \$98 may cost \$54 plus \$2 freight; the difference is the markup. This can also be expressed as a percentage:

$$\text{Markup} = \text{Selling Price} - \text{Cost}$$

$$\text{Markup Amount} = \$98 - (\$54 + \$2) = \$98 - \$56 = \$42$$

$$\%\ \text{Markup} = \frac{\text{Markup}}{\text{Selling Price}} \times 100 = \frac{\$42}{\$98} \times 100 = 42.9\%$$

The term *keystone markup* is used to indicate that the markup is 50 percent (i.e., the selling price is exactly double the cost of the goods).

Markup can be used in checking that an adequate differential between cost and selling price is being maintained. It allows the retailer to calculate an appropriate selling price. For example, what price must be used to maintain a markup of 46 percent on an item that costs \$38 (+ \$2 freight)?

$$\text{Selling Price} = \text{Cost} \times \frac{100}{100 - \text{Markup}\ \%}$$

$$\text{Selling Price} = (\$38 + \$2) \times \frac{100}{100 - 46\ \%} = \$40 \times \frac{100}{54\%} = \$74.07$$

Markup also permits calculation of an acceptable invoice cost for an item. How much can be paid (+ \$1 freight) for an item selling at \$49 if the required markup is 43 percent?

$$\text{Cost} = \text{Selling Price} \times \frac{100 - \text{Markup}\ \%}{100}$$

$$\text{Cost} = \$49 \times \frac{100 - 43\ \%}{100} = \$49 \times \frac{57\%}{100} = \$27.93$$

$$\text{Invoice Cost} = \$27.93 - \$1\ \text{freight} = \$26.93$$

The accompanying table shows the kinds of information that are typically available for sales and end-of-month inventories (in thousands of dollars at retail). These figures will be used to calculate percentage change, stockturn, and stock-to-sales ratios in the following examples.

Sales and End-of-Month Inventory Figures
(Thousands of Dollars)

Month	Sales This Year	Sales Last Year	Stock at End of Month	Stock-to-Sales Ratio	Sales Percent Change
Jan			52.1		
Feb	16.0	15.2	66.7	3.4	5.3
Mar	23.8	20.1	73.7	3.3	18.4
Apr	20.6	20.9	68.0	3.5	<1.4>
May		19.9	75.4	3.3	
Jun		22.0	77.2	3.4	
Jul		23.9	73.6	3.2	
Aug		20.6	84.0	3.6	
Sep		24.3	87.3	3.5	
Oct		28.2	90.0	3.1	
Nov		23.1	94.2	3.9	
Dec		42.5	64.7	2.2	
Jan		21.7	60.3	3.0	
Total		**282.4**	**967.2**		
Average		*23.5*	*74.4*		

Percentage change is the difference between this year's and last year's figures, expressed as a percent of last year's figure. The basic formula and its use with the figures for February through April in the table are shown here (in full amounts).

$$\% \text{ Change} = \frac{\text{This Year} - \text{Last Year}}{\text{Last Year}} \times 100$$

$$\frac{\$16{,}000 - \$15{,}200}{\$15{,}200} \times 100 = 5.3\% \text{ for February}$$

$$\frac{\$23{,}800 - \$20{,}100}{\$20{,}100} \times 100 = 18.4\% \text{ for March}$$

$$\frac{\$20{,}600 - \$20{,}900}{\$20{,}900} \times 100 = -1.4\% \text{ for April}$$

February and March results are favorable; April is unfavorable and would be shown in brackets or parentheses in a tabulation, thus: <1.4>.

Stockturn, also called stock turnover, is the rate at which inventory is sold. It is calculated as net sales dollars divided by the average inventory value at retail. Average inventory is the sum of the first-of-the-year inventory plus the following twelve month-end inventories, divided by thirteen. (Stockturn can also be calculated as the annual cost of goods sold divided by the average inventory at cost.) From the table, total net sales are $282,400; average monthly inventory is $74,400 (13 months' total of $967,200 divided by 13).

$$\text{Stockturn} = \frac{\text{Net Sales}}{\text{Average Inventory}} = \frac{\$282{,}400}{\$74{,}400} = 3.8$$

The stock-to-sales ratio is particularly useful in planning inventories. The inventory at the beginning of a month divided by that month's sales shows how many months' worth of inventory is on hand. Using figures from the table, the January end-of-month inventory would be divided by February's sales, as shown below:

$$\text{February Stock-to-Sales Ratio} = \frac{\text{Stock at end of January}}{\text{Sales in February}} = \frac{\$52{,}100}{\$15{,}200} = 3.4$$

The stock-to-sales ratio is used to determine the amount of inventory to be kept on hand.

$$\frac{\text{Total Annual Sales}}{\text{12 months}} = \text{Average Monthly Sales}$$

Using information from the table and a stockturn of 3.8, if average monthly sales are $23,500, stock levels should be maintained at approximately $90,000.

$$\frac{\$282{,}400}{12} = \$23{,}533 \text{ (rounded down to \$23,500)}$$

$$\$23{,}500 \times 3.8 = \$89{,}300 \text{ (rounded up to \$90,000)}$$

At season's end, it is important for stock levels to be low enough to allow for addition of merchandise for the new season. For months when higher levels of sales are anticipated, the stock can be increased. However, it is desirable to end the year with a lower inventory—January is usually a slow selling month. (Most retailers close their books January 31, having used "closeout" sales during this normally "slow" month to reduce inventory levels still further.)

Knowing when to mark down prices to sell slow-moving merchandise is extremely important. The retailer must be able to make room for new stock that will bring in new sales. If an inventory is held constant—if reductions are not taken—the stock becomes very uninteresting over time. For this reason, a considerable portion of an inventory is marked down before it is sold—in many businesses, half or more—and the average markdown percent is substantial. The reason for marking down prices need not be poor buying, or competition, but rather a changing marketplace—customers constantly want new merchandise. To be effective, a pricing program should plan for markdowns after a certain selling period, and merchandise should be dated to implement the program. After the first markdown is taken, repeated markdowns should be taken until all the merchandise is sold. The timing of markdowns is also related to the stockturn. Any item that has not sold in 25 percent more time than the average is not selling acceptably and should be marked down.

$$\text{Acceptable Selling Period} = \frac{\text{Weeks in a Year} \times 1.25}{\text{Stockturn}} = \frac{52 \times 1.25}{3.8} = 17.1 \text{ weeks}$$

If one-half of a group of items has not been sold in one-half of the acceptable selling period, what remains of the group should be marked down ($17.1 \div 2 = 8.5$ weeks). Sales goals for shorter time frames are also related to the acceptable selling period.

$$\frac{\text{Time Available for Sale}}{\text{Acceptable Selling Period}} = \text{Percent of Stock to be Sold}$$

$$\frac{\text{4 Weeks}}{\text{17.1 Weeks}} \times 100 = 23.4\%$$

In-season markdowns typically begin at one-fourth off and progress at four-week intervals to one-third and one-half off the original price, with subsequent reductions by one-fifth of the reduced sale price. Out-of-season merchandise is usually marked down on a shorter schedule (i.e., 2–3 weeks), with the first reduction being one-third.

Retailing Terminology

Although there is little specialized language or jargon in retailing, there are some terms the property manager should know so he or she can understand and participate in conversations with retailing personnel.

Back order Part of an order that the vendor has not filled on time but still intends to ship.

Breakeven point The sales volume at which revenues and costs are equal.

Consignment Merchandise shipped for future sale or other purpose for which title (ownership) remains with the shipper (consignor).

Cumulative mark-on The difference between the total cost and the total original retail value of all goods handled to date.

Free on board (FOB) A shipping term indicating delivery without charge. *FOB destination* means seller pays freight to destination (the buyer); *FOB origin* means buyer pays all freight from point of shipment or other designated place.

Initial markup The difference between the merchandise cost (including freight) and the original retail price placed on the goods expressed as a percentage of the retail value; also called *initial mark-on.*

Loss leader An item sold at a lesser markup than would normally be obtained on that item in order to increase store traffic.

Maintained markup The difference between the cost of goods sold and net sales; also called *maintained mark-on.*

Markdown A reduction in the original or previous retail price of an item stated as a percentage of net sales.

Markup The difference between merchandise cost and the retail price; also called *mark-on* or *margin.*

Markup percentage The difference between cost and retail price expressed as a percentage of retail (or, less commonly, as a percentage of cost).

Net terms Requiring payment for the billed amount of the invoice; no cash discount is allowed.

Stock turnover A measure of how quickly merchandise has been sold; the number of times during a year that the average inventory is sold (also called *stockturn*).

Appendix B

Insurance and Risk Management

The cost of insurance has risen dramatically since the late 1990s, and the administration of claims has taken several turns. Many years ago it was not unusual for a landlord to be sued for an accident, and the entire claim would be handled by the landlord's insurance company. Today, a claim against a landlord is likely to go beyond the landlord to involve the property management company and any vendors or contractors that may have been involved in the facilities where the accident took place. Additionally, insurance companies are keeping track of claims from specific properties and/or owners and, if the claims are too numerous, they may deny coverage in the future; alternatively, they may provide the coverage but at much higher premiums. All of these events have required shopping center owners and managers to pay much more attention to risk management and insurance administration.

Protection against financial loss is what links insurance to risk management, and insurance against many of the hazards that could produce financial loss is essential for the profitability of a shopping center. Although an insurance and risk management program is vital to a successful shopping center, the property manager is not expected to have specific expertise in these matters. However, to manage real property effectively, the property manager must be able to assist the shopping center owner in assessing risks and establishing appropriate insurance coverages for the property.

A well-insured shopping center is one that is prepared for loss. Because shopping centers are generally larger and costlier than many other types of property investments, many shopping center developers and owners are more concerned about protection against major risks on the property than about minor losses. They carry high deductibles in order to pay lower premiums and concentrate on major coverages. Insurance is a major component of a good risk management program.

Risk Management

Risk represents uncertainty, and many uncertainties affect the shopping center each day. In shopping centers, there are hundreds of potential risks or *loss exposures,* ranging from individual tenants' spaces to common areas and the structures themselves. Wherever people gather in one location, as they do in a shopping center, the number of risks increases. A shopper can suffer a bodily injury for which the center may be held liable. The common area may be defaced (*vandalism*), or a *windstorm* may blow down a fence surrounding the parking lot. Even a federally imposed guideline can be considered a risk if the owner must abide by it or face litigation. Insurance is one way to protect against economic losses.

Defining Risk Management

Risk management prepares the owner for the financial demands of claims arising from accidents and lawsuits; it gives the shopping center owner and manager, as well as their creditors protection against such claims. Thus, insurance serves as a financial shield against risk. By managing risk, shopping center owners increase their profits both directly and indirectly. Direct protection takes the form of financial support when damage occurs. Indirect protection results from periodic inspection of the property for loss exposures taking taking appropriate action to eliminate and/or reduce risk. A regularly inspected property will likely be better controlled and managed than one that has not been so scrutinized. Thus, risk management encompasses prevention of and preparation for the financial demands of unexpected accidents or litigation.

An effective risk management program offers a level of peace of mind to the shopping center owner and the investors. With an adequate amount of insurance coverage, the investor may try to reduce the loss from various hazards, insure the remainder, then assume the cost of the lessened risks. Risk management can also improve the quality of investment decisions. After identifying all the potential loss exposures from locating in a region with a high crime rate, and being unable to find reasonable insurance coverage, the developer may ultimately decide that the project is unwise. Risk management is a primary issue that shopping center managers must confront, and insurance is just one of the ways to manage risk.

Insurance in Risk Management

Insurance companies do not prevent losses; they offer financial protection against the consequences of such losses. Insurance is based on the probabilities that events will occur in various climates, regions, areas, or neighborhoods. From a statistical review of many factors, rates are determined for a given exposure. The insurance company pools together the premiums paid to it and thus has the funds to pay for claims as they are made.

Obtaining Insurance. The insurance policy is a legal contract which is prepared by an underwriter and issued by an insurance company. The shopping center owner's insurance agent should negotiate the insurance contract, and the owner's primary concerns are the amounts and types of insurance that should be carried. The amount will depend on the value of the property, the types of stores at the shopping center, and the types of consumers it attracts. The types of coverages will depend on the potential risks.

It is important to find an insurance agent who specializes in writing policies for income properties and more specifically, shopping centers. Insurance agents act as independents, or they represent a single company as "direct writers" or "exclusive agents." Even more important than this distinction are the credentials, experience, and training of the particular agent. Although there are many professional designations insurance agents can earn, the most prestigious is the CPCU, which stands for Chartered Property Casualty Underwriter. The insurance agent should review the loss exposures at the property with the owner and the manager, offer suggestions, answer questions, review the owner's objectives, and propose a program of appropriate insurance coverages in keeping with the risk management plan.

The person charged with finding insurance coverage for the shopping center should examine the reputations of potential insurers. A proven track record, a wide selection of policies, prompt processing of claims, and thorough service are all considerations in the evaluation of an insurance company. *Best's Insurance Report: Property–Casualty*, published annually by A. M. Best Company in Oldwick, New Jersey, is an independent source for such data. Of particular interest are three activities of an insurance company:

1. *Coverage*—the insurer's ability to provide the appropriate contract for the exposures.
2. *Capacity*—the insurer's ability to offer insurance policies and limits that meet the needs of the buyer.
3. *Claims*—the insurer's capabilities to process claims quickly and efficiently.

Also to be evaluated are the means that the insurer uses to handle sales, underwriting, loss control, policy issuance, claims records, and policy renewals.

As part of the decision-making process, the property owner should assess property values on a replacement-cost basis. When insurance is based on "actual cash value," an amount is deducted for depreciation—the loss of value—based on the age of the insured property. Such a plan may penalize the insured when a loss occurs because it covers only the original cost of the item, and inflation precludes replacement at the same (original) cost. Newer package policies often provide full replacement cost coverage if insurance is at 80 percent of value at the time of loss. In deciding on the amount of coverage to purchase and the type of policy to carry, the owner and the manager must understand the exact coverage provided under each policy being considered. If some coverage will be limited, there could be major effects on the shopping center's profits because a particular loss may not be covered.

Once policies are in effect, the insurance company's performance must be evaluated on a continual basis. Of concern are whether the agent and the insurer are providing the expected services and how quickly claims are processed. Comments of other insured parties may also be taken into account. If there are problems with an insurance carrier and service does not improve, it may be necessary to start the process all over again. Sometimes a simple warning that a policy may be dropped is enough to improve the services provided by the agent and the insurer.

Factors Affecting Rates and Premiums. Essentially, property insurance rates are based on four factors:

1. *Construction*—the materials used in building the shopping center structure. Interior materials and the layout and design of the shopping center are also evaluated. Of concern are the susceptibility of materials to fire, the presence (or absence) of a fire sprinkler system, and other perils.
2. *Occupancy*—the types of tenants in the shopping center. Most tenants are retailers, but more and more service tenants (doctors' offices, dry cleaners, cinemas) are leasing space in shopping centers. Of importance is the greater exposure of one tenant (a restaurant) compared to another (a women's apparel store); the greater the risk, the higher the premium.
3. *Protection*—actions taken to protect the property and reduce its exposure to loss. Systems such as sprinklers, parapets, fire doors, and fire "divisions," used effectively, ultimately reduce premiums and underwriting problems. Prevention activities such as fire drills, meetings with tenants to discuss fire safety, and periodic store inspections may ultimately reduce both the threat of fire or other losses and insurance rates.
4. *Exposure*—external hazards that increase the dangers to the property. These include vulnerability to physical hazards such as might result from being located near a chemical manufacturing plant (e.g., property damage and potential liability in the event of an explosion) and weather-related perils such as tornados, hurricanes, or hailstorms. Geologic perils such as earthquakes and volcanic eruptions are other possibilities.

When underwriters review a property for coverage, they often look at the losses that similar businesses in the area have suffered. Some plans offer rate credits to those businesses that have active loss-prevention programs.

Coinsurance. A coinsurance clause requires the insured to carry insurance equal to a specified percentage of the value of the property at the time of the loss to avoid a penalty. If less insurance is carried, the insurer pays for only a part of the loss. Under an 80-percent coinsurance clause, for example, the insured must have coverage equal to 80 percent of the replacement cost of the property at the time of the loss in order to receive 100 percent reimbursement (up to the policy limit)—otherwise, the insured is penalized, and the loss is shared between the insurer and the insured. In essence, the insurer is agreeing to a rate reduction if a coinsurance clause is included. As an example, consider a building worth \$100,000 that, because of coinsurance (at 80 percent), must have \$80,000 of coverage. As long as the building's value remains at \$100,000, 100 percent of losses will be covered (up to the policy limit). However, if the amount of coverage remains at \$80,000 and the value of the property increases to \$150,000, the insured will have to pay the difference because the amount of insurance required to cover the increased property value is \$120,000 (\$150,000 × .80 = \$120,000). In this case, the insured will receive two-thirds of the value for a partial loss, and only the maximum value of the policy (i.e.,

80 percent of the original value) for a total loss. The following equations show how this works.

$$\frac{\text{Amount carried}}{\text{Amount required at time of the loss}} \times \text{Amount of Loss} = \text{Dollar amount received}$$

$$\frac{\$80{,}000}{\$80{,}000} \times \$10{,}000 = \$10{,}000 \text{ (100\% coverage)}$$

$$\frac{\$80{,}000}{\$120{,}000} \times \$10{,}000 = \$6{,}666 \text{ (insured must pay the remaining \$3,334)}$$

$$\frac{\$80{,}000}{\$80{,}000} \times \$100{,}000 = \$80{,}000 \text{ (because policy limit = 80\% of original value)}$$

Another approach is called an *agreed amount endorsement*. In this case, the insurer and the insured agree that the property will be insured for a specific amount for a specific period of time. The insured need not worry about being uninsured so long as the agreed amount of insurance is carried; the insurer will always honor the full amount of the loss up to the face value of the policy. An inflation clause may be included so the amount of insurance is automatically increased by a predetermined percentage periodically during the policy term—e.g., for an annual policy, inflation may be calculated each quarter.

Regardless of the method used to determine the amount of insurance coverage, annual review of all the insurance policies for the property is recommended. In several areas of the United States, real estate values have skyrocketed over the past ten years, and it would be quite easy to be underinsured. Should there be a major loss, the shopping center owner may be unable to rebuild the shopping center from insurance proceeds, due to insufficient insurance funds.

Record Keeping. A fully qualified insurance agent will handle insurance record keeping and inform the property manager of policy expiration dates, premium payments, inspection reports, and loss history. However, the management agreement usually specifies whether the owner or the manager will maintain insurance records and coverages. In practice, the manager usually obtains and monitors insurance coverage, maintaining a cross-index of renewal and follow-up dates. If the owner obtains and pays for the insurance, the manager may still have responsibility for monitoring the program. In that case, the manager must alert the owner to new risks that arise during the policy term and prepare renewal data for the owner at lease 90 days before the term expires. The manager will likely have to maintain records of losses and inspections as well.

Ultimately, it simplifies matters if the manager handles all insurance administrative matters, including the decision-making process. The manager knows what happens on the property day-to-day and can usually maintain a more thorough and efficient insurance program.

Applying Risk Management Concepts

Risk can be static (pure) or dynamic (speculative). Speculative risks are the uncertainties involved in any business decision resulting in either a financial gain or loss. The decision to buy or build a shopping center is such a risk. Static risks are created by the shopping center's construction, tenancy, maintenance, and location. Static risks create loss or premium costs but no gains other than insurance payments for actual damage claims. Once a buyer becomes an owner, the dynamic risks become static.

Careful planning can minimize loss exposures. Location, design, leasing, and operations may affect the amount of risk at a shopping center, and these are factors that managers can try to control. A risk-management decision-making model can help the manager develop an appropriate program. Risk management has three modes—planning, action, and decision making—and each of these modes has numerous components.

Planning. This first mode comprises three stages. The first is *identification* of all possible loss exposures on the property. This can be accomplished by studying blueprints of the property and making a comprehensive inspection. This is followed by *analysis* of the probability that an event will actually occur and the frequency at which it may recur. Frequent losses generally have limited financial impact, but some exposures can cause severe loss. As an example of the latter, earthquakes are difficult to anticipate, and when a destructive one occurs, many shopping centers are not covered. The third stage is *selection* of the actions to be taken in managing specific risks.

Action. There are four possible actions for dealing with a specific risk.

1. *Avoidance* is chosen when it is possible to avoid a risk and the cost of avoidance is less than that of assumption. For example, the risks of losses from damage to a building can be avoided by not owning any buildings. However, the money lost because of unwillingness to accept the risks involved in building ownership usually will outweigh any benefits of avoiding such ownership. A more appropriate act of avoidance involves elimination of a known risk or employment of methods to control that risk within the context of ownership or operation.

2. *Control* involves taking active steps to reduce loss exposures for both people and things. This includes *loss control* measures to protect customers and employees from injury (e.g., fire drills). It also includes *property preservation* measures such as installation of sprinkler systems and use of fire-resistant materials. Such things are generally under the control of the property owner and his or her representatives. (The property manager must take responsibility to control losses at the shopping center.) Private associations that specialize in loss prevention (e.g., the National Safety Council, insurance companies) can be resources for information and services. The federal government, under the

Occupational Safety and Health Act of 1970 (OSHA), establishes standards and provides funding for specific services. Some of the OSHA safety standards that affect shopping centers are listed below.

- Walking and working surfaces
- Means of entering and exiting
- Powered platforms, handlifts, and vehicle-mounted work platforms
- Hazardous materials
- Personal protective equipment
- General environmental control
- Medical and first aid
- Fire protection
- Compressed gas and compressed air equipment
- Material handling and storage

If an inspector discovers that the shopping center or a tenant at the shopping center is violating an OSHA requirement, a citation will be issued describing the violation and requiring that the employer or the owner must remove the hazard or correct the condition within a specific time frame.

3. *Retention* can be intentional (active) or unintentional (passive). In an active retention, the risk manager consciously decides that the shopping center owner will pay the consequences of a known exposure. This may be done when the probability of loss is very low and essentially can be ignored. Passive retention is often the result of ignorance because a risk is unknown or unobserved (e.g., an old mine shaft beneath the property).

4. *Transfer* is the action related specifically to insurance. Risk is transferred to a professional risk bearer through property, casualty, life, and health insurance policies. Often such transfer is combined with some form of retention or control. A noninsurance transfer may be affected via a hold-harmless agreement; however, such an agreement is only as good as the financial ability of the issuer to honor the agreement.

Decision Making. In this mode, the manager reviews the selection criteria and assigns the actions to treat the loss exposure. This may involve convincing the shopping center owner of the effectiveness of the risk management program, especially if it will be costly to implement or if a less-costly insurance plan would reduce the coverage. Because several people may be involved in this decision-making process, the management agreement should set forth the limits of the manager's authority and indicate the approvals needed for major decisions regarding insurance matters. With selection criteria approved in advance, the manager knows the parameters for planning the program and can implement the program as soon as decisions are made. The *transfer* of risk to the insurance company requires the advice and assistance of the insurance agent. *Control* activities generally require the insurance company employees to work continually with the shopping center staff and tenants. Specific risk *retentions* must be monitored and notes made of various risks to be *avoided* and eliminated.

Types of Insurance Coverage

There are many factors to consider when insuring a shopping center, including the size and type of the center, the center's location, the center's physical characteristics, and local ordinances, financial institutions, and insurers. Basically there are two types of insurance to be obtained—*property insurance,* which covers damage to the shopping center, and *liability insurance,* which covers injuries to third parties or damage to others' property. Often the two are packaged as a Special Multiperil Policy, which may incorporate other types of coverages as well.

Property Insurance

Basic coverage for property is often established under a fire and extended insurance policy with an extended coverage endorsement that covers not only damage from fire and lightning but also damage caused by windstorms, civil commotions, vehicles, aircraft, hail, explosions, riots, and smoke. Property policies can also cover consequential losses—income losses that occur because of the insured damage—and so-called specialty losses.

Fire Insurance. A standard fire policy offers only limited coverage; it essentially provides the insured with coverage only for damage caused by fire, lightning, and the removal of property from the premises. Claims under a standard fire policy are paid on an *actual cash value (ACV)* basis—the person who handles the claim must determine the replacement cost with materials of "like" kind and quality and subtract an amount for depreciation.

Fire is a constant threat on any type of property, and it is one of the main reasons that property owners buy insurance. Fire kills, and it puts people out of work. It destroys property. All property owners need protection against the financial consequences of fire.

Lightning—a natural electrical charge—strikes properties less frequently than does fire. Nevertheless, when lightning does strike, it can destroy property. Most insurance policies provide coverage for damage to property caused by lightning and consequent fire.

Most states require that specific information be provided in the fire insurance policy.

- Terms of the policy.
- Description of the property.
- Losses covered.
  The standard fire policy protects the shopping center owner from losses caused by fire or lightning. The insured may choose and pay for coverage for other items. No insurance policy covers damages caused by war or nuclear attacks.
- Amounts covered.
  A fire insurance policy is intended to pay the insured for the amount of the damage—no more and no less. The standard fire policy attempts to put the insured back in the same financial position as when the contract was signed or when the loss occurred.

- Suspension.
  The standard fire policy is suspended—not cancelled—when either of the following occurs: (1) a hazard increases in some way, with the insured's control or knowledge; or (2) during any period that the shopping center, for any reason, stands vacant for more than 60 consecutive days.
- Cancellation.
  A standard fire insurance policy holds that both the tenant and the landlord have cancellation rights, provided that both parties adhere to the specific guidelines that are stated in the contract.
- Subrogation.
  Most insurance companies insist on this clause in their contracts. Basically, the clause states that the insurer assumes all rights to recover amounts paid to the insured for damage caused by a third party. However, it is not unusual for a landlord and tenant to enter into an agreement whereby each agrees not to make a claim against the other in any loss that is covered by insurance. The insurance company must agree to such a provision, which is known as a *mutual waiver of subrogation*.
- Apportionment.
  This is the pro rata distribution over several policies held by the same insured.

Extended Coverage. This provides the insured with coverage beyond the perils of fire and lightning—including windstorms, hail, riots, civil commotions, vehicles, explosions, aircraft, and smoke. Intentional, destructive acts of vandalism done to the property can be insured under a *vandalism and malicious mischief (VMM)* endorsement. There are many other property insurance coverages that can be considered to provide as broad protection as is needed.

Crime Insurance. The high cost and limited availability of insurance coverage might prevent many owners from buying crime insurance. Coverage for crime should be tailored to the needs of the shopping center. Shoplifting and theft are major problems, especially in large shopping centers, and insurance companies cannot afford to cover all such losses. Some shopping center owners, or individual tenants in the shopping center, may want to obtain coverage for burglary, robbery, theft, and employee crime. Shopping centers have limited crime exposure, but many tenants have high exposure. Therefore, tenants are generally more concerned with crime insurance than are property owners.

Special Coverage. Shopping center owners can also purchase insurance that covers specific risks in their areas. Flood insurance and earthquake insurance are examples. A flood is an overflow of water that comes from a lake, river, or ocean. Floods can devastate regions and destroy properties. A business located in an area susceptible to such water overflows should have flood insurance and may be required by law to obtain such coverage. Flood insurance is available from the federal government. Earthquakes occur because of movements of the earth's surface. They are possible in almost any region but mainly in those areas located along a geologic fault. Most shopping centers do not carry earthquake insurance because, compared to other risks, the probability of a destructive earthquake occurring is low.

Specialty Contracts. Basically, the shopping center owner and the retailer/tenant should consider four types of specialty policies.

- *Accounts payable* insurance covers risks associated specifically with the destruction of payment records.
- *Valuable papers* insurance covers the loss of important papers such as blueprints or leases.
- *Plate glass* insurance covers accidental glass breakage and the subsequent board-up service. It also insures against possible damage to glass caused by the application of acid or other chemicals.
- *Rent loss* insurance pays the contract rent to the property owner during the restoration of the property. Most leases provide that tenants' rents are abated during restoration of a building that suffers a casualty loss.

Business Interruption Coverage. One form of this type of insurance covers *indirect damages*—the loss of profits resulting from direct damage. If the operation of the shopping center is interrupted, tenants would lose business as a result. In that case, retailers measure their damages in terms of their losses in sales volume. The insurance would cover not only the profits lost but also all of the expenses that have been incurred because of the interruption of business and the efforts to reduce the loss.

Contingent business interruption results when one supplier's product is so important that interruption of its delivery or availability (because of damage to the supplier) causes a loss to the distributor. An example would be the loss of business a bakery store would incur because its bread supplier was burned out.

Extra expense insurance covers extra expenses that are the result of continuing business in the event of damage. An example would be the cost to fly in parts and the overtime wages paid to maintenance workers to expedite repairs of a fire-damaged elevator.

Liability Insurance

An employee's act of negligence that causes injury to a customer or damage to another's property may result in the shopping center being held responsible for monetary damages. Because the person who makes the liability claim is a "third party," liability insurance is referred to as "third party insurance." Shopping center owners carry liability coverage, not only because the cost of paying a legal suit is high, but also because of the amounts of damages awarded to injured parties by the courts.

Some owners of large shopping centers will carry liability in amounts approaching 25 to 50 million dollars. Anchor tenants, who are required to reimburse landlords for their share of liability coverage will often resist paying their share of the premiums on such high coverage. They will typically be willing to pay the premiums on limits in the area of one million dollars in coverage with the landlord being responsible for anything above that figure.

Boiler and Machinery Liability. The extensive heating and cooling systems in shopping centers are insured under this type of coverage. The policy provides protection for damage to the operating machinery in the building, including air-conditioning units, generating systems, heating systems, and electrical control panels. Coverage includes repairs to existing units, any costs up to a fixed dollar amount (e.g., $1,000) that will expedite the repair process, any consequent damage to others' property (for which the insured is liable), and new equipment (coverage is automatically added, on installation), but *not* damage caused by wear and tear, corrosion, and erosion.

General Liability Insurance. A typical general liability policy provides one or more of the following three coverages: bodily injury liability, property damage liability, and medical payments. A single policy may be used to cover different scheduled hazards. Specific examples include the following:

- *Owners, Landlords, and Tenants Liability (OLT).* This type of policy provides coverage for problems that arise out of ownership, maintenance, or use of the insured premises and all operations necessary and incidental to it.
- *Contractual Liability.* This type of coverage is common in shopping centers because of the serious problems raised by contracts which require one party to assume liability for another party's conduct. For example, a lease may include a hold-harmless clause that shifts to the tenant the landlord's liability for building defects or for acts of negligence by the tenant or by any other person, including the landlord.
- *Medical Payments Insurance.* This type of coverage reimburses medical, hospital, and funeral expenses to members of the public who are injured on the premises—regardless of liability. Medical payments insurance may be added to certain liability policies. It surpasses the medical payments provision in the general liability contract and imposes no prerequisites of negligence on the part of the insured.
- *Personal Injury Liability.* Many shopping center owners choose to add personal injury liability coverage to their general liability policies. This type of insurance is particularly important for shopping centers because of the frequency of incidents of shoplifting and subsequent arrest. Many shopping center tenants also carry this type of coverage. Personal injury includes libel, slander, invasion of privacy, false arrest or imprisonment, and wrongful eviction.
- *Comprehensive General Liability.* This type of policy provides the broadest protection against liability claims. It covers premises/operations, elevators/escalators, products, completed operations, and owners' protective liability. Many separate endorsements can be added to this policy to broaden the coverage even further.

Workers' Compensation. The theory behind this type of insurance is that an employer must assume responsibility for injuries or illnesses that arise out of or during the course of a worker's employment. Workers' compensation insurance provides unlimited coverage for death benefits, medical expenses, lost wages, and disability payable to the insured—the employee. The premium paid by the employer will depend on payroll size, job classifications, and the claims experience of the insured parties. The shopping center owner, individual retailers, and the merchants' association will all have to carry this type of insurance if they have a certain number of employees—the standards (number of employees) are established by the states.

Note that insurance as a method of risk management substitutes regular payment of insurance premiums for the unpredictable cost of an economic loss, based on the probability of a particular type of loss occurring.

Appendix C

Basic Math for Shopping Center Managers

While most professionals in the shopping center industry would agree that the most essential element of good shopping center management is good people skills, shopping center managers must also be good at record keeping and accounting. The math of shopping centers is not all that complicated once one understands some of the basics involved. In all accounting and math functions there is one answer and only one answer. Close is not good enough. The tenant and the landlord both expect to pay what is agreed upon and nothing more; on the reverse side, nothing less.

Accuracy and timeliness is critical for billings, sales reports, traffic counts, financial records, etc. In this section the most common calculations and the likely variations that the shopping center manager is likely to encounter will be discussed. Even if the shopping center manager does not do the math, he or she should be able to check it for accuracy and therefore must have a basic understanding of the theories and calculations involved.

Pro rata share is a common term in the allocation of common area costs, taxes, insurance, some marketing funds and sometimes, even utilities. Pro rata share means each tenant's share is based on the part of the whole they occupy. The whole in most shopping centers means the Gross Leasable Area (GLA) which is the total of the areas of the shopping center meant for occupancy or as defined in the leases. Generally, GLA does not include hallways, public restrooms, electrical rooms, etc.

1) Gross Leasable Area

Assume a common area maintenance budget as follows:

Landscaping	\$ 28,400
Sweeping	\$ 23,500

Electricity	$ 18,600
Water	$ 12,700
Repairs	$ 42,300
Insurance	$ 41,300
Security	$ 37,600
Trash removal	$ 21,300
Supervision 10%	$ 22,500
Total budget:	$248,200

Assume this particular shopping center has a gross leasable area of 132,600 square feet. A tenant signs a new lease of 2,400 square feet. The tenant's pro rata share of the whole is calculated by dividing the 2,400 square feet by the 132,600 feet and the pro rata share is:

2,400 ÷ 132,600 = .0181 or 1.81% of the whole

Note: Almost all property owners carry the pro rata calculations out to four points past the decimal point.

If the common area costs of the shopping center were $248,200 for the year, the tenant's share would be:

$248,200 × .0181, or $4,492.42

From time to time a strong national tenant or a leading local tenant will have the negotiating strength to have limitations placed on the costs. If this same tenant were to negotiate a limit of no more than $3,600 per year, the tenant would be billed only the $3,600 and the landlord would absorb the additional $892.42. It would not be appropriate to bill the other tenants for the balance not paid by this tenant as this should be a landlord cost. An exception is the example of a mall where the anchor tenant is not obligated to pay full mall CAM charges and the shop tenants leases require them to pay these charges.

2) Leased Area

Some leases indicate that a tenant will pay his pro rata share based on the leased area of a shopping center. The theory is that the tenants who have leases are the only ones using the facilities and therefore should pay all of the cost. If the shopping center is 90 percent leased, the denominator for the calculations is as follows:

132,600 square feet × .90 = 119,340 square feet leased

The tenant's pro rata share is:

2,400 square feet ÷ 119,340 square feet or .0201 (2.01%)

The tenant will pay a larger portion of the costs based on this formula. The tenant's share of the above costs of $248,200 would be as follows:

$248,200 × .0201 = $4,988.82

3) Common Area Maintenance Bill Backs

Common area maintenance bill backs have become one of the most contentious items between landlords and tenants. Tenants feel frustrated that they have no control over the costs, and on the other hand, landlords feel they are just billing back the legitimate costs of operating a shopping center. It becomes critical to make sure the calculations are accurate and in accordance with the lease terms, no matter how complicated. In malls there are likely to be two budgets, one for the overall shopping center which includes all tenants, including anchors, and a second budget for operating the mall's common area, which does not include anchors or out parcel tenants. The denominator for each of these budgets will be different.

Gross leasable area of the shopping center	1,250,000 square feet
Anchor tenants	800,000 square feet
Out parcel tenants	100,000 square feet
Mall shop space	350,000 square feet

To illustrate the allocations, assume a shop space of 3,000 square feet in the mall. This tenant's pro rata share would be:

Overall shopping center: 3,000 square feet ÷ 1,250,000 square feet = 0.0024%

Mall maintenance expenses: 3,000 square feet ÷ 350,000 square feet = .0086%

4) Common Area Costs with a Maximum

Some anchor tenants and some large national tenants may have the negotiating strength to get limits on the amount of common area maintenance they may pay. The lease language will often indicate that the tenant will pay his or her share, but not to exceed a given figure. It might seem that it would be easy to just bill that agreed upon maximum figure, but the tenant will want to see how much the actual charges were, and will expect to be billed only the maximum. Assume a particular supermarket is 50,000 square feet, occupies 26.45 percent of the shopping center of 189,036 square feet, and has a 10 percent common area maintenance (CAM) supervision provision. It also has a lease provision limiting common area costs to $4.00 per square foot per year, but the actual costs are $6.32. The tenant would receive a statement with all of the costs itemized in reasonable detail and the calculation would be as follows:

Total billable CAM costs	$1,194.707.52
Supermarket share .2645	$ 316,000.00
CAM Supervision fee 10%	$ 31,600.00
Total	$ 347,600.00
Maximum under lease $4.00/square foot	$ 200,000.00
Net bill to supermarket	$ 200,000.00

Most likely the supermarket will still want copies of all of the bills and may challenge anything they do not agree with even though it will not change this billing. They are entitled to a full accounting, even if they do not owe the total amount.

5) Multiple Denominators

Every lease is negotiated separately and often has varying reimbursement provisions. While this may be an accounting nightmare, the shopping center owner either needed or wanted the tenant badly enough to make concessions. The administration of the various provisions is not that difficult if one just thinks through the terms, separates out the needed changes, sets up the proper adjustments, and makes sure that they are clear in the billings.

As an example, it is not unusual for a restaurant that faces a mall to have its own trash removal service. The restaurant would not want to pay for its pro rata share of the shopping center's trash removal as that would be a double billing to this tenant. The same situation can arise with insurance premiums, real estate taxes, etc. Some shopping centers have as many as seven or eight separate denominators (expense pools) because of the exceptions in the leases. While setting up the different pools is time consuming, it is fairly straightforward, and each tenant is entitled to the "deal" that they negotiated. A sample showing a trash exception is calculated as follows:

Scottsdale Fashion Plaza Year End CAM Expenses

Service	Cost
Landscaping	$ 24,000
Sweeping	$ 18,200
Electricity	$ 12,200
Water	$ 9,600
Insurance	$ 18,500
Trash removal	$ 27,600
Repairs	$ 16,500
Total expenses	$126,600

The shopping center has 22,400 square feet. Tenant A occupies 1,200 square feet and has no exceptions with a 10 percent CAM supervision fee. Tenant B occupies 2,100 square feet, has a 15 percent CAM supervision fee and handles its own trash removal. Because tenant B is not part of the trash removal pool, it will have less square footage and therefore a smaller denominator. The two billings would be prepared as follows:

Tenant A

Total common area costs	$126,600.00
Less trash removal of $27,600	$ 99,000.00
Tenant's pro rata share is .0536, or	$ 5,306.40
(Trash removal equals $27,600 × tenant's square footage share of 22,400, less 2,100.) = 20,300 divided into 1,200 which is .0591	$ 1,631.16
Net charges:	$ 6,937.56
Plus supervision fee 10%	$ 693.76
Total annual CAM charges:	$ 7,631.32
Monthly CAM charges (rounded):	$ 636.00

Tenant B

Total common area costs	$126,600.00
Tenant's pro rata share .0938	$ 11,875.08
Credit on trash removal $27,600 × .0938	($ 2,588.88)
Net charges	$ 9,286.20
Plus supervision fee 15%	$ 1,392.93
Total annual CAM charges:	$ 10,679.13
Monthly CAM charges (rounded):	$ 890.00

It is possible but not probable that every line item in the budget could have a different denominator (expense pool) because of lease exceptions; each line item would then need a separate calculation.

6) Rents per Square Foot

Rent per square foot is a very common figure in shopping centers. It is the basis for comparison by the tenant and the landlord. Most parts of the country use an annual rate per square foot, but California often quotes rents on the basis of monthly rate per square foot. It is important that each party understand the terms being used by the other in a negotiation or discussion.

If the store space is 3,000 square feet and the annual rental is $72,000 the annual rental rate per square foot is:

$72,000 ÷ 3,000 square feet = $24.00 per square foot

The monthly rental rate per square foot is:

$24.00 ÷ 12 = $2.00 per square foot

Natural Breakpoint for Percentage Rent

Most shopping center leases contain a percentage rent provision. Most often the percentage rent is paid on the gross sales, less some agreed upon deductions and, in most cases minus the minimum rent paid. The *natural breakpoint* is the point at which the tenant's volume of sales multiplied by a predefined percentage rate is equal to the base rent stated in the lease and beyond which the tenant will begin to pay percentage rent. To calculate the natural breakpoint, you need to know the minimum rent and the percentage rent rate. As an example, the annual minimum rent for a tenant will be $84,600 on 3,525 square feet, and the percentage rental rate will be 6 percent. The calculation of the natural annual breakpoint is as follows:

Subtract the breakpoint from the sales and multiply that number by 6 percent:

$2,350,000 (sales) − 1,410,000 (breakpoint) = $940,000 of sales above the breakpoint

= $940,000 × .06 = $56,400

Another way of calculating this would be:

On a yearly basis, $84,600 ÷ .06 = $1,410,000 (annual breakpoint)

On a monthly basis, $1,410,000 ÷ 12 = $117,500 (monthly breakpoint)

If the tenant's annual sales are below $1,410,000, there is no percentage rent due. If the tenant's sales are above $1,410,000 the tenant will owe 6 percent of all sales above that figure. If the tenant's sales were $2,350,000 for the year, the calculation would be as follows:

$2,350,000 × .06 = $141,000

However, the tenant has already paid the minimum rent of $84,600 so that must be deducted as follows:

$141,000 − $84,600 (minimum rent) = $56,400

The tenant will owe an additional $56,400 of percentage rent.

7) Sales per Square Foot

Because it is useful to compare a tenant's sales production with like tenants, this comparison must be based on sales per square foot, as gross sales only are not as useful. To calculate the sales per square foot one divides the sales by the square footage as follows:

Gross sales of $2,350,000 ÷ 3,525 square feet = $666.67 per square foot

This figure can now be compared to similar tenants in the shopping center and to the publication *Dollars & Cents of Shopping Centers* to determine if this tenant is doing well or having problems.

8) Breakpoint per Square Foot

Quite often shopping center managers will evaluate a tenant and its rental rate by looking at the breakpoint per square foot. That calculation, based on the example in section 6, is as follows:

$1,410,000 ÷ 3,525 square feet = $400,00 per square foot

9) Artificial or Negotiated Breakpoint

There are many reasons why a tenant or a landlord may not wish to use the natural breakpoint. If the breakpoint is lowered the landlord benefits, and if the breakpoint is increased the tenant benefits. A landlord may lease a space to a tenant who wants the space improved to meet their standards and the landlord may not have the funds. The negotiation may be such that the tenant will pay for the improvements but increase the breakpoint in order to recover those costs from percentage rent.

Space	3,600 square feet
Rent	$90,000
Percentage rental rate	6% (.06)
Natural breakpoint =	$1,500,000

Assuming a cost of improvements of $600,000 and a 10-year recovery rate by the tenant, the tenant may negotiate an artificial breakpoint of $2,500,000 to allow for the recovery. The calculation is as follows:

Natural breakpoint	$1,500,000
Recovery per year	$ 60,000
60,000 ÷ .06	$1,000,000
Artificial breakpoint	$2,500,000

On the other hand, a landlord may be asking for a market rent of $25,00 per square foot and a desired tenant agrees to take the space, but wants to pay only $20.00 per square foot. The landlord may agree to the lower rental figure but ask that the breakpoint be lowered below the natural breakpoint so the landlord can recover the loss more quickly. Assuming a space of 4,200 square feet and a percentage rental rate of 5 percent, the calculation would be as follows:

Space of 4,200 square feet at $25.00 per square foot =	$ 105,000 annual rent
Tenant wants 4,200 square feet at $20.00 per square foot =	$ 84,000 annual rent
Natural breakpoint of $84,000 ÷ .05 =	$1,680,000 annually

The landlord will want to make up the difference of $21,000 if sales are good so he may ask for the breakpoint to be reduced to $1,260,000 as follows:

Natural breakpoint =	$1,680,000 annually
$21,000 ÷ .05 =	$ 420,000 annually
Artificial or negotiated breakpoint =	$1,260,000 annually

There is no right or wrong sales breakpoint, but rather the proper figure is one that both parties agree to.

10) Declining Percentage Rent Rate

Most small merchants will not be granted a declining percentage rental rate as they generally do not produce the volume to justify it. However, supermarkets, department stores and some high volume merchants have negotiated a declining percentage rental rate on the theory that the higher their sales volume, the less likely it is because of the shopping center; therefore, the shopping center should participate less in the higher sales. As an example, assume a national dress store occupies 4,000 square feet with an annual rental rate of $80,000. The basic percentage rental rate was set at 5 percent of gross from the natural breakpoint of $1,600,000, but declining to 4 percent above $2,000,000 in sales and .3 percent on sales above $2,500,000. Assuming that the dress store had sales of $2,600,000, the rental calculation would be as follows:

\$1,600,000 to \$1,999,999 = \$399,999 × .05	\$ 19,999.95
\$2,000,000 to \$2,499,999 = \$499,999 × .04	\$ 19,999.96
\$2,500,000 to \$2,600,000 = \$100,000 × .04	\$ 4,000.00
Total percentage rent =	\$ 43,999.91
Plus minimum rent =	\$ 80,000.00
Total rental due =	\$123,999.91

11) Split Percentage Rent Rate

It is not unusual for a landlord and a tenant to disagree over the specific percentage rental rate, with the landlord wanting a 6 percent rate and the tenant wanting a 5 percent rate. Now and then one will see a split rate with 6 percent to the breakpoint and 5 percent thereafter. This gets to the breakpoint faster, but the tenant only pays 5 percent on any sales above the breakpoint. Using a 1,500 square foot store at \$25.00 per square foot minimum rent, we will compare the three options: 6 percent to the breakpoint with 5 percent thereafter; a flat 6 percent; and a flat 5 percent:

Split Percentage Rent Rate

	6% to the breakpoint, 5% thereafter	6% flat	5% flat
Sales	\$700,000	\$700,000	\$700,000
Breakpoint	\$625,000	\$625,000	\$750,000
Sales subject to % rent	\$ 75,000	\$ 75,000	-0-
Percentage due	\$ 3,750	\$ 4,500	-0-

The tenant sales are \$750 from the flat 6 percent rate and the landlord gains an additional \$3,750 from the flat 5 percent rate.

Offsets or Deductions From Percentage Rents

While it is almost never done on new leases, there are some older leases that allowed a strong anchor tenant to deduct certain expenses from percentage rents. The items that could be deducted were most often common area costs, insurance and/or taxes. Most owners and tenants realize that these charges have nothing to do with percentage rents and can resist giving the deductions. As an example, an anchor tenant may demand the right to deduct real estate taxes from percentage rents and do so on a cumulative basis. This would mean that there may be no percentage rents due for the first few years of the lease, though the tenant pays the taxes. The first time percentage rents become due, the tenant could deduct any and all taxes paid for past years from the percentage rent due in that year. The better provision for the landlord is for the deductions to apply on an annual basis only. To simplify this example, we will use real estate taxes only:

Minimum rental rate	\$ 765,000
Breakpoint of 5%	\$15,300,000
Sales	\$18,600,000
Percentage rent due	\$ 165,000 (\$3,300,000 × .05)
Taxes paid this year	\$ 93,000
Net percentage rent due	\$ 72,000

12) Occupancy Costs – Rent and Charges as a Percent of Sales

One of the ways shopping center managers evaluate tenants is to look at the tenant's occupancy costs compared to the tenant's sales. Generally, occupancy costs include the base rents, plus the common area maintenance, taxes, and insurance. In today's market most owners feel that occupancy costs should be 15 percent or less, but there are many merchants that operate above those levels and do not feel it is a problem. New merchants will almost always operate above those figures, but it should only be for a short period of time. Supermarkets, drug stores, department stores, hardware stores, etc., could not operate at anything close to 15 percent on an ongoing basis. The comparison is as follows:

SCOTTSDALE PLAZA SHOPPING CENTER
CURRENT YEAR Sales/Rental Analysis

	Sales	Rent	Charges	Total	Occupancy Cost
Men's wear	$407,000	$45,000	$14,967	$59,967	14.73%
Women's wear	$328,000	$27,500	$10,168	$37,668	11.48%
Shoes	$568,200	$57,200	$18,304	$75,504	13.29%
Cleaners	$197,680	$28,600	$10.816	$39,416	19.94%

The men's wear store is close to the 15 percent, but if they are paying their rent on time and no problems are indicated, there would be no reason for concern. The cleaners, however, is well above the 15 percent level, and management might want to either look over their situation for problems or meet with the tenant to discuss the situation. If this is a new tenant, there is no real reason for concern. Occupancy cost alone is not a full measure of how a tenant is doing, but it is another tool for evaluating the merchants.

13) Consumer Price Index Calculations

Landlords in many parts of the country have consumer price index (CPI) provisions in their leases to protect against inflation. Anchor tenants and large national tenants will not sign leases with a consumer price index, but most often they will make some provisions for increasing the rents on a long term lease arrangement.

The lease provision should be quite clear as to which index will be used, what month it will be effective and which month of the index will be used to measure the change. Generally, most landlords use an index at least three months prior to the change date to be sure all the data is in and the change can be calculated before the due date. If the rent is to be increased in February, most likely the lease will call for the October index to be used as it comes out in November and everything can be calculated prior to the due date. There are two ways to calculate the increase; they are shown below. The tenant occupies space of 1,400 square feet and has a current base rent of $36,400. The rent is to increase in February and the lease calls for the October index to be used both as the base index and trigger index.

The first method of calculation is:

Base rent	$36,400
October index of previous year	161.4
October index of current year	166.4
Percent increase	3.1

Calculations would then be:

Increase per year:

$36,400 × .031 (3.1%) = $1,128.40

New annual rent:

$36,400 + $1,128.40 = $37,528.40 per year

Monthy rent:

$37,528.40 ÷ 12 = $3,127.36

The second method is as follows:

Base rent	$36,400
$36,400 ÷ 161.40 =	$225.53
$225.53 × 166.4 =	$37,527.63
$37,527.63 ÷ 12 =	$3127.30 monthly

The second method brings one to a slightly lower rental figure. Many landlords will calculate the change both ways and then use the lower to bill the tenant to avoid any future disputes. Either way is acceptable, but the landlord should be consistent. Most landlords will provide the tenant with the calculation made and, in most cases with a copy of the government notice on the actual amount of the change.

Consumer Price Index – Floor and Ceiling

Because the consumer price index has gone well over 10 percent per year from time to time, some tenants do not mind the rental increase but ask that the amount of the increase be limited. It is not unusual for the tenant to ask for an upper limit of 6 percent per year. Generally, if the landlord is willing to take the risk of an upper limit, the landlord will want to be sure that it does not fall too low and may ask for a minimum increase of 4 percent in any given year. Such an agreement provides some benefits to both parties. The effect of such an agreement will be:

If the actual CPI is between 4 percent and 6 percent, the rental increase will be the actual percentage of the increase in the index. If the CPI is less than 4 percent, the actual increase to the tenant will be 4 percent. If the CPI is above 6 percent, the actual rental increase to the tenant will be limited to 6 percent per the agreement. The following examples show these calculations:

Increase between 4 percent and 6 percent:

Base rent	$45,000
Base index	161.4
1 year index	169.5
Percentage increase	5.02
New rent	$47,259
($45,000 × 1.0502)	

Increase below 4 percent:

Base rent	$45,000
Base index	161.4
1 year index	166.2
Percentage increase	2.97
Minimum per lease	4%
New rent	$46,800.00
($45,000 × 1.04)	

Increase above 6 percent:

Base rent	$45,000
Base index	161.4
1 year index	172.7
Percentage increase	7.0
Maximum per lease	6.0
New rent	$47,700
($45,000 × 1.06)	

Another variation on the consumer price increase is one that limits the increase on an annual basis, but allows it to go to the full index every fifth year. In this example, assume that the annual limit is 4 percent. The calculation would be:

Base year rent	$52,000.00
Year 1 (CPI increase of 5.3% limited to 4%)	$54,080.00
Year 2 (CPI increase of 5.5% limited to 4%)	$56,243.20
Year 3 (CPI increase of 5.3% limited to 4%)	$58,492.93
Year 4 (CPI increase of 5.2% limited to 4%)	$60,832.65
Year 5 (CPI 5.1 percent – actual figures now used to bring CPI up to full $52,000 × 1.2640 =	$65,728.00

The next year the maximum goes back to 4 percent per year. The tenant has had the benefit of the lower rents and the landlord then gets the full adjustment every fifth year.

It is also not unusual to see marketing fund contributions and even some common area items set up to be increased by the consumer price index on an annual basis. The calculations for these items would be done in exactly the same way as a rental increase. Using a marketing fund contribution as an example it would be calculated as follows:

Initial marketing fund contribution	$900.00/ year
Initial Consumer Price Index	161.4
Trigger Index	166.4
Percent of Increase (166.4 ÷ 161.4) =	3.1
New contribution $900.00 × 1.031 =	$927.90/year

14) Allowable Building Area

Most communities have a maximum building area on a given site. Either in the initial development calculations or when there is a desire to expand the shopping center, one may have to determine the maximum building area for the specific site. One typical limitation is to allow for one square foot of building for every four square feet of land:

If we desire final building area of	158,000 square feet
We will need 4 times that in land area or	632,000 square feet
Total land needed =	790,000 square feet
(43,560 square feet per acre)	18.14 acres

15) Parking Ratios

Most communities require a minimum parking ratio in our shopping centers. A very common number is 5 spaces per thousand square feet of leasable area. Generally, it is a little more complicated than having one figure that works for every parking need in the shopping center as restaurants and theaters often require more parking than general retail; however, the calculations are done the same way.

If we know we have 138,000 square feet of retail and the city requirement is five spaces per thousand square feet, we can calculate the number of spaces needed as follows:

138,000 ÷ 1,000 =	138
138 × 5 spaces required =	690 parking spaces required

16) Effective Rent

The term "effective rent" means the rent that is available after the necessary expenses have been deducted. Those expenses are generally free rent, a leasing commission, and any tenant improvements. In very poor markets it is possible to make a deal with no effective rent, but that is a rare situation. To make the illustration simple, we will use a five year lease term, space of 1,500 square feet, and rent of $25.00 per square foot. It is a triple net lease, the leasing commission is 5 percent, and we have given the tenant a $5.00 per square foot improvement allowance. We have not given any free rent. The calculation is as follows:

Base rent 1,500 × $25.00 = $37,500 × 5 years =	$187,500
Tenant improvements $5.00 × 1,500 =	(7,500)
Leasing commission $187,500 × .05 =	(9,375)
Net effective rent =	$170,625
Net effective rent per square foot $170,625 ÷ 5 =	$34,125
$34, 125 ÷ 1,500 square feet =	$22.75 per square foot

17) Rental and/or Expense Pro Ration

A very common calculation is that of the pro ration of base rents, common area charges, marketing fund contributions, or other similar items. If a tenant opens its shop on any other day than the first of the month, a pro rated rental amount will be due. There is often great confusion as to what figures to use and how to calculate the pro ration. Most often the lease will spell out the basis for any pro ration. Generally, the lease will either specify a 360-day year or a 365-day year. If the lease specifies a 360-day year, every month is assumed to be 30 days. On the other hand, if the lease spells out a 365-day year, every month will be pro rated based on the actual number of days in that month. If the lease is not specific on the subject, most landlords will use a 360-day month as it is much easier and is consistent from month to month. Whichever approach one uses, it should be used all of the time and not changed for each calculation, especially if each change favors the landlord.

The following example uses the 360 day, or 30-day month approach. Assuming that the tenant's monthly rent is $4,320.00 and the tenant opened for business on the 12th of the month, the pro ration for that month would be as follows:

Opening on the 12th day of the month means the tenant will be open 19 of the 30 days of the month. (One might assume to deduct 12 from 30 and conclude that it is 18 days the tenant is open, but the 12th is also a working day, so that day counts as well.)

Monthly rent of $4,320.00 ÷ 30 days =	$144.00 per day
$144.00 × 19 =	$2,736 for the month

The common area, taxes, and insurance would also be pro rated for the same month. Assume in this case the monthly estimate for that month is $932.00.

$932.00 ÷ 30 =	$31.07 per day
$31.07 × 19 =	$590.27 for the month

It is also helpful to show the calculation where the 365-day year is set up in the lease. Assuming that the month in question is March, which has 31 days and that the same tenant opens on the 12th of the month, the calculation would be:

$4,320.00 ÷ 31 days =	$139.35 per day
$139.35 × 20 (days open) = 20 days	$2,787.10

The common area calculation would be:

$932.00 ÷ 31 =	$30.06 per day
$30.06 × 20 (days open) =	$601.29

It is important when administering the lease that the tenants are accurately billed for their charges. The shopping center manager and lease administrator need to understand the examples provided above and any other exceptions to the lease so that the tenants are accurately billed for their charges per their lease.

Appendix D

References and Resources

The following lists represent potential resources the shopping center manager can consult for additional information. They are not intended to be all-inclusive but rather to identify publications and organizations that may be useful to the shopping center manager. *Books in Print* and *Periodicals in Print,* published annually by R. R. Bowker and available in libraries, list current publications by author, title, and subject.

Books

Development

A Beginner's Guide to Architectural Services (Washington DC: The American Institute of Architects, 1989).

Developing Retail Entertainment Destinations (Washington DC: Urban land Institute Second edition, 2001).

New Uses for Obsolete Buildings (Washington DC: Urban Land Institute, 1996).

Parking Requirements for Shopping Centers: Summary Recommendations and Research Study Report (Washington, D.C.: ULI—The Urban Land Institute,1999).

Parking Standards (Washington DC: Urban land Institute, 2002).

Schwanke, Dean: *Mixed-Use Development Handbook Second Edition* (Washington, D.C.: ULI—The Urban Land Institute, 2003).

Shopping Center Development Handbook, Third Edition (Washington DC: Urban land Institute, 1999).

Shopping Center Redevelopment and Renovation (New York: International Council of Shopping Centers, 2000).

You and Your Architect (Washington DC: The American Institute of Architects).

Leasing

Halper, Emanuel B.: *Shopping Center and Store Leases* (New York: Law Journal Press, 2003).

Leasing Small Shopping Centers (New York: International Council of Shopping Centers 1997).

Senn, Mark A.: *Commercial Real Estate Leases: Forms, Second Edition* (New York: John Wiley & Sons, Inc., 1990).

Senn, Mark A.: *Commercial Real Estate Leases: Preparation and Negotiation, Second Edition* (New York: John Wiley & Sons, Inc., 1990).

Crafting Lease Clauses Volume III: 1999–2001 (New York: International Council of Shopping Centers, 2001).

Management and Operations

Alexander, Alan A.: *Common Area Maintenance (CAM) Administration* (New York: International Council of Shopping Centers, 2002).

Alexander, Alan A.: *Shopping Center Rent Administration* (International Council of Shopping Centers,1990).

Alexander, Alan A., Muhlebach, Richard F.: *Business Strategies for Real Estate Management Companies, Second Edition* (Chicago: Institute of Real estate Management, 2004).

Alexander, Alan A., Muhlebach, Richard F.: *Operating Small Shopping Centers* (New York: International Council of Shopping Centers, 1997).

Before Disaster Strikes: Developing an Emergency Procedures Manual, 3rd Edition (Chicago: Institute of Real Estate Management, 2005).

Developing a Shopping Center Business Plan (International Council of Shopping Centers).

Glossary of Real estate Management Terms (Chicago: Institute of Real Estate Management, 2003).

Guide to Writing A Shopping Center Security Manual (New York: International Council of Shopping Centers, 2003).

Graffiti Removal Manual (Providence, R.I.: Keep Providence Beautiful).

Halper, Emanuel B.: *Shopping Center and Store Leases* (New York: Law Journal Seminars-Press, Inc., 1984).

Roof Maintenance (Englewood, Colo.: The Roofing Industry Educational Institute, 1988).

Watson, John A.: *Commercial Roofing Systems* (Reston, Va.: Reston Publishing Company, Inc., 1984).

Marketing and Advertising

Fraser, Kim: *Marketing Small Shopping Centers* (International Council of Shopping Centers, 1991).

Shopping Center Marketing (New York: International Council of Shopping Centers, 2001).

Magazines and Newsletters

CarlsonReport (Indianapolis: Report Communications, monthly).

Chain Store Age Executive (with *Shopping Center Age*) (New York: Lebhar-Friedman, Inc., monthly).

Commercial Lease Law Insider (New York: Brownstone Publishing, Inc., monthly).

JonesReport (Indianapolis: Report Communications, monthly).

Journal of Property Management (Chicago: Institute of Real Estate Management, bimonthly).

Retail Construction (Cumming, GA, monthly).

Retail Traffic (New York: Primedia Publications, monthly).

Shopping Center Business (Atlanta: France Publications, monthly).

Shopping Center Management Insider (New York: Brownstone Publishers, Inc., monthly).

Shopping Centers Today (New York: International Council of Shopping Centers, monthly).

Shopping Center World (Atlanta, Ga.: Communication Channels, Inc., monthly).

Urban Land (Washington, D.C.: ULI—The Urban Land Institute, monthly).

Market Research

The U.S. Department of Commerce, Bureau of the Census, compiles demographic data on an ongoing basis. *The Census Catalog and Guide* is published every decade. The *Census of Retail Trade* is published every five years in years ending in two and seven. *Current Business Reports* compiles data on monthly retail trade sales and inventories. *American Housing Survey* compiles data on housing quality and costs, neighborhood quality, personal income, and other statistics of interest to retailers. The *CPI Detailed Report* is a monthly report of changes in the Consumer Price Index. The Bureau of Labor Statistics conducts and publishes a *Survey of Consumer Expenditures* that describes American spending patterns by merchandise categories. Updated census data are published each year in *Statistical Abstract of the United States* available from the Government Printing Office in Washington, D.C.

In addition, there are numerous nongovernmental sources for demographic data. *American Demographics* and *The Numbers News* are published monthly by American Demographics Press in Ithaca, New York. *Metro Insights* is published annually by DRI/McGraw-Hill in Lexington, Massachusetts. *Rand McNally Commercial Atlas & Marketing Guide* is published annually by Rand McNally & Company in Skokie, Illinois. The *REIS Reports* covering retail market analyses for major metropolitan areas are issued from New York City. *Survey of Buying Power,* published annually as a supplement to *Sales and Marketing Management* (New York: Bill Communications Inc.), provides information related to sales performance, market potential, marketing strategies, and selection of advertising media and markets.

Targeted data compilations that focus census statistics are available from several private companies, including the following:

CACI in Fairfax, Virginia
CDP Marketing Information Corporation in Hauppauge, New York
Claritas in Alexandria, Virginia

Donnelley Marketing Information Services in Stamford, Connecticut
Intelligent Charting, Inc., in Perth Amboy, New Jersey
National Decision Systems in Encinitas, California
Survey Sampling, Inc., in Fairfield, Connecticut
Clartias Dealmakers, in New Jersey.

Directories and other listings of retailers and leasing information are published periodically. Most are issued annually; a few are published twice a year or on another schedule. Many are special issues of trade magazines.

The Book on Value Retailing (St. Petersburg, Fla.: *Value Retail News*).
Lists off-price and outlet discount tenants, with their existing locations and people to contact.

Centermation Systems Food Court Special Report.
An annual survey published in *Carlson Report* (Indianapolis: Report Communications).

Chain Store Guide—Directory of Leading Chain Stores in the United States (New York: Business Guides, Inc., annual).
A listing of chain stores with five or more locations—by category and by state—showing company name, address and telephone number, number of stores, area of activity, and people to contact.

Dealmakers Weekly
A newsletter published 48 times a year and affiliated with TKC Consulting, Center Leasing & Development Corp.

Directory of Major Malls (Spring Valley, New York: JOMURPA Publishing Inc., annual).
A listing of shopping centers (existing and planned), developers, retailers, and markets in the United States and Canada.

Directory of Shopping Centers in the United States (Chicago: National Research Bureau, division of Automated Marketing Systems, Inc., annual).
A three-volume compilation of information on shopping centers (size, tenants, age, ownership, etc.), leasing agents, and other center personnel.

Factory Outlet World: Third Edition (Suffern, New York: DPN Enterprises, Inc., 1985).
A listing of retailers, developers, centers, and services to the off-price/outlet industry.

The Franchise Annual Directory (Lewiston, N.Y.: Info Franchise News).
A listing of hundreds of franchise opportunities.

Leasing Opportunities (New York: International Council of Shopping Centers).
Published annually, this book lists retailers with expansion plans for the coming year, giving space and location requirements and type of center desired.

Retail Tenant Directory.
An annual listing of tenants in large and small shopping centers in the United States published by *Monitor* magazine.

Reports of surveys of operating income and expenses for shopping centers and for various retailers are also available. Such information is useful for comparison purposes; however, the reader should bear in mind that the passage of time renders such data less reliable for current planning.

Fairchild's Financial Manual of Retail Stores (New York: Fairchild Publications, Book Division, annual).

A survey of the operating income and expenses of retail stores.

Income/Expense Analysis: Shopping Centers (Chicago: Institute of Real Estate Management, annual).

A resource on shopping center financial data, this publication provides timely information focused on income and expenses.

The SCORE:Shopping Center Operations, Revenue and Expenses (New York: International Council of Shopping Centers, periodic).

Professional Organizations

The Institute of Real Estate Management (IREM) is an association of property management professionals, including shopping center managers. Headquartered in Chicago, Illinois, IREM offers courses and seminars on property management topics and publishes numerous books and periodicals, including the annual *Income/Expense Analysis: Shopping Centers* and the bimonthly *Journal of Property Management (JPM)*. In addition, monthly meetings of local chapters provide opportunities to hear timely speakers and network with other shopping center management professional who are working towards their CPM® designation.

The International Council of Shopping Centers (ICSC) holds national and regional meetings and offers courses on shopping center marketing, leasing, management, and development. Headquartered in New York City, ICSC publishes *Leasing Opportunities,* an annual directory of shopping centers and retailers, and *Research Quarterly,* a report of shopping center statistics (size, sales, vacancies, etc.) as they are changing. They offer two designations: Certified Shopping Center Manager (CSM) and Certified Marketing Director (CMD).

The Urban Land Institute (ULI), an association of developers, architects, and others interested in land use, is headquartered in Washington, D.C. They publish *Dollars & Cents of Shopping Centers* and a series of *Dollars & Cents* special reports on fashion malls and other specialty retail centers comparing income and expenses with particular focus on individual merchandise categories.

ULI and ICSC have done considerable research on shopping center parking requirements. Information on other aspects of parking design, including parking for handicapped people, may be sought from the Institute of Transportation Engineers in Washington, D.C., publishers of *ITE Journal.*

Glossary

ACCREDITED MANAGEMENT ORGANIZATION® (AMO®) A designation conferred by the Institute of Real Estate Management on real estate management firms that are under the direction of a CERTIFIED PROPERTY MANAGER® and comply with stipulated requirements as to accounting procedures, performance, and protection of funds entrusted to them.

Adaptive use Conversion of an existing structure for a new use, e.g., a former post office converted to a shopping center.

All risk insurance Insurance that covers losses caused by all perils except those specifically excluded in the policy contract.

American Institute of Architects (AIA) A policy-making organization founded in 1857 and headquartered in Washington D.C., that fosters professionalism and accountability among its membership of licensed architects and promotes design excellence. The AIA also established guidelines for and publishes various construction related documents that are universally accepted in the architecture and engineering management professions.

Anchor pad A parcel of land occupied by an anchor tenant excluding parking area.

Anchor parcel A parcel of land occupied by an anchor tenant including its parking area.

Anchor tenant A major shopping center tenant that will draw the majority of customers to the site. Normally an anchor tenant occupies a large space in a desirable location in the shopping center. Often there are two or more anchor tenants, depending on the type and size of the shopping center.

Ancillary tenant A shopping center tenant that occupies a smaller space and a location that is secondary in relation to the anchor tenant.

Artificial breakpoint A dollar amount of gross sales that is negotiated to be higher or lower than the natural breakpoint. All sales above the artificial breakpoint are subject to percentage rent.

Asset management A specialized field of property management that involves the supervision of an owner's real estate assets at the investment level. An *asset manager* typically has a more active role in the acquisition, disposition, and divestiture of the real estate investment than a property manager normally does and may have only a superficial involvement with day-to-day operations. (See also *property management.*)

Asset manager One who is charged with supervising an owner's real estate assets at the investment level.

Assignee One to whom some right or interest is transferred, either for the individual's own enjoyment or in trust, i.e., the person receiving an assignment.

Assignment The transfer, in writing, of an interest in a bond, mortgage, lease or other instrument. The transfer of one person's interest or right in a property (e.g., a lease) to another. Also, the document by which such an interest or right is transferred. Specifically, the document used to convey a leasehold is called an assignment of lease. The assignor of a lease remains liable unless released by the landlord.

Assignor One giving some right or interest, i.e., the person making an assignment.

Base rent Minimum monthly rent payments as set forth in a retail lease, exclusive of pass-through expenses, percentage rents, and other additional charges. (See also *minimum rent.*)

Breakpoint In retail leases, the point at which the tenant's percentage rent (percentage rate times sales) is equal to the base rent and beyond which the tenant will begin to pay overages; also called *natural breakpoint* and calculated by dividing the percentage rate into the base rent amount. Sometimes tenant and landlord negotiate an *artificial breakpoint* that allows the tenant to begin paying percentage rent either before or after the natural breakpoint is reached.

Build-to-suit An arrangement between a shopping center developer and a large space user (supermarket, department store, fast food franchise, bank, etc.) whereby the developer agrees to construct the tenant's building according to the tenant's detailed specifications. The tenant then leases the building and the site from the developer.

Business interruption insurance A form of property insurance which provides coverage against the loss of rents resulting from damage to the building or content as by fire or other peril.

Buyout A form of concession whereby an owner arranges to pay for the rest of a tenant's lease term so that the tenant will relocate to the owner's shopping center or move out of a space that the owner wants to use for another tenant.

Cap A limit to the amount of an expense (e.g., CAM, real estate taxes) a tenant is obligated to pay.

Capitalization rate A percentage rate of return used to determine the value of a property based on its income stream; also called *cap rate.*

Cash flow The amount of spendable income from a real estate investment. The amount of cash available after all payments have been made for operating expenses, debt service (mortgage principal and interest) and capital reserves as well as ordinary operating expenses, but excluding income taxes.

Center court In an enclosed mall, a location midway between two department store anchors.

Central business district The central shopping or business area in an urban environment, usually the place where real estate values are highest; also called downtown.

Certificate of Occupancy A document issued by a municipal building department (or other appropriate governmental authority) verifying that a building or a portion of a building (a floor, an office, a store or other demised space) is in compliance with the applicable building, zoning, and other codes; this is also referred to as an occupancy permit. Commonly abbreviated as C of O or C.O., the certificate of occupancy permits the building or space to be occupied for its designated use.

CERTIFIED MARKETING DIRECTOR® (CMD®) A professional designation granted by the International Council of Shopping Centers (ICSC) to individuals who meet specific education and experience requirements and pass the qualifying exam.

CERTIFIED PROPERTY MANAGER® (CPM®) The professional designation conferred by the Institute of Real Estate Management on those individuals who distinguish themselves in the areas of education, experience, and ethics in property management.

CERTIFIED SHOPPING CENTER MANAGER® (CSM®) A professional designation granted by the International Council of Shopping Centers (ICSC) to individuals who meet specific education and experience requirements and pass the qualifying exam.

Chain store One of a group of stores operating under the same ownership that carries similar goods. National, regional, and local chains are defined in terms of the geographic areas they serve and the number of stores they operate.

Change of use The process of changing the function of a structure without changing its exterior dimensions.

Cold calling The process of calling on prospects to interest them in leasing space.

Common area agreement A separate agreement, usually between an anchor tenant and a shopping center owner, that sets standards for maintenance of the common area and states how the related expenses will be distributed between the parties. It may also prohibit the shopping center owner from making changes to the common areas (e.g., relocating entrances or adding a pad or outlot building) without the written approval of each signatory to the agreement. Such an agreement may also be established among multiple owners of a mixed-use development (MXD) or other similar property, in which case it may also address removal of the common area manager for nonperformance.

Common area maintenance (CAM) charges The amount the tenant will pay to maintain the common areas of the shopping center (e.g., landscaping, parking areas, etc.).

Community shopping center A shopping center commonly anchored by a junior department store, discount store, or variety store and having 150,000–400,000 square feet of GLA, often configured as a large open-air strip with three or more anchors.

Concession An economic incentive granted by an owner of real estate to encourage the leasing of space or the renewal of a lease. Concessions usually affect the total economic value of a lease.

Construction loan A short-term loan covering the cost to develop a project, usually funded by one or more commercial banks.

Consumer Price Index (CPI) A way of measuring consumer purchasing power by comparing the current cost of goods and services to those of a selected base period: formerly referred to as cost-of-living index. Sometimes used as a reference point for rent escalations in leases. The CPI is published by the U.S. Department of Labor, Bureau of Labor Statistics.

Convenience shopping center A small shopping center (5,000–30,000 square feet of GLA), sometimes anchored by a quick-stop food store and usually occupied by service-oriented businesses; often designed in a strip.

Cosmetic maintenance Work done on a building that enhances its appearance but does not contribute materially to its operations or preservation.

Cost-benefit analysis A projection of the impact of a particular change on operating income (NOI) and cash flow, comparing that impact to the cost of making the change.

Declining percentage rent A negotiated percentage rent structure such that the tenant pays a smaller percentage of gross sales after a specific sales volume is reached.

Deferred maintenance Ordinary maintenance of a building that, because it has not been performed, negatively affects the use, occupancy and value of the building.

Demographic profile The social and economic statistics of a specific population, including population size and density and characteristics of individuals such as age, education, occupation, and income.

Depreciation In real estate, the loss of value due to all causes, including physical deterioration (ordinary wear and tear), structural defects, and changing economic and market conditions (see also *obsolescence*). The tax deduction that allows for exhaustion of property by allocation of its cost over its estimated useful life.

Discretionary income Money available for spending after physical needs (food, clothing, shelter) have been met and taxes have been paid.

Disposable income The amount of personal income (i.e., wages) left over after all statutory deductions such as federal, state, and local income taxes and social security benefits. The amount of income the consumer actually has available to spend or save.

Doing business as More commonly seen as the abbreviation *dba*, it represents the business name assumed by a sole proprietor or the trade name of a business as opposed to its legal name.

Effective gross income The estimated gross income less allowances for vacancies and rent losses; the total amount of income actually collected during a reporting period.

Emergency maintenance Unscheduled repairs that must be done immediately to prevent further damage or to minimize danger to life or property.

Enclosure The conversion of part of the common area of an open-air shopping center to a fully enclosed mall by addition of a roof and walls.

Equity The interest or value that an owner has in real estate over and above the mortgage and other financial liens against it; outright ownership.

Estoppel certificate A document by which the tenant states the terms of the lease, including the amount of rent to be paid over the entire term of the lease; commonly requested by the landlord in conjunction with a transfer of ownership or in relation to financing.

Ethics The discipline dealing with what is right or wrong, good or bad, often related to duty or obligation. The rules of conduct or code of principles recognized in respect to a particular class of human activity.

Exclusive A right granted to the tenant that restricts the owner from leasing space in the same shopping center to other retailers that sell similar merchandise, usually defined in an *exclusive use* clause. Care must be taken in granting exclusives because such limitation of competition may violate antitrust regulations. When granted, exclusives must be taken into account when prospecting for and leasing to additional retail tenants.

Exhibit An attachment to a lease document that elaborates on points agreed to in the lease.

Feasibility study Analysis done to discover the practicality, possibility and reasonableness of a proposed undertaking (e.g., real estate development), especially regarding proposed costs and revenues.

Food court An area in a shopping center, usually in an enclosed mall, where different kinds of foods are available from individual vendors selling from separate stalls; typically there is a shared (common) seating area for customers.

Franchise An exclusive right to sell a product or perform a service; in retailing, an individual purchases this right from a chain store or other type of parent corporation and operates the store according to the rules and regulations of the franchisor.

Frontage The section of a store that faces the street or the pedestrian walkway in a mall; also refers to window display area and entrance.

Go dark A provision sometimes included in a shopping center lease that allows a tenant to cease operations at the property if a predefined event occurs (e.g., annual sales at the location are below an agreed-upon dollar amount).

Gross leasable area (GLA) The size of an individual tenant's space, usually measured in square feet. The total square footage of floor space in all store areas of a shopping center (excluding common area space); also called floor area.

Gross lease A lease whereby the landlord (lessor) is responsible for paying all property expenses (e.g., taxes, insurance, utilities, repairs, etc.), and these costs are factored into the rent paid by the tenant (lessee). (Compare *net lease*.)

Ground lease A lease for land only.

Guarantor One who acts as a surety or gives security, as for payment of a debt. In real estate, one who agrees to assume responsibility for a financial obligation of another in the event the other person cannot perform (e.g., payment of rent under a lease).

HVAC The universally recognized standard abbreviation for the science of providing an environment with the correct temperature, humidity, air movement, air cleanliness, ventilation and acoustical level. HVAC is the acronym for heating, ventilating and air conditioning.

Institute of Real Estate Management (IREM) A professional association of men and women who meet established standards of experience, education, and ethics with the objective of continually improving their respective managerial skills by mutual education and exchange of ideas and experience. The Institute is an affiliate of the NATIONAL ASSOCIATION OF REALTORS®. (See also *CERTIFIED PROPERTY MANAGER®*.)

Insurance A means of reducing economic risk in which funds are accumulated from a group of insured parties and used to pay the losses of an individual member of the group. As a form of risk management, insurance substitutes regular payment of insurance premiums for the unpredictable cost of an economic loss, based on the probability of a particular type of loss occurring.

Intercept survey A market research method often used at shopping centers in which customers at the shopping center are stopped at random and asked questions concerning their shopping habits and their likes, dislikes and preferences regarding their shopping experience.

International Council of Shopping Centers (ICSC) Membership organization of retailers, developers, owners, managers, leasing agents marketing personnel, and other professionals who provide services to those in the shopping center industry.

Investment value The price that an investor bound by special circumstances and restraints will agree to pay. (Compare *market value*.)

Keystone markup In retailing, a standard markup that sets a selling price for merchandise at double its cost.

Kickout A lease provision that provides the right of early lease termination based on a specific event such as the tenant not achieving a specific annual sales volume or the occupancy of the shopping center dropping below a specific percentage of spaced leased or occupied.

Kiosk A booth or stall set up in a shopping center, sometimes on a temporary basis, to sell goods such as seasonal merchandise and small impulse-purchase items.

Lease A contract between the property owner or landlord (lessor) and a tenant (lessee) that transfers to the tenant the right to use a piece of property for a specified period of time under certain conditions.

Leasing agent The individual directly responsible for renting space in a shopping center. Leasing agents may be employed by brokerage firms, management organizations, or development companies; in some states, they are required to be licensed as real estate brokers.

Life cycle The total number of years of operations of a system or a piece of equipment from its installation to replacement or removal: also known as operating life cycle.

Lifestyle shopping center A large shopping center with streetscape architecture design in an open-air layout with upscale fashion tenants, gift, jewelry, and specialty merchants, fine dining and possibly entertainment (e.g., multi-screen theater). The second generation of lifestyle shopping centers include residential space above the retail and smaller formatted department stores.

Maintenance The effort expended to keep a property in good physical and operating conditions and appearance.

Management agreement A legal contract between the owner of a property and a person who agrees to manage it. This agreement establishes the manager's duties, authority, and compensation and states the owner's obligations to insure the property, provide sufficient funds for its operation, and assure its compliance with building and construction codes and environmental regulations.

Management fee The monetary consideration paid monthly or otherwise for the performance of management duties, usually defined in the management agreement as a percentage of the gross rental income of the property and/or as a minimum monthly amount.

Marketing Promotion of a store or retail center through advertising and public relations programs.

Marketing fund An account controlled by the landlord that is specifically for funding shopping center promotions and advertising and to which all merchants in the center must contribute a predetermined amount as stated in their leases. (Compare *merchants' association*.)

Marketing plan A short-term business tool to generate profits by increasing business.

Market rent The rent a retail site could command under prevailing market conditions.

Market research The gathering of information about a trade area and a particular retail site—usually pertaining to population, economy, local industries, per capita expenditures, competing retail sites, and sales potential.

Market share The portion of consumer dollars spent on a particular merchandise category that a given retailer can capture.

Market value The price at which a seller would willingly sell an item (e.g., a property) and a buyer would willingly buy it in an open market.

Merchandising The buying, promoting, and selling of goods.

Merchants' association An organization formed in shopping centers and controlled by the tenants to plan promotions and advertisements for the good of the center as a whole and usually established as a not-for-profit corporation. All tenants are required to participate, and both tenants and landlord pay dues. (Compare *marketing fund*.)

Minimum rent The rent which will always be due each month in a tenant's lease term, regardless of sales volume and exclusive of any additional charges; often used in conjunction with a percentage rent arrangement; sometimes called fixed minimum rent. (See also *base rent*.)

Mixed-use development (MXD) A large-scale real estate project having three or more significant revenue-producing uses (e.g., retail, office, residential, hotel, recreation), incorporating significant physical and functional integration of project components (thus an intensive use of land), and conforming to a coherent plan.

Modernization The removal or upgrading of original or existing features of a property, primarily to reflect technological improvements such as energy-saving equipment.

Mortgage A written instrument that creates a lien upon real estate as security for the payment of a specified debt. See also *permanent loan*.

Multi-use development A term applied to multiple uses of a single site and encompassing densely configured developments that achieve physical and functional integration but include only two uses, mixed-use developments as such, and developments with two or more uses but lacking physical and functional integration (usually because of large scale, low density, or lack of a coherent plan). (Compare *mixed-use development*.)

Natural breakpoint The natural breakpoint is a mathematical formula calculated by dividing the annual base or minimum rent by the percentage rent rate. All sales above the breakpoint are subject to percentage rent.

Negotiation The process of bargaining between landlord and tenant to reach a mutually profitable agreement on rental rates, term of the lease, and other points.

Neighborhood shopping center A shopping center typically anchored by a supermarket or drugstore and having 30,000–150,000 square feet of GLA.

Net lease A lease under which the tenant pays a prorated share of some or all operating expenses. In retail leasing, the tenant pays a prorated share of property taxes under a net lease, prorated shares of both property taxes and insurance under a net-net lease, and prorated shares of all operating expenses (including common area maintenance) under a triple-net lease. (Compare *gross lease.*)

Net operating income (NOI) The money available to an owner or developer after deducting a property's operating expenses from its effective gross income. (Debt service is deducted from NOI to determine cash flow.)

Newsletter A periodical report devoted to news of and for a specific interest group, such as the tenants in a shopping center.

Obsolescence Lessening of value due to being out-of-date (obsolete) as a result of changes in design and use; an element of depreciation. *Physical obsolescence* (deterioration) results from deferred maintenance; *functional obsolescence* is an internal condition of a property related to its design or use; and *economic obsolescence* is an inability to generate enough income to offset operating expenses, usually due to conditions external to the property (changes in populations and/or land uses, legislation, etc.).

Occupancy breakeven When the income from the property is equal to operating expenses and debt service.

Occupancy cost The retail tenant's cost for the leased space, including base and percentage rent plus pass-through prorations (operating expenses, taxes, insurance, CAM costs).

Off-price shopping center A type of specialized shopping center whose tenants offer brand-name merchandise at large discounts (20 percent to 60 percent) off normal retail prices because special bulk purchases allow cost savings to be passed on to the customer. (Compare *outlet center.*)

Operating expenses All expenditures made in connection with operating a property with the exceptions of debt service and income taxes.

Option In a retail lease, a statement of the tenant's right to obtain a specific condition within a specified time (typically covering renewal, extension of the term, expansion of the space, or cancellation of the lease); often incorporated into the lease as an addendum.

Outlet shopping center A type of specialized shopping center dominated by factory outlet stores that sell manufacturers' surplus merchandise (factory seconds, irregulars, or overruns); usually the manufacturer operates the store, eliminating the retail markup. (Compare *off-price center.*)

Outlot In a shopping center, a site that is not attached to the main center; also called out parcel or *pad* space. The term is often applied to freestanding space in the parking lot.

Overage Rent Percentage rent paid in addition to the minimum or base rent.

Pad site A land area occupied by a free standing building within the parking area of a shopping center or other property type.

Parking area ratio The relationship between the square footage of the parking area and the square footage of the building.

Parking index The number of parking spaces per 1,000 square feet of GLA in a shopping center.

Pass-through charges The portion of operating expenses of the property that is prorated among the tenants, usually including real estate taxes, insurance on the property, and common area maintenance (CAM) costs; also sometimes called tenant charges and billback items. (See also *net lease.*)

Pedestrian mall In a downtown shopping area, a blocked off set of streets containing stores where people can shop without interference from automobile traffic.

Percentage rent Rent paid by a tenant based on a percentage of gross sales or net income; often set against a guaranteed minimum or base rent and therefore considered *overage.*

Permanent loan A long-term loan used to finance the purchase of an existing project or to replace the construction loan for a new development; a mortgage.

Physical life The length of time for which a building is a sound structure; this often depends on the quality of maintenance.

Points An upfront percentage fee paid for a loan—one point equals one percent of the face value of the loan—that increases the yield to the lender.

Power shopping center A large strip shopping center anchored by several large promotional, warehouse, or specialty stores that dominate their merchandising categories and having very few small shops; originally called *promotional centers.*

Powertown A shopping center that combines the large box stores of a power center with entertainment and shop tenants with more landscaping and customer amenities found in a power center.

Preleasing The leasing of a large retail project before and during construction to assure a high occupancy level when completed; often required to obtain financing.

Preventive maintenance A program of regularly scheduled inspection and care that allows potential problems to be prevented or at least detected and solved before major repairs are needed.

Pro forma A financial statement or projection developed by the developer of a proposed shopping center or owner of an existing shopping that projects costs for construction, financing and leasing costs: also projects gross income, operating expenses, and net operating income.

Property management The operation of income-producing real estate as a business, including leasing, rent collection, maintenance of the property, and general administration. Usually, this is performed by a person other than the owner, someone who acts as the owner's agent—a professional property manager.

Property manager The person who supervises the day-to-day operations of a property (e.g., a shopping center) according to the owner's objectives. Referred to as a shopping center manager when specifically managing a shopping center.

Pro rata share A tenant's share of operating expenses—e.g., common area maintenance, taxes, insurance, etc.—computed as a percentage by dividing the gross leasable area (GLA) of the tenant's space by the GLA of the shopping center.

Prospecting The search for potential tenants by advertising, referrals, canvassing, and cooperation with other brokers.

Psychographic profile A qualitative methodology for compiling information about people's individual personality and lifestyles; it goes beyond a demographic profile to uncover personal preferences and attitudes that statistical numbers do not reveal: a tool of market research. (See also *demographic profile*.)

Qualification The process of evaluating a prospective tenant to determine its ability to fulfill the terms of the lease, especially the payment of rent and other charges. Retail tenants are also evaluated on their ability as merchants and their compatibility with the array of tenants in the shopping center.

Reciprocal easement agreement (REA) In shopping centers, an agreement between anchor tenant(s) and landlord regarding rights of use of each other's property, specifically the use of each other's parking area for customer parking.

Recycling The reprocessing of various materials (e.g., paper, glass, aluminum, and various types of plastic) into usable products.

Regional mall A large shopping center anchored by two or three major retailers, at least one of which is a full-line department store, and usually developed as enclosed malls having 400,000–1,000,000 square feet of GLA.

Rehabilitation The restoration of a property to its original condition, without changing its basic use.

Retailing The selling of goods and services to the ultimate consumer. (See also specialized terminology in appendix A.)

Retail merchandising unit (RMU) A portable sales or display structure, similar to a kiosk, used for selling goods within the interior common are of a mall.

Sales analysis A comparative evaluation of tenants' sales for specified periods (e.g., one-month or one-year intervals) to measure growth and change, commonly on a per-square-foot basis. In shopping centers, sales analysis is used to evaluate prospective tenants, compare retailers within merchandise categories, and measure the success of the center as a whole.

Sales potential The total number of consumer dollars available to retailers for the entire trade area.

Sales tax A tax on the transfer of personal property (as distinguished from a tax on the property itself), usually measured as a percentage of the purchase price. It is added to the selling price and collected by the seller for the governmental agency (state, local) imposing it.

Sales volume The total dollar sales for a specified period, usually a year; also stated in dollars per square foot and often used as a measure of a retailer's success and for comparison of retailers to each other and within their merchandise categories.

Shadow space In line shop space in a shopping center with one or more anchor tenants.

Shell space The condition of a tenant's space before occupancy and before any tenant improvements to it. For retail space, definition may vary with regional location and type of shopping center.

Shopping center A group of commercial establishments planned, developed, owned, and managed as a unit related in location, size, and type of shops to the trade area the unit serves and providing on-site parking in definite relationship to the types and sizes of stores.

Specialty shopping center A type of shopping center often dominated by food, specialty gift, and fashion tenants and typically having 50,000–300,000 square feet of GLA. They do not have traditional anchor tenants. Many such shopping centers have been created by conversion of an existing old building (adaptive use) in a tourist-oriented area, usually perpetuating an architectural theme suggested by the site; also known as theme shopping centers.

Standard metropolitan statistical area (SMAS) A division of U.S. census data designating a central city and contiguous jurisdictions with a population exceeding 50,000.

Stock turnover The rate at which inventory is sold in a retail store, normally expressed on turns per year; also called *stockturn.*

Strip shopping center A shopping area consisting of a group of stores in a row.

Super regional mall A shopping center anchored by at least four anchor stores and having more than 1,000,000 square feet of GLA.

Temporary tenant A tenant that rents for a short period of time, often on a seasonal or month-to-month basis, usually occupying a kiosk or cart in the common area. A temporary tenant program may also be called a specialty leasing program.

Tenant improvement allowance Funds allowed by the landlord for the tenant's use in improving the shell space prior to move in, the amount being negotiable.

Tenant mix The combination of retailers and service vendors leasing space in a shopping center.

Trade area The geographic area from which a shopping center will obtain most of its customers, usually subdivided into primary, secondary, and tertiary trade area zones. The size of the trade area depends on the type of center, location of competition, and other factors.

Traffic count The number of automobiles passing an intersection or point along a street within a given period of time; in a mall, the number of pedestrians entering the shopping center. In shopping center development, these counts are used by market researchers to determine whether a site will support a proposed center.

Urban Land Institute An independent nonprofit research and educational organization dedicated to improving the quality and standards of land use and development.

Use clause A lease provision that restricts a retail tenant's use of the rented space by indicating what can and cannot be sold.

Vacancy rate The ratio of vacant space to total rentable space (GLA), expressed as a percentage.

Valuation The determination of value or worth. Valuation of real estate is handled by a professional appraiser. There are three approaches to determining property value. In the *cost approach,* the value of real property is based on the cost to replace the improvements on it—either to reproduce the improvements using the same materials or to replace them using modern materials and techniques. In the *market approach,* value is determined by comparing the property to similar properties that have been sold recently. In the *income approach,* value is based on the property's ability to generate income. All three approaches should be used to determine value most accurately.

View corridor The area in a parking lot that cannot be occupied by a building that obstructs the view of existing tenants or building.

Workletter An addendum to the tenant improvement clause of a retail lease that lists in detail all the work to be done for the tenant by the landlord.

Zoning A legal mechanism whereby local governments regulate the use of privately owned real property to prevent conflicting land uses and promote orderly development.

Zoning variance An exception made to a prevailing zoning ordinance that does not constitute a change in the legally applicable zoning.

Index